Cruise Ships

William Mayes

Published by Overview Press Limited
MAYES HOUSE, VANSITTART ESTATE, ARTHUR ROAD,
WINDSOR, BERKS, ENGLAND, SL4 1SE
TEL: +44 (0) 1753 620237   FAX: +44 (0) 1753 832430
www.overviewpress.co.uk

the **leading** guide to the cruise industry

contents

Contents

ISBN 978 0 9547206 6 7

This fifth edition fully revised and updated, published November 2014.

First edition published September 2005.

Second edition published August 2007.

Third edition published September 2009.

Fourth edition published September 2011

Front cover: The **Saga Sapphire** at Ny Alesund, Spitzbergen. *(William Mayes)*

Frontispiece: The **Aidamar** in Hamburg prior to her naming. *(William Mayes)*

Back cover: The **Aidastella** in Hamburg. *(William Mayes)*

Design by Miles Cowsill and Lily Publications Limited, PO Box 33, Ramsey, Isle of Man IM99 4LP

Printed by Printer Trento, Italy

the **leading** *guide to the cruise industry*

introduction

In the three years since the publication of the fourth edition of Cruise Ships there has been a great deal of change within the industry. Many of what might be thought of as traditional cruise ships have gone, most for scrap, but fortunately, a few to serve in static roles as hotel ships, including the elegant *Saga Ruby*. A large number have not been replaced and several small operators have ceased to trade.

There has been much encouragement from readers to produce a fifth edition so after much updating and photo sorting, here it is. Many friends have again supplied their best photographs and others have provided information, leads to information, corrections and other helpful remarks and I encourage you all to do so again. In a book of this sort it is almost impossible to avoid the occasional error or out of date piece of information. That said, the text is believed to be correct to 15th October 2014 and the late news to 31st October.

Maintaining the entry requirements for the book at 30 overnight berths has meant missing out some interesting smaller ships, although some of the most fascinating of this group have been included. The sheer volume of research required to lower this limit makes their inclusion somewhat impractical. However, I believe that each edition is an improvement on the previous one both in coverage and accuracy, and accordingly, I again stake my claim.

Without the Internet this book would be almost impossible to produce, and without the resources of IHS-Fairplay's on–line register Sea-web it would have been very much more difficult. Sea-web allows all sorts of links to be followed easily and quickly and thus represents a great improvement over the printed register books of the past.

Special thanks are due, again, to Rick Frendt ,who has generously supplied me with thousands of pictures over the past few years, to Captain Mark M Amielanczyk whose photographs and helpful remarks are always appreciated, to Ted Scull for pictures and encouragement, not to mention 30 years of friendship, to Jonathan Boonzaier for help with the Far East operators and to Alf Sims, Bill Lawes, Martin Grant and Matthew Sudders in particular for continuing to allow me to use some of their best pictures once again.

Sadly, Andy Kilk, a good friend for more than 25 years and prolific supplier of colour slides for all of that time, is no longer with us, but will long be remembered for his pictures in many books and magazines worldwide.

William Mayes

Mayes House

Windsor

England

SL4 1SE

william.mayes@overviewpress.co.uk

the **leading** *guide to the cruise industry*

a guide to using this book

Criteria for Inclusion In compiling this book I have attempted to include in the main section all sea-going passenger cruise ships listed as having overnight accommodation for more than 30 passengers. All roll-on roll-off vessels, regardless of their passenger capacity, have been excluded unless, at the time of compilation, the ship was in use exclusively as a cruise ship. Overnight passenger vessels that previously provided cabin accommodation, but which in their current roles (day cruise or gambling ships, generally) no longer do so are included within the other sections. In addition, a few significant passenger-carrying vessels that have never had overnight accommodation and some interesting vessels with fewer than 30 berths have been included. A small number of the more important river and canal operations are also included.

Place Names All countries, cities and towns have been given the English version of their name most commonly used, unless the local version is now generally used by English speakers.

List of Vessels The layout is as follows:

Name	Gross Tonnage	Year Built	Service Speed (knots)	Prop. method Screws	Passenger Capacity Normal	Max.	Crew Number	Length	Beam All in Metres	Draft	Flag
VESSEL NAME	5619gt	1965	16.0k	D2	280p	302p	91c	116.8m	16.5m	5.3m	HR

Gross Tonnage is now mainly listed under the 1969 convention, and is a measure of the volume of the ship. The tonnages used are generally those given by Lloyds Register, unless the author has reason to doubt those figures, in which case other sources have been used. In theory, all vessels laid down or significantly altered since 1982 and employed on international voyages, should be measured under the 1969 convention, but this is not always the case. Where a tonnage figure is given which is not in accordance with the 1969 convention the entry is marked with a ‡. Gross tonnage is now a unit-less measure of the volume of all of a ship's enclosed spaces from the keel to the funnel, measured to the inside of the hull framing. This volume is then multiplied by a factor, which is dependent upon the type of ship, to give a figure for gross tonnage. It is technically incorrect to refer to gross tons or tons, but for ease of reference the gross tonnage column figures have a gt after them.

Service Speed is generally that quoted by the company, and may be significantly less than the ship's top speed.

Machinery and Screws Machinery types are shown as follows with the number of screws after the type code.

Steam Turbine	ST	Steam Turbine with Electric Drive	SE
Steam Reciprocating	SR	Diesel	D
Diesel with Electric Drive	DE	Sail with Diesel Assistance	SD

Normal Passenger Capacity, **Maximum Passenger Capacity** and **Crew Numbers** are again those quoted by the company where possible, or from other authoritative sources if these are considered more reliable. In some cases the numbers quoted are berthed (b) and deck or unberthed (d). For school ships or training ships (s) is used to denote students or trainees. Passenger and crew numbers change from time to time, so the figures quoted here are a snapshot at the time of publication.

Dimensions are given in metres to one decimal place. Length is overall length. Beam is moulded breadth, which may be less than the width of the ship above the hull. Draught is full load draught.

Ownership Within this book ships are only listed as chartered if they are chartered from a company that is not part of the same group, as many ships are owned by one-ship companies within a group but operated by other group companies.

Many ships are chartered from owners unconnected with the operator. I have tried to list these ships

The ***Royal Clipper*** sailing from Piran, Slovenia *(William Mayes)*

under the operator with whom they spend most time. One area where it has been particularly difficult to deal with is the Arctic and Antarctic expedition ships, especially those owned by Russian companies but marketed throughout the world by a number of tour operators. In all cases I have tried to present the information in the most logical and accessible way, but suggestions for future improvement will be welcomed. There are some occasions when a ship appears more than once, under different operators. Examples of reasons why this happens are where a ship is to be transferred or sold and the sale is already known about before the book closed for press or in a situation where a ship is chartered to different operators at different times of the year.

Some companies are not currently operating or have no ships. Where there is a good likelihood that operations will resume, the company has been included in the relevant section. Similarly, some vessels were laid up. Those with a good chance of going back into service have also been included in the main sections.

Residential Cruise Ships are currently being advertised in both the United States of America and the United Kingdom. Only one such ship, THE WORLD, is currently in service and although others are projected, and have been for some time, at the time of publication none had ordered or acquired a ship.

Flag (and country codes) used throughout this book are the ISO 3166 standard code as follows.

Names of ships are shown in capitals throughout this book. Ship name derivations are given where

AE United Arab Emirates	FI Finland	KN St Kitts & Nevis	RU Russia
AN Netherlands Antilles	FJ Fiji	KP North Korea	SA Saudi Arabia
	FO Faroe Islands	KR South Korea	SE Sweden
AR Argentina	FR France	KY Cayman Islands	SG Singapore
AU Australia	GB United Kingdom	KZ Kazakhstan	SL Sierra Leone
AX Aland Islands	GD Grenada	LR Liberia	SN Senegal
BB Barbados	GE Georgia	LU Luxembourg	TG Togo
BE Belgium	GI Gibraltar	MH Marshall Islands	TH Thailand
BM Bermuda	GL Greenland	MM Myanmar	TR Turkey
BR Brazil	GR Greece	MT Malta	TT Trinidad & Tobago
BS Bahamas	HK Hong Kong	MX Mexico	TV Tuvalu
BZ Belize	HN Honduras	MY Malaysia	TZ Tanzania
CA Canada	HR Croatia	NI Norwegian International	UA Ukraine
CK Cook Islands	ID Indonesia		US United States
CL Chile	IL Israel	NL Netherlands	VC St Vincent & Grenadines
CN China	IM Isle of Man	NO Norway	
CO Columbia	IN India	NZ New Zealand	VE Venezuela
CY Cyprus	IS Iceland	OM Oman	VN Vietnam
DE Germany	IT Italy	PA Panama	VU Vanuatu
DK Denmark	JM Jamaica	PF French Polynesia	WF Wallis & Futuna
EC Ecuador	JP Japan	PH Philippines	ZA South Africa
EG Egypt	KH Cambodia	PL Poland	
ES Spain	KI Kiribati	PT Portugal	
	KM Comoros	PW Palau	

known and relevant either to the sphere of operation or to the owner. Some of these derivations are continuations of earlier themes and are perhaps less relevant today than formerly, but serve to link the current operation with earlier history of the owner.

IMO numbers are allocated by the International Maritime Organisation to each ship for life as an easy means of identification.

Acknowledgements

I would like to thank the following individuals, without whose help this would have been a less good book.

Mark M Amielanczyk, Jonathan Boonzaier, Ian Boyle, Philippe Brebant, Miles Cowsill, Rick Frendt, Martin Grant, Philip Hall, Clive Harvey, John Hendy, Kelvin Holmes, Trevor Jones, the late Andy Kilk, Bill Lawes, Doreen Lawes, Ben Lyons, Chris Mason, Brenda Mayes, Richard Mayes, Peter Plowman, Richard Osborne, Gillian Ridgway, Tom Rinaldi, Ted Scull, Richard Seville, Alf Sims, Matthew Sudders, David Trevor-Jones and Nick Widdows.

The **Insignia** at Dubrovnik *(William Mayes)*

Istanbul line-up - **MSC Lirica**, **Costa Favolosa**, **MSC Fantasia** and **Marina** *(William Mayes)*

the **leading** *guide to the cruise industry*

a brief review of events in
the cruise industry

A massive clear out of older ships has occurred during the past three years and although in number they have been replaced, and in capacity replaced many times, the balance between the small number of large groups and the large number of small operators has continued to move in favour of the former, as much of the scrapping has been ships of the latter. While the large groups continue to invest billions of dollars in new ships, with the exception of a very small group, the smaller operators simply cannot afford to buy new ships and with the supply of small and medium sized second-hand vessels drying up, it is likely that more small cruise companies will simply cease trading. As can be seen from the changes section of this book, several have already given up.

Bucking the trend, however, are Viking Ocean Cruises and Ponant Cruises both of whom have new ships on order. The former is complete new start up, an offshoot of Viking River Cruises, and has demonstrated its commitment with orders for four mid-sized ships.

Although not buying new ships, Portuscale Cruises has also bucked the trend by bringing back into service four of the former Classic International Cruises ships, and the flagship, *Funchal*, is looking better than ever despite her 53 years.

We have seen the loss of the first large cruise ship in an accident that should never have happened. The loss of the *Costa Concordia* had a short-term effect of cruise bookings for Costa, but appears now to have been largely forgotten by would-be passengers. One legacy from the accident, however, appears to be a tightening up of bridge visits while ships are at sea by some, but not all operators.

Political unrest, particularly around the Mediterranean continues to restrict cruise itineraries with Libya, Egypt, Israel, Lebanon, Syria and Ukraine off most cruise operators visiting list for the time being. Some of those may come back on stream in 2015, but it is likely that both Syria and Libya will be no-go areas for the foreseeable future.

The German market seems to have taken over from that of the United Kingdom as the fastest growing market in Europe, but the global picture sees China emerging as the region with most potential, and it is entirely possible that in a few years China could be home to the world's largest cruise market. The fact that Carnival Corporation, Fincantieri and the China State Shipbuilding Corporation have recently entered into a memorandum of agreement hints at things to come.

In the next edition of Cruise Ships, currently planned for late 2017, the face of cruising may be quite different.

The *Saga Pearl II* at Skjolden, Norway *(William Mayes)*

The view from the bridge of the *Louis Aura*, leaving Kos *(William Mayes)*

the **leading** *guide to the cruise industry*

section I Cruise Ships

ABOU MERHI CRUISES

The Company Abou Merhi Cruises is a subsidiary of Abou Merhi Lines, a Lebanese shipowner with a small fleet of vehicle carriers. A previous experiment with ORIENT QUEEN, while producing a fine ship, was badly timed and that ship is now Louis Cruises' LOUIS AURA.

Address 3rd Floor, Atrium Building, BP 175016, Weygand Street, Beirut, Lebanon

Telephone +961 1 969 999

Website www.aboumerhicruises.net

Area operated Eastern Mediterranean

ORIENT QUEEN II	7478gt	1989	16.5k	D2	282p	282p	139c	117.4m	16.8m	4.5m	MT

ORIENT QUEEN II was built by Union Naval de Levant SA (yard number 175) at Valencia, Spain as the VISTAMAR for Mar Line Universal Shipping, a subsidiary of Hoteles Marinos. In 2000 she was transferred to Vistamar Canarias and two months later to Servicios Maritimos Litoral, based in The Netherlands, both without change of name. In November 2006 she was purchased by Venetian catering firm Ligabue. VISTAMAR was chartered by Plantours & Partner for a number of years, but left the company in spring 2012 to join Plein Cap Crosieres. That charter may not have taken place as the ship was sold to Abou Merhi Lines, refitted and renamed as the ORIENT QUEEN II. IMO 8701193

ADVENTURE CANADA

The Company Adventure Canada was founded by the Swan family in 1987 to specialise in travel to remote parts of Canada. Subsequently charters/spaces were taken on a number of small ships. Cruise North Expeditions, founded in 2005, was part of the Inuit-owned Makivik Corporation, based in Canada. The company previously operated the USHUAIA, now operated by Antarpply Expeditions. Following the arrest of the company's chartered ship, the LYOBUV ORLOVA, the business was merged with Adventure Canada. The area of operation remains Northeast Canada and Greenland. For 2011 and 2012 the Cruise North programme was merged with Adventure Canada's CLIPPER ADVENTURER sailings, and the same ship was used in 2013, but in 2014 Adventure Canada has taken a charter of the OCEAN ENDEAVOUR.

Address 14 Front Street South, Mississauga, Ontario, L5H 2C4, Canada

Telephone +1 905 271 4000 **Fax** +1 905 271 5595

Website www.adventurecanada.com

Area operated Canada

OCEAN ENDEAVOUR	12907gt	1982	17.5k	D2	198p	198p	c	137.1m	21.0m	5.8m	MH

OCEAN ENDEAVOUR was built by Stocznia Szczecinska (yard number B492/03) in Szczecin, Poland as the KONSTANTIN SIMONOV, the third of a series of seven ships for the Baltic Shipping Company. She operated as a ferry serving the ports of Leningrad, Riga and Helsinki. From 1992 she ran for Baltic Shipping Company subsidiary, Baltic Line. In 1996 she passed to Pakartin Shipping and was renamed FRANCESCA. Her Australian employment failed and she was eventually laid up in Wilhelmshaven, Germany. In 2000 she was acquired by Silver Cruises and renamed THE IRIS for operation by Mano Maritime. In 2010 she was sold to Kristina Cruises for rebuilding to replace the KRISTINA REGINA on international voyages and was renamed KRISTINA KATARINA. Kristina Cruises failed in 2013 and the ship was acquired by FleetPro Ocean (formerly International Shipping Partners), renamed OCEAN ENDEAVOUR and chartered out as an accommodation ship in the Shetland Islands. She has now been chartered for the 2014/15 winter to Adventure Canada, who will limit the passenger capacity to 198. IMO 7625811

Abou Merhi Cruises' *Orient Queen II* at Rhodes *(Rick Frendt)*

Adventure Canada's *Ocean Endeavour* as *Kristina Katerina* at Las Palmas *(William Mayes)*

ALASKAN DREAM CRUISES

The Company Alaskan Dream Cruises commenced operations in 2011, when it acquired laid up vessels from bankrupt former owners operating in Alaska. The parent company is Allen Marine, an Alaska-based tour operator and boat builder, established in 1970.

Address 1512 Sawmill Creek Road, Sitka, Alaska 99835, United States of America

Telephone +1 907 747 8100 **Fax** +1 907 747 4819

Website www.alaskandreamcruises.com

Area operated Alaska

ADMIRALTY DREAM	514gt	1979	8.5k	D1	54p	58p	21c	43.5m	8.5m	2.0m	US
ALASKAN DREAM	490gt	1986	13.0k	D2	36p	40p	15c	32.0m	9.4m	2.0m	US
BARANOF DREAM	c500gt	1980	9.0k	D1	50p	50p	21c	43.5m	8.5m	2.0m	US

ADMIRALTY DREAM was built by Blount Marine Corporation (yard number 225) at Warren, Rhode Island, USA as the NEW SHOREHAM II. She was acquired by Cruise West and renamed SPIRIT OF COLUMBIA in 1993. When Cruise West collapsed in 2010 she was acquired by the newly formed Alaskan Dream Cruises and renamed ADMIRALTY DREAM. IMO 8963727

ALASKAN DREAM was built by Nichols Brothers Boatbuilders (yard number S 81) at Freeland, Washington for Glacier Bay Cruises and Tours as the EXECUTIVE EXPLORER. She was acquired by Ambassadors International at the end of 2005, but did not enter service until the autumn of 2006 as the CONTESSA. She was surrendered to MARAD on the bankruptcy of Majestic America Line in 2008, and subsequently purchased by Alaskan Dream Cruises, who renamed her ALASKAN DREAM. IMO 8978679

BARANOF DREAM was built by Blount Marine Corporation (yard number 234) at Warren, Rhode Island, USA as the PACIFIC NORTHWEST EXPLORER. She became Cruise West's SPIRIT OF ALASKA in 1988 and was laid up in 2009. Cruise West went out of business in 2010 and she was acquired by Alaskan Dream Cruises and renamed BARANOF DREAM. It is thought that she has not yet entered service. IMO 8963715

ALL LEISURE GROUP

The Company All Leisure Group is the holding company of All Leisure Holidays, in turn the owner of Voyages of Discovery, Swan Hellenic and Discover Egypt. In April 2009 the business of Hebridean Island Cruises was bought out of administration. The group purchased the ALEXANDER VON HUMBOLDT at auction in 2009 from the bankrupt Club Cruise. This ship was chartered to Turkish operator Bam Tur for the 2011 season, but after a major refit entered service for Voyages of Discovery in December 2012. Shortly afterwards the DISCOVERY was chartered to Cruise and Maritime Voyages. In May 2012 the tour operator Page and Moy (now trading as Travelsphere) was acquired. That company had previously operated cruises for its own account, but does not currently do so.

Address Compass House, Rockingham Road, Market Harborough, Leicestershire, LE16 9QD, England

Telephone +44 1858 581364

Website www.allleisuregroup.com

HEBRIDEAN ISLAND CRUISES

The Company Hebridean Island Cruises was established in 1988 to purchase and convert the car ferry COLUMBA for operation as the small luxury cruise ship HEBRIDEAN PRINCESS in the waters of Western Scotland. The company was a subsidiary of Hebridean Cruises plc, which purchased Hebridean Island Cruises from its previous owner in 1998. An expansion of operations occurred in 2001 with the acquisition of the former Renaissance Cruises' ship RENAISSANCE SIX, which was refitted and renamed HEBRIDEAN SPIRIT. The new ship operated on worldwide itineraries. In 2006 the company was renamed as Hebridean International Cruises Limited. In August 2007 58% of the share capital was acquired by Stonefield Castle Group. With the economic downturn in the United Kingdom biting hard, the company sold the HEBRIDEAN SPIRIT at short notice in the spring of 2009, and returned to its roots. The sale of the HEBRIDEAN SPIRIT was completed on 7 April 2009 and on the following day the company went into administration. Within three weeks the business and the ship was sold to All Leisure Group and renamed as Hebridean Island Cruises. The Hebrides, after which the company is named, is an archipelago off the Western coast of Scotland, comprising the Inner and Outer Hebrides. They include Skye, Lewis, Harris and Islay.

Address Kintail House, Carleton New Road, Skipton, North Yorkshire, BD23 2DE

Telephone +44 1756 704747

Website www.hebridean.co.uk

Area operated Scotland, the Scottish Isles and occasionally Norway and round Britain in segments

HEBRIDEAN PRINCESS	2112gt	1964	14.5k	D2	49p	49p	38c	71.6m	13.3m	2.7m	GB

HEBRIDEAN PRINCESS, the former MacBrayne car ferry COLUMBA underwent a massive transformation in 1989 to become one of the most exclusive cruise ships in the world. Hall Russell (yard number 912) at Aberdeen, Scotland built her as one of a trio of side-loading car ferries for service to the Western Isles from Oban. In 1973 David MacBrayne and the Caledonian Steam Packet Company (both British Government owned) were merged into Caledonian MacBrayne, and the ship was eventually re-registered under that organisation. In 1988 she was sold to Leisure and Marine Holdings (trading as Hebridean Island Cruises) and converted into the luxury country house style cruise ship HEBRIDEAN PRINCESS. In 1998 the company and the ship were sold to Hebridean Cruises plc, but the style of operation remained unchanged. During the summer of 2006 HM Queen Elizabeth II chartered the ship for a week of Scottish cruising. IMO 6409351

SWAN HELLENIC

The Company The origins of what is now Swan Hellenic go back to the 1930's when the Hellenic Travellers Club ran cruises and tours to Greece and Asia Minor. Following the end of the Second World War, W F & R K Swan, who then owned the club, re-introduced Hellenic cruises. The first of these cruises was undertaken in 1954 aboard the 1,700 ton 1952-built MIAOULIS, chartered from Nomikos Lines. It was in the following year that Sir Mortimer Wheeler, the celebrated archaeologist, began his connection with the firm, of which he was later to become Chairman. In that year the company operated its second cruise aboard the AEGAEON, owned by the Greek Typaldos Lines, and by then more than 40 years old. W F & R K Swan (Hellenic) Ltd, trading as Swans Hellenic Cruises used another of that company's ships, the MEDITERRANEAN, between 1956 and 1958. Typaldos also provided the ADRIATIKI for ten cruises between 1957 and 1961. By the early 1960's a pattern of three early and three late season cruises aboard the ANKARA, chartered from Turkish Maritime Lines, had emerged. At the start of the next decade the number of cruises undertaken each year had steadily increased and a replacement was sought for the ANKARA, which was by now more than 45 years old, and only partly air-conditioned. The vessel selected was the ORPHEUS of Epirotiki, and she served Swans well for 22 years. In the meantime, P&O had bought Swans Hellenic Cruises in 1983 from Trust House Forte (who had acquired the company in 1968), and continued to develop the business by gradually extending the cruising season. Later the company was restyled as Swan Hellenic. In 1995, the ORPHEUS was replaced by the newly built MINERVA, based on the hull of an unwanted Russian research vessel, but completed and fitted out as a very suitable ship to take the business forward. Initially taken on a four-year charter, this was extended to the spring of 2003, when the laid-up R EIGHT, renamed as the MINERVA II, replaced her. Ken Swan died in August 2005, and subsequently Carnival Corporation (by then owner of Swan Hellenic) decided to transfer the MINERVA II to Princess Cruises as the ROYAL PRINCESS. In February 2007 Carnival announced that the Swan Hellenic brand was not going to be revived. Just three weeks later Lord Sterling acquired Swan Hellenic from Carnival, but within a short time had sold the brand to Voyages of Discovery. The company started trading again in spring 2008, using the company's earlier ship, the MINERVA, on which a six-year charter had been secured. Swan Hellenic has subsequently re-entered the European river cruise market.

Address Compass House, Rockingham Road, Market Harborough, Leicestershire, LE16 7QD, England

Telephone +44 1858 410456

Website www.swanhellenic.com

Areas operated Mediterranean and Northern Europe in summer, Far East, India and Arabia, or South America in winter

MINERVA	12892gt	1996	16.0k	D2	362p	394p	157c	133.0m	20.0m	5.1m	BS

MINERVA was partially constructed by the Sudostroitelnyy Zavod Okean Shipyard (yard number 1) at

All Leisure Group's **Minerva** at Thesalonika *(Martin Grant)*

All Leisure Group's **Hebridean Princess** at Oban *(Rick Frendt)*

Nikolaev in the Ukraine as the research vessel OKEAN. Her keel was laid in 1987 and she was launched in 1989 but not completed. She was purchased by V-Ships and towed to the Mariotti shipyard in Genoa for completion as a passenger ship. On completion in 1996 she was chartered to the Peninsular and Oriental Steam Navigation Company for use by Swan Hellenic Cruises, as a replacement for the smaller ORPHEUS, and given the name MINERVA. At the end of her charter in 2003 she was returned to V-Ships, who succeeded in setting two new charters for her. For the summer of 2003 she became the SAGA PEARL for the 'over 50' tour operator, Saga Cruises, and in the winter she took the name EXPLORER II for Abercrombie & Kent's expedition cruises. For summer 2004 she was operated by Saga again, reverting to her Saga name. In November 2004 she took up winter employment with Abercrombie & Kent, but for the summer she operated for Phoenix Reisen as the ALEXANDER VON HUMBOLDT. In January 2007 it was announced that Voyages of Discovery had taken the ship on long-term charter. Some six months later the group acquired Swan Hellenic and so the perfect match was to return the renamed MINERVA to that organisation. The ship continued to serve her 2008 winter in the Antarctic where she was marketed in conjunction with Abercrombie and Kent, and where passenger numbers were limited to 200. MINERVA was chartered to Phoenix Reisen for the return leg of her Antarctic season in spring 2010. However, the ship is not expected to return to Antarctica in the near future and now operates exclusively for Swan Hellenic all year round. Over the winter of 2011/12 Minerva had a major refit that included the addition of extra balconies and a forward facing observation lounge. Minerva is the Roman name for Athena, the Greek goddess of (amongst other things) wisdom. IMO 9144196

VOYAGES OF DISCOVERY

The Company Voyages of Discovery is a brand of the United Kingdom registered All Leisure Group. Its origins are in the Schools Abroad business that started offering educational cruises in 1984. The cruises, mostly run during school holidays and using a variety of chartered Greek ships, were popular with both adults and children and so the company expanded into the mainstream cruise market. For a while, in the early 1990s, the company was Greek-owned and operated the EMERALD SEAS, although in that era the company was known as Discovery Cruises. The Greek company failed in the mid 1990s and came back under UK control. Voyages of Discovery has chartered a number of ships over the years including the AEGEAN I and the AEGEAN SPIRIT (formerly Costa's ENRICO C). Until 2004 the company operated the DISCOVERY from May to November on charter from Discovery World Cruises (founded by Gerry Herrod), but now also markets itself under that name in the USA following its recent acquisition of that business, together with the DISCOVERY. For 2008 the company also operated the OCEAN MAJESTY under exclusive charter between March and May on a series of Mediterranean, Black Sea and Red Sea Cruises. Until 2010 Voyages of Discovery operated at least one schools cruise each year, with those in 2009 and 2010 being to the Eastern Mediterranean in the October half-term. The DISCOVERY was chartered to British tour operator Shearings for three cruises in the summer of 2011. From spring 2013, following a major refit, DISCOVERY started a charter to Cruise and Maritime Voyages, but just a year later All Leisure Group announced that the DISCOVERY would be taken out of sevice at the end of 2014. In August 2014 reports of her sale were accompanied by the news that her CMV charter would be terminated early.

Address Compass House, Rockingham Road, Market Harborough, Leicestershire, LE16 9QD, England

Telephone +44 1858 410456

Website www.voyagesofdiscovery.com

Area operated Europe, Red Sea, Scandinavia, Middle East, Far East and Australia

| DISCOVERY | 20216gt | 1971 | 18.0k | D2 | 698p | 758p | 350c | 168.7m | 24.6m | 7.5m | BM |
| VOYAGER | 15396gt | 1990 | 18.8k | D2 | 520p | 556p | 214c | 150.7m | 19.8m | 5.7m | BS |

DISCOVERY was built by Rheinstahl Nordseewerke (yard number 414) at Emden in Germany as the ISLAND VENTURE for Norwegian Cruiseships (a joint venture between Fearney & Eger and Lorentzen), to be chartered to Flagship Cruises for service between New York and Bermuda, along with her sister, the SEA VENTURE. The service could not support two ships, so the ISLAND VENTURE was put up for charter. Princess Cruises was in search of a replacement for the CARLA C, so chartered the ISLAND VENTURE and renamed her as the ISLAND PRINCESS in 1972. She passed to The Peninsular & Oriental Steam Navigation Company with the Princess Cruises business in 1974. In 1999 she was sold to Ringcroft Investment and chartered to Hyundai Merchant Marine as the HYUNDAI PUNGAK for

All Leisure Group's *Discovery* *(Bill Lawes)*

All Leisure Group's *Voyager* at Killybegs *(Rick Frendt)*

American Cruise Lines' *American Star* in New York *(Rick Frendt)*

cruising from South Korea. Having acquired three ships, the market could not sustain this number of berths and the ship was laid up before being sold to Gerry Herrod, the founder of Orient Lines. She was taken to Tuzla in Turkey and refitted as the PLATINUM in 2001. From 2002 she operated for Herrod's own Discovery World Cruises on South American itineraries in winter and on Voyages of Discovery educational cruises in summer, as the DISCOVERY in both roles. Herrod retired in 2004 and Voyages of Discovery operated the ship under its own name and as Discovery World Cruises. Later the DISCOVERY was operated only under the Voyages of Discovery brand until the end of 2012, after which she underwent a major refit. Subsequently she has been chartered to Cruise and Maritme Voyages for two years but will be withdrawn at the end of 2014. The most famous ship to bear the name DISCOVERY was undoubtedly that of Captain Robert Falcon Scott, who used the ship for the National Antarctic Expedition of 1901-1904. That ship is currently preserved in Dundee, Scotland. IMO 7108514

VOYAGER was built by Union Naval de Levante (yard number 185) at Valencia, Spain as the CROWN MONARCH for Crown Cruise Lines, a subsidiary of Effjohn Intl. The ship operated cruises in the Caribbean and South Pacific until being chartered to Singaporean interests for use as the casino cruise ship NAUTICAN in 1995. The Singaporean authorities banished the ship from its waters a few months later, and it moved up to Hong Kong, where it operated as the WALRUS until replaced by the CT NEPTUNE in April 2005. The ship was returned to Sea Containers, the then owners of former Effjohn company Silja Line, and was laid up awaiting new employment. In 2006 she was sold to Dutch operator Club Cruise for US$21 million and was chartered by new Spanish operator, Vision Cruceros, for whom she operated as the JULES VERNE. From the spring of 2008 she operated as the ALEXANDER VON HUMBOLDT, although for the first two months she was named ALEXANDER VON HUMBOLDT II. She replaced a previous ship of the same name, now Swan Hellenic's MINERVA. Following the ship's owner going into administration the ship was arrested in Bremerhaven, and remained in that position for some time. Phoenix Reisen were expecting to have the ship operational again by late spring 2009, but in view of likely delays chartered the ATHENA as a temporary replacement. The ship was eventually sold at auction in November 2009 to All Leisure Group, who chartered her to Phoenix Reisen for the 2010 summer season. Following an extensive refit in Genoa she was chartered to Bamtur for the 2011 summer season, after which she was laid up and refitted again. For Voyages of Discovery she was renamed VOYAGER and entered service in December 2012. For four summers from 2013 the VOYAGER is chartered to Belgian operator All Ways Croisieres for an 80-day programme. IMO 8709573

ALL WAYS CROISIERES

The Company All Ways Croisieres is a Belgian travel business, part of the Genairgy Group, that sells and operates river cruises and sells ocean cruises aboard other company's ships. A recent additional activity has been the provision of its own custom cruises on board the chartered VOYAGER.

Address Avenue Victor Rousseau 149, 1190 Forest, Brussels, Belgium

Telephone +32 2 344 9088

Website www.all-ways.be

Area operated Northern Europe

VOYAGER	15396gt	1990	18.8k	D2	520p	556p	214c	150.7m	19.8m	5.7m	BS

VOYAGER For details see under Voyages of Discovery (All Leisure Group)

AMBIENTE KREUZFAHRTEN

The Company Ambiente Kreuzfahrten is a German company. Having previously used Classic International's PRINCESS DAPHNE and ATHENA (now AZORES), when that company collapsed Ambiente was left without a ship and withdrew temporarily from the cruise market. The company returned in 2014 with the charter of Portuscale's AZORES from March to November. However, poor bookings resulted in the early termination of the charter and Ambiente Kreuzfahrten has indicated that it intends to close.

Address Stresemannstrasse 30, D10963 Berlin, Germany

Telephone +49 30 814050 500 **Fax** +49 30 814050 555

Website www.ambientekreuzfahrten.de

Area operated Northern Europe and the Mediterranean

| AZORES | 16144gt | 1948 | 16.5k | D2 | 552p | 659p | 185c | 160.0m | 21.0m | 7.6m | PT |

AZORES For details see under Portuscale Cruises

AMERICAN CRUISE LINES

The Company American Cruise Lines was established in 2000. The business expanded into stern-wheeler operation in 2011.

Address 741 Boston Post Road, Suite 200, Guildford, Connecticut 06437-2743, United States of America

Telephone +1 203 458 5700 **Fax** +1 203 453 7385

Website www.americancruiselines.com

Area operated East Coast USA from New England to Florida, Snake and Columbia Rivers, and the Mississippi. Alaska from June 2012.

AMERICAN EAGLE	1148gt	2000	12.5k	D2	49p	49p	22c	51.2m	13.1m	2.0m	US
AMERICAN GLORY	1148gt	2002	12.5k	D2	49p	49p	22c	51.2m	13.1m	2.0m	US
AMERICAN SPIRIT	1973gt	2005	14.0k	D1	100p	100p	27c	65.2m	13.9m	2.0m	US
AMERICAN STAR	1973gt	2007	14.0k	D1	100p	100p	27c	65.2m	13.9m	2.0m	US
INDEPENDENCE	2169gt	2010	14.0k	D2	104p	104p	27c	73.0m	15.4m	2.0m	US
QUEEN OF THE MISSISSIPPI	gt	2012	12.0k	D2	150p	150p	c	90.0m	16.1m	2.3m	US
QUEEN OF THE WEST	2115gt	1994	11.0k	DE1	120p	120p	47c	70.1m	15.2m	2.1m	US

AMERICAN EAGLE was built by Chesapeake Shipbuilding (yard number 78) at Salisbury, Maryland, USA for the company. At the time of writing the AMERICAN EAGLE was sale-listed on Chesapeake Shipbuilding's website and is currently laid up at Salisbury. IMO 8972340

AMERICAN GLORY was built for the company by Chesapeake Shipbuilding (yard number 80). IMO 8972338

AMERICAN SPIRIT was built by Chesapeake Shipbuilding (yard number 82). IMO 9283124

AMERICAN STAR was delivered by Chesapeake Shipbuilding (yard number 86) in the summer of 2007. IMO 9427615

INDEPENDENCE was built at Chesapeake Shipbuilding (yard number 90) and was delivered in the spring of 2010. IMO 9583366

QUEEN OF THE MISSISSIPPI was built for the company by Chesapeake Shipbuilding (yard number 97) at Salisbury, Maryland. Launched on 3 August 2011, she entered service in June 2012 and was the first new overnight Mississippi sternwheeler for more than 20 years. She was named by cruise expert Phyllis Dale in Nashville on 25 August 2012.

QUEEN OF THE WEST was built at the Nichols Brothers Boatbuilders Yard (yard number S110) at Freeland, Washington State, USA for the American West Steamboat Company. That business was later absorbed in Ambassadors International's Majestic America Line, which ceased trading in 2008. In September 2009 the ship was acquired by American Cruise Line offshoot Blue Spruce LLC and underwent a major renovation over the winter of 2010/11. She operates on the Snake and Colombia Rivers. IMO 8642957

Cruise ships on order

NEWBUILD 1	gt	2015	12.0k	D2	150p	150p	c	90.0m	16.1m	2.3m	US
NEWBUILD 2	gt	2015	12.0k	D2	175p	175p	c	m	m	m	US
NEWBUILD 3	gt	2016	12.0k	D2	p	p	c	m	m	m	US
NEWBUILD 4	gt	2017	12.0k	D2	p	p	c	m	m	m	US

NEWBUILD 1, 2, 3 and **4** are stern-wheelers under construction by Chesapeake Shipbuilding. The first was launched on 30 June 2014, for operation on the Mississippi. The second, slightly larger will be used on the Columbia and Snake Rivers.

American Cruise Lines' *Queen of the Mississippi* *(company picture)*

Pearl Cruises' *Pearl Mist* at Baltimore *(Jonathan Boonzaier)*

American Steamboat Company's *American Queen* at Natchez Steamboat Landing *(Matthew Sudders)*

PEARL SEAS CRUISES

The Company Pearl Seas Cruises is a subsidiary of American Cruise Lines. The order placed with the Irving Shipyard was for two vessels, but with the long delays in completing the first ship, the order for the second was cancelled.

Address 741 Boston Post Road, Suite 200, Guildford, Connecticut 06437, United States of America

Telephone +1 203 458 5700 **Fax** +1 203 453 7385

Website www.pearlseascruises.com

Area operated East Coast America from Canada (including the Great Lakes) to the Caribbean.

PEARL MIST		5109gt	2014	17.0k	D2	210p	210p	c	99.0m	16.8m	3.5m	MH

PEARL MIST was built by the Irving Shipyard (yard number 6092) in Halifax, Nova Scotia. The order was originally for two ships, but serious delays in the delivery of the PEARL MIST led to the cancellation of the second ship. It appears that, in October 2010, the company rejected the ship on the grounds that it did not meet some regulatory requirements, an allegation that the shipyard refuted. All cabins on the ship have private balconies.The ship finally entered service in June 2014, having been completed by Chesapeake Shipbuilding. IMO 9412701

AMERICAN QUEEN STEAMBOAT COMPANY

The Company The Great American Steamboat Company was formed to acquire and bring back into service the American Queen. Operations began in the spring of 2012. It subsequently became the American Queen Steamboat Company.

Address 40 South Main Street, 21st Floor, Memphis, TN 38103, United States of America

Telephone +1 888 749 5280

Website www.americanqueensteamboatcompany.com

Area operated The Mississippi, Ohio, Columbia and Snake Rivers

AMERICAN EMPRESS	3388gt	2003	14.0k	DE2	223p	223p	84c	109.7m	16.4m	3.8m	US
AMERICAN QUEEN	10159gt	1995	10.0k	SR1	444p	481p	180c	127.5m	25.9m	2.6m	US

AMERICAN EMPRESS was built at the Nichols Boatbuilders Yard (yard number S142) at Freeland in Washington State, USA for the American West Steamboat Company as the EMPRESS OF THE NORTH. That business was absorbed into Majestic America Line in 2006. After Majestic America Line failed she was handed over to MARAD and was laid up in Portland. She was purchased by the American Queen Steamboat Company in 2013 and resumed sailing on the rivers of the Pacific Northwest in 2014 as the AMERICAN EMPRESS, following her christening by Claudette Waggoner, wife of the company's CEO. IMO 9263538

AMERICAN QUEEN was built by the McDermott Shipyard (yard number 296) in Amelia, Louisiana, USA for the Delta Queen Steamboat Company and remains the largest river steamboat ever built. In 2006 the company was acquired by Ambassadors International to become part of its Majestic America Line. With the collapse of Majestic America Line she was returned to her mortgage holder, MARAD, and laid up at Violet, Louisiana. She was subsequently moved to Beaumont, Texas and was acquired by Great American Steamboat Company, now restyled as the American Steamboat Company. IMO 9084542

ANDANDO CRUISES

The Company Andando Cruises is a Galapagos Islands tour and cruise operator, which operates three smaller ships in addition to the MARY ANNE.

Address Moises Brito s/n y Las Ninfas, Apartado 1721-0088, Puerto Ayora, Galapagos, Ecuador

Telephone +593 2 323 7330

Website www.andandotours.com

Area operated Galapagos Islands

MARY ANNE		395gt	1997	8.0k	SD1	24p	34p	20c	65.8m	7.9m	4.8m	EC

MARY ANNE was built by Workshop Marine Radunia-Spawmet (yard number 1104), Gdansk, Poland and completed by Gebr. Freidich KG Schiffswert in Kiel as the MARY ANNE for Segeltouristik Meyer zur Heyde 'Mary Anne' Betriebs GmbH & Co KG of Germany. In 2003 she was renamed MARY ANNE II and her flag changed from that of Germany to Panama. She appears to have been acquired by Angermeyer Cruises (now Andando Cruises) in 2009, when she reverted to her original name. IMO 8976413

ANTARCTICA XXI

The Company Antarctica XXI is a Chilean Tour operator specializing in fly cruises to Antarctica from Punta Arenas, with flights to King George Island in the South Shetland Islands. From November 2009 to January 2010 the company operated the PROFESSOR MULTANOVSKIY, but for the past four years has taken space on the OCEAN NOVA. The company also sells space on the SEA EXPLORER.

Address O'Higgins 1170, Punta Arenas, Chile

Telephone +56 61 2614100 **Fax** +56 61 2614105

Website www.antarcticaxxi.com

Area operated Antarctica

OCEAN NOVA	2183gt	1992	12.0k	D1	68p	68p	34c	72.8m	11.3m	3.7m	BS
SEA EXPLORER	4200gt	1991	15.5k	D2	71p	114p	70c	90.3m	15.3m	4.0m	MH

OCEAN NOVA For details see under Quark Expeditions (TUI Group).

SEA EXPLORER For details see under Clipper Group.

ANTARPPLY EXPEDITIONS

The Company Antarpply Expeditions is an Argentinean tour operator specializing in cruises to Antarctica.

Address Gobanador Paz 633, 1st Floor, 9410 Ushuaia, Argentina

Telephone +54 2901 433636 **Fax** +54 2901 437728

Website www.antarpply.com

Area operated Antarctica

USHUAIA	2923gt	1970	12.0k	D2	88p	88p	38c	84.8m	15.6m	5.5m	KM

USHUAIA was built as the US Government research vessel RESEARCHER by the American Shipbuilding Co (yard number 198) at Lorain, Ohio, USA. Launched in 1968, she was not completed until 1970. She was renamed as the MALCOLM BALDRIGE in 1988 and was sold to Argentinean company Ushuaia Adventure in 2001, when she took her current name. Cruise North seasonally chartered her from 2005, but she is now operating on charter to Antarpply Expeditions. In December 2008 she suffered a severe grounding in Wilhelmina Bay, Antarctica but was repaired at Punta Arenas and returned to service. Ushuaia is the capital city of the Argentine province of Tierra del Fuego and is the world's southernmost city. IMO 6901907

ARCTIC UMIAQ LINE

The Company Arctic Umiaq Line is a Greenland owned company, which was founded in 1774 as Den Kongelige Gronlandske Handel (Royal Greenland Trading Company) and first started operating ships on its own account in 1797. In 1985 the company was taken over by the Greenland Home Rule Administration and then became Gronlands Handel (Greenland Trading). The company was later restyled as KNI Service and subsequently KNI Pilersvisoq. In January 1993 the company was split into two, with the container shipping going to the newly formed Royal Arctic Line and the passenger ships being placed with another new company, Arctic Umiaq Line. Both companies remained Greenland Government owned. Arctic Umiaq Line ceased trading on 31 March 2006 as it was then decided to maintain links along the Greenland coast by air rather than by sea. The company was then sold to Arctic Travel Group, a new company established by three Danish travel agencies. The service lasted only until September 2006, when the company collapsed due to financial difficulties. Two ships quickly found buyers, but the third did not. As a result the Greenland Government required Royal Arctic Line and Air Greenland to jointly form a new Arctic Umiaq Line to operate the ship on the west coast of

Antarpply Expeditions' **Ushuaia** off Ushuaia *(Rick Frendt)*

Arctic Umiaq Line's **Sarfaq Ittuk** at Qaqortoq *(Rick Frendt)*

Ayravata Cruises **Paukan 1947** as **Pandaw** *(company picture)*

Greenland.

Address Aqqusinersuaq 52, PO Box 1580, DK 3900 Nuuk, Greenland

Telephone +299 349190 **Fax** +299 322450

Website www.aul.gl

Area operated Cruises and passenger services on the west coast of Greenland

SARFAQ ITTUK		2118gt	1992	13.0k	D1	104p	249p	22c	72.8m	11.3m	3.3m	GL

SARFAQ ITTUK was built by the Orskov Shipyard (yard number 156) in Frederikshavn, Denmark for the Greenland Government owned KNI Pilersvisoq, as a coastal passenger ship with a capacity for 150 passengers. In 1999/2000 the ship was lengthened by 23 metres by Stocznia Remontowa at Gdansk, Poland. IMO 8913899

ATOLL EXPLORER CRUISES

The Company Atoll Explorer Cruises is a trading name of Universal Enterprises, a Maldives based company that also operates a supply ship in the islands. The company previously owned the ISLAND EXPLORER (ex NORDNORGE), which was used initially as a cruise ship, and later as a static hotel and diving ship. That ship has now been sold for scrap.

Address Level 7, Aagadhage, Boduthakurufaanu Magu, Male, Maldive Islands

Telephone +960 300 2006

Website www.atollexplorer.com

Area operated Maldive Islands

ATOLL EXPLORER		297gt	1964	13k	D2	40p	40p	c	50.3m	11.6m	3.0m	MV

ATOLL EXPLORER was built by the Burton Shipyard (yard number 357) at Port Arthur, Texas, USA as CAMPECHE SEAL. In 1986 she became the AQUANAUT EXPLORER for Cayman Islands based Dive and Sail Holidays. She was renamed as THE EXPLORER in 1993 and took her current name in 1995, when acquired by Universal Enterprises. IMO 7101231

AURORA EXPEDITIONS

The Company Aurora Expeditions is an Australian adventure company specialising in small group expeditions. In addition to its own operation of the POLAR PIONEER, the company takes space on a number of other ships.

Address Suite 12, Level 2, 35 Buckingham Street, Surry Hills, Sydney 2010, New South Wales, Australia

Telephone +61 2 9252 1033 **Fax** +61 2 9252 1373

Website www.auroraexpeditions.com.au

Area operated Antarctica, generally from Argentina between November and March and the Arctic in summer

POLAR PIONEER		1753gt	1982	12.0k	D1	54p	54p	23c	71.6m	12.8m	4.5m	RU

POLAR PIONEER was built by Oy Laivateollisuus Ab (yard number 342) at Turku, Finland as the AKADEMIK SHULEYKIN for the Russian Hydrometeorological Institute. She was transferred to the Arctic and Antarctic Research Institute in 1994 and to the Russian Government controlled Marine Service in 1997. In 2001 she was refitted as a polar expedition ship and registered as the POLAR PIONEER. IMO 8010324

AYRAVATA CRUISES

The Company The Irrawaddy Flotilla Company was established by Scottish merchants in 1865. By the 1920s the company was running more than 650 vessels on the rivers of Burma and had become the largest privately owned fleet of ships in the world. In 1942 the entire fleet was scuttled as an act of denial when the Japanese invaded the country. The company became operational again at the end of the Second World War, but in 1948 after the British had left Burma, the company handed over its fleet to the Inland Water Transport Board. The Irrawaddy Flotilla Company name was revived in 1995 by

Ayravata Cruises' *Paukan 2012* *(company picture)*

Baltic and Black Sea Cruise Company's *Adriana* in Nice when operating for Plein Cap *(Rick Frendt)*

Birka Cruises' *Birka Paradise*, now *Birka Stockholm* in Stockholm *(William Mayes)*

historian Paul Strachan when he restored the 1947-built PANDAW. In 2003 the name of the company was changed to Ayravata Cruises.

Address Number 25, Ground Floor, 38th Street, Kyauktada Township, Yangon, Myanmar.

Telephone +95 1 380877

Website www.ayravatacruises.com

Area operated The rivers of Myanmar

PAUKAN 1947	gt	1947	11.0k	D1	32p	32p	c	47.7m	11.5m	0.8m	MM
PAUKAN 2007	gt	2007	12.0k	D1	55p	55p	30c	55.8m	11.6m	1.1m	MM
PAUKAN 2012	gt	2012	10.0k	D1	32p	32p	20c	42.0m	10.0m	0.8m	MM

PAUKAN 1947 was one of six similar vessels commissioned by the Burmese Government-owned Inland Water Transport Board. She was built by Yarrows on the River Clyde in Scotland as the river passenger and cargo vessel PANDAW. In 1998 she underwent conversion to a luxury river cruise ship and was operated for five years by a new Irrawaddy Flotilla Company. That charter ended and she was subjected to another major refit for her current operator. She appears to have been renamed PAUKAN 1947 in about 2012.

PAUKAN 2007 was built by the Myanmar Shipyard at Yangon (Rangoon), Myanmar for the company. Paukan is the old name for Bagan, a city on the banks of the Irrawaddy River, the capital city of the First Myanmar Empire.

PAUKAN 2012 was built by the Ahlone Shipyard in Yangon.

BALTIC & BLACK SEA CRUISE COMPANY

The Company Baltic and Black Sea Cruise Company is a Russian cruise operator.

Address Ulitsa Efimova 4a, St Petersburg, Russia

Telephone +7 812 324 7091

Website www.bbscc.ru

Area operated Black Sea

ADRIANA		4490gt	1972	15.0k	D2	240p	298p	100c	103.7m	14.0m	4.5m	KN

ADRIANA was built by the United Shipyard (yard number 54) at Perama, Greece for Hellenic Mediterranean Lines as the AQUARIUS. She was both the first cruise ship for that company and the first such vessel to be built in Greece. With her long raked bow she was a very elegant ship, and made an attractive sight on her Greek Island cruises during the summer. She did spend a few winters in the Caribbean, but served mostly in the Mediterranean. The ACHILLE LAURO hijacking in 1985 had a particularly bad effect on the business of Hellenic Mediterranean Lines, and in 1986 her mortgagees seized the AQUARIUS. She was sold to Adriatic General Shipping, part of the Yugoslav Jadrolinija company and began operating in the Adriatic Sea as the ADRIANA. She often ran cruises on charter to German tour operators. In 1997 she passed to Marina Cruises of Nice and in February of the following year commenced cruising under the Plein Cap banner, a role in which she continued until 2010. In 2008 she was renamed ADRIANA III. She was acquired by Tropicana Cruises for cruising around Cuba in 2010 and renamed ADRIANA. In 2014 ADRIANA is scheduled to operate in the Black Sea for BBSCC. IMO 7118404

BAMTUR

The Company Bamtur is a Turkish tour operator and travel agency, which chartered the ALEXANDER VON HUMBOLDT for a number of cruises in 2011. It is not known which, if any vessel will be in service in 2015.

Address Saskinbakkal Kazim Ozalp Sk, Kulun Apt, B Blok no 22/2, 34740 Suadiye Kadikoy, Istanbul, Turkey.

Telephone +90 216 444 0157 **Fax** +90 216 355 0299

Website www.bamtur.com

Area operated Greek islands from Istanbul

BEIHAI HUAMEI CRUISE

The Company Beihai Huamei Cruise is a Chinese company. It is uncertain if this ship is currently operating.

ORIENTAL PRINCESS	11513gt	1976	22.5k	D2	402p	750p	200c	137.9m	20.5m	5.6m	KH

ORIENTAL PRINCESS was built for the Spanish Ybarra Line as the CANGURO CABO SAN JORGE by Union Naval de Levante (yard number 131) at Valencia, Spain. When taken over by Trasmediterranea in 1981 she was renamed CIUDAD DE SANTA CRUZ DE LA PALMA, simplified during the following year to CIUDAD DE PALMA. In 2005 she was sold to Horizon Corporation of China, and for a single season in 2005 was chartered to operate as the DALMATINO for Italian Enermar for service between Italy and Croatia. The service ended after the summer season and the ship was later arrested and laid up in Choggia, Italy. She moved to China and was expected to be renamed as PRINCESS ANGEL. In the event she took the name OCEAN PRINCESS in 2006 for short cruises from China to Vietnam. She was renamed ORIENTAL PRINCESS in 2008. She was acquired by Beihai Huamei Cruise in 2010. IMO 7387718

BELMOND ROAD TO MANDALAY

The Company Belmond Road to Mandalay is a Myanmar cruise operator, which is part of Orient-Express Hotels. Orient Express Hotels was one of the luxury brands of the now defunct Sea Containers Inc.

Address 1st Floor, Shackleton House, 4 Battle Bridge Lane, London, SE1 2HP, United Kingdom

Telephone +44 203 117 1300

Website www.belmond.com

Area operated Irrawaddy River, Myanmar

ROAD TO MANDALAY	1650gt	1964	11.0k	D2	118p	118p	80c	101.6m	11.6m	1.4m	MM

ROAD TO MANDALAY was built by Ewald Berninghaus in Cologne, Germany as the river cruise ship NEDERLAND. She was to have been renamed ELBERESIDENZ, but was instead sold to Burmese interests in 1994 and renamed ROAD TO MANDALAY for river cruising. The ship has recently undergone a major refit and returned to service in August 2009. IMO 8642969

BIRKA CRUISES

The Company Birka Line is a Finnish (Aland Island) owner of ro-ro freighters that also operates a cruise ship on 22 hour duty free and party cruises from Stockholm. For a while the company owned the BIRKA QUEEN, built as the ROYAL VIKING SKY, but her operation was not totally successful and she was chartered to Princess Cruises as the GOLDEN PRINCESS before being sold to Star Cruises. The Baltic cruise business began in 1971, but stepped up a gear with the arrival of the purpose built BIRKA PRINCESS in 1986. That ship was sold to Louis Cruise Lines in 2006, becoming the SEA DIAMOND. She sank in April 2007 following contact with rocks off the Greek island of Santorini. Birka Line was taken over by Aland Island ferry operator, Eckero Line in 2007.

Address Stadsgardsterminalen, Box 15131, SE10465 Stockholm, Sweden

Telephone +46 8 702 7230

Website www.birka.se

Area operated 22 hour cruises from Stockholm, Sweden to Mariehamn plus some longer Baltic Sea cruises

BIRKA STOCKHOLM	34924gt	2004	21.0k	D2	1468p	1800p	219c	176.9m	28.0m	6.6m	SE

BIRKA STOCKHOLM was built by Aker Finnyards (yard number 442) at Rauma, Finland for Birka Line as the BIRKA PARADISE. She was designed to attract a younger clientele than that usually associated with her former fleet mate, the BIRKA PRINCESS. She was renamed BIRKA STOCKHOLM in 2013. IMO 9273727

Blount's *Grande Caribe* in New York *(Rick Frendt)*

Bohai Cruise Company's *Zhong Hua Tai Shan* as *Costa Voyager* at Corfu *(Martin Grant)*

Aida Cruises' *Aidabella* off Cannes *(William Mayes)*

BLOUNT SMALL SHIP ADVENTURES

The Company American Canadian Caribbean Line was founded in 1966 by Captain Luther Blount to serve the demand for small ship cruising in American coastal waters. The ships are all shallow draft, have retractable wheelhouses to allow access to rivers that would otherwise be inaccessible, and are fitted with a bow ramp to allow direct disembarkation onto secluded beaches. Luther Blount died in 2006, at the age of 90. In November 2006, the company's third ship, the NIAGARA PRINCE, passed into the ownership of Rhode Island College, Roger Williams University and Wentworth Institute of Technology; a $6.5 million legacy from inventor and philanthropist Blount. In early 2007 she was renamed LUTHER'S LEGACY. However, she remained unused so the company bought her back in 2008 and reinstated her original name. The name of the company was later changed to Blount Small Ship Adventures.

Address 461 Water Street, PO Box 368, Warren, Rhode Island 02885, United States of America

Telephone +1 401 247 0955 **Fax** +1 401 247 2350

Website www.blountsmallshipadventures.com

Area operated Caribbean and Central America (winter), East Coast USA and Canada (summer)

GRANDE CARIBE	761gt	1997	10.0k	D2	100p	100p	17c	55.6m	11.9m	2.0m	US
GRANDE MARINER	829gt	1998	10.0k	D2	100p	100p	17c	56.0m	11.9m	1.9m	US
NIAGARA PRINCE	667gt	1994	10.0k	D2	84p	94p	17c	53.0m	12.2m	2.0m	US

All three ships were built for the company by Blount Industries (yard numbers 294, 298 and 287) at Warren, Rhode Island, USA. IMO 8978631 8978643 and 8978629

BLU CRUISES

The Company Blu Cruises, part of the Alilauro Group of high-speed ferry operating companies, operates 3- and 4-day cruises and charters in the Bay of Naples.

Area operated The Bay of Naples but may not still be operating

CAPRI	900gt	1962	13.5k	D2	56p	56p	17c	62.0m	9.8m	2.8m	PT

CAPRI was built by Cantieri Navale Cassaro (yard number 115) at Messina, Sicily as the general cargo ship BASILUZZO for Societa di Navigazione NaviSarMa Spa. She later became part of the Si.Re.Mar. fleet. She was acquired by Cycladic Cruises in 1985 and renamed CITY OF ANDROS, with the intention of having her rebuilt as a cruise ship. That was eventually completed in 1992 in Piraeus. In 2003 she was acquired by Blu Cruises and renamed as the CITALIA after an extensive refit. She was renamed as the CAPRI in 2007. IMO 5037644

BLUE LAGOON CRUISES

The Company Blue Lagoon Cruises was founded in 1950 by New Zealander, Captain Trevor Withers, initially as a tuna boat charter business. In 1966 he sold the business to Captain Claude Miller, a well-known New Zealand ship owner. Blue Lagoon Cruises is now a subsidiary of South Sea Cruises Ltd.

Address PO Box PDO52, Denarau, Nadi, Fiji Islands

Telephone +679 675 0500

Website www.bluelagooncruises.com

Area operated Fiji

FIJI PRINCESS	1258gt	1998	15.0k	D2	68p	76p	20c	55.5m	15.0m	2.1m	FJ
MYSTIQUE PRINCESS	1533gt	1996	11.5k	D2	72p	108p	24c	55.3m	12.5m	2.8m	FJ

FIJI PRINCESS was built by Chantiers Navale (yard number B234) at Marseilles, France as the RIVAGE MARTINIQUE for Rivages Croisieres. She was renamed PEARL OF SEYCHELLES in 2001 and joined the fleet of her present owner in 2004 as the FIJI PRINCESS. IMO 9199907

MYSTIQUE PRINCESS was built by Astilleros Servicios Navales (yard number 111) at Valdivia, Chile for Blue Lagoon Cruises. IMO 9131395

BOHAI CRUISE COMPANY

The Company Bohai Ferry Company is a 2014 entrant in the cruise market. The company is a well-established Chinese ferry operator, which has now branched out into cruising, using a new company. Cruise services were due to commence on 26 August 2014.

Address 2 Huanhai Lu, Zhifu Qu, Yantai, Shandong, Peoples Republic of China

Area operated Cruises from Yantai, China

ZHONG HUA TAI SHAN	24427gt	2000	28.0k	D2	836p	920p	360c	180.4m	25.5m	7.3m	PA

ZHONG HUA TAI SHAN, another first new ship, was built as one of a pair of high-speed cruise ships for Royal Olympic Cruises of Greece by Blohm & Voss (yard number 961) in Hamburg as the OLYMPIC VOYAGER. Political unrest in the Eastern Mediterranean meant that her intended service was curtailed and she was put to work more mundane than the 'Three Continents in a Week' circuit for which she was built. Difficulties with the International Olympic Organisation led to the company restyling itself as Royal Olympia Cruises and the ship was renamed OLYMPIA VOYAGER. The company within ROC that owned the ship filed for bankruptcy, starting the process that led to the complete failure of the group. The ship was auctioned and acquired by the V-Ships group. Renamed VOYAGER, she was chartered to Iberojet, initially being marketed as GRAND VOYAGER. She was formally renamed in late 2005. Iberocruceros acquired the ship in 2009 and she was transferred to Costa late in 2011 and renamed COSTA VOYAGER. In 2014 she was sold by Costa to Bohai Ferry Company and renamed ZHONG HUA TAI SHAN, although Lloyds Register shows this as CHINESE TAISHAN. IMO 9183506

CAPTAIN COOK CRUISES (FIJI)

The Company Captain Cook Cruises was an Australian family-owned business, established by Captain Trevor Haworth on 26 January (Australia Day) 1970 to operate sightseeing cruises in Sydney Harbour. The Australian parts of the company were sold to Adelaide-based Sea Link Travel Group in 2011. The Fiji part of the business appears to have been retained. The company also operates three day vessels in the islands.

Address Denarau Marina, Nadi, Fiji Islands

Telephone +67 9 670 1823

Website www.captaincook.com.fj

REEF ENDEAVOUR	3125gt	1996	13.5k	D2	130p	140p	35c	73.6m	14.0m	3.7m	FJ

REEF ENDEAVOUR was built at the Fiji Marine Shipyard & Slipways (yard number 920) at Suva, Fiji. She operates cruises in the Fiji Islands. IMO 9012666

The company also operates the day vessels CITY OF NADI, FIJI ONE and SPIRIT OF THE PACIFIC in the Fiji Islands.

CAPTAIN COOK CRUISES (SYDNEY)

The Company Captain Cook Cruises was an Australian family-owned business, established by Captain Trevor Haworth on 26 January (Australia Day) 1970 to operate sightseeing cruises in Sydney Harbour. The Australian parts of the company were sold to Adelaide-based Sea Link Travel Group in 2011. The company now operates 13 day ships in Sydney Harbour.

Address No 6 Jetty, Circular Quay, Sydney, New South Wales 2000, Australia

Telephone +61 2 9206 1111 **Fax** +61 2 9251 4725

Website www.sealinktravelgroup.com.au

Area operated Murray River and day cruises in Sydney Harbour

MURRAY PRINCESS	c1500gt	1986	6.0k	D1	120p	120p	30c	67.0m	15.0m	1.2m	AU

MURRAY PRINCESS was built at Goolwa, Australia as a stern-wheel river cruise ship, and is currently operating in the Murray River.

CARNIVAL CORPORATION and PLC

The Company In 1972, entrepreneur Ted Arison purchased the 1960 built Canadian Pacific Steamships' transatlantic liner EMPRESS OF CANADA, renamed her MARDI GRAS, and began operating her on cruises from Miami. Arison had been involved in Norwegian Caribbean Lines, so was no stranger to the Caribbean cruise trade. Who, in 1972, could have foreseen that from these modest beginnings Carnival would, by the end of the century, have become the largest cruise-ship owning group in the world. This transformation has come about not only by building new ships, but also by means of an ambitious acquisition programme. Commencing with the purchase of Holland America Line in 1989, Seabourn in 1992, a 50% stake in Costa Crociere (Airtours had the other 50% and Carnival also acquired just under 30% of Airtours) in 1997, Cunard in 1998 and finishing (to date) with the acquisition of the remaining 50% share in Costa Crociere in 2001. There was also the hard fought merger with P&O Princess Cruises in 2003 to form a dual listed company (on the London and New York stock exchanges). P&O Princess itself was a relatively new company, albeit with a long and impressive pedigree, having been formed as recently as the autumn of 2000 when P&O (The Peninsular and Oriental Steam Navigation Company) de-merged its cruising businesses. One potential acquisition that did not happen was the purchase of Premier Cruise Line in 1991, following uncertainty over earnings in the wake of the first Gulf War. The operational name Carnival Corporation came into use in 1993. Where not operating for an international clientele the marketing area of each subsidiary is shown after the company name. The operating companies within the group are shown in alphabetical order, but the section headed 'structure' may be useful for viewing how this conglomerate developed. In late 2006 Carnival Corporation announced its intention to enter into a joint venture with Germany's TUI AG, under which the latter company would have owned 5% of the new business. However, the proposal fell foul of the regulatory process and did not proceed. In 2007 Carnival Corporation entered into a joint venture with Spain's Iberojet, under which Carnival now owns 75% of that business. This would seem to serve two purposes in that it gives Carnival a toehold in the Spanish market, hot on the heels of Royal Caribbean's acquisition of Pullmantur, and also provides another outlet within the group for ships that are no longer considered to be 'front line' vessels. Shortly after this acquisition Carnival sold Wind Star Cruises to Ambassadors International's Majestic America Line. Carnival Corporation's ships are currently estimated to contain about 50% of the world's cruise ship berths.

Address Carnival Place, 3655 N.W. 87th Avenue, Doral, Miami, FL 33178-2428 United States of America

Carnival House, 100 Harbour Parade, Southampton SO15 1ST, United Kingdom

Website www.carnivalplc.com or www.carnivalcorp.com

Structure Holding Company Carnival Corporation and plc

Carnival Cruise Lines, Costa Crociere, Holland America Line and Carnival UK report directly to Carnival Corporation.

Cunard Line, Princess Cruises UK operations, and P&O Cruises form Carnival UK.

Aida Cruises and Iberocruceros report through Costa Crociere.

Princess Cruises, P&O Australia and Seabourn report through Holland America Line.

AIDA CRUISES

The Company The origins of Aida Cruises can be traced back to 1991, when one of the results of German reunification was the acquisition of former East German Deutsche Seereederei and its single ship, the ARKONA, by West German investors. In 1994 the order was placed for the first new ship, a radically different vessel from the ARKONA, and one that was intended to offer the German equivalent of Club Med at sea. At this time the ARKONA was on charter to another German company, Seetours, then part of TUI, but later acquired by Deutsche Seereederei. At the end of September 1999 it was announced that P&O and Seetours, as the German cruising business was now styled, had agreed to form a new venture, Aida Cruises, to develop the German cruise market. The company had been operating the AIDA since 1996, but lacked the finance to invest in further ships; indeed the AIDA had been sold to NCL in 1997 and chartered back. The AIDA was reacquired and almost immediately P&O placed the order for two similar, but slightly larger ships. All three Aida vessels were then registered in London. With the merger of P&O Princess and Carnival Corporation, Aida Cruises was moved from the control of P&O Princess to Costa Cruises, and the ships were re-registered from London to Genoa.

Aida Cruises' *Aidacara* in Copenhagen *(William Mayes)*

Aida Cruises' *Aidastella* in Hamburg *(William Mayes)*

Aida Cruises' *Aidavita* at Civitavecchia *(William Mayes)*

With the demise of A'Rosa's ocean cruise business, that organisation's single ocean cruise ship (AIDABLU – formerly CROWN PRINCESS) was transferred to Aida. It had been intended that the A'Rosa brand would also operate her sister, the REGAL PRINCESS, but that ship remained with Princess Cruises, latterly being transferred to P&O Cruises (Australia). Germany is the world's third largest market for cruise passengers, and is currently one of the fastest growing, thus justifying the order for a further quartet of ships, the first of which replaced the AIDABLU, transferred within the Carnival Group to Ocean Village. That order for four ships was later extended to six vessels. A seventh ship was ordered in 2010. Aida Cruises caters only for German speaking passengers. In 2012 Aida Cruises carried 633,000 passengers. Aida Cruises is managed by Costa Crociere.

Address Am Strande 3d, 18055 Rostock, Germany

Telephone +49 381 4440 **Fax** +49 381 444 8888

Website www.aida.de

Areas operated Mediterranean, Atlantic Isles, Scandinavia, Middle East and the Caribbean

AIDAAURA	42289gt	2003	19.4k	DE2	1266p	1582p	389c	203.2m	28.1m	6.2m	IT
AIDABELLA	69203gt	2008	21.0k	DE2	2050p	2500p	607c	252.0m	32.2m	7.2m	IT
AIDABLU	71304gt	2010	21.8K	DE2	2192p	2192p	607c	253.3m	32.2m	7.3m	IT
AIDACARA	38557gt	1996	21.0k	D2	1180p	1230p	369c	193.3m	27.6m	6.2m	IT
AIDADIVA	69203gt	2007	21.8k	DE2	2050p	2500p	607c	252.0m	32.2m	7.2m	IT
AIDALUNA	69203gt	2009	21.0k	DE2	2050p	2500p	607c	252.0m	32.2m	7.2m	IT
AIDAMAR	71304gt	2012	21.0k	DE2	2192p	2500p	646c	252.0m	32.2m	7.2m	IT
AIDASOL	71304gt	2011	21.8k	DE2	2192p	2192p	607c	252.0m	32.3m	7.2m	IT
AIDASTELLA	71304gt	2013	21.0k	DE2	2192p	2500p	646c	252.0m	32.2m	7.2m	IT
AIDAVITA	42289gt	2002	19.4k	DE2	1266p	1582p	389c	203.2m	28.1m	6.2m	IT

AIDAAURA was built by the Aker MTW Yard (yard number 4) in Wismar, Germany for Aida Cruises and named by Heidi Klum. IMO 9221566

AIDABELLA was delivered by the Meyer shipyard (yard number 660) in the spring of 2008, and named by Eva Padberg. IMO 9334868

AIDABLU is the first ship in a series of three vessels that are slightly larger than the AIDADIVA class. She was built by Meyer Werft (yard number 680) at Papenburg, Germany, and was floated out on 5 January 2010. She was based in Northern Europe for the first part of 2010, following her naming on 9 February by international designer Jette Joop. IMO 9398888

AIDACARA was built by Kvaerner Masa Yards (yard number 1337) at Turku, Finland for Arkona Touristik of Germany as the AIDA. Her godmother was Christiane Herzog. As a result of the financial difficulties of her owners, the ship was sold to Norwegian Cruise Line in 1997, but chartered back. She was re-purchased by Arkona Touristik in 1999, and the operating company was restyled as Aida Cruises. The AIDA was renamed AIDACARA in 2001 in anticipation of the delivery of the first of the pair of ships under construction in Germany. IMO 9112789

AIDADIVA is the first of a series of four ships ordered from the Meyer shipyard (yard number 659) at Papenburg, Germany. The order was later amended with the addition of two more ships with a slightly higher passenger capacity, and at that time the fourth ship in this series had her specification changed to match the new pair. The ship was named in Hamburg on 20 April 2007 by Maria Galleski, winner of a competition held in conjunction with local newspaper the Hamburger Abendblatt. The AIDADIVA spent her first season in the Mediterranean based at Palma de Majorca and later in the Canary Islands, based in Tenerife. IMO 9334856

AIDALUNA is the last of the first series of three ships built by Meyer (yard number 666) and was named in Palma, Majorca on 4 April 2009 by model Franziska Knuppe. She then repositioned to Northern Europe before spending the winter in the Canary Islands. IMO 9362542

AIDAMAR was built by Meyer Werft at Papenburg (yard number 690) and delivered in April 2012. She was named at a spectacular ceremony in Hamburg as part of the port's 823rd birthday celebrations on 12 May by Sissi Kuhlmann, in the presence of the AIDABLU, AIDALUNA and AIDASOL. IMO 9490052

AIDASOL is the second of the enhanced AIDADIVA class ships built by Meyer (yard number 689) at Papenburg and was named by Bettina Zwickler in Kiel on 9 April 2011. IMO 9490040

AIDASTELLA is the final ship in the series of seven built by Meyer at Papenburg (yard number 695). She was christened by ten godmothers, chosen from Aida Cruises staff (8) and one each from the shipbuilders and the design house, on 16 March 2013 at Warnemunde. IMO 9601132

AIDAVITA was built at Wismar in Germany by Aker MTW (yard number 3) for Aida Cruises. She was christened by Doris Shroder-Kopf. IMO 9221554

Cruise ships on order

AIDAPRIMA	124500gt	2015	16.0k	DE2	3286p		p		c	300.0m	37.6m	8.1m	IT
NEWBUILDING 2	124500gt	2016	16.0k	DE2	3283p		p		c	300.0m	37.6m	8.1m	IT

AIDAPRIMA and **NEWBUILDING 2** are under construction by Mitsubishi Heavy Industries at Nagasaki in Japan (yard numbers 2300 and 2301). The AIDAPRIMA will be the first of company's ships to be based year-round in Hamburg and her open decks will be equipped to cope with the sometimes unpredictable weather in Northern Europe. Originally due for delivery in spring 2015, she will be delivered approximately six months late and will spend her first winter based in Dubai. She was launched on 3 May 2014. IMO 9636955 and 9636967

CARNIVAL CRUISE LINES

The Company Carnival Cruise Lines began operations in 1972 with the MARDI GRAS (formerly the EMPRESS OF CANADA); an inauspicious start as she ran aground on her maiden voyage. In 1979 she undertook a series of Pacific cruises from Los Angeles, and earlier had undertaken an epic 41-day Mediterranean cruise. Her former running mate on Canadian Pacific's transatlantic service, the EMPRESS OF BRITAIN, suitably renamed CARNIVALE, joined her at the end of 1975. A third ship, the S A VAAL of the South African Marine Corporation (earlier the TRANSVAAL CASTLE of the Union Castle Mail Steamship Company), renamed FESTIVALE, joined the fleet in 1977 following her closing the joint Union Castle/Safmarine service between Southampton and South Africa. The first new ship was ordered shortly afterwards, and entered service in January 1982 as the TROPICALE. All of these ships have now left the Carnival Cruise Lines fleet. The delivery of the TROPICALE, however, signalled the start of what has proved to be the most expansive passenger shipbuilding programme of the past 50 years, and by 1987 Carnival Cruise Lines was carrying more passengers than any other cruise line. Carnival Cruise Lines has developed a strong affiliation with Italian shipbuilder Fincantieri, who have built eight of the most recent twelve ships. The company employs around 43,000 staff and in 2013 carried approximately 4.5 million passengers.

Address Carnival Place, 3655 N.W. 87th Avenue, Miami, FL 33178-2428, United States of America

Telephone +1 305 599 2600 **Fax** +1 305 406 4779

Website www.carnival.com

Areas operated Caribbean, Mexico, Alaska, East Coast USA, Mediterranean and Australia

CARNIVAL BREEZE	128052gt	2012	22.5k	DEP2	3690p	4724p	1386c	305.5m	37.2m	8.2m	PA
CARNIVAL CONQUEST	110239gt	2002	22.5k	DE2	2984p	3700p	1150c	290.2m	35.5m	8.2m	PA
CARNIVAL DREAM	128251gt	2009	22.5k	DEP2	3646p	4631p	1367c	304.2m	37.0m	8.2m	PA
CARNIVAL ECSTASY	70526gt	1991	19.5k	DE2	2056p	2606p	920c	260.8m	31.5m	7.8m	PA
CARNIVAL ELATION	70390gt	1998	19.5k	DEP2	2052p	2606p	920c	260.8m	31.5m	7.8m	PA
CARNIVAL FANTASY	70367gt	1990	19.5k	DE2	2056p	2610p	920c	260.8m	31.5m	8.0m	PA
CARNIVAL FASCINATION	70538gt	1994	19.5k	DE2	2056p	2606p	920c	260.8m	31.5m	7.8m	BS
CARNIVAL FREEDOM	110320gt	2007	22.5k	DE2	2980p	3700p	1150c	290.2m	35.5m	8.2m	PA
CARNIVAL GLORY	110239gt	2003	22.5k	DE2	2980p	3700p	1150c	290.2m	35.5m	8.2m	PA
CARNIVAL IMAGINATION	70367gt	1995	19.5k	DE2	2056p	2634p	920c	260.8m	31.5m	7.8m	BS
CARNIVAL INSPIRATION	70367gt	1996	19.5k	DE2	2054p	2658p	920c	260.8m	31.5m	7.8m	BS
CARNIVAL LEGEND	85942gt	2002	22.0k	DEP2	2132p	2680p	930c	292.5m	32.2m	7.8m	MT
CARNIVAL LIBERTY	110320gt	2005	22.5k	DE2	2974p	3700p	1160c	290.2m	35.5m	8.2m	PA
CARNIVAL MAGIC	128048gt	2011	22.5k	DEP2	3690p	4724p	1367c	304.2m	37.0m	8.2m	PA
CARNIVAL MIRACLE	85942gt	2004	22.0k	DEP2	2124p	2680p	934c	292.5m	32.2m	8.0m	PA
CARNIVAL PARADISE	70390gt	1998	19.5k	DEP2	2052p	2606p	920c	260.8m	31.5m	7.8m	PA
CARNIVAL PRIDE	85920gt	2001	22.0k	DEP2	2124p	2680p	930c	292.5m	32.2m	7.8m	PA
CARNIVAL SENSATION	70538gt	1993	19.5k	DE2	2056p	2658p	920c	260.8m	31.5m	7.8m	BS
CARNIVAL SPIRIT	85920gt	2001	22.0k	DEP2	2124p	2680p	930c	292.5m	32.2m	7.8m	MT
CARNIVAL SPLENDOR	113323gt	2008	22.5k	DE2	3006p	4914p	1160c	290.0m	25.5m	8.2m	PA

Carnival Cruise Lines' *Carnival Breeze* in Venice *(Rick Frendt)*

Carnival Cruise Lines' *Carnival Fascination* off Nassau *(Rick Frendt)*

Carnival Cruise Lines' *Carnival Inspiration* at Cozumel *(Richard Mayes)*

Carnival Cruise Lines' *Carnival Liberty* at Civitavecchia *(Rick Frendt)*

Carnival Cruise Lines' *Carnival Magic* at Cozumel *(Rick Frendt)*

Carnival Cruise Lines' *Carnival Spirit* in Sydney *(Alf Sims)*

CARNIVAL SUNSHINE	103881gt	1996	19.0k	DE2	3002p	3360p	1040c	272.3m	35.5m	8.3m	BS
CARNIVAL TRIUMPH	101509gt	1999	19.0k	DE2	2754p	3470p	1100c	272.2m	35.5m	8.2m	BS
CARNIVAL VALOR	110239gt	2004	22.5k	DE2	2980p	3783p	1180c	290.2m	35.5m	8.2m	PA
CARNIVAL VICTORY	101509gt	2000	19.0k	DE2	2754p	3470p	1100c	272.2m	35.5m	8.2m	PA

CARNIVAL BREEZE was built at Fincantieri's Monfalcone shipyard (yard number 6201). After an inaugural season based in Barcelona she moved to Miami in November 2012 for Caribbean cruising. She was named in Miami on 8 December 2012 by Tracy Wilson Mourning, the founder of Honey Shine, a mentoring programme for young girls. IMO 9555723

CARNIVAL CONQUEST was built by Fincantieri (yard number 6057) at Monfalcone, Italy. Interestingly, the forward section of the hull was built at the Sestri yard in Genoa and towed to Monfalcone for completion. She was named by former US Congresswoman Lindy Boggs. The CARNIVAL CONQUEST currently operates Caribbean cruises from Fort Lauderdale and Miami. IMO 9198355

CARNIVAL DREAM was built by Fincantieri (yard number 6151) and was delivered in September 2009. She then operated cruises in the Mediterranean Sea before moving to New York, where actress Marcia Gay Harden named her on 12 November. After a series of cruises from New York she then took up station at Port Canaveral for alternate 7-day Eastern and Western Caribbean itineraries. She now operates from New Orleans. IMO 9378474

CARNIVAL ECSTASY was built by the Helsinki, Finland shipyard of Masa Yards (yard number 480) and delivered in 1991 as the ECSTASY, the second of the Fantasy class. Following her naming ceremony by television personality Kathie Lee Gifford in New York, the ECSTASY began cruising from Miami in June 1991. The Carnival prefix was added to her name in November 2007. She now operates to the Bahamas and Caribbean from Miami. IMO 8711344

CARNIVAL ELATION is the seventh ship in the Fantasy class and was delivered in 1998 by Kvaerner Masa Yards (yard number 491), Helsinki, Finland as the ELATION. Named by Shari Arison, she was the first large passenger ship to use pod propulsion. She was renamed as the CARNIVAL ELATION in November 2007. In spring 2010 she was chartered by the Royal Canadian Mounted Police for use as an accommodation ship at Vancouver in connection with the Winter Olympic Games. Her itineraries include short cruises from New Orleans. IMO 9118721

CARNIVAL FANTASY is the first ship in an eight ship series ordered from Wartsila and its successors in Finland. She was delivered as the FANTASY by Masa Yard's Helsinki shipyard (yard number 479) in 1990, following the failure of Wartsila Marine Industries, and was immediately employed on cruises from Miami. Her original godmother was Jeanne Farcus. She was renamed with the Carnival prefix in 2007. She now cruises to the Caribbean from Charleston, South Carolina. IMO 8700773

CARNIVAL FASCINATION is the fourth of the Fantasy class (yard number 487), delivered by Masa Yards, Helsinki, Finland and entered service as the FASCINATION in 1994. Renamed in October 2007, the CARNIVAL FASCINATION is now employed on cruises to the Bahamas from Jacksonville. In 2010 she had 98 new balconies fitted. IMO 9041253

CARNIVAL FREEDOM was built by Fincantieri (yard number 6129) at the Breda Shipyard in Venice. After being named by businesswoman Kathy Ireland, her first season featured Mediterranean cruises followed by a repositioning trip to the Caribbean. She now operates Eastern, Western and Southern Caribbean cruises from Fort Lauderdale and Galveston. IMO 9333149

CARNIVAL GLORY is another product of the Monfalcone, Italy shipyard of Fincantieri (yard number 6059). She was named by astronaut Dr Sally Ride. The CARNIVAL GLORY now operates Caribbean cruises from Miami. IMO 9198367

CARNIVAL IMAGINATION is the fifth member of the Fantasy class (yard number 488) and was delivered to Carnival Cruise Lines as the IMAGINATION by Masa Yards, Helsinki, Finland in 1995. Her godmother was Jodi Dickinson. CARNIVAL IMAGINATION is currently based in Los Angeles for Mexican Riviera cruises. IMO 9053878

CARNIVAL INSPIRATION entered service with Carnival as the INSPIRATION in 1996, following her naming by Mary Ann Shula. She was renamed as the CARNIVAL INSPIRATION in late 2007 and now operates short Mexico cruises from Los Angeles. She is the sixth ship to be constructed by Masa Yards, Helsinki, Finland in the Fantasy class (yard number 489). IMO 9087489

CARNIVAL LEGEND was delivered in 2002 by Kvaerner Masa Yards (yard number 501) at Helsinki, Finland, as the third of the Spirit class for Caribbean cruising. Following her naming by Dame Judi

Dench, she was the first Carnival ship to cruise in Europe as she undertook a number of voyages from Harwich, England prior to heading for New York. She now covers the entire West Coast of the USA from Alaska to Hawaii. She also operates seasonally in Australia. IMO 9224726

CARNIVAL LIBERTY was built by Fincantieri (yard number 6111) at Monfalcone, Italy. After being christened by actress Mira Sorvino in Civitavecchia, Italy on 19 July 2005, the ship commenced a series of summer cruises in the Mediterranean, based at that port. Her current employment is Bahamas and Caribbean cruises from Port Canaveral. IMO 9278181

CARNIVAL MAGIC was named by Lindsey Wilkerson of St Judes' Childrens' Hospital following delivery by Fincantieri (yard number 6167) at Monfalcone. She spent the summer of 2011 in the Mediterranean after which she moved to Galveston, Texas to operate Caribbean itineraries. IMO 9378486

CARNIVAL MIRACLE was built by Kvaerner Masa Yards (yard number 503) in Helsinki, Finland. Her godmother is Jessica Lynch. For 2014 the ship is cruising in Alaska and to Hawaii and Mexico. IMO 9237357

CARNIVAL PARADISE is the final member of the eight ship Fantasy class (yard number 494), and when delivered to Carnival Cruise Lines as the PARADISE in 1998 became the world's first totally smoking-free ship (funnel excepted, we assume). She later quietly dropped her non-smoking status. Her godmother is television newswoman Paula Zahn. The ship had the Carnival prefix added to her name in 2007 and now sails on short cruises from Tampa, Florida to the Caribbean. IMO 9120877

CARNIVAL PRIDE is the second of the Spirit class ships and was delivered by the Helsinki, Finland shipyard of Kvaerner Masa Yards (yard number 500) at the end of 2001 for alternate 7-day Eastern and Western Caribbean cruising based at Port Canaveral, Florida. She now operates a variety of itineraries from Baltimore, Maryland and Tampa. Her godmother is US space travel pioneer Tamara Jernigan. IMO 9223954

CARNIVAL SENSATION is the third member of the Fantasy class. Following the failure of Wartsila Marine Industries in November 1989, the order was cancelled. The contract was renewed with Masa Yards, Helsinki, Finland (yard number 484) in 1991 and the ship joined Carnival's growing Caribbean fleet as the SENSATION in 1993. Her godmothers were Gerry Donnelly, Vicki Freed, Roberta Jacoby and Cherie Weinstein. She was renamed as the CARNIVAL SENSATION in 2007 and now sails to the Bahamas and the Caribbean from Port Canaveral. In early 2009 she had 98 new balconies added. IMO 8711356

CARNIVAL SPIRIT is the name-ship of the Spirit class. When delivered by Kvaerner Masa Yards (yard number 499) of Helsinki, Finland in 2001, she became Carnival Cruise Lines' first ship to serve the Alaska and Hawaii markets, although she is now based in Australia. Her godmother is Elizabeth Dole. IMO 9188647

CARNIVAL SPLENDOR is the first ship in a new class, built by Fincantieri (yard number 6135), at the Sestri yard at Genoa, Italy. Following her delivery she was named by broadcaster and musician Myleene Klass in Dover on 10 July 2008 and was based in the UK for a summer season of cruises in Northern Europe. The ship now serves the East Coast USA market from New York, Norfolk and Miami. IMO 9333163

CARNIVAL SUNSHINE was Carnival Cruise Lines' first 100,000+ gross ton cruise ship. At the time of her delivery, as the CARNIVAL DESTINY, by Fincantieri's Monfalcone, Italy yard (yard number 5941) in 1996 she was the largest passenger ship ever built. Her godmother is Lin Arison. After a major rebuild in 2013 the ship re-entered service as the CARNIVAL SUNSHINE, and was again christened by Lin Arison. The ship now operates Bahamas cruises from Port Canaveral. IMO 9070058

CARNIVAL TRIUMPH was built by Fincantieri (yard number 5979) at Monfalcone, Italy and delivered in 1999, as the second ship in the Destiny class. She currently cruises to the Western Caribbean from New Orleans and Galveston. Her godmother is Madeleine Arison. IMO 9138850

CARNIVAL VALOR was built by Fincantieri (yard number 6082) at Monfalcone, Italy. The CARNIVAL VALOR is employed on various Caribbean itineraries from Barbados and San Juan. She was named by NBC's Today programme presenter Katie Couric. IMO 9236389

CARNIVAL VICTORY is the third member of the Destiny class, built by Fincantieri (yard number 6045) at Monfalcone, Italy and delivered in 2000. She now operates from Miami to the Caribbean. Her godmother is Mary Frank. IMO 9172648

Carnival Cruise Lines' *Carnival Splendor* in Istanbul *(William Mayes)*

Carnival Cruise Lines' *Carnival Sunshine* in Venice *(Matthew Sudders)*

Carnival Cruise Lines' *Carnival Victory* in New York *(Theodore W Scull)*

Cruise ship on order

CARNIVAL VISTA	c135000gt	2016	22.5k	DE2	3611p	4500p	1367c	330.0m	38.4m	8.5m	PA

CARNIVAL VISTA is on order from Fincantieri's Monfalcone shipyard (yard number 6232). IMO 9614141

COSTA CROCIERE

The Company The origins of the Costa Line date from 1924 when the brothers Federico, Eugenio and Enrico Costa bought their first cargo ship. It was not until after the Second World War that the business entered passenger shipping. In 1947 the small MARIA C, and in 1948 the ANNA C and ANDREA C were the first passenger ships for what had now become known as Linea C. The company was initially involved in the post-war migrant trades, but subsequently built up a route network linking South America with Mediterranean ports. In 1959 the FRANCA C (built in 1914 and still around as the static ship DOULOS) became the first Costa Line ship to be exclusively allocated to American cruising. This major Italian passenger line was re-styled Costa Armatori S.p.A. in 1967 and in the following year the company introduced Caribbean fly-cruises based in San Juan. In 1986, in response to changed markets, the company was renamed Costa Crociere S.p.A. and thereafter was involved solely in cruise operations. In 1993 the French Croisieres Paquet became part of Costa, and two years later the company began cruises to Havana. In December 1996 the shareholders accepted a joint bid by Airtours of the United Kingdom and Carnival Corporation, and so the last major Italian passenger ship operator ceased to be independent. In spring 2001 Carnival Corporation acquired Airtours' holding in Costa, and the latter company then became a full subsidiary. Subsequently Costa has taken control of both Aida Cruises and Iberocruceros for management purposes. In 2010 a new Paquet Croisieres began operation using the COSTA ALLEGRA. It is thought that Costa has licenced the Paquet name to a new French operator in order to test the market. In 2011 Paquet used Iberocruceros' GRAND MISTRAL, and the GRAND VOYAGER from the same source was used for a series of Red Sea cruises from December 2011 to March 2012. With the arrival of the COSTA NEORIVIERA in 2013 Costa set up a new sub-brand for its smaller ships, with greater emphasis on smaller ports and longer port calls. The loss of the COSTA CONCORDIA in January 2012 was a serious blow to the company.

Address Piazza Piccapietra 48, GE 16121 Genoa, Italy

Telephone +39 10 548 3751 **Fax** +39 10 469 4114

Website www.costacruises.co.uk, www.costacruise.com, www.costacrociere.it

Areas operated Mediterranean, Scandinavia, Middle East, Far East, South America and the Caribbean

COSTA ATLANTICA	85619gt	2000	22.0k	DEP2	2114p	2680p	897c	292.5m	32.2m	8.0m	IT
COSTA CELEBRATION	47263gt	1987	21.5k	D2	1498p	1910p	620c	223.3m	28.0m	7.6m	PT
COSTA CLASSICA	52926gt	1991	18.5k	D2	1308p	1680p	590c	220.6m	30.8m	7.3m	IT
COSTA DELIZIOSA	92720gt	2010	21.6k	DEP2	2260p	2826p	921c	294.0m	32.3m	8.1m	IT
COSTA FASCINOSA	113216gt	2012	19.6k	DE2	3012p	3780p	1110c	290.2m	35.5m	8.3m	IT
COSTA FAVOLOSA	113216gt	2011	19.6k	DE2	3016p	3780p	1100c	290.2m	35.5m	8.3m	IT
COSTA FORTUNA	102587gt	2003	20.0k	DE2	2716p	3470p	1027c	272.2m	35.5m	8.2m	IT
COSTA LUMINOSA	92720gt	2009	21.6k	DEP2	2260p	2826p	921c	294.0m	32.3m	8.1m	IT
COSTA MAGICA	102587gt	2004	20.0k	DE2	2716p	3470p	1027c	272.2m	35.5m	8.2m	IT
COSTA MEDITERRANEA	85619gt	2003	22.0k	DEP2	2114p	2680p	897c	292.5m	32.2m	8.0m	IT
COSTA NEORIVIERA	48200gt	1999	19.0k	DE2	1244p	1807p	470c	216.0m	28.8m	6.9m	IT
COSTA NEOROMANTICA	56769gt	1993	18.5k	D2	1356p	1697p	596c	220.5m	30.8m	7.3m	IT
COSTA PACIFICA	114288gt	2009	21.5k	DE2	3000p	3780p	1100c	290.2m	35.5m	8.3m	IT
COSTA SERENA	114147gt	2007	21.5k	DE2	3000p	3780p	1100c	290.2m	35.5m	8.2m	IT
COSTA VICTORIA	75166gt	1996	22.0k	DE2	1928p	2394p	790c	252.9m	32.3m	7.8m	IT

COSTA ATLANTICA is the first example within Carnival Corporation of similar designs being used for ships built for more than one operator. The COSTA ATLANTICA is a sister to the CARNIVAL SPIRIT class of ships and was delivered to the company by Kvaerner Masa Yards (yard number 498), Helsinki, Finland in June 2000. Her sister ship, the COSTA MEDITERRANEA, was delivered during 2003. The COSTA ATLANTICA is currently based in China. IMO 9187796

COSTA CELEBRATION was built by Kockums (yard number 597), at their Malmo, Sweden shipyard. She was delivered in 1987 as the CELEBRATION to Carnival Cruise Lines for that company's

Costa Crociere's **Costa Atlantica** in Dover *(William Mayes)*

Costa Crociere's **Costa Celebration** as **Grand Celebration** in Piraeus *(William Mayes)*

Costa Crociere's **Costa Classica** off Santorini *(Rick Frendt)*

Costa Crociere's **Costa Deliziosa** in Amsterdam *(William Mayes)*

Costa Crociere's **Costa Favolosa** at Barcelona *(William Mayes)*

Costa Crociere's **Costa Magica** at Valletta *(William Mayes)*

Caribbean cruising operation. In 1989 the CELEBRATION collided with, and sank, the Cuban vessel CAPITAN SAN LOUIS but sustained only minor damage herself. She was transferred within the group to Iberocruceros in July 2008 and renamed GRAND CELEBRATION. In 2014 she was transferred to the Costa fleet and it was reported that she would be renamed COSTA CELEBRATION. IMO 8314134

COSTA CLASSICA, ordered in July 1987, was the first new passenger ship to be built for Costa Line since the elegant EUGENIO C of 1966. Built by Fincantieri (yard number 5877) at Venice, Italy, she was floated out of her building dock in February 1991 and delivered at the end of that year. In 2000 she was due to have been lengthened by Cammell Laird at Birkenhead, England, but while the ship was on her way to the shipyard a dispute arose and the lengthening didn't take place, despite the shipyard having constructed the new centre section. The COSTA CLASSICA was based in China until October 2011. She now operates in the Mediterranean and in late 2014 is to be renamed as COSTA NEOCLASSICA.IMO 8716502

COSTA DELIZIOSA was built by Fincantieri (yard number 6164). The forward section was built in Ancona, while the after section came from the Breda yard in Venice. She completed sea trials in November 2009 and was named by Tala Dionisi, in Dubai on 23 February 2010, while on her maiden voyage. The COSTA DELIZIOSA operates in many geographical areas worldide. IMO 9398917

COSTA FASCINOSA was built by Fincantieri (yard number 6189) in the Marghera yard, and delivered in 2012. COSTA FASCINOSA operates mainly in the Mediterranean. IMO 9479864

COSTA FAVOLOSA was delivered by Fincantieri (yard number 6188) in June 2011, having been built in the Breda yard. She was named in Trieste on 2 July by Italian actress Margareth Made. The ship currently operates in Europe and South America. IMO 9479852

COSTA FORTUNA was built by Fincantieri at the Sestri yard (yard number 6086) in Genoa, Italy and was named by Italian actress Maria Grazia Cucinotta. The COSTA FORTUNA currently operates in Europe and South America. IMO 9239783

COSTA LUMINOSA was built by Fincantieri (yard number 6155) at the Breda yard in Venice. She sails in Northern and Southern Europe and the Caribbean Sea. Her godmother is Olympic fencing champion Valentina Vezzali. The COSTA LUMINOSA currently operates in Europe, the Middle East, Far East, the Caribbean and South America. IMO 9398905

COSTA MAGICA was built by Fincantieri at the Sestri yard (yard number 6087) in Genoa, Italy. She currently operates in summer in the Baltic and Mediterranean Seas, and winters in the Caribbean. IMO 9239795

COSTA MEDITERRANEA was built by Kvaerner Masa Yards (yard number 502) at Helsinki, Finland. The COSTA MEDITERRANEA currently operates in the Caribbean Sea in winter and the Mediterranean Sea and Northern Europe in summer. IMO 9237345

COSTA NEORIVIERA, the first new ship for Festival Cruises, was delivered by Chantiers de l'Atlantique (yard number J31), St Nazaire, France as the MISTRAL. Following the collapse of Festival Cruises she was purchased by her builder, now part of the Alstom Group and eventually chartered to Iberojet. She was marketed initially as the IBEROSTAR MISTRAL. Subsequently she was renamed as the GRAND MISTRAL in 2004, when acquired by the company. She was rebuilt in 2007 with additional balcony cabins at the stern. She joined the Costa fleet in 2014 after a refit, as the COSTA NEORIVIERA. She currently operates in the Mediterranean, Indian Ocean and the Far East. IMO 9172777

COSTA NEOROMANTICA is a near sister to the COSTA CLASSICA and was delivered to the company by the Venice shipyard of Fincantieri (yard number 5899) in September 1993. In winter 2006/7 she cruised from South American and Caribbean ports, returning to Europe for the summer. In 2009 she spent the summer in the Mediterranean Sea before moving on to the east coast of Africa en route to the Far East where she was based in 2010. She currently operates in the Mediterranean Sea. The COSTA ROMANTICA was dry docked from late October 2011 to early February 2012 when she had a major rebuild incorporating new passenger decks, cabins and clip on balconies. She was renamed as COSTA NEOROMANTICA and operates mainly in the Mediterranean. IMO 8821046

COSTA PACIFICA was built by Fincantieri (yard number 6148) at the Sestri yard, Genoa. She was named by international pop star Noa, and spent her first 18 months in the Mediterranean Sea on a variety of itineraries. She now operates in both Northern and Southern Europe and from South America. IMO 9378498

COSTA SERENA was built by Fincantieri (yard number 6130) at Sestri, Genoa. Her godmother is actress

Costa Crociere's **Costa neoRomantica** *(Jonathan Boonzaier)*

Costa Crociere's **Costa Serena** in Palma *(William Mayes)*

Costa Crociere's **Costa Victoria** off Mykonos *(Rick Frendt)*

Costa Crociere's **Costa neoRiviera** at Valletta *(William Mayes)*

Cunard Line's **Queen Elizabeth** off Calshot *(William Mayes)*

Cunard Line's **Queen Mary 2** off Calshot *(William Mayes)*

Marion Cotillard. The COSTA SERENA spends much of her time in the Mediterranean Sea, operating from her home port of Savona, but for 2014/15 will also venture to the Far East. IMO 9343132

COSTA VICTORIA is one of a pair of ships ordered from Bremer Vulkan at Bremen, Germany (yard number 107) at the end of 1993. Her keel was laid in November 1994 and she was floated out of her building dock less than ten months later. She was delivered in July 1996. The second ship of this pair (to have been named COSTA OLYMPIA) was not delivered due to the bankruptcy of the shipyard, but was later bought and completed for Norwegian Cruise Line as the NORWEGIAN SKY. The COSTA VICTORIA operated in South America during the winter of 2011/12 and moved to China during 2012. IMO 9109031

Cruise ship on order

COSTA DIADEMA	c132500gt	2014	22.0k	DE2	3708p	4928p	1240c	305.0m	37.0m	8.0m	IT

COSTA DIADEMA was ordered from Fincantieri on 4 August 2011, and is due in service late in 2014. IMO 9636888

The company also owns the THOMSON DREAM, on charter to Thomson Cruises, who have an option to purchase.

CUNARD LINE

The Company In 1840 Samuel Cunard's British and North American Royal Mail Steam Packet Company inaugurated the first North Atlantic steamship mail service under a contract with the Admiralty for which the latter would pay the sum of £55,000 per annum. This company soon became known as the Cunard Line. The 1,135-ton wooden paddle steamer BRITANNIA took the first sailing on 4th July 1840 between Liverpool, Halifax and Boston. By 1848 Cunard Line was operating a weekly transatlantic service using nine steamers. During the 1850's Mediterranean services were established and by the time of Samuel Cunard's death in 1865 the company had built up an impressive route network served by modern ships. To raise capital for new ships, the company, along with its associated companies, was merged into the new Cunard Steam Ship Company Limited in 1878, and two years later the public were invited to subscribe for £800,000 of the issued capital of £2,000,000. The next 50 years was a period of growth, spurred on to a great extent by the rivalry with the many emerging European and American shipping companies. In 1881, Cunard's SERVIA was the first ship to be lit by electric light, and twelve years later the CAMPANIA was the company's first twin-screw vessel. Steam turbines began to power the fleet in 1905 with the arrival of the CARMANIA. In 1907, the company's largest and most prestigious ships to date, the 31,000 gross ton sisters LUSITANIA and MAURETANIA entered service, each taking the 'Blue Riband' for Cunard. In fact, with the exception of the UNITED STATES, the MAURETANIA was the ship that held the record for the longest – from 1907 to 1929. With the arrival in 1914 of the 45,000-ton AQUITANIA the company could maintain the weekly New York service with just these three ships. After the end of the First World War, Cunard acquired the former German owned 52,000 ton IMPERATOR and renamed her BERENGARIA. During the depression of the early 1930's it became necessary for Cunard Line to merge with the White Star Line to form Cunard-White Star Limited in order to secure British Government finance to pay for the building of the 81,000 ton QUEEN MARY. To maintain the New York service with just two ships a second 'Queen' was ordered in 1936, but due to the outbreak of war the QUEEN ELIZABETH did not enter Cunard service until 1946. The company's first ship designed with cruising in mind was the 1949 built CARONIA; painted in three shades of green, she served the lucrative American market. The QUEEN MARY made her last transatlantic voyage in 1967 and was sold eventually for use as a hotel and museum at Long Beach, California. The last voyage of the QUEEN ELIZABETH took place the following year, and in early 1969 the QUEEN ELIZABETH 2 made her debut on the North Atlantic. Trafalgar House Investments Limited acquired Cunard in 1971, and in the same year the first of Cunard's new generation of cruise ships, the 14,000-ton sisters CUNARD ADVENTURER and CUNARD AMBASSADOR began sailing in the Caribbean. The former was sold to Klosters (the forerunner of Norwegian Cruise Line) in 1976 and the latter was converted for use as a livestock carrier following a fire in 1974. The CUNARD PRINCESS (launched as the CUNARD CONQUEST) and the CUNARD COUNTESS, both 18,000 tons, were the next cruise ships to join the fleet and were again used in the Caribbean. These were sold to other operators in 1995/96. Norwegian America Cruises, together with the elegant near-sisters SAGAFJORD and VISTAFJORD, was acquired in 1983 and retained as a separate brand for a number of years. Trafalgar House Investments was taken over towards the end of 1996 by the Norwegian construction and engineering group Kvaerner, and thus Cunard became Norwegian owned. Cunard didn't fit well into the Kvaerner group, so was sold to a consortium led by Carnival in May 1998. That company subsequently acquired the remaining shares from the other members of the consortium. Cunard's first new vessel

Cunard Line's **Queen Victoria** off Calshot *(William Mayes)*

Holland America's **Amsterdam** in Sydney *(Alf Sims)*

Holland America's **Eurodam** at St. Thomas *(Rick Frendt)*

subsequent to the acquisition, the QUEEN MARY 2, entered service in January 2004, thus ending almost a quarter of a century of no investment in new ships. The CARONIA (formerly VISTAFJORD) left the Cunard fleet in the autumn of 2004 when she began a new career with Saga Holidays.

The previously announced QUEEN VICTORIA, due for delivery in 2005 never materialised in the Cunard fleet, instead being diverted to P&O Cruises as the ARCADIA. Subsequently the new QUEEN VICTORIA was ordered from Fincantieri. Before the entry into service of the new ship, the disposal of the QUEEN ELIZABETH 2 was announced. She had been sold to a company owned by the Government of Dubai for $100 million, to become a hotel, conference centre, museum and tourist attraction, and undertook her final, one way, cruise to Dubai in November 2008. A new QUEEN ELIZABETH joined the fleet in October 2010. Cunard Line is managed as part of Carnival UK. In 2015 the Queen Mary 2 will re-create the first Atlantic crossing of the Britannia, although rather more comfortably.

Address Carnival House, 100 Harbour Parade, Southampton SO15 1ST, United Kingdom

Telephone +44 845 678 0013 **Fax** +44 2380 657353

Website www.cunard.com or www.cunard.co.uk

Areas operated Europe, the Caribbean, the Americas and World Cruises (QUEEN MARY 2 also Atlantic crossings)

QUEEN ELIZABETH	90901gt	2010	22.0k	DEP2	2014p	2200p	820c	294.0m	32.3m	7.9m	BM
QUEEN MARY 2	148528gt	2003	29.3k	GDEP4	2620p	3090p	1292c	345.0m	41.0m	10.3m	BM
QUEEN VICTORIA	90049gt	2007	22.0k	DEP2	1980p	2144p	818c	294.0m	32.3m	7.9m	BM

QUEEN ELIZABETH was ordered as a near sister to the QUEEN VICTORIA from Fincantieri (yard number 6187) at Monfalcone, near Venice, Italy. Her keel-laying ceremony was held on 2 July 2009 and she was floated out on 5 January 2010. She was named by HM Queen Elizabeth II on 11 October 2010 in Southampton. IMO 9477438

QUEEN MARY 2 was built by Chantiers de l'Atlantique (yard number G32) at St Nazaire in France in 2003 as the first traditionally hulled liner for more than a quarter of a century. In a tragic accident on 15 November 2003 eleven shipyard workers and members of their families died when a gangway collapsed during a celebratory open day aboard the ship. The QUEEN MARY 2 was delivered at the end of the year and made a triumphant entrance to the Port of Southampton for the first time on 26 December 2003. HM Queen Elizabeth II named the ship in Southampton on 8 January. Following her maiden voyage to Fort Lauderdale on 12 January 2004 she spent the spring in the Caribbean before undertaking a varied programme of cruises from both Southampton and New York, between which she undertook Atlantic crossings. In 2006 she undertook a trip around South America, which attracted rather more adverse publicity than might have been thought necessary after she put one pod out of action on leaving Fort Lauderdale. In 2007 she undertook her first World Cruise. IMO 9241061

QUEEN VICTORIA was ordered as a replacement for the previous ship intended to carry this name (now P&O Cruises' ARCADIA), from Fincantieri (yard number 6127) at Monfalcone, Italy. Her keel was laid in May 2006 and the ship floated out in January 2007. HRH The Duchess of Cornwall named the QUEEN VICTORIA in Southampton on 10 December 2007. During her first season she operated a series of fly cruises based in the Mediterranean, but has subsequently been firmly based in Southampton. IMO 9320556

HOLLAND AMERICA

The Company The Nederlandsch Amerikaansche Stoomvaart Maatschappij (Netherlands American Steamship Company) came into being on 18 April 1873 to operate transatlantic liner services in competition with the other already well-established European steamship lines. The company gradually built up its services, fleet and reputation, and in 1898 adopted the yellow, green and white funnel colours which were to identify its ships for more than 70 years. The company was officially established as De Holland Amerika Lijn N.V. (The Holland America Line Ltd.) in 1896, a name by which it had been known unofficially for many years. The company was able to operate during most of the First World War as The Netherlands was a neutral country, but that didn't stop the loss of a number of ships to mines and later to submarine and surface attack. After the war, the Depression began to set in and the operations of the company started to be scaled back at the end of the 1920's. However, Holland America's passenger shipping was less severely affected than that of some other liner companies and by 1934 the STATENDAM was in need of a running mate on the New York service. That running mate was to be the NIEUW AMSTERDAM of 1938, Holland America's most elegant ship and certainly one of the best looking passenger liners ever built.

At the beginning of the Second World War the company moved its headquarters from Rotterdam to Willemstad, Curacao even though The Netherlands attempted to remain neutral. In 1940 Germany overran its small neighbour and in the accompanying air raids the Holland America office was destroyed. After the end of the war the first new passenger ships were the predominantly tourist class ships RYNDAM (1951) and MAASDAM (1952), for the North Atlantic service. The company then began to think more positively about using ships for cruising in the off-season. Although the NIEUW AMSTERDAM had already proved successful in this role, the newer ships were not really suitable. The next delivery, however, had been built with an eye to cruising and entered service in 1956 as the STATENDAM. A running mate was now required for the NIEUW AMSTERDAM, and thus the ROTTERDAM with her revolutionary profile and thin uptakes in place of a funnel arrived in 1959. During the 1960's and 1970's cruising increased its importance to the company's revenues and a pair of former Moore McCormack liners were acquired for this purpose. As if to add emphasis to the change in direction, a new house flag, hull colour and an orange and blue funnel marking were introduced. The grand old NIEUW AMSTERDAM made the last scheduled transatlantic crossing for the Holland America Line in 1971, bringing to an end almost 100 years of the Rotterdam to New York passenger service. She remained in a cruising role for a further two years before being sold to Taiwanese breakers at the end of 1973. That year also saw the entry into service of the first new passenger ship for almost a quarter of a century, the 9,000-ton PRINSENDAM. Sadly she was to have a very short life as she was lost in the Gulf of Alaska on 11th October 1980 following an engine room fire. However, she had established the popularity of Alaskan cruising and in the following year both the ROTTERDAM and the STATENDAM served this market. In 1983, just before the delivery of the new NOORDAM and NIEUW AMSTERDAM, the company merged fully with its recently acquired subsidiary, Westours Inc., to form Holland America Westours Inc. In 1985 this name was further changed to Holland America Line – Westours Inc. July 1987 saw the new holding company Holland America Line N.V. take a 50% stake in Windstar Cruises Inc. and in the following year the company acquired Home Lines Inc. with its two ships, the ATLANTIC (not operated by Holland America and later sold to Premier Cruise Lines) and the HOMERIC, renamed the WESTERDAM. Later in 1988 Holland America purchased the remaining 50% of Windstar.

In November 1988 agreement was reached for Carnival Holdings Ltd to acquire the cruise and tour businesses of the Holland America group for $625 million. The first major effect of the takeover was the ordering of three (later increased to four) new ships from Fincantieri, beginning with the STATENDAM, delivered in 1993. The 1959-built ROTTERDAM was retired in September 1997; her replacement, delivered shortly afterwards was the sixth ship to bear that name. The WESTERDAM left the fleet in 2002 and joined fellow Carnival subsidiary Costa in Europe. Thereafter a steady stream of new-buildings joined the premier brand fleet of Holland America. In recent years the company has diversified its itineraries and now commits more ships to Europe each summer. In 2010 the management of Seabourn was transferred to Holland America Line.

Address 300 Elliott Avenue West, Seattle, WA 98119-4198, United States of America

Telephone +1 206 281 3535 **Fax** +1 206 281 7110

Website www.hollandamerica.com

Areas operated Worldwide

AMSTERDAM	62735gt	2000	22.5k	DEP2	1380p	1872p	615c	237.8m	32.2m	8.1m	NL
EURODAM	86273gt	2008	21.9k	DEP2	2104p	2671p	929c	285.2m	32.2m	8.0m	NL
MAASDAM	55575gt	1993	20.3k	DE2	1258p	1625p	580c	219.2m	30.8m	7.7m	NL
NIEUW AMSTERDAM	86273gt	2010	21.9k	DEP2	2106p	2671p	929c	285.2m	32.2m	8.0m	NL
NOORDAM	82897gt	2006	22.0k	GDEP2	1924p	2388p	820c	285.2m	32.2m	8.0m	NL
OOSTERDAM	82305gt	2003	22.0k	GDEP2	1916p	2388p	817c	285.2m	32.2m	8.0m	NL
PRINSENDAM	39051gt	1988	21.8k	D2	835p	870p	470c	204.0m	28.9m	7.2m	NL
ROTTERDAM	61849gt	1997	22.5k	DE2	1404p	1708p	600c	237.9m	32.2m	7.5m	NL
RYNDAM	55819gt	1994	20.3k	DE2	1260p	1633p	580c	219.2m	30.8m	7.7m	NL
STATENDAM	55819gt	1993	20.3k	DE2	1260p	1621p	580c	219.2m	30.8m	7.7m	NL
VEENDAM	57092gt	1996	20.3k	DE2	1350p	1621p	580c	219.2m	30.8m	7.7m	NL
VOLENDAM	61214gt	1999	20.2k	DE2	1432p	1837p	615c	237.0m	32.3m	8.1m	NL
WESTERDAM	82348gt	2004	22.0k	GDEP2	1916p	2388p	817c	285.2m	32.2m	8.0m	NL
ZAANDAM	61396gt	2000	20.2k	DE2	1432p	1837p	615c	237.0m	32.3m	8.1m	NL
ZUIDERDAM	82305gt	2002	22.0k	GDEP2	1916p	2388p	817c	285.4m	32.2m	7.8m	NL

AMSTERDAM is the third ship to be named in honour of the capital city of The Netherlands, and was delivered to Holland America by Fincantieri (yard number 6052), Venice, Italy during 2000. Initially she was named AMSTERDAM I as there was already a ship on the Bahamas register named AMSTERDAM. Following her 2002 world cruise she was deployed on cruises to Alaska and the Caribbean Sea. The AMSTERDAM spends time in Alaska and South America. IMO 9188037

EURODAM was built by the Breda (Venice) yard of Fincantieri (yard number 6149). She is the first ship of the so-called Signature class, a development of the Vista class of ship, and was named by Her Majesty Queen Beatrix of the Netherlands in Rotterdam on 1 July 2008. The EURODAM spends time in Europe each summer and on the US East Coats and the Caribbean at other times. IMO 9378448

MAASDAM is the second of three ships ordered from Fincantieri (yard number 5882) at Monfalcone, Italy on 25 November 1989, and the fifth MAASDAM to have been in the Holland America line fleet. The ship entered service under the Bahamas flag in December 1993, following her naming by actress June Allyson, and was transferred to the Dutch flag in 1996. Her current itineraries include South America and the East Cost of the USA and Canada. Maasdam is a village situated to the south of Rotterdam. IMO 8919257

NIEUW AMSTERDAM was built in two parts, the forward section at the Sestri yard and the after section at the Breda yard of Fincantieri (yard number 6181). She was later moved to the Marghera yard for fitting out. After a rather unfortunate choice of name for the preceding ship (EURODAM), the company has revived a traditional name. She will be the fourth of the company's ships to bear this former name for New York City. The NIEUW AMSTERDAM was named in Venice on 4 July 2010 by HRH Princess Maxima of the Netherlands. The NIEUW AMSTERDAM currently operates in the Mediterranean and Caribbean Seas. IMO 9378450

NOORDAM has a name incorporating the northerly compass point together with the traditional Holland America 'Dam' ending. She is the second ship of this name and the last in a series of four vessels built for the company by Fincantieri (yard number 6079) in Italy. Her godmother, actress Marlee Matlin, named the ship at a ceremony in New York on 22 February 2006. The NOORDAM cruises in the Far East and Australia. IMO 9230115

OOSTERDAM was built by Fincantieri (yard number 6076) in Italy as the second ship in what has emerged as a four ship series (with a fifth similar ship eventually becoming P&O Cruises' ARCADIA). Her name is derived from the easterly point of the compass. HRH Princess Margriet of The Netherlands named her in Rotterdam. IMO 9221281

PRINSENDAM was built by Wartsila Marine Industries (yard number 1296) at their Turku, Finland yard, for Kloster's Royal Viking Line of Oslo as the ROYAL VIKING SUN. She was to be the penultimate ship built for this company, which had been owned since 1984 by Norwegian Caribbean Line. In 1994 she was sold to Cunard Line but retained her name. Following the partial amalgamation of Cunard and Seabourn, she was transferred to the Seabourn fleet and renamed the SEABOURN SUN. Considered to be unsuitable as a fleet-mate for the trio of yacht-like ships in the Seabourn fleet, she was transferred to fellow Carnival subsidiary Holland America Line as the second PRINSENDAM in 2002. Her dedication was carried out by Rose Abello, Eva Andresen, and Linda Ehlenberger, representing all of the employees of Holland America Line. During late 2009 and early 2010 the ship had a major refit that included the addition of 22 cabins and a new bar. The PRINSENDAM generally offers longer voyages but will spend time in Europe in 2015. IMO 8700280

ROTTERDAM was ordered in January 1995 from the Marghera, Venice yard of Fincantieri in Italy (yard number 5980) as a larger and faster version of the STATENDAM class, but particularly as a replacement for the much-loved 1959-built ROTTERDAM. She was named by HRH Princess Margriet in December 1997 and is the sixth Holland America ship to bear the name of the second largest city and busiest seaport in The Netherlands. The ROTTERDAM is generally based in Europe but in 2015 will undertake a round-Africa voyage. IMO 9122552

RYNDAM is the final member of the trio of cruise ships (and the third ship to bear this name) ordered from the Monfalcone, Italy yard of Fincantieri (yard number 5883) on 25 November 1989. She began her commercial career under the Bahamas flag with a ten day Caribbean cruise on 20 October 1994, after being named by Madeleine Arison, wife of Micky Arison. She was re-flagged to the Netherlands in 1996, and cruises in Northern and Southern Europe and the Caribbean Sea. She has been based in Dover for several summers but after the end of her 2015 European Season she will head for the Far East and eventually Australia (by then as a P&O ship). IMO 8919269

STATENDAM is the lead ship in a series of three sisters ordered from Fincantieri (yard number 5881)

Holland America's *Maasdam* sailing from Funchal *(William Mayes)*

Holland America's *Prinsendam* in Istanbul *(William Mayes)*

Holland America's *Rotterdam* at Flam *(Rick Frendt)*

at Monfalcone, Italy on 25 November 1989. She was the first ship to be ordered for Holland America Line following the takeover by Carnival, and entered service on 25 January 1993. She is the fifth ship to bear this name, the origins of which are unclear. The name may refer to a settlement near the Dutch town of Geertruideaberg, but is more likely a reference to the Staten, the Government in the early days. She was named by Lin Arison (the widow of Ted Arison) and originally registered under the ownership of Windsurf Ltd of Nassau, Bahamas but was transferred to the Dutch flag under Holland America Line ownership in 1996. In spring 2010 she was chartered by the Royal Canadian Mounted Police for use as an accommodation ship at Vancouver in connection with the Winter Olympic Games. In her current season the STATENDAM cruises to Alaska, Mexico and the Caribbean Sea. IMO 8919245

VEENDAM became the fourth member of the STATENDAM class when ordered from Fincantieri's Marghera shipyard (yard number 5954) in Venice, Italy on 3 December 1993. She was delivered in May 1996 and, after being named by the actress Debbie Reynolds, entered commercial service at the end of that month. She had a large complement of British deck and engineering officers due to a shortage of suitable Dutch personnel. She retained her Bahamas registry for a number of years before switching to the Dutch flag. She was partially rebuilt in 2009, resulting in a gross tonnage increase of 1,300. The VEENDAM is named in honour of a town in the eastern part of The Netherlands, close to Groningen. The VEENDAM cruises from New York to Bermuda and in South America. IMO 9102992

VOLENDAM, named after a small town on the coast of the inland sea, the Ijssel-Meer, was delivered by the Venice, Italy yard of Fincantieri (yard number 6035) in 1999. Tennis player Chris Evert christened the ship on 12 November 1999 in Fort Lauderdale. The VOLENDAM currently cruises on the US Pacific Coast and the Far East and Australia. IMO 9156515

WESTERDAM was built by Fincantieri (yard number 6077) in Italy as the third ship in a series of four. Her name is derived from the western point of the compass. Her godmother, actress Renee Soutendijk named the ship in a ceremony held in Venice on 25 April 2004. The WESTERDAM cruises in Alaska, on the Pacific Coast and to Mexico. IMO 9226891

ZAANDAM takes her name from a town that now forms part of the northern suburbs of Amsterdam. Delivered by the Venice yard of Fincantieri, (yard number 6036), she was named by actresses Mary-Kate and Ashley Olsen. The ship operates to Hawaii, Alaska and South America. IMO 9156527

ZUIDERDAM has a name incorporating the southern compass point together with the traditional Holland America 'Dam' suffix. This ship is the first of a series of five vessels (then six – one of which was cancelled and another became P&O Cruises' ARCADIA) ordered from Fincantieri (yard number 6075) in Italy. American journalist Joan Lunden named the ship in Fort Lauderdale on 14 December 2002. The ZUIDERDAM cruises in the Caribbean Sea and to Europe in 2014/15. IMO 9221279

Cruise Ship on order

KONINGSDAM	c99500gt	2016	22.0k	DEP2	p	2560p	c	297.0m	35.0m	8.3m	NL

KONINGSDAM, Under construction at Finantieri's Breda yard (yard number 6241) near Venice. She will be the largest Holland America Line ship to date and will be the lead ship in the so-called 'Pinnacle Class'. IMO 9692557

IBEROCRUCEROS

The Company Iberojet was, until February 2007, part of Orizonia Corporation, Spain's largest travel company. Iberojet was a relative newcomer to the growing market for cruising amongst Spaniards. During the early part of 2005 the company was also operating the GRAND LATINO, now Fred. Olsen's BOUDICCA. In February 2007, Carnival Corporation signed a letter of intent with Iberojet's owners to form a joint venture targeting the Spanish Market. The fleet is to be grown by cascading older units from the various Carnival Corporation fleets. Under the terms of the agreement, Carnival Corporation owned 75% of the joint venture, with the remainder in the hands of Orizonia. Costa Crociere manages the company, and in 2009 Carnival Corporation acquired the remaining 25% of Iberocruceros. Carnival Cruise Lines' CELEBRATION and HOLIDAY joined the fleet in 2008 and 2010 respectively. Iberocruceros caters for Spanish speaking passengers and operates predominantly from Barcelona. With a weak Spanish economy and much competition in the Spanish market, first the GRAND VOYAGER and then GRAND MISTRAL were transferred to Costa. The ships are all registered in Madeira. Iberocruceros is now a trading name of Costa Crociere. In May 2014 Costa Crociere announced the closure of Iberocruceros with effect from the end of 2014. Late in 2014 the GRAND CELEBRATION was transferred to Costa.

Holland America's **Volendam** in Sydney *(Richard Seville)*

Holland America's **Westerdam** at Half Moon Cay *(Rick Frendt)*

P&O Cruises' **Adonia** off Calshot *(William Mayes)*

P&O Cruises' *Arcadia* at Zakinthos *(Kelvin Holmes)*

P&O Cruises' *Aurora* off Calshot *(William Mayes)*

P&O Cruises' *Azura* off Calshot *(William Mayes)*

Address Piazza Piccapietra 48, GE 16121 Genoa, Italy

Telephone +34 010 54831 **Fax** +34 015 483360

Website www.iberocruceros.es

Area operated Mediterranean Sea and South America

GRAND HOLIDAY	46052gt	1985	21.5k	D2	1452p	1848p	660c	221.6m	28.0m	7.5m	PT

GRAND HOLIDAY was the second new ship ordered by Carnival Cruise Lines, being delivered from the Aalborg Vaerft shipyard (yard number 246) at Aalborg, Denmark in June 1985 as the HOLIDAY. She underwent a major refit during the winter of 2009/10 and was transferred to Iberocruceros as the GRAND HOLIDAY. IMO 8217881

P&O CRUISES

The Company As the ownership of this company changes over the years since its de-merger from the Peninsular and Oriental Steam Navigation Company, it is easy to forget that this is the descendant of the company that invented cruising. Its history of passenger services goes back to 1837 and the formation of the Peninsular Steam Navigation Company (the peninsula being Iberia), which later became The Peninsular and Oriental Steam Navigation Company, or P&O as it is both universally and affectionately known. The company was founded as the Peninsular Steam Navigation Company to fulfill the new British Admiralty-controlled mail contract serving Vigo, Oporto, Lisbon, Cadiz and Gibraltar from Falmouth. In 1840, a new company was set up with liability limited by Royal Charter; the Peninsular and Oriental Steam Navigation Company had been born. P&O invented cruising in 1844 when it advertised a 'Grand Tour' by sea from Southampton to Gibraltar, Malta, Athens, Smyrna, Jaffa and Alexandria utilising three ships, the LADY MARY WOOD, the TAGUS and the IBERIA. This voyage was recorded in William Makepeace Thackeray's 'Notes of a Journey from Cornhill to Grand Cairo'. Subsequently round trips from Southampton to destinations such as Constantinople and Alexandria were offered.

In 1904 the company advertised its first proper cruise on a ship refitted specifically for that purpose. The 6,000-ton VECTIS had been adapted to carry just 150 first-class passengers. Ten years later, after the company had merged with the British India Steam Navigation Company, its fleet totalled 197 ships. That year also saw the company relieved of almost two-thirds of its fleet for war service as hospital ships, troop transports and armed merchant cruisers. P&O lost 17 ships during the First World War, and subsidiary companies lost a further 68.

In December 1918 one of the most significant acquisitions took place when P&O purchased 51% of the share capital of the Orient Steam Navigation Company. The Orient Line had been a joint operator with P&O on the Australian Mail Contract for some time. By 1921 the company had reintroduced its long haul services to India (weekly), China (fortnightly) and Australia (four-weekly). In the 1920's P&O and Orient Line between them took delivery of more than twenty new passenger liners, most of which were used on the Australian service. Cruising began again in 1925 when the RANCHI undertook a cruise to Norway for her maiden voyage. For the 1929 season, P&O offered a total of 15 cruises, including some aboard the new VICEROY OF INDIA, the first turbo-electric ship for the company.

The combined fleets of the companies within the P&O Group peaked in the mid 1920's, when more than 500 ships ranging from the excursion vessels and coasters of the General Steam Navigation Company, to the modern refrigerated cargo ships of New Zealand Shipping Company and Federal Steam Navigation, and the state of the art passenger liners of P&O and Orient Line were owned.

The Second World War took its toll on the P&O Group with the loss of 156 ships including such passenger liners as the VICEROY OF INDIA, RAWALPINDI, CATHAY, STRATHALLAN, ORONSAY and ORCADES. By the late 1940's commercial aviation was beginning to take a hold, so the passenger fleet renewal programme concentrated on fewer but larger and faster ships. When these ships came on stream between 1947 and 1954 they cut the sailing time to Australia from five to four weeks.

In 1955 both P&O and Orient Line ordered what were to be their last passenger liners, the CANBERRA and the ORIANA. These were fast ships and shaved another week off the Australian run; ORIANA recorded a speed of 30.64 knots on trials. These two ships came under full common ownership in 1961 when P&O acquired the remaining minority interests in Orient Line and restyled its passenger operations as P&O-Orient Lines. The 1960's saw a general downturn in line voyages and a reduction in the number of ships operated, a trend that was to continue into the 1970's when cruising became a vital employment for ships between line voyages.

In 1971 the company underwent a massive re-organisation when the activities of more than 100 subsidiaries operating 239 ships were structured into a number of operating divisions. The Passenger Division, the forerunner of P&O Cruises, commenced with 13, including the last two large ships of British India, NEVASA and UGANDA. During the early 1970's times were really bad for the passenger liner with relatively young ships being sent for scrap becoming a regular occurrence. Princess Cruises was acquired in 1974 and the almost new SPIRIT OF LONDON was transferred to that company. By the late 1970's the CANBERRA and ORIANA served the UK cruise market and the ARCADIA was employed in Australia. In 1981 the ORIANA replaced the ARCADIA in Australia, and the UK was left with just the CANBERRA and the SEA PRINCESS, newly transferred from Australia. CANBERRA was out of P&O service for much of 1982 when she was requisitioned for use in the Falklands War. In 1986 SEA PRINCESS was switched to the Princess Cruises fleet, leaving just the CANBERRA to service the UK.

With the withdrawal of the CANBERRA imminent, P&O Cruises ordered its first new ship for the British market, the ORIANA, which was delivered in 1995. The CANBERRA was scrapped in 1997 and her replacement was the ARCADIA (formerly STAR PRINCESS and now PACIFIC PEARL). The P&O Cruises fleet grew at an impressive rate and the 2005 brochure offered cruises on six ships (including the ADONIA, now transferred back to Princess Cruises as the SEA PRINCESS), a choice not seen since the early 1970s.

P&O Princess Cruises became an independent company on its demerger from the Peninsular & Oriental Steam Navigation Company in 2000. In early 2003 P&O Princess began talks with Royal Caribbean on a possible merger, but shareholders eventually voted for a merger with Carnival Corporation, which occurred in the autumn of that year. In 2003 the Ocean Village subsidiary was formed, but that business closed at the end of the summer season in 2010. The most recent fleet additions have either come from Princess Cruises or are based on Princess Cruises design, as is the current ship on order. P&O Cruises is the principal constituent of Carnival UK.

Address Carnival House, 100 Harbour Parade, Southampton SO15 1ST, England

Telephone +44 2380 655000 **Fax** +44 2380 657030

Website www.pocruises.com

Areas operated Mediterranean, Scandinavia, positioning voyages to the Caribbean and world cruises, all from Southampton. Fly cruises in the Mediterranean, Caribbean and South America

ADONIA	30277gt	2001	18.0k	DE2	710p	801p	381c	181.0m	25.5m	5.8m	BM
ARCADIA	84342gt	2005	22.0k	DEP2	1996p	2388p	866c	285.1m	32.2m	7.8m	BM
AURORA	76152gt	2000	25.0k	DE2	1878p	2290p	850c	270.0m	32.2m	7.9m	BM
AZURA	115055gt	2010	22.5k	DE2	3100p	3597p	1200c	289.6m	36.0m	8.5m	BM
OCEANA	77499gt	2000	21.0k	DE2	2022p	2272p	875c	261.0m	32.3m	8.0m	BM
ORIANA	69840gt	1995	24.0k	D2	1822p	1928p	800c	260.0m	32.2m	7.9m	BM
VENTURA	116017gt	2008	22.5k	DE2	3092p	3597p	1239c	289.6m	36.0m	8.5m	BM

ADONIA was built by Chantiers de l'Atlantique (yard number Z31) at St Nazaire, France as the R EIGHT for Renaissance Cruises. Following the failure of that company in the autumn of 2001 she was laid up at Gibraltar. During 2002 it was announced that Swan Hellenic had taken her on a seven-year charter, to commence service in April 2003 following a major re-fit, as the MINERVA II, replacing the smaller MINERVA. In 2006 Carnival Corporation purchased the ship and in spring 2007 she was transferred to Princess Cruises as the ROYAL PRINCESS, the second ship to bear this name. Her Princess cruises began in the Mediterranean, after which she moved to South America. She was transferred to P&O Cruises as ADONIA in May 2011 and named by Dame Shirley Bassey in Southampton. Adonia is the female version of the name Adonis. IMO 9210220

ARCADIA was laid down for Holland America Line (yard number 6078) by Fincantieri at Marghera, Venice in Italy. Prior to delivery she was transferred to the Cunard line as the QUEEN VICTORIA. In the spring of 2004, she was again transferred – this time to P&O Cruises as part of a major fleet reorganisation within the British parts of Carnival – to become the ARCADIA when delivered in April 2005. She continues the tradition established by the previous ship of this name as an adults-only vessel. Named by Dame Kelly Holmes, she is the fourth P&O ship to bear the poetic name for an area of what is now the Greek Peloponnese, the peninsula south of the Isthmus of Corinth that makes up the southern part of Greece. In late 2008 the ship received a new block of 34 cabins at the stern during a refit at the Lloydwerft shipyard at Bremerhaven. IMO 9226906

P&O Cruises' **Oceana** off Calshot *(William Mayes)*

P&O Cruises' **Oriana** at Rhodes *(William Mayes)*

P&O Cruises' **Ventura** in Southampton *(William Mayes)*

AURORA was built by Jos. L. Meyer (yard number 640) at Papenburg, Germany as the second purpose built cruise ship for the British market. Ordered in 1998, she was delivered in the spring of 2000, named by HRH The Princess Royal, and after an abortive maiden voyage has settled down as a popular and successful member of the P&O Cruises fleet. Engine problems at the start of her World Cruise in 2005 gained much press coverage, but despite the best journalistic efforts it proved extremely difficult to find anyone with a bad word to say about either the company or the ship. During her 2008 world cruise she again suffered mechanical problems, leading to the loss of several port calls. Aurora, goddess of the dawn, was the name chosen for the ship as a link to the dawning of a new millennium. IMO 9169524

AZURA was ordered late in 2006 from Fincantieri (yard number 6166) and was built at Monfalcone. She was named in Southampton in 2010 by ballerina Darcy Bussell. IMO 9424883

OCEANA was built by Fincantieri (yard number 6044) at Monfalcone, Italy as the OCEAN PRINCESS for Princess Cruises' operations in the Caribbean and to Alaska. In the autumn of 2002 she was renamed OCEANA and transferred to P&O Cruises to serve the British market, operating predominantly from the United Kingdom. In Southampton a double naming ceremony (with ADONIA, now SEA PRINCESS) was performed by HRH The Princess Royal and her daughter Zara Phillips. The ship's first season commenced with Caribbean fly-cruises before she took up her Southampton based itineraries. She is now based in Southampton year-round. The second ship to bear the name, Oceana is the feminine form of Oceanus, the Roman god of the ocean. IMO 9169550

ORIANA was the first purpose built cruise ship for the British market, and when she entered service in 1995 she very quickly became a favourite and set the standard that many others have yet to achieve. This sturdily built, classically elegant ship was ordered from the Jos. L. Meyer yard (yard number 636) at Papenburg in 1993, becoming, at the time of her delivery, the largest passenger ship to be built in Germany. HM Queen Elizabeth II named her in Southampton. In addition to cruises from Southampton, the ORIANA has undertaken a number of world cruises, but for the 2004 UK winter season pioneered a new programme in the Caribbean and around South America. Her regular cruising pattern now centres on Southampton, with a winter World Cruise. In 2006, following a major refit, the ORIANA was moved from the UK registry to that of Bermuda in order to allow weddings to be performed on board. The ORIANA had another major refit in the autumn of 2011 during which all of her children's facilities were removed and the space refilled with cabins, to make her an adults-only ship. In 2012 ORIANA undertook a world cruise, but from 2013 has been based in Southampton year-round. This is the second ORIANA to have served the company; a name given to the poetic huntress and heroine, a character associated with Queen Elizabeth I of England by contemporary writers. IMO 9050137

VENTURA was built by Fincantieri (yard number 6132) at the Monfalcone shipyard in Italy, and based on a design that can be traced back to the first 100,000+ ton ship for Princess Cruises, the GRAND PRINCESS. She was named on 15 April 2008 by actress Dame Helen Mirren in Southampton. IMO 9333175

Cruise ship on order

BRITANNIA	c141000gt	2015	22.0k	DE2	3611p	p	c	330.0m	38.4m	8.6m	BM

BRITANNIA is on order from Fincantieri (yard number 6231) at Monfalcone and is due for delivery in 2015. IMO 9614036

P&O CRUISES AUSTRALIA

The Company Although P&O had always had a cruising presence in Australia, until the mid-1970's with regular line voyages and 'between voyage cruising' and in later years with the 1954-built ARCADIA and subsequently the 1960-built ORIANA, the permanent presence ended with the sale of the latter ship to Japan at the end of 1986. That all changed in 1988, however, when P&O acquired Sitmar Line and its Australian based cruise ship, the FAIRSTAR (built in 1957 as the Bibby Line troopship OXFORDSHIRE). A one-ship operation continued with the FAIRSTAR until 1997, then the FAIR PRINCESS until 2000, followed by the PACIFIC SKY until 2003 when the PACIFIC PRINCESS (see Princess Cruises) joined the fleet on a part time basis. Subsequently, the company has benefited from the replacement programmes elsewhere within the group with Carnival's JUBILEE and Costa's COSTA TROPICALE joining the growing fleet. For management purposes the company has recently been re-styled as Carnival (Australia), but it is too soon to know whether the P&O Cruises Australia marketing name is likely to disappear in the immediate future. In 2006 the PACIFIC SKY was sold to Spanish operator Pullmantur and renamed SKY WONDER. In 2009 the OCEAN VILLAGE TWO joined the fleet

P&O Cruises Australia's **Pacific Jewel** at Moreton Bay *(David Robinson)*

P&O Cruises Australia's **Pacific Pearl** off Sydney *(Alf Sims)*

Princess Cruises' **Crown Princess** arriving at Kusadasi *(William Mayes)*

as the PACIFIC JEWEL, and one year later the OCEAN VILLAGE followed her as the PACIFIC PEARL, thus reuniting the last three Sitmar ordered ships in the same fleet for the first time since 1997. In 2013 management of the company was moved from Carnival UK to Holland America Line. In November 2015 Holland America Line's RYNDAM and STATENDAM will join the fleet as the PACIFIC ARIA and PACIFIC EDEN, although which name will be given to which ship is not yet apparent.

Address Level 5, 15 Mount Street, North Sydney, NSW 2060, Australia

Telephone +61 2 8424 8838 **Fax** +61 2 8424 9161

Website www.pocruises.com.au

Areas operated Australasia, South East Asia and the Pacific Islands

PACIFIC DAWN	70285gt	1991	19.5k	DE2	1596p	2020p	696c	245.1m	32.3m	8.1m	GB
PACIFIC JEWEL	70310gt	1990	19.5k	DE2	1708p	1950p	677c	245.1m	32.3m	7.9m	GB
PACIFIC PEARL	63786gt	1989	19.5k	DE2	1592p	1800p	514c	245.6m	32.2m	7.7m	GB

PACIFIC DAWN was the last ship ordered by Sitmar Line, but was delivered to the P&O Group for service with Princess Cruises as the REGAL PRINCESS by the Monfalcone yard of Fincantieri (yard number 5840). She has undertaken interesting South East Asian itineraries, and was due to be transferred to fellow group company A'Rosa Cruises in 2004. This transfer did not occur and she remained in the Princess fleet. However, she was then due to transfer to Ocean Village in November 2006. This transfer did not take place either as her sister the AIDA BLU (formerly CROWN PRINCESS and now the PACIFIC JEWEL) was transferred instead. She joined the P&O Cruises Australia fleet in the autumn of 2007, as the PACIFIC DAWN. IMO 8521232

PACIFIC JEWEL is one of the last pair of ships ordered by Sitmar Line in 1988 prior to that company being acquired by P&O. Built by Fincantieri (yard number 5839) at Monfalcone, Italy, she was delivered to Princess Cruises in 1990 as the CROWN PRINCESS. Princess employed her on a variety of itineraries including European cruises until the summer of 2002, when she was transferred within the Group to the newly formed A'Rosa Cruises of Germany, taking the name A'ROSA BLU. On the sale of A'Rosa's river cruise business in 2004, she was transferred to Aida Cruises and renamed as the AIDABLU. In spring 2007 she passed to Ocean Village and following a three-week refit emerged as the OCEAN VILLAGE TWO. She was transferred to P&O Cruises Australia in 2009 as the PACIFIC JEWEL. IMO 8521220

PACIFIC PEARL was laid down in May 1988 as the SITMAR FAIRMAJESTY by Chantiers de l'Atlantique (yard number B29) at St Nazaire, France for the Sitmar Line. That company passed into the ownership of the P&O Group in September 1988, and the ship was subsequently delivered as the STAR PRINCESS in the spring of 1989 for service within P&O's Princess Cruises division. In late 1997 the ship was transferred to P&O Cruises for operation within the UK passenger fleet and was renamed ARCADIA, thus reviving a traditional P&O name. She cruised from the UK in the summer and in the Caribbean during the winter until the spring of 2003, when she was transferred to Ocean Village and renamed OCEAN VILLAGE in a ceremony performed by Ulrika Jonsson. She was based in the Mediterranean in summer and the Caribbean in winter. On the closure of Ocean Village in the autumn of 2010 she was transferred to P&O Cruises Australia as the PACIFIC PEARL. IMO 8611398

PRINCESS CRUISES

The Company Princess Cruises began operation in December 1965 when Stanley McDonald, a Seattle industrialist, chartered the 1949-built, Canadian Pacific Railway ship PRINCESS PATRICIA, from where the new company took its name. The first cruises were to the west coast of Mexico, and they were so successful that the ship was chartered again the following year. By the 1967/68 season a larger ship was needed, and the company was fortunate to obtain the charter of the recently completed 12,000-ton ITALIA, marketed as PRINCESS ITALIA but not renamed. During the next season a second ship, Costa Line's CARLA C, marketed as PRINCESS CARLA, joined the ITALIA, allowing that ship to inaugurate cruises to Alaska. In the autumn of 1970 her owners needed the CARLA C, so Princess Cruises was again a one-ship company. The recently built ISLAND VENTURE became unexpectedly available for charter in late 1972 and, renamed ISLAND PRINCESS, quickly established her position in the Princess fleet, where she remained for 27 years. In 1973 the ITALIA was returned to her owners, and in the following year the Peninsular & Oriental Steam Navigation Company, in a move designed to strengthen its American operation, bought out Princess Cruises and transferred the SPIRIT OF LONDON (renamed SUN PRINCESS) to the company, later purchasing the ISLAND PRINCESS and her sister the SEA VENTURE (renamed PACIFIC PRINCESS). The popularity of American cruising

Princess Cruises' *Grand Princess* at Barcelona *(William Mayes)*

Princess Cruises' *Island Princess* at Vancouver *(Rick Frendt)*

Princess Cruises' *Pacific Princess* in Istanbul *(William Mayes)*

undoubtedly received a boost in the mid-1970s when the PACIFIC PRINCESS starred in the US television series 'The Love Boat'. The first new ship for the growing Princess company was the 1984-built ROYAL PRINCESS, and two years later the SEA PRINCESS (formerly Swedish America Line's KUNGSHOLM) joined the fleet following a downturn in UK cruising, thus giving Princess five relatively modern ships. By 1988, however, it was apparent that the P&O Group was once again falling behind the market leaders as the US cruise market boomed. P&O had no new ships on order for Princess, and its largest ship, the ROYAL PRINCESS, was only 44,000 tons compared with the 70,000 ton ships that other lines were preparing to take into their fleets. Sitmar Line, facing various difficulties became available and P&O quickly snapped up this business for $210 million in September 1988, taking into the Princess fleet a mixed bag of older, but popular tonnage, but more importantly contracts for three large ships due for imminent delivery.

Sitmar Line had commenced trading just after the Second World War using two surplus US ships converted to carry around 800 passengers in fairly basic accommodation. Initially the company sailed in the migrant trades between the Mediterranean and Central America and the Caribbean. A little later the company acquired its third ship and entered the emigrant trade from the United Kingdom to Australia. By 1963, the star of the fleet was the former Bibby Line troopship OXFORDSHIRE, then running as the FAIRSTAR. With the acquisition in the late 1960's and the conversion for luxury cruising in 1970/71 of the former Cunard liners CARINTHIA (FAIRSEA) and SYLVANIA (FAIRWIND), the company quickly established itself at the luxury end of the US cruise market. The first new ship for the company was the FAIRSKY (latterly P&O Australia's PACIFIC SKY and later Pullmantur's ATLANTIC STAR), delivered in 1984, and in 1986 the company ordered its largest ship to date, the SITMAR FAIRMAJESTY. However, that ship, along with two slightly larger ships ordered a little later, were actually delivered to the P&O Group, following the takeover.

The Princess story subsequently has been one of rapid expansion, keeping the company at the forefront of the premium US cruise market. The company commissioned two series of new ships in the 1990's. The SUN PRINCESS was the lead ship in a class of four vessels, but the GRAND PRINCESS was the forerunner of a much larger class of similar ships of around 110,000 gross tons. Princess Cruises became part of the new P&O Princess Cruises in 2000, when the cruise operations of the Peninsular & Oriental Steam Navigation Company were de-merged to form a new publicly listed company. Following talks on a possible merger with Royal Caribbean, the shareholders chose instead a merger with Carnival Corporation, which took place in 2003. SEA PRINCESS and OCEAN PRINCESS were sent, with little change to their interiors, to the P&O Cruises fleet in 2003, with the latter company relinquishing its Grand Class ship order to Princess. The transfer back to Princess of the former of this pair may indicate that it's not that easy to quickly adapt large ships from one market to another. With the transfer of ROYAL PRINCESS to P&O Cruises in 2005, and the REGAL PRINCESS to P&O Cruises in Australia during 2007, the oldest ship in this fleet is the 1995-built SUN PRINCESS. Princess Cruises now regularly base a number of cruise ships in Europe each summer, including two in Southampton. Two ships of a totally new design were ordered in 2010, ROYAL PRINCESS being the first of these.

Address 24844 Avenue Rockefeller, Santa Clarita, California 91355, United States of America

Telephone + 1 310 553 1770 **Fax** +1 310 832 0728

Website www.princesscruises.com

Areas operated North and South America, Caribbean, Mediterranean, Scandinavia, Pacific Islands and the Far East

CARIBBEAN PRINCESS	112894gt	2004	22.5k	DE2	3112p	3796p	1200c	289.0m	36.0m	8.0m	BM
CORAL PRINCESS	91627gt	2002	24.0k	GDE2	2000p	2590p	895c	294.0m	32.2m	8.0m	BM
CROWN PRINCESS	113651gt	2006	22.5k	DE2	3082p	3842p	1200c	288.6m	36.0m	8.5m	BM
DAWN PRINCESS	77441gt	1997	21.4k	DE2	1998p	2250p	924c	261.3m	32.3m	8.1m	BM
DIAMOND PRINCESS	115906gt	2004	22.1k	DE2	2674p	3290p	1099c	290.0m	37.5m	8.0m	GB
EMERALD PRINCESS	113651gt	2007	22.5k	DE2	3078p	3825p	1200c	288.6m	36.0m	8.5m	BM
GOLDEN PRINCESS	108865gt	2001	22.5k	DE2	2636p	3209p	1100c	289.5m	36.0m	8.5m	BM
GRAND PRINCESS	107517gt	1998	22.5k	DE2	2602p	3209p	1150c	289.5m	36.0m	8.5m	BM
ISLAND PRINCESS	91627gt	2003	24.0k	GDE2	1974p	2590p	900c	294.0m	32.2m	8.0m	BM
OCEAN PRINCESS	30277gt	1999	18.0k	DE2	676p	800p	375c	181.0m	25.5m	5.8m	BM
PACIFIC PRINCESS	30277gt	1999	18.0k	DE2	676p	800p	375c	181.0m	25.5m	5.8m	BM
REGAL PRINCESS	142714gt	2014	22.0k	DE2	3560p	4340p	1346c	330.0m	38.4m	8.6m	BM
ROYAL PRINCESS	142714gt	2013	22.0k	DE2	3560p	4340p	1346c	330.0m	38.4m	8.6m	BM

RUBY PRINCESS	113561gt	2008	22.5k	DEP2	3084p	3861p	1200c	290.0m	36.0m	8.5m	BM
SAPPHIRE PRINCESS	115875gt	2004	22.1k	DE2	2674p	3290p	1100c	290.0m	37.5m	8.0m	GB
SEA PRINCESS	77499gt	1998	21.4k	DE2	1950p	2250p	830c	261.3m	32.3m	8.1m	BM
STAR PRINCESS	108977gt	2002	22.5k	DE2	2594p	3211p	1105c	289.5m	36.0m	8.5m	BM
SUN PRINCESS	77441gt	1995	21.5k	DE2	2022p	2250p	825c	261.3m	32.3m	8.1m	BM

CARIBBEAN PRINCESS, ordered from the Monfalcone yard of Fincantieri (yard number 6067) was destined for P&O Cruises for service in the growing British cruise market. Following a cascading of ships from Princess to P&O, this vessel was switched to Princess Cruises for service in the Caribbean Sea as the CARIBBEAN PRINCESS. She is currently operating itineraries to Canada and New England and the Caribbean, but in the summer of 2015 will be based in Northern Europe. Her godmother is actress Jill Whelan. IMO 9215490

CORAL PRINCESS was built by Chantiers de l'Atlantique (yard number C32) at St Nazaire, France for Princess Cruises as the company's first gas turbine powered ship. She was named in the Panama Canal by Mireya Moscoso, the President of Panama and currently cruises in the Caribbean, through the Panama Canal and to Alaska and the Mexican Riviera. IMO 9229659

CROWN PRINCESS was ordered from Fincantieri (yard number 6100) in April 2003 in place of the sixth ship in the Holland America Vista class. The forward section of her hull was actually built in Fincantieri's Sestri shipyard at Genoa and bears the yard number 1100. Her godmother, American media personality Martha Stewart, named the ship at Brooklyn on 14 June 2006. This is the second ship of this name. For 2014/15 she operates on the west coast of North America including Alaska and Mexico. IMO 9293399

DAWN PRINCESS is the second ship in the SUN PRINCESS class and was built by Fincantieri (yard number 5955) at Monfalcone, Italy. She was christened by the original Love Boat cast. For 2014 to 2016 she cruises in the Pacific Ocean, based for most of the year in Australia. IMO 9103996

DIAMOND PRINCESS was laid down by Mitsubishi Heavy Industries (yard number 2181) in Japan as the SAPPHIRE PRINCESS, but following a major fire on board the DIAMOND PRINCESS while fitting out, the two ships exchanged names. She was christened by Yoshiko Tsukada, wife of the president of Mitsubishi, and currently operates in Australia, South East Asia and from Japan. IMO 9228198

EMERALD PRINCESS debuted in the Mediterranean before moving to the Caribbean in autumn of 2007. She was built by Fincantieri (yard number 6131) at Monfalcone, and now spends the summer in Europe and the winter in the Caribbean. Her godmothers are famous television mothers and daughters from the Brady Bunch and Happy Days, Florence Henderson, Susan Olsen, Marion Ross and Erin Moran. IMO 9333151

GOLDEN PRINCESS was built by Fincantieri (yard number 6050) at Monfalcone, Italy as the second of the GRAND PRINCESS Class. She was named by British actress Jane Seymour on 2 October 2001 in Fort Lauderdale and is the second ship in the Princess fleet to bear this name, the first being the former ROYAL VIKING SKY chartered in the 1990's, now the BOUDICCA of Fred. Olsen Cruise Lines. The GOLDEN PRINCESS currently cruises in Alaska, the Mexican Riviera and from Australia. IMO 9192351

GRAND PRINCESS was built as the first 100,000+ ton cruise ship for the P&O Group by Fincantieri (yard number 6956) at Monfalcone, Italy. Her godmother is actress Olivia de Havilland. In a major refit in the Bahamas in the spring of 2011 the ship had her Skywalkers Disco removed. Her current areas of operation are the west coast of North America, including Alaska, Mexico and Hawai'i. IMO 9104005

ISLAND PRINCESS is the second of a pair of ships built for the company by Chantiers de l'Atlantique (yard number D32) at St Nazaire, France, and a sister to the CORAL PRINCESS. She takes the name of one of the pair of ships upon which the long success of Princess Cruises was founded. Her godparents are Jamie Sale and David Pelletier, Canadian Olympic pairs ice skating champions. Her summer itineraries centre on the splendours of Alaska, while later in the year she cruises to the Caribbean and through the Panama Canal. For the summer of 2015 the ISLAND PRINCESS will be in the Mediterranean. IMO 9230402

OCEAN PRINCESS was built by Chantiers de l'Atlantique (yard number O31) at St Nazaire, France for Renaissance Cruises as the R FOUR. Renaissance Cruises filed for bankruptcy in the autumn of 2001 and the ship was laid up. P&O Princess Cruises acquired the R FOUR in 2002 and renamed her TAHITIAN PRINCESS. She was used for year round cruising based at Tahiti. This appeared to be a condition of acquisition of the ship, which received French Government subsidies when built, on the

Princess Cruises' **Regal Princess** in Piraeus *(William Mayes)*

Princess Cruises' **Sapphire Princess** at Mazatlan *(Rick Frendt)*

Princess Cruises' **Sea Princess** at Skagway *(Rick Frendt)*

basis that she would be operated for a number of years in French Polynesia. The TAHITIAN PRINCESS, whose godmother was Tonita Flosse was renamed OCEAN PRINCESS in late 2009. She currently spends much of the year in the South Pacific and Australia with a visit to Europe in the summer. IMO 9187899

PACIFIC PRINCESS was built as the R THREE for Renaissance Cruises by Chantiers de l'Atlantique (yard number N31) at St Nazaire, France for year round service in French Polynesia. Renaissance Cruises filed for bankruptcy in the autumn of 2001 and the ship was laid up. P&O Princess Cruises acquired the R THREE in 2002, and renamed her PACIFIC PRINCESS, reviving a name from the company's early days. Her godmother was Gabi Hollows. The ship currently operates in Alaska and the South Pacific. IMO 9187887

REGAL PRINCESS was built by Fincantieri (yard number 6224) at Monfalcone, and sailed from Venice on her maiden voyage on 20 May 2014. Her first cruises were in Europe after which she will move to the Caribbean, returning to Europe for the summer of 2015. IMO 9584724

ROYAL PRINCESS was built by Fincantieri (yard number 6223) at Monfalcone and christened in Southampton in May 2013 by HRH the Duchess of Cambridge. The ROYAL PRINCESS is currently operating in the Caribbean, but returns to Northern Europe in 2015 for a programme that includes several round-Britain cruises. IMO 9584712

RUBY PRINCESS was built by Fincantieri (yard number 6150) at Monfalcone, Italy, and was named by Trista and Ryan Sutter at Fort Lauderdale on 6 November 2008. She serves the Caribbean and Mediterranean markets, but in the summer of 2014 was based in Southampton. IMO 9378462

SAPPHIRE PRINCESS was laid down as the DIAMOND PRINCESS by Mitsubishi Heavy Industries (yard number 2180) in Japan, but following a major fire and consequent delay in delivery, she exchanged names with her sister under construction at the same yard. She was named by Alaskan First Lady Nancy Murkowski. The ship is currently based full time in South East Asia and Japan. IMO 9228186

SEA PRINCESS was built by Fincantieri (yard number 5998) at Monfalcone, Italy as the SEA PRINCESS for Princess Cruises. As the second ship to bear this name, she subsequently cruised in the Caribbean and to Alaska before being transferred to P&O Cruises as the ADONIA for operation from Southampton in the spring of 2003. With P&O Cruises she operated as an adult-only ship, and in addition to her UK based itineraries undertook a half-world cruise in 2004. The ADONIA transferred back to Princess Cruises in April 2005, reverting to the name SEA PRINCESS and was christened by English actress Joanna Lumley. The SEA PRINCESS is based full-time in Australia, and in 2015 will undertake a world cruise from there. IMO 9150913

STAR PRINCESS, the second ship to carry this name, is the third of the GRAND PRINCESS class to be built by Fincantieri (yard number 6051) at Monfalcone, Italy. Her godmother is Gunilla Antonini, the wife of the executive chairman of Fincantieri. The ship's 2003/2004 itineraries included Mexico, Alaska, Australia, Japan, China and the Far East, and a positioning voyage from Bangkok to Venice to commence a summer 2004 season in the Mediterranean. In March 2006 she suffered a major fire, which started on a balcony, damaging more than 100 cabins and putting the ship out of service for some time. She currently operates on the west coast of the USA, including Alaska and Mexico. IMO 9192363

SUN PRINCESS was built by Fincantieri (yard number 5909) at Monfalcone, Italy, as the lead ship in what was eventually to become a series of four. She was christened by Lady Dorothy Sterling, wife of the then chairman of P&O. She cruises in South East Asia, the Pacific Ocean and from Australia, but will be moving to the Japanese market. IMO 9000259

Cruise ship on order

NEWBUILD 1	c143000gt	2017	22.0k	DE2	3560p	4340p	1346c	330.0m	38.4m	8.6m	BM

NEWBUILD 1 was ordered on 30 July 2014 at Fincantieri and will be built at the Monfalcone shipyard. IMO 9753038

SEABOURN CRUISE LINE

The Company Seabourn Cruise Line was founded in 1987 by the Norwegian industrialist Atle Brynestad, now owner of Seadream Yacht Club, with the aim of providing the highest level of personal service to its passengers. In 1991 25% of the company was acquired by Carnival. A further 25%

passed to Carnival in 1996, and the remaining stock was acquired in 1998, at which time Seabourn was put under the management of Cunard, Carnival's premium brands division. Cunard's yacht-like SEA GODDESS I and II and the ROYAL VIKING SUN were transferred to the Seabourn operation and appropriately renamed. The SEA GODDESSES subsequently passed to Seadream Yacht Club. The Seabourn operation was separated from Cunard in 2005, when the latter company came under the wing of Princess Cruises, and it was thought then that Carnival Corporation was preparing to dispose of Seabourn, so it came as something of a surprise when the company announced the order for two new ships in late 2006. Operational control of Seabourn was passed to Holland America Line in 2010. In 2014 and 2015 the three original members of the fleet, SEABOURN LEGEND, SEABOURN PRIDE and SEABOURN SPIRIT will be delivered to Windstar Cruises.

Address 300 Elliott Avenue West, Seattle, WA 98119, United States of America

Telephone +1 866 755 5619

Website www.seabourn.com

Areas operated Worldwide

SEABOURN LEGEND	9961gt	1992	19.0k	D2	208p	212p	150c	135.0m	19.0m	5.2m	BS
SEABOURN ODYSSEY	32346gt	2009	19.0k	DE2	450p	450p	330c	198.0m	25.6m	6.4m	BS
SEABOURN QUEST	32477gt	2011	19.0k	DE2	450p	450p	330c	198.0m	25.6m	6.4m	BS
SEABOURN SOJOURN	32346gt	2010	19.0k	DE2	450p	450p	330c	198.0m	25.6m	6.4m	BS
SEABOURN SPIRIT	9975gt	1989	19.0k	D2	208p	212p	150c	133.8m	19.0m	5.2m	BS

SEABOURN LEGEND was to have been the third ship of the series for Seabourn Cruise Line. However, the company did not exercise the option, although Royal Viking Line effectively later took it up. She was delivered to that company by Schichau Seebeckwerft (yard number 1071), Bremerhaven as the ROYAL VIKING QUEEN in 1992. By this time the three original Royal Viking ships had left the company, so the fleet consisted of only this ship and the ROYAL VIKING SUN. She was renamed QUEEN ODYSSEY in 1994 and passed to Seabourn in 1996, becoming the SEABOURN LEGEND. She has been sold to Windstar Cruises with delivery in 2015. IMO 9008598

SEABOURN ODYSSEY was built by Mariotti (yard number 62). The hull was constructed at San Giorgio di Nogaro, in the Gulf of Venice and towed to Genoa where the superstructure was added and the ship fitted out. Uniquely, all of the passengers on the maiden voyage were designated as the ship's godparents. The SEABOURN ODYSSEY undertook Seabourn's first world cruise in 2010. IMO 9417086

SEABOURN QUEST was built by the Mariotti shipyard (yard number 64) at Genoa. She was named by American actress Blythe Danner on 20 June 2011 in Barcelona. IMO 9483126

SEABOURN SOJOURN was built by the Mariotti shipyard (yard number 63) in Genoa. The keel was laid on 1 July 2008. The ship was named at Greenwich, London by UK model Twiggy in June 2010. IMO 9417098

SEABOURN SPIRIT was the second ship to be delivered to Seabourn by Schichau Seebeckwerft (yard number 1070) at Bremerhaven in Germany, and christened by Aagot Brynestad. In November 2005 the SEABOURN SPIRIT became the first cruise ship to be attacked by pirates off the coast of Somalia. The SEABOURN SPIRIT has been sold to Windstar Cruise with delivery in spring 2015. IMO 8807997

Cruise ship on order

NEWBUILD 1	c40350gt	2016	19.0k	DE2	604p	604p	420c	198.0m	25.6m	6.4m	BS

NEWBUILD 1 is on order at Fincantieri for delivery in 2016. She will be an enlarged version of the SEABOURN ODYSSEY class ships. IMO 9731171

CELEBRATION CRUISE LINE

The Company Celebration Cruise Line is a subsidiary of Imperial Majesty Cruise Line, a company formed in 1999 to operate the OCEAN BREEZE (formerly the SOUTHERN CROSS of 1955). In 2003 the REGAL EMPRESS was acquired as a replacement for the OCEAN BREEZE, but with the SOLAS regulation changes looming in 2010 it was decided to retire the REGAL EMPRESS and begin again with a very different type of ship. At $33 million, the BAHAMAS CELEBRATION represents a very significant investment.

Address 2419 East Commercial Boulevard, Suite 302, Fort Lauderdale, FL33308, United States of America

Princess Cruises' **Star Princess** off Oslo *(Martin Grant)*

Seabourn Cruises' **Seabourn Quest** arriving at Rhodes *(William Mayes)*

Seabourn Cruises' **Seabourn Spirit** in Venice *(William Mayes)*

Telephone +1 954 414 1336

Website www.bahamascelebration.com

Area operated West Palm Beach to Freeport, Bahamas

BAHAMAS CELEBRATION	35855gt	1981	21.8k	D2	1004p	1250p	375c	205.3m	24.0m	5.8m	BS

BAHAMAS CELEBRATION was built by Howaldtswerke-Deutsche Werft (yard number 164) at Kiel in Germany as the PRINSESSE RAGNHILD for Norwegian ferry operator Jahre Line's Kiel to Oslo service. The Company merged with Norway Line in 1991 and was restyled as Color Line. During the following year, the ship underwent a significant rebuild in Spain, including lengthening by 33.5 metres, and the addition of extra decks. In 2005 she was displaced by the new COLOR FANTASY and began a new service linking Bergen and Stavanger in Norway with Hirtshals in Denmark. In January 2008 the route closed and she transferred to the Oslo to Hirtshals service. That service closed in May 2008 and the ship was laid up. She was subsequently acquired for Celebration Cruise Line's service and refitted in the Bahamas. IMO 7904891

CLASSIC CRUISES OF NEWPORT

The Company Classic Cruises of Newport is a US company, part of Atlantic Stars Hotels and Cruises, operating small sailing vessels from Newport, Rhode Island.

Address Christies Landing, Newport, Rhode Island 02840-3455, United States of America

Telephone +1 409 849 3033

Website www.cruisearabella.com

Area operated Summer - New England, winter – Virgin Islands

ARABELLA	208gt	1983	10.0k	SD1	40p	49p	9c	47.7m	7.4m	3.8m	US

ARABELLA was built by Palmer Johnson (yard number 186) at Sturgeon Bay, Wisconsin, USA as the research vessel CENTURION. She was acquired by Altantic Star Lines in 2001, converted to a three-masted sailing yacht and renamed ARABELLA. She is marketed by Classic Cruises of Newport. IMO 8201272

CLIPPER GROUP

The Company Clipper Group is a Danish ship owner that controls around 250 vessels, of which about 100 are owned. The origins of this company are in Armada Shipping, formed in 1972 by Torben Jensen and Jorgen Dannesboe. In 1991 the partnership broke up and Torben Jensen took the ships with a Clipper prefix name and started Clipper Group. Jensen stayed in Houston, from where he had been operating since 1980, but set up a head office in Switzerland. In 1997 the head office moved to Nassau, and two years later Clipper Group entered into a joint venture with two Danish banks. In 2005 the company moved its headquarters to Denmark. During 2008 the company acquired 50% of Miami-based International Shipping Partners. However, in early 2009 that shareholding was sold back to ISP's management. Clipper Group owns 15% of Danish ferry operator DFDS, has a major share in a number of Danish domestic routes and owns SeaTruck Ferries, operating between England, Ireland and Northern Ireland.

Address Clipper House, Sundkrogsgade 19. DK2100, Copenhagen, Denmark

Telephone +45 4911 8000

Area operated Does not operate for its own account. Ships are chartered out.

GEMINI	19093gt	1992	18.4k	D2	819p	916p	470c	163.8m	22.5m	5.4m	MH
SEA ADVENTURER	4376gt	1975	14.0k	D2	122p	122p	79c	100.0m	16.2m	4.7m	BS
SEA DISCOVERER	4954gt	2007	10.0k	DP2	226p	226p	74c	91.4m	15.2m	3.8m	US
SEA EXPLORER	4200gt	1991	15.5k	D2	114p	114p	70c	90.3m	15.3m	4.0m	MH
SEA VOYAGER	4954gt	2001	10.0k	DP2	226p	226p	74c	91.4m	15.2m	3.8m	BS
SILVER DISCOVERER	5218gt	1989	18.0k	D2	120p	120p	70c	103.0m	15.4m	4.3m	BS

GEMINI was built by Union Naval de Levante (yard number 197) at Valencia, Spain for Effjohn Group's Crown Cruise Line as the CROWN JEWEL. Cunard marketed her from 1993 as the CUNARD CROWN JEWEL before passing to Star Cruises in 1995 when she was renamed as the SUPERSTAR GEMINI. She operated cruises to Japan from her Taiwan base, but in the autumn of 2005 moved back to

Celebration Cruise Line's **Bahamas Celebration** at Freeport *(Rick Frendt)*

Clipper Group's **Gemini** when operating for Quail Cruises *(William Mayes)*

Club Med's **Club Med 2** at Portofino *(Richard Mayes)*

Singapore to cruise in the Straits of Malacca and the Andaman Sea. She was sold to Clipper Group of Denmark in 2007, and remained under charter to Star Cruises. In 2009 she was to have operated for Spanish company, Vision Cruises, in place of the JULES VERNE (now ALEXANDER VON HUMBOLDT) but that company apparently sub-chartered the vessel to Golden Star Cruises and pulled out of cruising. Although Golden Star Cruises was advertising this ship at the same time as the VISION STAR, she was actually renamed GEMINI in March 2009 and was then chartered to Quail Cruises for six months. For her first three months she operated from Valencia, before taking a series of Eastern Mediterranean cruises. Her charter continued with her charterer restyled as Happy Cruises and subsequently she had a winter based in Cuba and for 2011 operated in Northern Europe during the summer. Happy Cruises folded in September 2011 and the GEMINI was laid up at Tilbury, England. She served briefly as an accommodation ship at the London Olympic Games in 2012, but then went back into lay up at Tilbury. In July 2014 she was chartered to Petrofac for use as an accommodation ship at Dales Voe in Shetland. IMO 9000687

SEA ADVENTURER (Formerly CLIPPER ADVENTURER) For details see under Quark Expeditions (TUI).

SEA DISCOVERER was built by Atlantic Marine (yard number 4243) at Jacksonville, Florida, USA for American Classic Voyages as the CAPE COD LIGHT. That group declared bankruptcy in 2001 and the ship may never have actually been completed. She was laid up at Green Cove Spring, Florida. In early 2007 Hornblower Marine Services purported to have acquired her and her sister. That transaction was never completed. She was renamed COASTAL QUEEN 2 in late 2007. In 2008 she was purchased by Clipper Group and was renamed CLIPPER DISCOVERER. At some stage it was proposed that the ship would be used by Waterfront Lifestyles International to provide floating retirement homes at Port Canaveral, Florida under the name VALENCIA. That never happened and she was renamed SEA DISCOVERER in late 2009. Subsequently she has been used as an accommodation ship for several off shore wind farm projects in the UK. At the time of writing she was serving in a similar role off the German island of Borkum. IMO 9213131

SEA EXPLORER (Formerly CORINTHIAN II) For details see under Quark Expeditions (TUI).

SEA VOYAGER was built as the CAPE MAY LIGHT by Atlantic Marine (yard number 4242) at Jacksonville, Florida, USA for American Classic Voyages. In 2001 she made three cruises in each direction between Buffalo and Quebec City, and was to have commenced a series of New England cruises from Providence, Rhode Island. It is not certain if these took place before the company filed for bankruptcy. Hornblower Marine Services was thought to have acquired the ship in 2007, but that transaction was never completed. She was reported to have been renamed COASTAL QUEEN 1 in 2007. In 2008 she was purchased by Clipper Group and was renamed initially as CLIPPER VOYAGER. During 2009 it was planned for Waterfront Lifestyles International to use the ship as floating retirement homes at Port Canaveral, Florida, under the name ALEGRIA. That did not happen. In late 2009 she was renamed SEA VOYAGER and in 2010 was used as an accommodation ship for UN relief workers in Haiti. In 2011 she was chartered to Comfort at Sea as an accommodation vessel for construction workers in Deception Bay, Canada. Later she is believed to have been used as accommodation by St Mary's College, Maryland. Reports suggest that following a refit she will enter service for Rivages du Monde on Saint Lawrence Seaway cruises as the SAINT LAURENT PRESTIGE in 2015. IMO 9213129

SILVER DISCOVERER (Formerly Clipper Odyssey) For details see under Silversea Cruises.

CLUB MED CRUISES

The Company Club Med Cruises is a division of the French travel company Club Med, which was founded in 1950 by former Belgian water polo champion, Gerard Blitz (1912-1990). The company's first holiday village was opened on the Spanish island of Mallorca. Ownership passed to Baron Edmond de Rothschild in 1961 and in 2004 French hotel group Accor became the largest shareholder, eventually selling its stake in 2006.

Address 11 Rue de Cambrai, 75957 Paris Cedex 19, France

Telephone +33 153 353553

Website www.clubmed.com

Area operated Summer in the Mediterranean Sea and winter in the Caribbean Sea

| CLUB MED 2 | 14983gt | 1992 | 15.0k | SD2 | 372p | 419p | 200c | 187.0m | 20.0m | 5.1m | FR |

CLUB MED 2 was built by Societe Nouvelle des Ateliers et Chantiers du Havre (yard number 282) at Le Havre, France, as one of a pair of sister ships for Club Med. The other of this duo was sold to Windstar Cruises. CLUB MED 2 is a 5-masted ship and is managed by V-Ships. IMO 9007491

COMPAGNIE DU FLEUVE

The Company Compagnie du Fleuve is a Senegalese company, recently formed to restore and operate the BOU EL MOGDAD.

Address BP 266, Saint-Louis, Senegal

Telephone +221 961 5689 **Fax** +221 961 8320

Website www.compagniedufleuve.com

Area operated Senegal

BOU EL MOGDAD	650gt	1954	7.0 k	D2	56p	56p	22c	52.0m	10.0m	2.5m	SN

BOU EL MOGDAD is a former river boat from French colonial days in West Africa, that operated on the Senegal River from 1954 until about 1968. She was built in The Netherlands for Messageries du Senegal and plied between the northern coastal town of Saint-Louis and Kayes in Mali, to link the first capital of Senegal with the many inland trading posts. Abandoned by the company around 1968, the ship was used for humanitarian missions for a number of years, and later as a local cruise ship before again falling into disuse. Acquired by her current owner in 2005 and now fully restored, she operates as far as the border with Mauritania, but also undertakes coastal trips along the Atlantic shores of Senegal and Mauritania. The ship's name recalls that of El Hadj Boa El Mogdad Seck, the Mauritanian diplomat and explorer, the first African to receive France's Legion d'Honneur.

CORAL PRINCESS CRUISES

The Company Coral Princess Cruises is an Australian company, founded by Captain Tony Briggs, which pioneered Great Barrier Reef cruising in 1984 with a converted Second World War Fairmile class submarine chaser. The company commissioned its first purpose built vessel, the CORAL PRINCESS, in 1988. The company has been involved in a co-operation agreement with Captain Cook Cruises since 2008.

Address PO Box 2093, Cairns, Queensland 4870, Australia

Telephone +61 7 4040 9999 **Fax** +61 7 4035 5995

Website www.coralprincesscruises.com

Area operated Australia's Great Barrier Reef, New Zealand, Papua New Guinea and Melanesia

CORAL PRINCESS	730gt	1988	10.0k	D2	50p	54p	12c	35.0m	13.3m	2.4m	AU
CORAL PRINCESS II	729gt	1985	10.0k	D2	46p	48p	12c	37.3m	12.0m	2.4m	AU
OCEANIC DISCOVERER	1779gt	2005	14.0k	D2	72p	72p	20c	63.1m	13.0m	3.0m	AU

CORAL PRINCESS was built by Carrington Slipways (yard number 204) at Newcastle, New South Wales, Australia. IMO 8804696

CORAL PRINCESS II was built by North Queensland Engineers & Agents (yard number 121) at Cairns, Queensland, Australia as the catamaran CORAL CAT. In 1990 she was renamed SPICE ISLANDER and took her current name in 1996 when acquired by Coral Princess Cruises. IMO 8409240

OCEANIC DISCOVERER was built as the OCEANIC PRINCESS by North Queensland Engineers & Agents (yard number 220) at Cairns, Queensland, Australia for the company. She was renamed as the OCEANIC DISCOVERER in October 2006. IMO 9292747

CROISIEUROPE

The Company CroisiEurope is a French family-owned operator of river cruise ships, established in 1976 by Gerard Schmitter as Alsace Croisieres. The company adopted its current name in 1997 and operates 26 river cruise ships, including LA BELLE DE CADIX, which also ventures out into the Atlantic Ocean on its Spanish coastal itineraries.

Address 12 Rue de la Division Leclerc, 67000 Strasbourg, France

Telephone +33 3 8876 4444 **Fax** +33 3 8832 4996

Coral Princess Cruises' **Coral Princess** *(Peter Plowman)*

Croisimer's **La Belle de l'Adriatique** at Split *(Martin Grant)*

Coral Princess Cruises' **Oceanic Discoverer** *(company picture)*

Website www.croisieurope.com

Area operated The Spanish rivers and Atlantic coast (this ship)

LA BELLE DE CADIX	2038gt	2005	12.0k	D3	176p	176p	45c	110.0m	11.4m	3.0m	BE

LA BELLE DE CADIX was built by Meuse & Sambre Chantier Naval (yard number 24) at Beez sur Meuse in Belgium. IMO 9068938

CROISIMER

The Company CroisiMer is the newly created coastal cruise division of the French river cruise operator CroisiEurope, which was established in 1976. A further two sisters to the 'Adriatic' were ordered from the same shipyard, but all records of these have disappeared, so it is likely the orders for LA BELLE DU BOSPHORE and LA BELLE DES CYCLADES were cancelled.

Address 12 Rue de la Division Leclerc, 67000 Strasbourg, France

Telephone +33 3 8876 4444 **Fax** +33 3 8832 4996

Website www.croisieurope.com

Area operated The Adriatic Sea, Red Sea and the Canary Islands

LA BELLE DE L'ADRIATIQUE	2995gt	2007	12.0k	D3	198p	198p	43c	110.0m	12.8m	3.0m	BE

LA BELLE DE L'ADRIATIQUE was built by Meuse & Sambre Chantier Naval (yard number 30) at Beez sur Meuse in Belgium. It is thought that she was originally going to be named MARCO POLO. She operates on the Dalmacian coast in summer and moves to Egypt, Jordan and the Red Sea in winter. IMO 9432799

CRUCEROS AUSTRALIS

The Company Cruceros Australis is a Chilean company, founded in 1990 to operate short cruises in and around Patagonia.

Address Avenida El Bosque Norte 0440 Piso 11, Las Condes, Santiago 6780235, Chile

Telephone +56 2 2442 3115 **Fax** +56 2 2203 5173

Website www.australis.com

Area operated Patagonia, Tierra del Fuego and Cape Horn

MARE AUSTRALIS	2664gt	2002	12.0k	D2	126p	126p	40c	71.8m	13.4m	3.2m	CL
STELLA AUSTRALIS	4508gt	2010	12.0k	D2	200p	210p	c	89.0m	14.6m	3.5m	CL
VIA AUSTRALIS	2716gt	2005	12.0k	D2	128p	128p	40c	72.3m	13.4m	3.3m	CL

MARE AUSTRALIS, **STELLA AUSTRALIS** and **VIA AUSTRALIS** were built by Astilleros y Servicios Navales (yard numbers 132, 159 and 145) at Valdivia, Chile for Nisa Navegacion, a Chilean operator of ferries and cargo ships within the same corporate grouping as Cruceros Australis. The MARE AUSTRALIS is currently laid up. IMO 9265677, 9534676 and 9334088

CRUISE AND MARITIME VOYAGES

The Company Cruise and Maritime Voyages is a trading name of South Quay Travel & Leisure Ltd. The cruise business was formed to take on the operation of the MARCO POLO when Transocean Tours filed for bankruptcy in 2009. This company is associated with Cruise and Maritime Services International, the former UK agency for both Classic International Cruises and Louis Cruise Lines. Subsequently Majestic International's OCEAN COUNTESS was chartered for two years, being replaced in 2013 by Voyages of Discovery's DISCOVERY. A seasonal charter of ASTOR for line voyages and Australian cruising began in November 2013, but later CMV took full control of the ship. In 2014 CMV took over the sales and marketing of Passat Kreuzfahrten, operator of the DELPHIN. For 2015 the DISCOVERY is replaced by Portuscale's AZORES. CMV also offered two cruises aboard Portuscale's FUNCHAL in October 2014.

Address Gateway House, Stonehouse Lane, Purfleet, Essex RM19 1NS, United Kingdom

Telephone +44 1708 893100

Website www.cruiseandmaritime.com

Area operated Northern and Southern Europe, the Caribbean Sea and South America from the UK, plus line voyages to Australia and Australian cruising

ASTOR	20704gt	1987	16.5k	D2	578p	600p	278c	176.3m	22.6m	6.1m	BS
AZORES	16144gt	1948	16.5k	D2	552p	659p	185c	160.0m	21.0m	7.6m	PT
DISCOVERY	20216gt	1971	18.0k	D2	708p	758p	350c	168.7m	24.6m	7.5m	BM
MARCO POLO	22080gt	1965	19.5k	D2	800p	850p	350c	176.3m	23.6m	8.2m	BS

ASTOR was ordered by the South African Marine Corporation, as a replacement for the 1981-built ASTOR, from Howaldtswerke-Deutsche Werft (yard number 218) at Kiel, Germany. During construction however, the company decided to abandon its plans to re-start the Cape Town to Southampton liner service and in a complicated series of moves the ship was delivered as the ASTOR to Ireland Blyth and registered in Mauritius. After only eighteen months she was sold to the Black Sea Shipping Company of Odessa as the FEDOR DOSTOEVSKIY. In 1991 she was registered under the ownership of a SOVCOMFLOT group company. She subsequently performed a number of charters and was then chartered to Transocean Tours as the ASTOR under a long-term arrangement. In 2006 she was acquired by German-based Premicon, but remained on charter to Transocean Tours. That company collapsed in 2009 and Premicon set up a new Transocean to continue operating the ship in the German market from 2010. In 2014 CMV took over the marketing of the ship. IMO 8506373

AZORES For details see under Portuscale Cruises.

DISCOVERY For details see under Voyages of Discovery (All Leisure Group).

MARCO POLO was built in what was then East Germany by Mathias-Thesen-Werft (yard number 126) at Wismar, Germany as one of a series of five liners for the Black Sea Shipping Company and the Baltic Shipping Company. The ALEKSANDR PUSHKIN entered service for the Baltic Shipping Company in the summer of 1965 with a series of cruises before taking up her intended employment on the service from Leningrad to Montreal during the following spring. From 1975 she was mainly used for cruising and from 1979 was on a five-year charter to Transocean. In 1985 she was transferred to the Far Eastern Shipping Company of Vladivostok and over the next few years she undertook charters to CTC Lines for cruising from Sydney, Australia. Following a brief lay-up in Singapore she was sold in 1991 to Shipping and General (Orient Lines) and sent to Greece for a major refit that took almost three years to complete. As the MARCO POLO she proved to be both popular and successful with her out of the way itineraries. Norwegian Cruise Line subsequently acquired Orient Lines in 1998, but the operation retained its own identity. NCL closed Orient Lines in 2007 and sold the ship to Global Maritime of Greece, from whom she was chartered by Transocean Tours until the end of 2009. Cruise & Maritime voyages took her on charter from the beginning of 2010 for, it is thought, five years. Marco Polo, the great Italian traveller, was born in 1254 on the Dalmatian island of Korcula, which at that time belonged to Venice. His epic journey along the Silk Road through Asia lasted 24 years and resulted in the production of the greatest travelogue ever written. IMO 6417097

TRANSOCEAN KREUZFAHRTEN

The Company Transocean Tours Touristik was a German tour company, established in 1954, operating ocean cruises and river cruises on the waterways of Europe for German-speaking passengers. In a move away from its core market, the company positioned the ARIELLE (then Louis Cruise Lines' AQUAMARINE) for a number of ex-UK cruises for British passengers in 2007, and the MARCO POLO performed a similar programme in 2008 and 2009. The company subsequently sub-chartered the MARCO POLO to Cruise and Maritime Voyages of the UK, an offshoot of its former UK general sales agent, but eventually Transocean Tours filed for insolvency in September 2009. Premicon, the owner of the ship decided to establish a new Transocean Kreuzfahrten, which commenced trading in 2010 after the ASTOR (the line's only remaining ship) had undergone a major upgrade. Sales, marketing and the ASTOR were taken over by Cruise & Maritime Voyages in 2014. Both Transocean and CMV operate river cruise vessels.

Telephone +49 421 33360 **Fax** +49 421 3336 100

Website www.transocean.de

Area operated Northern Europe and the Mediterranean Sea

ASTOR	20704gt	1987	16.5k	D2	578p	578p	278c	176.3m	22.6m	6.1m	BS

ASTOR For details see under Cruise & Maritime Voyages

Cruise and Maritime Voyages' *Astor* at Tilbury *(William Mayes)*

Cruise and Maritime Voyages' *Marco Polo* at Tilbury *(Peter Godliman)*

Deilmann's *Deutschland* off Cuxhaven *(William Mayes)*

CVC

The Company CVC is a major Brazilian travel and tour operator that has previously chartered ships for its own account. Since January 2010 CVC has been 64% owned by the investment house Carlyle Group. The company relies on Pullmantur for most of its ships, but has chartered from other operators. CVC also markets other cruise ships during the Brazilian summer, notably those of Iberocruceros, Costa and MSC. For 2014, however, it appears that CVC is not operating ships for its own account but is selling space on a variety of vessels.

Website www.cvc.com.br

Area operated Brazil

DEILMANN CRUISE

The Company Peter Deilmann set up his cargo handling business Deilmann Reederei in 1972, and within a year had established Peter Deilmann Cruises as a company offering cruises in the premium sector. He withdrew from the cargo business in 1979 to concentrate on cruising. Until 2004 the company also operated the small cruise ship BERLIN, but this has now been returned to her owners. Peter Deilmann died in 2004 and the company passed into the hands of his daughters. The company also operated a fleet of river cruise ships on the waterways of Europe until June 2009, when that part of the business filed for bankruptcy. In August 2010 German investment house Aurelius took a majority stake in the company, but this was sold on to Callista Private Equity in early 2014. In July 2014 travel group FTI took over the travel agent marketing for Germany, Austria and Switzerland.

Address Am Holm 25, 23730 Neustadt in Holstein, Germany

Telephone +49 4561 3960 **Fax** +49 4561 8207

Website www.deilmann-kreuzfahrten.de

Area operated Worldwide

| DEUTSCHLAND | 22496gt | 1998 | 20.0k | D2 | 520p | 576p | 280c | 175.3m | 23.0m | 5.8m | DE |

DEUTSCHLAND was built by Howaldtswerke Deutsche Werft (yard number 328) at Kiel, Germany for grand style cruising for Peter Deilmann Cruises. IMO 9141807

DENIZ CRUISE AND FERRY LINES

The Company Deniz Cruise and Ferry Lines is a Turkish operator formed in 2004 to acquire and operate these two former Turkish Maritime Lines passenger and car ferries. The Istanbul Chamber of Shipping has a lead role in the owning consortium.

Address Site B1 Block no 2, Floor 8 D, 18 Kozyatagi, Kadikoy, Istanbul, Turkey

Telephone +90 216 380 9797 **Fax** +90 216 380 9384

Website www.denizline.com.tr

Area operated Greek Island cruises from Istanbul and charters (and ferry services)

| ANKARA | 10870gt | 1983 | 18.5k | D2 | 268p | 564p | 90c | 127.6m | 19.4m | 5.4m | TR |
| SAMSUN | 10870gt | 1985 | 18.5k | D2 | 274p | 564p | 90c | 127.6m | 19.4m | 5.4m | TR |

ANKARA was built by Stocznia Szczecinska im. A Warskiego (yard number B490/03) at Szczecin, Poland. She was to have been the MAZOWIA for Polska Zeluga Baltycka, but was completed as the ANKARA and delivered to Turkish Maritime Lines as part of a debt repayment programme. She generally operated between Turkey and Italy, sometimes through the Corinth Canal. Turkish Maritime Lines was privatised in a piecemeal fashion between 2003 and 2005 and this ship was taken up by her current owner. She was extensively refurbished in 2005/6. For the summer of 2011 the ship was chartered to Adriatica Traghetti for use on its ferry service from Bari in Italy to Durres in Albania. Ankara, known as Ancyra in classical times, became the capital of the new Turkish Republic in 1923. IMO 7615672

SAMSUN was built as a sister to the ANKARA by Stocznia Szczecinska im. A Warskiego (yard number B490/04) at Szczecin, Poland for Turkish Maritime Lines. She was renovated in 2005/6 when acquired as part of the Turkish privatisation programme. During 2010 the SAMSUN was chartered to Bamtur. Samsun is a port city on Turkey's Black Sea coast. IMO 7615684

Deniz Cruise Lines' *Samsun* in Istanbul *(William Mayes)*

Disney Cruise Line's *Disney Dream* at Castaway Cay *(Rick Frendt)*

Disney Cruise Line's *Disney Magic* off Villefranche *(William Mayes)*

DESERT ISLAND CRUISING

The Company Desert Island Cruising Ltd is an associated company of Leisure Park Management Ltd, a UK operator of camp and caravan sites and holiday letting properties.

Address Wharf Road, Crowle, Scunthorpe, Lincolnshire, DN17 4JS United Kingdom

Telephone +44 1724 712884

Website www.desert-island-cruising.com

Area operated The Maldives

YASAWA PRINCESS	917gt	1985	11.0k	D2	60p	66p	25c	55.0m	11.0m	2.5m	FJ

YASAWA PRINCESS was built by the Fiji Marine Shipyard & Slipways (yard number 81) at Suva, Fiji for Blue Lagoon Cruises. Her current operator acquired her in December 2007 without a change of name. Yasawa is the main island in the western Fiji Yasawa group of islands. IMO 8325638

DISCOVERY FLEET CRUISES

The Company Discovery Fleet Cruises is a Philippines-based company founded in 2012, specialising in diving cruises.

Address JTKC Center, 2155 Chino Roces Ave, 1231 Makati City, Philippines

Telephone +63 2 5195674

Website www.discoveryfleet.com

Area operated Diving cruises in the Philippines

DISCOVERY ADVENTURE	394gt	1988	11.0k	D2	32p	32p	30c	42.6m	8.5m	2.0m	PH
DISCOVERY PALAWAN	539gt	1973	10.5k	D1	32p	32p	30c	50.0m	8.6m	3.0m	PH

DISCOVERY ADVENTURE was built by the Fiji Marine Shipyard & Slipways (yard number 84) at Suva, Fiji for Blue Lagoon Cruises of Fiji as the NANUYA PRINCESS. She was acquired by her current owner in 2012 and renamed YASAWA LEGEND. She will be renamed DISCOVERY ADVENTURE when her refit is completed. IMO 8908014

DISCOVERY PALAWAN was built by Scheepswerf Appingedam (yard number W488) at Appingedam in the Netherlands as the Danish training ship HANS CHRISTIAN ANDERSON. She moved to the Philippines in 2007 and was acquired by her current owner in 2012 and renamed DISCOVERY PALAWAN. IMO 7219844

DISNEY CRUISE LINE

The Company Disney Cruise Line is part of the Disney Corporation leisure group.

Address PO Box 10238, Lake Buena Vista, Florida 32830-0238 United States of America

Telephone +1 407 566 3500 **Fax** +1 407 566 3541

Website www.disneycruise.com

Area operated Caribbean Sea, Mexican Riviera and Europe

DISNEY DREAM	129690gt	2011	22.0k	DE2	2500p	4000p	1458c	339.8m	37.0m	8.3m	BS
DISNEY FANTASY	129750gt	2012	22.0k	DE2	2500p	4000p	1458c	339.8m	37.0m	8.3m	BS
DISNEY MAGIC	83969gt	1998	21.5k	DE2	1750p	2834p	945c	294.1m	32.3m	8.0m	BS
DISNEY WONDER	83308gt	1999	21.5k	DE2	1750p	2834p	945c	294.1m	32.3m	8.0m	BS

DISNEY DREAM was ordered from Jos. L. Meyer (yard number 687) at Papenburg, Germany in February 2007 She was delivered in December 2010, and her godmother, at a naming ceremony on 19 January 2011 was singer Jennifer Hudson. IMO 9434254

DISNEY FANTASY was ordered from Jos. L. Meyer (yard number 688) at Papenburg, Germany in February 2007 and delivered in early 2012. She was christened by Mariah Carey. IMO 9445590

DISNEY MAGIC was built by Fincantieri (yard number 5989) at the Breda shipyard, Venice, Italy. The forward section of the ship was built at the company's Ancona shipyard and towed to Venice to be completed and joined to the after section. The ship's godmother is Patty Disney, wife of Roy Disney.

DISNEY MAGIC underwent a major refit in 2013, as a result of which additional structures increased her gross tonnage by about 600. IMO 9126807

DISNEY WONDER was built by Fincantieri (yard number 5990) at Breda, Italy for Disney Cruise Line. It is thought that this was the first ship to be christened by a cartoon character, the honour going to Tinkerbell. IMO 9126819

EMERAUDE CLASSIC CRUISES

The Company Emeraude Classic Cruises is a member company of the Apple Tree Group, a tourism, land, development, import and distribution business based in French Indo-China, Myanmar, Thailand and India.

Address 46 Le Thai To Street, Hanoi, Vietnam

Telephone +84 4 3935 1888 **Fax** +84 4 3825 5342

Website www.emeraude-cruises.com

Area operated Halong Bay, Vietnam

EMERAUDE	700gt	2003	10.0k	D2	78p	78p	35c	56.0m	10.0m	2.6m	VN

EMERAUDE was built by the Song Cam Shipyard in Vietnam as a replica 1910 French colonial steamer. She now operates overnight cruises in Halong Bay.

ETSTUR

The Company Etstur is a Turkish tour operator, established in 1991, with a worldwide programme of land tours. Although the company has sold cruises on other lines, it is only recently that it has started to offer cruises for its own account.

Address Bagdat Caddesi 55, 34725 Kiziltoprak, Istanbul, Turkey

Telephone +90 216 542 9999 **Fax** +90 216 349 8640

Website www.etstur.com

Area operated Eastern Mediterranean

AEGEAN PARADISE	23287gt	1990	16.0k	D2	650p	650p	315c	174.0m	24.0m	6.5m	BS

AEGEAN PARADISE was built by Ishikawajima – Harima Heavy Industries (yard number 2987) at the Tokyo shipyard in Japan as the ORIENT VENUS for Japan Cruise Line. She operated mainly in the charter cruise trades but had been laid up for several years. After a major re-build, in 2005 she became the CRUISE ONE of First Cruise Group, now Hainan Enterprises, but it is not thought that she saw active service under that name. Delphin Kreuzfahrten chartered her for operation commencing in December 2006, but an over-running refit delayed her entry into service until spring 2007. She operated for Delphin as the DELPHIN VOYAGER until the autumn of 2010 when that company was declared bankrupt. She was returned to her owner and renamed HAINAN EMPRESS in January 2011, but was almost immediately chartered by Happy Cruises as the HAPPY DOLPHIN, for whom she operated briefly in the Eastern Mediterranean until the company folded in September 2011. For the summers of 2012, 2013 and 2014 she has been chartered to Etstur as the AEGEAN PARADISE. Her ultimate owner is Global Maritime Group of Greece. IMO 8902333

FRED. OLSEN CRUISE LINES

The Company The business we know today as Fred. Olsen Cruise Lines has its origins in the ship owning firm founded in 1886 by Frederik Olsen. By the early 1900's the business had expanded to embrace routes between Norway and Europe, Britain and the Mediterranean. The latter was a particularly important development as it introduced the company to the fruit trades from the region. The Canary Islands later became the focus of this trade, and the Olsen family still has significant investments in that area including a ferry operation. In 1906 the company began to carry passengers between Norway and the River Tyne, in northeast England, and Fred. Olsen developed the North Sea business, which probably peaked with the introduction of the BRAEMAR on the route from Harwich to Oslo in 1985. Olsen first started to offer what might now be regarded as proper cruises in 1966 with the arrival of the dual purpose BLACK WATCH and BLACK PRINCE. The first of these was jointly ordered by Fred. Olsen and the Bergen Line to serve the latter company's North Sea trades in the

Emeraude Classic Cruises' **Emeraude** in Halong Bay, Vietnam *(Theodore W Scull)*

Etstur's **Aegean Paradise** at Santorini *(William Mayes)*

Fred. Olsen's **Balmoral** at Rouen *(William Mayes)*

summer under the name JUPITER and to begin a new era for the Olsen's by offering cruises to the Canary Islands from London in the winter as the BLACK WATCH. The impressive vehicle deck space was occupied on the northbound leg by Canary Islands fruit, destined for the tables of Northern Europe. The second ship was ordered by Olsen for its own account, but in 1970 the company entered into a similar arrangement with the Bergen Line and she became the VENUS in summer and the BLACK PRINCE in winter. The BLENHEIM, a larger version of the twins was delivered to the company in 1970.

The arrangement between Olsen and the Bergen Line came to an end in 1986 and the BLACK WATCH became the property of the latter. Fred. Olsen retained the BLACK PRINCE and had her converted for full cruise ship operation by Wartsila at Turku in Finland, principally by means of the installation of 125 cabins on her vehicle deck. A second cruise ship, a new BLACK WATCH joined the fleet in 1996. The third ship for this gently expanding company appeared in 2001 in the form of the BRAEMAR and a fourth ship (BOUDICCA) arrived in 2006, closely followed by the announcement of a fifth (BALMORAL). The BLACK PRINCE was withdrawn from service in the autumn of 2009, and sold for further service in Venezuela. Fred. Olsen Cruise Lines specialises in cruises for British passengers, and are also the UK General Sales Agents for Star Clippers.

Address Fred Olsen House, White House Road, Ipswich, Suffolk, IP1 5LL England

Telephone +44 1473 292200 **Fax** +44 1473 292201

Website www.fredolsencruises.com

Area operated Ex-UK to Scandinavia, the Mediterranean, South America, Caribbean and Grand Voyages

BALMORAL	43537gt	1988	19.0k	D2	1350p	1400p	510c	217.9m	28.2m	6.8m	BS
BLACK WATCH	28613gt	1972	18.5k	D2	804p	892p	330c	205.5m	25.2m	7.5m	BS
BOUDICCA	28551gt	1973	20.0k	D2	755p	880p	329c	205.5m	25.2m	7.6m	BS
BRAEMAR	24344gt	1993	18.5k	D2	929p	988p	371c	195.1m	22.5m	5.4m	BS

BALMORAL was built for the Greek owned Royal Cruise Line by Jos. L. Meyer (yard number 616) at Papenburg, Germany as the CROWN ODYSSEY. She was to have been one of a pair of ships, but in the event the second vessel was either never ordered or cancelled before work began. Royal Cruise Line became part of the Kloster group around 1990, but the company retained its identity until 1996 when it was absorbed into Norwegian Cruise Line and the ship was renamed NORWEGIAN CROWN. In May 2000 the ship was transferred to Orient Lines and reverted to her original name for 'exploration cruising' worldwide. In early 2003 it was announced that the ship would be returned to Norwegian Cruise Line as the NORWEGIAN CROWN, following a downturn in Orient Lines' business and reverting to her previous NCL name. She operated to Bermuda, and handled the longer South American itineraries for NCL before being sold to Fred. Olsen Cruise Lines in 2006, for delivery in late 2007. When handed over to the company in November 2007, the ship went immediately to the Blohm & Voss shipyard in Hamburg to be refitted and to have a new 30-metre mid section fitted. That structure had already been completed by Schichau Seebeckwerft in Bremerhaven, and towed to Hamburg in October. Unfortunately, the ship's delivery back to Fred. Olsen Cruise Lines was delayed, and with work still to be completed the BALMORAL missed her maiden voyage. In the spring of 2008 the company experimented with a first season of Mediterranean fly cruises with the BALMORAL before repositioning to Dover for a series of UK based cruises. Balmoral Castle and Estate is HM Queen Elizabeth II's private residence in Scotland, purchased by Queen Victoria in 1848. IMO 8506294

BLACK WATCH was built as the first of a trio of ships for the new Royal Viking Line consortium, one of the first purpose-built luxury cruise ships, for worldwide service. When delivered by the Helsinki shipyard of Wartsila (yard number 395) as the ROYAL VIKING STAR she introduced a new and impressive profile. As built she was 21,847 gross tons and carried a mere 539 passengers in luxurious surroundings. She was lengthened by Schichau Seebeckwerft in Bremerhaven in 1981, giving her an increased passenger capacity of 829. In 1988 she was transferred to Kloster Cruise (owners of the Royal Viking Line since 1984) and three years later was given the name WESTWARD. She was transferred within the group to Royal Cruise Line in 1994 and renamed as the STAR ODYSSEY. Olsen purchased her in 1996 through an intermediary (Olsen and Kloster were both Oslo shipping families and there was a certain amount of rivalry between the two) and following a refit she entered service on ex-UK cruises as the BLACK WATCH. In 2005 she underwent a major refit, including the replacement of her engines. The Scottish army regiment, the Black Watch, was established in 1725 and until recent years only drew its recruits from Perthshire, Angus and Fife. The Black Watch was incorporated into a larger Scottish Regiment in 2006. IMO 7108930

BOUDICCA was built by Wartsila (yard number 396) at Helsinki, Finland as the ROYAL VIKING SKY for the new Royal Viking Line of Oslo. She was 21,891 gross tons as built. During 1982 Schichau Seebeckwerft at Bremerhaven lengthened her by 28m. In 1987 she was transferred to the fleet of Norwegian Caribbean Line (Kloster Cruise), the parent company (Klosters had acquired Royal Viking Line in 1984) and was renamed SUNWARD. In 1992 she passed to Birka Line, an Aland Island based shipping company, and was renamed BIRKA QUEEN for the company's short Baltic cruises. This venture was unsuccessful and the ship was chartered back to Klosters from October 1992 to May 1993. She was then chartered to Princess Cruises as the GOLDEN PRINCESS for Alaska cruising for three years, before passing to Star Cruises in 1996 as the SUPERSTAR CAPRICORN for Asian cruising. Surplus to requirements, in 1998 she was chartered to Hyundai Merchant Marine Co as the HYUNDAI KUMGANG for cruises from Korea. At the end of the charter in 2001 she reverted to the name SUPERSTAR CAPRICORN and was laid up. In 2004 she operated as the GRAND LATINO for Spanish operator Iberojet, but was sold in early 2005 to Fred. Olsen Cruise Lines, to enter service at the end of 2005 as the BOADICEA, following a major refit and re-engining by Blohm & Voss in Hamburg. This name was later revised to the alternative spelling BOUDICCA. Boadicea, Queen of the Iceni, led her people in battle against the Romans in Britain around 60 A.D., and remains one of Britain's greatest heroines. IMO 7218395

BRAEMAR is the second of a pair of ships ordered by Commodore Cruise Line from the Valencia shipyard of Union Naval de Levante (yard number 198). She was delivered in 1993 as the CROWN DYNASTY and operated alongside her sister, the CROWN JEWEL. At the end of the following year Commodore Cruise Line entered into an arrangement with Cunard that involved the latter company in the marketing of Commodore's ships. She became the CROWN MAJESTY for a charter to Majesty Cruise Line in 1997, and later that year was renamed as the NORWEGIAN DYNASTY for Norwegian Cruise Line. She reverted to her original name for Commodore again in 1999. Fred. Olsen Cruise Lines acquired the ship as their third vessel in 2001 and following a refit by Blohm & Voss in Hamburg; she entered service in August of that year under the name BRAEMAR. In May 2008 she was again sent to the Blohm & Voss shipyard in Hamburg, where she was lengthened by 31 metres. She re-entered service in July 2008, and takes her name from the site on Royal Deeside in Scotland, home to the Braemar Gathering and Highland Games since 1813. IMO 9000699

FTI TOURISTIK

The Company FTI Touristik is a German travel operator, making a first move into cruising for its own account with the acquisition of the former SPIRIT OF ADVENTURE.

Address Landsberger Strasse 88, D 80339 Munchen, Germany

Website www.fti-cruises.com

Area operated Mediterranean Sea

BERLIN	9570gt	1980	17.0k	D2	412p	412p	180c	139.3m	17.5m	4.8m	MT

BERLIN was the ship by which Peter Deilmann entered the ocean cruise market. She was built by Howaldtswerke-Deutsche Werft (yard number 163) at Kiel, Germany as the BERLIN for a consortium of German investors in which Deilmann held a small share. Late in 1982 she was chartered to Blue Funnel Cruises of Singapore, an associated business of the Straits Steamship Company, as a replacement for the CENTAUR, which had in turn been chartered to St Helena Shipping. She was renamed PRINCESS MAHSURI. Blue Funnel's Far East and Australian operation was already in decline and she was returned to her owners a year early in 1984, when she reverted to her original name. She was lengthened by 17 metres in 1986 at Rendsburg, Germany and continued to operate for Deilmann until that company terminated her charter at the end of 2004, following which she was laid up until purchased by Saga, with delivery at the end of 2005. In the meantime she secured a charter for Metropolis Tur, for whom she operated as the ORANGE MELODY. For her new service with Saga she was renamed as the SPIRIT OF ADVENTURE, although it was originally thought that she would be named SAGA OPAL. The ship finished her service with the company in May 2012 and was sold to and immediately put into service by FTI as the FTI BERLIN. The ship later reverted to her original name, BERLIN. IMO 7904889

GALA TRAVEL

The Company Gala Travel is a trading name of Sotomayor Neira J, a Galapagos Island tour operator.

Address Avenida de los Shyris 1000, y Holanda, Quito, Ecuador

Fred. Olsen's **Black Watch** off Calshot *(William Mayes)*

Fred. Olsen's **Boudicca** at Olden *(Rick Frendt)*

Fred. Olsen's **Braemar** at Flam *(Rick Frendt)*

Telephone +593 2 243 0345 **Fax** +593 2 245 0775

Area operated Galapagos Islands

TROPIC SUN	‡790gt	1967	12.5k	D2	48p	48p	25c	51.8m	10.1m	3.0m	EC

TROPIC SUN was built by R Dunston (yard number S850) at Hessle in England as the HUMBER GUARDIAN for the British Transport Docks Board, which later became Associated British Ports. She passed through a number of owners, only changing name once, in 1993 to TROPIC SUN, before arriving with her current owner in 2002. IMO 6726826

G ADVENTURES

The Company GAP Adventures was founded in Toronto by Trinidadian Bruce Poon Tip in 1990, pioneering land tours to Ecuador, Belize and Peru. In September 2004 the company acquired the EXPLORER, but that ship was lost on a cruise in November 2007 after striking ice off Antarctica. All of her passengers were rescued. As a stopgap measure the company chartered the Murmansk Shipping Company's POLARIS. The company acquired its current ship in early 2008 and following extensive refit she entered service in April 2009. The company re-styled itself as G Adventures in 2012. G Adventures also markets space on other vessels in the Greek Islands and the Galapagos Islands.

Address 19 Charlotte Street, Toronto, Canada M5V 2H5

Telephone +1 416 260 0999 **Fax** +1 416 260 1888

Website www.gadventures.com

Area operated Antarctica, Amazon, West Africa, North Atlantic and the Arctic

EXPEDITION	6334gt	1972	14.5k	D2	124p	140p	55c	105.2m	18.6m	4.6m	LR

EXPEDITION was built by Helsingor Skips & Maskinbygg (yard number 398) at Helsingor, Denmark as the car ferry KATTEGAT for Jydsk Faergefart of Denmark for the domestic Grenaa – Hundested service. In 1978 she was sold to P&O Ferries and renamed N F TIGER (the N F referring to the P&O Ferries subsidiary Normandy Ferries), for use on the Dover to Boulogne route. The Normandy Ferries operation along with the ship was sold to European Ferries (Townsend Thoresen) in 1985, when she was renamed TIGER. She was withdrawn from service in June 1986 and later that year was sold to Finlandshammen AB of Sweden for use on the summer service of Viking Line between Mariehamn and Kapellskar, and renamed ALANDSFARJAN. She continued in this role until May 2008, when replaced by the ROSELLA. She was immediately acquired by GAP Adventures and sent to what is now the STX shipyard at Rauma, Finland for conversion into an expedition cruise ship. During her first summer with GAP Adventures she was chartered by the Hurtigruten Group for three months. The ship conforms to ice class 1B. IMO 7211074

GENTING GROUP

The Group Star Cruises was established in 1993 by Malaysia's Genting Group, controlled by Lim Goh Tong. The company revolutionized the Asian cruise industry by operating large, modern cruise ships at internationally accepted levels of service and entertainment. In 2000 Star bought out Norwegian Cruise Lines in a deal that propelled it to the position of the third largest cruise line in the world. The Genting Group has its origins in the Genting Highlands Resort, which commenced in 1965. The group is now involved in the oil, power generation, property, paper and leisure industries. Lim Goh Tong passed away in October 2007. Genting is now based in Hong Kong.

In 2008 an agreement was reached with Apollo Management under which that organisation took 50% of the equity, and control of NCL. Subsequently, the Cruise Ferries business was closed when its sole ship, the WASA QUEEN, was sold for use as a ferry in the Adriatic Sea. Latterly Genting has reduced its holding in NCL to 27.7% by way of public offerings.

STAR CRUISES

The Company From its early foundations in 1993 to the present day, the development of Star Cruises has not been without difficulty, caused by a number of regional factors. The company acquired its first ships, the former Viking Line Baltic ferries ATHENA (the previous STAR AQUARIUS) and KALYPSO (STAR PISCES) in 1993, and these were followed by other good quality second-hand tonnage. It was not until 1998 that the first purpose built ship for the company's South East Asian itineraries entered the fleet, and the story subsequently has been one of alternate expansion and cut back as new markets

FTI Touristik's **Berlin** off Nice *(William Mayes)*

G Adventures' **Expedition** at Ushuaia *(Mark Oelbaum)*

Star Cruises' **Star Pisces** at Hong Kong *(Mark M Amielanczyk)*

Star Cruises' **SuperStar Gemini** (Jonathan Boonzaier)

Star Cruises' **Superstar Libra** (Mark M Amielanczyk)

Star Cruises' **Superstar Virgo** (Mark M Amielanczyk)

in the region have been explored and either developed or abandoned. Star Cruises recently sold the WASA QUEEN, thereby effectively closing down subsidiary Cruise Ferries. The name of the company is now Genting Hong Kong Limited, but it still trades as Star Cruises. The two small ships are generally used for charters and exclusive gambling cruises.

Address 1528 Ocean Centre, 5 Canton Road, Tsimshatsui, Hong Kong

Telephone +852 2317 7711 **Fax** +852 2317 5551

Website www.starcruises.com

Areas operated South East Asia

MEGASTAR TAURUS	3341gt	1989	16.0k	D2	72p	72p	80c	82.2m	14.0m	3.4m	PA
STAR PISCES	40053gt	1990	18.0k	D2	1180p	1900p	750c	176.6m	29.0m	6.0m	BS
SUPERSTAR AQUARIUS	51309gt	1993	18.0k	D2	1512p	2016p	614c	229.9m	28.5m	7.0m	BS
SUPERSTAR GEMINI	50764gt	1992	21.0k	D2	1530p	2156p	614c	229.8m	28.5m	6.8m	BS
SUPERSTAR LIBRA	42285gt	1988	17.0k	D2	1418p	1796p	609c	216.2m	28.4m	7.0m	BS
SUPERSTAR VIRGO	75338gt	1999	24.0k	DE2	1870p	2975p	1125c	268.6m	32.2m	7.9m	PA
THE TAIPAN	3370gt	1989	11.5k	D2	66p	130p	80c	82.2m	14.0m	3.4m	BS

MEGASTAR TAURUS was built by Flender Werft (yard number 647) at Lubeck, Germany for the Windsor Cruise Line as the LADY DIANA, but not delivered and later renamed LADY DI, before transferring to New Frontier Cruises of Hamburg as the AURORA I. She became the MEGASTAR TAURUS on acquisition by Star Cruises in 1995. The ship is currently laid up. IMO 8705266

STAR PISCES was built by Masa Yards (yard number 1298) at Turku, Finland as the car ferry KALYPSO for the Swedish partner in the Viking Line consortium, Rederi AB Slite. Following the financial difficulties encountered by that company, receivers were appointed and in 1993 the ship was sold (for $85 million compared to her building cost of $100 million) together with her sister, the ATHENA (now DFDS Seaways' PEARL SEAWAYS) to Star Cruises. She was rebuilt as the cruise ship STAR PISCES and has since been based in Hong Kong. In recent years she has operated overnight cruises out of Hong Kong. While these are geared mainly for gamblers, unlike the rest of the Hong Kong casino cruise fleet, she still offers a full range of cruise-type activities as well. IMO 8710857

SUPERSTAR AQUARIUS was built as the WINDWARD for Kloster Cruise of Nassau (Norwegian Caribbean Line) by Chantiers de l'Atlantique (yard number D30) at St Nazaire, France. When built, the ship was 39,217 gross tons and had a length of 190 metres. In 1998 she went to Lloydwerft at Bremerhaven, Germany to have a new 40 metre mid section inserted and was renamed NORWEGIAN WIND for the now re-styled Norwegian Cruise Line. In 2007 she was transferred to Star Cruises for short cruises based in Hong Kong for which she was renamed SUPERSTAR AQUARIUS. She is currently operating short cruises from Taiwan. IMO 9008421

SUPERSTAR GEMINI was built as the DREAMWARD for Kloster Cruise Line of Nassau (Norwegian Caribbean Line) by Chantiers de l'Atlantique (yard number C30) at St Nazaire, France. When built the ship was 39,217 gross tons and had a length of 190 metres. In 1998 she followed her sister, the NORWEGIAN WIND, into the Lloydwerft shipyard in Bremerhaven, Germany to have a new 40 metre mid section fitted, and was renamed NORWEGIAN DREAM for the now re-styled Norwegian Cruise Line. During the following year while on passage to Dover, England at the end of a cruise she was involved in a serious collision with the Evergreen container ship EVER DECENT. After disembarking her passengers at Dover she proceeded to Lloydwerft at Bremerhaven for repairs. The NORWEGIAN DREAM spent a number of summer seasons cruising from Dover to Baltic and Scandinavian destinations, but then moved to the Caribbean and Alaska. In 2008 she was expected to be replaced by the NORWEGIAN JADE, and a sale (which later fell through) was agreed with Louis Cruise Lines. Having spent more than two years laid up in Eleusis Bay, Greece she moved to Singapore, where, after a further period of lay up she was refitted for Star Cruises and renamed SUPERSTAR GEMINI. She is currently operating from Singapore. IMO 9008419

SUPERSTAR LIBRA was built as the SEAWARD for Kloster's Norwegian Caribbean Cruise Line by Wartsila (yard number 1294) at Turku, Finland and following her naming ceremony in New York she commenced cruising in the Caribbean. In 1997 she was renamed NORWEGIAN SEA. In September 2005 she was transferred within the group to Star Cruises and was renamed SUPERSTAR LIBRA to start a new cruise venture operating from Mumbai, India. That service finished after the Indian Government extended the territorial limits for gambling to 200 miles. She was laid up for a while but then operated a Taiwan programme. She now operates short cruises from Penang. IMO 8612134

SUPERSTAR VIRGO was built by Meyer Werft (yard number 647) at Papenburg, Germany for Star Cruises. She is the current flagship of the Star Cruises fleet and is a sister to the NORWEGIAN SPIRIT. She currently operates short cruises from Hong Kong. IMO 9141077

THE TAIPAN was built by Flender Werft (yard number 648), Lubeck, Germany for the Windsor Cruise Line as the LADY SARAH, but was not delivered. She was renamed AURORA II in 1991 when operating for New Frontier Cruises of Hamburg, and passed to Star Cruises in 1995, becoming the MEGASTAR ARIES. Following a period of lay up she was refitted and renamed GENTING WORLD. Subsequently she was renamed TAIPAN and currently operates gambling cruises from Penang. IMO 8705278

Cruise ships on order

NEWBUILD 1	c150000gt	2016	24.0k	3364p	p	2030c	330.0m	m	m	BS
NEWBUILD 2	c150000gt	2017	24.0k	3364p	p	2030c	330.0m	m	m	BS

NEWBUILD 1 and **2** are on order with Meyer Werft (yard numbers 711 and 712) at Papenburg. IMO9733105 and 9733117

GOTA CANAL STEAMSHIP COMPANY

The Company The Gota Canal Steamship Company (Rederi AB Gota Kanal) was founded on February 27, 1869. The JUNO was the second of the company's ships, and still remains in service after more than 130 years. The company is now part of the Stromma Turism & Sjofart Group.

Address Pusterviksgaten 13, SE41301 Gothenburg, Sweden

Telephone +46 31 806315 **Fax** +46 31 158311

Website www.gotacanal.se

Area operated The Gota Canal between Gothenburg and Stockholm, Sweden

DIANA	269gt	1931	10.0k	D1	56p	56p	12c	31.6m	6.8m	2.7m	SE
JUNO	254gt	1874	10.0k	D2	58p	58p	12c	31.5m	6.7m	2.7m	SE
WILHELM THAM	268gt	1912	10.0k	D1	50p	50p	12c	31.5m	6.7m	2.7m	SE

DIANA was built at the Finnboda Shipyard in Stockholm, Sweden. Built as a steamship, she was the last of that type in regular Swedish canal service when her steam engine was replaced by diesel in 1969. Diana was the Roman goddess of the hunt and of chastity.

JUNO was built by Motala Werkstad, at Motala in Sweden. She was to have been named DARWIN, but after shareholder objection she took the name JUNO. Her steam plant was replaced by diesel engines in 1956. Her name is that of the Roman goddess of marriage and motherhood. She is the oldest registered ship with overnight cabins.

WILHELM THAM was built by Motala Werkstad, at Motala, Sweden and is named after the Swedish industrialist and director of the Husqvarna Weapons Factory from 1876 to 1911. Her steam engine was replaced by diesel in 1965.

GRAND CIRCLE CRUISE LINE

The Company Ethel Andrus, a retired teacher, founded Grand Circle Travel in 1958. The business was purchased by Alan Lewis in 1985 and moved from its previous New York base to Boston. Grand Circle Cruise Line has taken on the operation of the three 'A' class ships from its associated company Overseas Adventure Travel and has recently expanded the fleet with the acquisition of the CORINTHIAN.

Address 347 Congress Street, Boston MA 02210, United States of America

Website www.gct.com

Area operated Dalmacia and the Mediterranean and Red Seas plus worldwide itineraries for the CORINTHIAN

ARETHUSA	1206gt	2008	13.6k	D2	50p	50p	21c	59.0m	10.7m	2.9m	MT
ARTEMIS	1206gt	2007	13.6k	D2	50p	50p	21c	59.0m	10.7m	2.9m	MT
ATHENA	1206gt	2007	12.5k	D2	50p	50p	21c	59.0m	10.7m	2.9m	MT
CORINTHIAN	4077gt	1990	15.0k	D2	100p	100p	70c	88.3m	15.3m	3.3m	MT

ARETHUSA, ARTEMIS and **ATHENA** were built by Brodosplit (yard numbers 509, 508 and 507) at the

Star Cruises' **The Taipan** at Penang *(Mark M Amielanczyk)*

Gota Canal's **Diana** *(company picture)*

Gota Canal's **Juno** *(company picture)*

Grand Circle's *Artemis* arriving at Rhodes *(William Mayes)*

Grand Circle's *Corinthian* *(Bill Lawes)*

Hansa Touristik's *Ocean Majesty* in Istanbul *(William Mayes)*

Split shipyard in Croatia for Overseas Adventure Travel, but have susequently been taken over by the parent company. IMO 9398022, 9398010, 9398008

CORINTHIAN was built by Cantieri Navale Ferrari (yard number 46) at La Spezia, Italy as the RENAISSANCE FOUR for Renaissance Cruises. She became the CLELIA II for Lindos Maritime in 1996. She was registered under the ownership of Goodwin Sands Marine as a private yacht, although in recent years she operated for Travel Dynamics on a long term charter. Orion Cruises acquired her in late 2009 with delivery in early 2011 on a ten-year bareboat charter, with purchase options. She was renamed as the ORION II. Orion Cruises surrendered the ship after only one season and she went back to Travel Dynamics briefly before being acquired by Grand Circle Cruise Line who renamed her CORINTHIAN. IMO 8708672

GUANGXI BEIBU GULF CRUISE

The Company Guangxi Beibu Gulf Cruise is a Chinese operator

Area operated Cruises from Beihai to Halong Bay

ORIENTAL QUEEN	7820gt	1981	18.0k	D1	p	p	c	137.8m	13.6m	6.0m	KH

ORIENTAL QUEEN was built by the Hudong Shipyard in Shanghai as the passenger and cargo vessel CHANG LUI. She was renamed LU XING JIA in 2000 and at some stage was converted into a passenger vessel. She was named ORIENTAL QUEEN in 2010 and is believed to be running cruises between China and Vietnam. IMO 8425115

HANSA TOURISTIK

The Company Hansa Touristik is a German travel company which also operates river cruises. The OCEAN MAJESTY is on seasonal charter from Majestic International Cruises.

Address Konigstrasse 20, D70173 Stuttgart, Germany

Telephone +49 711 2293 1690

Website www.hansatouristik.de

Areas operated Baltic, Northern Europe, Mediterranean and the Black Sea

OCEAN MAJESTY	10417gt	1966	20.0k	D2	500p	548p	235c	130.6m	19.2m	5.4m	PT

OCEAN MAJESTY For details see under Majestic International Cruises.

HERITAGE EXPEDITIONS

The Company Heritage Expeditions was founded in 1985 by biologist Rodney Russ. The AKADEMIK SHOKALSKY was chartered for a single voyage to the Ross Sea in January 2014.

Address 53B Montreal Street, Christchurch 8023, New Zealand

Telephone +64 3 365 3500 **Fax** +64 3 365 1300

Website www.heritage-expeditions.com

Areas operated Antarctica

SPIRIT OF ENDERBY	1759gt	1983	12.0k	D2	50p	50p	23c	71.6m	12.8m	4.7m	RU

SPIRIT OF ENDERBY is a marketing name used by Heritage Expeditions for the Far Eastern Hydrometeorological Research Institute of Vladivostok owned PROFESSOR KHROMOV. She was built by Oy Laivateollisuus Ab (yard number 345) at Turku, Finland. She operates for Heritage Expeditions in the southern summer. The ship had a major refurbishment in spring 2013. Enderby Land is an Antarctic landmass extending from Shinnan Glacier to William Scoresby Bay, discovered in 1831 by John Briscoe and named by him after the owners of his ship (the TULA), the Enderby Brothers of London. IMO 8010350

HERITAGE LINE

The Company Heritage Line is a Vietnamese organisation providing cruises from Ho Chi Minh City into the Mekong River and on to Cambodia. Three smaller vessels operate in Halong Bay.

Address A9-02 Nam Thien 2, Ha Huy Tap Street, Phu My Hung, District 7, Ho Chi Minh City, Vietnam

Telephone +84 8 377 38555

Website www.heritage-line.com

Areas operated Vietnam and Cambodia

| THE JAHAN | 1000gt | 2011 | 10.0k | D2 | 52p | 52p | 40c | 70.0m | 12.5m | 1.7m | VN |
| THE JAYAVARMAN | 700gt | 2009 | 10.0k | D2 | 54p | 54p | 40c | 58.0m | 11.0m | 1.6m | VN |

THE JAHAN was built locally and delivered in October 2011.

THE JAYAVARMAN The name Jayavarman was that of several kings of Cambodia from about the ninth century. The ship was built in the Ho Chi Minh City shipyard and is believed to have entered service in the autumn of 2009. The ship was originally to have been named MEKONG EXPLORER.

HNA CRUISES

The Company HNA Tourism Cruises Yacht Management Ltd is a new Chinese cruise company formed in 2012 and is part of Hainan Airlines Group.

Website www.hnacruises.com

Area operated China

| HENNA | 47678gt | 1986 | 21.5k | D2 | 1308p | 1965p | c | 223.2m | 28.0m | 7.5m | MT |

HENNA floated out of her building dock at the Kockums shipyard (yard number 596), Malmo, Sweden in October 1985, and was delivered eight months later to Carnival Cruise Lines as the JUBILEE. In 2004 she was transferred within the group to P&O Cruises Australia and renamed PACIFIC SUN by Olympian Lisa Curry-Kenny. On the arrival of the PACIFIC DAWN, the PACIFIC SUN moved from Sydney to Brisbane. She was sold to HNA in October 2012 and after a refit at the Sembawang shipyard in Singapore began sailing again on 26 January 2013 from her new base in Shanghai. IMO 8314122

HURTIGRUTEN GROUP (Norwegian Coastal Voyage)

The Company The Hurtigruten, the Norwegian Coastal Express, covers the 1,300 or so nautical miles from Bergen to Kirkenes, just ten miles from the Russian border in the far north of Norway, in a twelve-day round trip making 34 port calls. Most of the ships carry cars and other vehicles on decks accessed through side doors. All of the vessels perform a year-round lifeline service linking communities who have no other means of transport to the outside world. The Hurtigruten commenced in 1893 at which time the Norwegian Government entered into a four-year agreement with Vesteraalens Dampskibsselskab, providing the subsidy for a weekly service from Trondheim to Hammerfest in summer and to Tromso in winter. However, the story of the coastal service really begins around 1838, when the Norwegian Government paid for the construction and running costs of the steamer PRINS GUSTAV to trade between Trondheim and Hammerfest in the far north. The service only ran for about seven months each year, and then only sailed during daylight due to the lack of navigation markers north of Trondheim. Initially the service was monthly, but as new ships arrived it was extended south to Kristiansand and increased in frequency. The prime purpose of these early ships was the carriage of passengers and mail; most goods were still travelling in sailing vessels. During the 1860's the route passed in its entirety into the hands of private companies. The failure of the fish harvest in 1875/6 had the eventual result of reducing the lifeline service, as the various operating companies switched their investment to the more lucrative tourist trade. The outcome was the tendering of the service and the awarding of the agreement referred to above. In 1894 two further companies were licensed to operate the Coastal Express - Bergenske Dampskibsselskab and Nordenfjeldske Dampskibsselskab. Today the route is in the hands of just a single company, following the merger in 2006 of OVDS and TFDS, and as Government subsidies are again under scrutiny the service is once more turning to tourism as the main source of income on what has often been described as 'The World's Most Beautiful Voyage'.

OVDS or Ofotens og Vesteraalens Dampskibsselskab ASA can trace its origins back to 1881 when Captain Richard With established the Vesteraalens Dampskibsselskab. Ofotens Dampskibsselskab joined the Hurtigruten service in 1936 and in 1987 the two companies merged to form OVDS.

TFDS or Troms Fylkes Dampskibsselskab ASA was a major Norwegian ship owner at the time of the merger, with around 34 vessels. The company was founded in 1866 as Tromso Amts D/S, but assumed its current name in 1925. TFDS joined the Hurtigruten in 1979, when it purchased four ships from the Bergen Line. In 2003 the company became the major shareholder in Fjord Line, a ferry company that links Norway with Denmark.

HNA Cruises's **Henna** *(Mark M Amielanczyk)*

Hurtigruten's **Fram** off Lisbon *(Rick Frendt)*

Hurtigruten's **Kong Harald** off Floro *(Rick Frendt)*

Until recently, in addition to the ships listed here, the Hurtigruten Group operated more than 50 ferries along the coasts of Norway and was a major Norwegian bus operator, employing more than 3,400 people. However, recent financial difficulties have led to the sale of most of the company's assets that were not directly associated with the Hurtigruten service.

Address Frederik Langes Gate 14, Postbox 6144, 9291 Tromso, Norway

UK Office Bedford House, 69-79 Fulham High Street, London, SW6 3JW, England

Telephone +47 970 57030 UK Office +44 203 411 2236

Website www.hurtigruten.com and www.hurtigruten.co.uk

Area operated Norwegian coast – all ships, Spitzbergen, the Lofoten Islands, Greenland, Chile and Antarctica - FRAM

FINNMARKEN	15690gt	2002	18.0k	D2	628b	372d	85c	135.8m	21.5m	4.9m	NO
FRAM	11647gt	2007	16.0k	DEP2	348p	152d	70c	113.9m	20.2m	5.1m	NI
KONG HARALD	11204gt	1993	15.0k	D2	474b	148d	59c	121.8m	19.2m	4.7m	NO
LOFOTEN	2621gt	1964	15.0k	D1	153b	187d	40c	87.4m	13.3m	4.6m	NO
MIDNATSOL	16151gt	2003	15.0k	D2	638b	362d	74c	135.8m	21.5m	4.9m	NO
NORDKAPP	11386gt	1996	15.0k	D2	458b	164d	59c	123.3m	19.2m	4.7m	NO
NORDLYS	11204gt	1994	15.0k	D2	469b	153d	60c	121.7m	19.2m	4.7m	NO
NORDNORGE	11384gt	1997	15.0k	D2	451b	172d	57c	123.3m	19.2m	4.7m	NO
POLARLYS	11341gt	1996	15.0k	D2	473b	146d	63c	123.0m	19.2m	4.5m	NO
RICHARD WITH	11205gt	1993	15.0k	D2	464b	155d	57c	121.8m	19.2m	4.7m	NO
TROLLFJORD	16140gt	2002	15.0k	D2	640b	182d	74c	135.8m	21.5m	4.9m	NO
VESTERALEN	6261gt	1983	15.0k	D2	294b	226d	34c	108.6m	16.5m	4.6m	NO

FINNMARKEN was built by Kleven Verft (yard number 292) at Ulsteinvik in Norway. In the spring of 2010 she was chartered out as an accommodation vessel for 18 months for use at Chevron's Gorgon Project off Barrow Island, Australia, for which she was painted white. Additionally, the air conditioning system was upgraded and much of deck 7 was converted into a fitness area. The first FINNMARKEN served the coastal route from 1912. Finnmark is Norway's most northerly region, bordering Finland. IMO 9231951

FRAM was built by Fincantieri (yard number 6144) at Monfalcone, Italy. She is used mainly for cruising, particularly around Greenland, during the summer and then heads south to the Antarctic during the winter. She was named by HRH Crown Princess Mette Marit in Oslo on 19 May 2007. In late 2007, following a blackout, the FRAM collided with an iceberg in Antarctica, but was not seriously damaged. The ship is named in honour of the polar expedition ship Fram, now housed in the Oslo Maritime Museum, which took Fridtjof Nansen across the Arctic Ocean, Roald Amundsen on his race to the South Pole, and Otto Sverdruo on many Arctic voyages of discovery. IMO 9370018

KONG HARALD is named in honour of the King of Norway, who succeeded to the throne in 1991. The ship was built in Germany at the Stralsund shipyard of Volkswerft (yard number 101). IMO 9039119

LOFOTEN is the last surviving traditional Hurtigruten ship still in regular service. She was built by AS Akers Mekanik Verksted (yard number 547) at Oslo, Norway for Vesteraalens Dampskibsselskab (VDS). From 1988 she operated for Finnmark Fylkesrederi og Ruteselskap, who sold her to OVDS in 1996. In recent years she operated on the Hurtigruten during the winter, when the NORDNORGE went south to Antarctica, but now operates year round again as a result of the laying up of the NORDLYS. She takes her name from the Lofoten Islands, off the coast of central Norway. IMO 5424562

MIDNATSOL had her hull built at Bruce's Shipyard, Landskrona, Sweden, but was completed by the Fosen Yard (yard number 73) in Norway. Her name means Midnight Sun. IMO 9247728

NORDKAPP was built by Kvaerner Kleven Ulsteinvik (yard number 265) at Ulsteinvik in Norway. She is one of two ships that travelled to South America and Antarctica in the winter, but she no longer does so. Her name translates as North Cape, the most northerly point of mainland Norway. IMO 9107772

NORDLYS takes her name from the Northern Lights, in Latin the Aurora Borealis, or Red Dawn of the North. She was built in Germany at the Stralsund shipyard of Volksverft (yard number 102). In September 2011 she suffered a serious engine room fire. IMO 9048914

NORDNORGE was built by the Kvaerner Kleven Ulsteinvik shipyard (yard number 266) at Ulsteinvik in Norway. She sailed south to Antarctica in the winter for several seasons before being replaced by the FRAM. For the winter of 2008/9 she was laid up due to the continuing financial woes of her owner.

Hurtigruten's *Lofoten* (Bill Lawes)

Hurtigruten's *Midnatsol* at Molde (William Mayes)

Hurtigruten's *Nordnorge* at Molde (William Mayes)

Hurtigruten's *Vesteralen* at Geiranger *(Rick Frendt)*

Il Tur's *Halas 71* off Kos *(William Mayes)*

Japan Cruise Line's *Pacific Venus* in San Francisco *(Rick Frendt)*

She was then chartered from December 2008 to April 2009 as an accommodation ship in the Mediterranean, returning to her normal service at the end of the charter. Her name simply means North Norway. IMO 9107784

POLARLYS is a product of the Ulstein Verft yard (yard number 223) at Ulsteinvik, Norway. Her name translates as Polar Lights. IMO 9107796

RICHARD WITH was the name of the founder of the Vesteralens company, with which Ofotens later merged. This ship was built at Stralsund in Germany by Volkswerft (yard number 103). IMO 9040429

TROLLFJORD's hull was built by Bruce's Shipyard (yard number 246) at Landskrona, Sweden but the ship was completed by the Fosen Yard in Norway, where she acquired the build number 72. Trollfjord is one of the many fjords in the Vesteralen and Lofoten district of Norway. IMO 9233258

VESTERALEN was built by Kaarbos Mek. Verksted (yard number 101) at Harstad, Norway. The very first of the coastal express ships carried the name VESTERALEN, in honour of the Vesteralen Islands, a little to the north of the Lofoten Islands. VESTERALEN was also the name of the first coastal express ship. IMO 8019368

I D RIVA TOURS

The Company I D Riva Tours is a German owned travel and tour operator, running a large number of small coastal cruise ships on the Croatian coast. In addition to the ships listed here, there are about a dozen others that carry fewer than 30 passengers.

Address Neuhauser Str 27, D80331 Munich, Germany

Telephone +49 89 2311 000 **Fax** +49 89 2311 110022

Website www.idriva.com

Area operated Croatia

AMORE	297gt	2011		40p	40p	40.0m		HR
ANETA	113gt	1958		30p	32p	32.0m		HR
ANTONELA	197gt	2007		35p	35p	33.0m		HR
ATLANTIC	gt	2014		40p	40p	42.0m		HR
COLUMBO	220gt	2009		34p	37p	35.0m		HR
KAZIMIR	gt	2000		38p	38p	39.0m		HR
KRUNA MORA	274gt	1964		32p	32p	43.7m		HR
LASTAVICA	gt	2008		32p	32p	32.9m		HR
MACEK	199gt	2004		30p	32p	35.0m		HR
MILENA	gt	2012		38p	38p	35.0m		HR
NEREZINE	136gt	1922		32p	34p	29.8m		HR
OTAC IVAN	170gt	1953		34p	34p	33.0m		HR
PRINCESS ALOHA	170gt	2012		38p	38p	38,0m		HR
SVETI VID	gt	1955		32p	32p	35.5m		HR
VITA	gt	2014		38p	38p	37.0m		HR

All of the above vessels are believed to have been built locally in Croatia.

IL-TUR ISLETMELERI

The Company Il-Tur Ileri Turizm ve Yat Isletmeleri is a Turkish operator and organiser of exclusive tours in and around Turkey.

Telephone +90 549 334 2104

Website www.myhalas.com

Area operated Bosphorus and Gulf of Fethiye, Turkey, and as a hotel at Istinye, Istanbul

HALAS 71	678gt	1915	12.0k	D2	28p	28p	26c	52.0m	8.5m	3.2m	TR

HALAS 71 is now owned by Il-Tur Isletmeleri of Istanbul and operates on the Turkish coast as a very luxurious cruise vessel. She was built by Fairfield Shipbuilding and Engineering Company (yard number 502) at Govan on the River Clyde in Scotland, as one of the numerous steam ferries for service around Constantinople (now Istanbul) and the Bosphorus. Although completed in 1915, she was requisitioned by the Royal Navy and served as the dispatch steamer HMS WATERWITCH, and is one of

only two surviving vessels to have been present at the Gallipoli Campaign. She eventually reached her intended owner in 1923, taking the name HALAS, later HALAS 71, instead of her intended name RESIT PASA. She survived in her original role until the mid 1980's and after a period in lay-up she was rebuilt as the rather splendid ship she is today. She now operates charter cruises in summer and spends the winter as a boutique hotel in the Bosphorus. She appears to have reverted to the name HALAS 71 in June 2011. IMO 5140697

JAPAN CRUISE LINE

The Company Japan Cruise Line is part of SHK Group, a Japanese joint venture between the Shin Nohonkai, Hankyu and Kanpu ferry companies. The PACIFIC VENUS is marketed as Venus Cruise. A second ship, the ORIENT VENUS, was sold to Greek investors in 2005 and is now operating as AEGEAN PARADISE for Etstur.

Address 25 Hanshin Umeda 2-chome, Kita-ku, JP 530 0001 Osaka, Japan

Telephone +81 6 6347 7521 **Fax** +81 6 6341 8980

Website www.venus-cruise.co.jp

Area operated Asia and worldwide

| PACIFIC VENUS | 26594gt | 1998 | 20.8k | D2 | 532p | 720p | 180c | 183.4m | 25.0m | 6.5m | JP |

PACIFIC VENUS was built by IHHI (yard number 3095) in Tokyo. She operates cruises ranging in length from a few days along the Japanese coast, to several months around the world. IMO 9160011

KATARINA LINE

The Company Katarina Line is a Croatian travel and tour company. It owns none of the ships, but arranges and sells cruises on those listed here and a further 20 or so smaller vessels. Some ships are only available for charter.

Address Spinciceva 13, HR 51410 Opatija, Croatia

Telephone +385 51 603 400 **Fax** +385 51 271 372

Website www.katarina-line.com

Area operated Croatian coast

ADRIATIC QUEEN	gt		12.0k		30p	35p	c	40.0m	8.3m	3.0m	HR
AMALIA	gt	2013	9.0k	D2	36p	36p	c	37.4m	8.2m	m	HR
AZIMUT	gt	2003	9.0k	D2	38p	40p	c	32.0m	7.5m	m	HR
DALMATIA	gt	2011	8.5k	D2	38p	42p	c	37.0m	7.6m	m	HR
DIONIS	249gt	2010	9.0k	D1	38p	38p	c	33.0m	7.5m	m	HR
EMANUEL	306gt	2006	9.5k	D1	36p	36p	c	37.6m	7.0m	m	HR
EOS	264gt	2008	10.0k	D1	42p	45p	c	39.0m	7.8m	m	HR
FUTURA	gt	2013	9.0k	D2	38p	38p	7c	47.0m	9.0m	m	HR
KAPETAN BOTA II	168gt	2008	9.0k	D1	32p	36p	c	29.0m	7.0m	m	HR
LABRADOR	gt	1967	10.0k	D1	36p	40p	c	30.0m	7.0m	m	HR
LIBERTY	gt	2011	9.0k	D2	40p	40p	7c	45.0m	9.0m	m	HR
LOPAR	180gt	1954	9.0k	D1	28p	32p	c	27.5m	6.5m	m	HR
MERIDIJAN	249gt	2007	9.0k	D1	38p	43p	c	32.5m	7.5m	m	HR
OCEAN	gt	2010	9.0k	D2	40p	42p	c	36.0m	7.7m	m	HR
OMLADINAC	112gt	1943	7.5k	D1	32p	32p	c	27.8m	7.6m	m	HR
PACIFIC	gt	2012	10.0k	D1	40p	40p	7c	42.0m	8.0m	m	HR
PAPE I	gt	2008	8.5k	D1	30p	34p	c	29.0m	7.0m	m	HR
PLOMIN	164gt	1947	10.0k	D1	34p	36p	c	27.0m	7.2m	m	HR
PRESIDENT	gt	2011	10.0k	D2	40p	40p	7c	42.0m	9.0m	m	HR
PRESTIGE	gt	2014	10.0k	D2	40p	40p	7c	47.0m	9.0m	m	HR
PROVIDENCA	gt	2014	9.0k	D2	40p	40p	7c	46.0m	9.1m	m	HR
PROVIDNOST	gt	1950	8.0k	D1	30p	30p	c	23.0m	5.8m	m	HR
SKARDA	gt	2013	12.0k	D1	30p	30p	c	27.0m	7.0m	m	HR
SPALATO	gt	2012	9.0k	D1	36p	36p	c	36.7m	7.6m	m	HR
TOMA	gt	2003	8.5k	D1	30p	35p	c	28.0m	6.5m	m	HR
VAPOR	197gt	2005	10.0k	D1	36p	37p	c	33.0m	7.6m	m	HR

Katarina Line's *Futura* in Dubrovnik *(William Mayes)*

Katarina Line's *Spalato* at Dubrovnik *(William Mayes)*

Lindblad's *National Geographic Explorer* in Southampton *(Bill Lawes)*

| VIKTORIJA | 108gt | 1948 | 8.0k | D1 | 32p | 32p | c | 24.0m | 6.2m | m | HR |

All of the ships listed above were built locally in Croatia.

KLEINTOURS

The Company Kleintours is a Galapagos Islands based tour and cruise operator, which was established in 1983.

Address Av. Eloy Alfaro N 34-151 & Catalina, Aldaz, Quito, Ecuador

Telephone +593 2 2267 000 **Fax** +593 2 2442 389

Website www.galapagosecuador.com

Area operated Galapagos Islands

CORAL I	359gt	1980	10.0k	D2	36p	36p	10c	39.7m	8.4m	2.1m	EC
CORAL II	208gt	1963	10.0k	D1	20p	26p	10c	33.5m	7.5m	2.4m	EC
GALAPAGOS LEGEND	2890gt	1963	15.0k	D2	100p	110p	60c	91.5m	14.3m	4.2m	EC

CORAL I was built by KG Norderwerft in Hamburg, Germany as the TROPIC BIRD. She was acquired by Kleintours in 2002 and extended in 2005. IMO 8978875

CORAL II was built in The Netherlands by NV Scheepswerf Alphen as the AVANTE. She was acquired by Kleintours in 2002. IMO 8978887

GALAPAGOS LEGEND was built by Howaldtswerke (yard number 943) at Hamburg, Germany as the HELGOLAND for local services on the North Sea and Baltic coasts of Germany. She had been ordered from the Hanseatische Werft yard in Hamburg, but that yard was declared bankrupt so the order was transferred. She was chartered out from 1964 to 1966 under the name LARVIKSPILEN, but reverted to her original name at the end of that period. From 1966 to 1971 she served as a hospital ship in Vietnamese waters before returning to Europe. In 1972 she was purchased by Stena Reederei of Germany and became the STENA FINLANDICA. Three years later she was renamed BALTIC STAR for Seetouristik (later Forde Reederei) day cruises in the Baltic Sea. She was sold to her current owner in 2001, renamed the GALAPAGOS LEGEND and refitted as an overnight cruise ship. IMO 5404964

LINDBLAD EXPEDITIONS

The Company Lindblad Expeditions was founded in 1979 by Sven-Olof Lindblad, as a development from Lindblad Travel, which had been established some twenty years earlier by his father. From the spring of 2005 Lindblad teamed up with National Geographic in the marketing and operation of the company's expedition ships. At that time the ENDEAVOUR, was renamed as the NATIONAL GEOGRAPHIC ENDEAVOUR, and subsequently the other ships have taken the National Geographic prefix.

Address 96 Morton Street, 9th Floor, New York, NY 10014, United States of America

Telephone +1 212 765 7740

Website www.expeditions.com

Area operated Arctic, Northern Europe, the Americas and Antarctica, Galapagos Islands, Alaska and Baja California

NATIONAL GEOGRAPHIC ENDEAVOUR	3132gt	1966	15.0k	D1	96p	138p	63c	89.1m	14.0m	6.6m	EC
NATIONAL GEOGRAPHIC EXPLORER	6471gt	1982	17.5k	D2	148p	148p	34c	108.6m	16.5m	4.6m	BS
NATIONAL GEOGRAPHIC ISLANDER	1021gt	1995	14.0k	D2	48p	48p	20c	49.9m	13.5m	1.9m	EC
NATIONAL GEOGRAPHIC ORION	3984gt	2003	13.0k	D1	106p	106p	75c	102.7m	14.0m	3.8m	BS
NATIONAL GEOGRAPHIC SEA BIRD	630gt	1982	12.0k	D1	62p	70p	41c	46.3m	9.4m	2.4m	US
NATIONAL GEOGRAPHIC SEA LION	630gt	1982	12.0k	D1	62p	70p	41c	46.3m	9.4m	2.4m	US

NATIONAL GEOGRAPHIC ENDEAVOUR was once a fishing trawler, built by AG Weser (yard number 917) at Bremerhaven, Germany as the MARBURG for German owners. In 1982 she became the LINDMAR and during the following year was converted at Gothenburg into the cruise ship NORTH STAR for Fearney & Eger of Oslo. She entered service for North Star Line in 1983 on Scandinavian cruises, switching to the Mediterranean in the winter. In 1986 she was chartered to Exploration Cruises and Holidays of Seattle, USA for service on the Alaskan coast. Three years later her charterers were in financial trouble and the NORTH STAR was sold to the Caledonian Steamship Company, renamed CALEDONIAN STAR and chartered to Salen-Lindblad. From 1993 the ship was marketed in the UK by Noble Caledonia and in the USA by Special Expeditions. The latter company acquired the CALEDONIAN STAR in 1997, and in 2000 became Lindblad Expeditions, renaming the ship as ENDEAVOUR during the following year. In March 2005 she was renamed NATIONAL GEOGRAPHIC ENDEAVOUR. In November 2007 she assisted in the rescue operation for the sinking EXPLORER of GAP Adventures. The ship is now based full time in and around the Galapagos Islands. The most famous ENDEAVOUR was that of Captain James Cook, whose epic voyages of discovery took place between 1768 and 1771. IMO 6611863

NATIONAL GEOGRAPHIC EXPLORER was built by Ulstein Hatlo (yard number 176) at Ulsteinvik in Norway, as the MIDNATSOL. She was renamed MIDNATSOL II and laid up in 2003, following the delivery of the new MIDNATSOL. Her proposed sale to Canadian owners in 2005 fell through, and she returned to service on the Hurtigruten as the LYNGEN in the winter of 2005/2006. She also operated on the coastal voyage over the winter of 2006/2007. She was acquired by Lindblad for US$8.6m in October 2007 and after a major refit was renamed NATIONAL GEOGRAPHIC EXPLORER and entered service in the summer of 2008. She now operates in the Arctic and Antarctic with interesting positioning voyages between the two. IMO 8019356

NATIONAL GEOGRAPHIC ISLANDER is operated by Ecoventura and chartered to Lindblad for specific cruises. She was built by Chantiers Navale de Marseille (yard number B210) at Marseilles, France as the RIVAGES GUADELOUPE. Between 2002 and 2004 she was cruising in and around Scotland as the LORD OF THE HIGHLANDS (she is a near sister to LORD OF THE GLENS) for Highland Lord Steamship Company, but entered service in the Galapagos Islands as the ISLANDER in early 2005 for ETICA, by whom she is still owned. She took the National Geographic prefix in 2008, and is still based in the Galapagos Islands. IMO 9139878

NATIONAL GEOGRAPHIC ORION was built by Schiffswerft u Maschinenfabrik Cassens (yard number 236) at Emden, Germany as the ORION for Explorer Maritime Ltd of Greece. It is believed that she was laid down as the SUN EXPLORER. She began a long-term charter to Orion Expedition Cruises at the beginning of 2005, having previously operated for Travel Dynamics. Lindblad Expeditions bought Orion Expedition Cruises in 2013 and the ship was renamed NATIONAL GEOGRAPHIC ORION. She operates in the Pacific and Indian Oceans. IMO 9273076

NATIONAL GEOGRAPHIC SEA BIRD was owned by Majestic Alaska Boat Co and operated under charter to Lindblad, who later acquired the vessel in 2007. She was built by Nichols Bros (yard number S62) at Freeland, Washington State, USA as the MAJESTIC EXPLORER, but renamed as the SEA BIRD within nine months. Her NATIONAL GEOGRAPHIC prefix appeared late in 2007. Her current areas of operation are Alaska and Baja California. IMO 8966444

NATIONAL GEOGRAPHIC SEA LION is registered under the ownership of SPEX Sea Lion (now a Lindblad group company). She was built by Nichols Bros (yard number S63) at Freeland, Washington State, USA as the GREAT RIVERS EXPLORER, but became the SEA LION in 1989. Her prefix was added in 2008. She operates in Alaska, Panama and Costa Rica. IMO 8966456

LOUIS CRUISE LINES

The Company Louis began chartering passenger ships soon after the end of the Second World War, but did not actually begin owning its own vessels until the PRINCESSA MARISSA was acquired in 1987. The company also offers management services and is involved in the leisure industry. Louis was a major shareholder in the now defunct Royal Olympic Cruises, but stepped in to fill the breach with Louis Hellenic Cruises. Louis Hellenic Cruises was a Greek-registered company set up by Louis Cruise Lines principally to operate cruises calling at Turkish ports, a destination not available to Greek Cypriot flagged vessels. The company suffered a major setback on 5 April 2007 when the Group's newest ship, the SEA DIAMOND, hit rocks on the approach to Santorini and after evacuation of passengers and crew, sank 15 hours later, close to the island's ferry port. In order to continue to provide the SEA DIAMOND's itineraries, the THOMSON SPIRIT was used for the first half of April,

Lindblad's *National Geographic Sea Lion* at Juneau *(Rick Frendt)*

Louis Cruises' *Louis Aura* at Rhodes *(William Mayes)*

Louis Cruises' *Louis Cristal* approaching Istanbul *(William Mayes)*

followed by THE EMERALD and finally the OCEANIC II (formerly the MONA LISA) on charter for most of May. That was followed by the RUBY (OCEAN COUNTESS) and eventually the permanent replacement was the CRISTAL. Louis Hellenic Cruises appears to have been disbanded and the ships have been incorporated into the Louis Cruise Lines fleet. Louis Cruise Lines is a subsidiary of the Cypriot-quoted Louis plc. The AQUAMARINE and THE AEGEAN PEARL were both sold in 2010, and more recently the CORAL, THE EMERALD and SAPPHIRE were sold for scrap. From September 2014 the Piraeus based cruises were to be marketed as Celestyal Cruises and the ships on those services were expected to be renamed. However, by late September there was still no evidence of use of the new name.

Address Louis House, 11 Lemesos Avenue, 2112, Nicosia TT 21301, 1516 Nicosia, Cyprus

Telephone +357 255 88168 **Fax** +357 224 42949

Website www.louiscruises.com

Area operated Mediterranean Sea and charters, Greek Islands and Turkey from Piraeus

LOUIS AURA	15781gt	1968	20.0k	D2	710p	912p	315c	160.1m	22.8m	6.7m	MT
LOUIS CRISTAL	25611gt	1980	21.0k	D2	960p	1200p	180c	158.9m	25.2m	5.6m	MT
LOUIS OLYMPIA	37773gt	1982	19.0k	D2	1450p	1595p	540c	214.5m	28.4m	7.0m	MT
THOMSON MAJESTY	41662gt	1992	21.0k	D2	1464p	1800p	550c	207.3m	27.6m	5.8m	MT
THOMSON SPIRIT	33930gt	1983	18.0k	D2	1254p	1374p	209c	214.7m	27.2m	7.5m	MT

LOUIS AURA was built by AG Weser Werk Seebeck (yard number 935) at Bremerhaven, Germany as the STARWARD for Kloster's Norwegian Caribbean Cruise Line. She spent the bulk of her career with NCCL cruising in the Caribbean. In 1995 she became the BOLERO following her sale to Festival Cruises. For Festival she initially cruised in the Mediterranean but was later chartered out to other operators, including Britain's First Choice in 2000 and the now defunct Spanish Cruise Line in 2001. Following the collapse of Festival Cruises in early 2004 she was laid up at Gibraltar. She was registered under the ownership of Cruise Elenora in February 2004 and renamed as the ORIENT QUEEN in November 2004. She commenced service in the Eastern Mediterranean in the summer of 2005 for Abou Merhi Lines. In late 2005 she was positioned to Dubai but her programme there was unsuccessful. She was to have cruised from Beirut again in 2006, but further troubles in the area may have curtailed or prevented this programme in its entirety. In 2006 Abou Merhi Lines pulled out of the cruising market and chartered the ORIENT QUEEN to Louis Cruise lines for five years with an option to purchase. She was quickly chartered to the United States Military Sealift Command for the purpose of rescuing Americans stranded in Beirut. Subsequently she was chartered to Delphin Kreuzfahrten for a world cruise in place of the delayed DELPHIN VOYAGER. For 2011 she operated from Genoa and Marseille. In 2013 she was renamed LOUIS AURA and currently operates the company's Cyprus sailings in peak summer and is chartered out at other times. IMO 6821080

LOUIS CRISTAL as we see her now was completed in 1992 by the Rauma Yard at Rauma, Finland as the SALLY ALBATROSS, using the lower hull parts of the previous SALLY ALBATROSS destroyed by fire in 1991 while refitting in Stockholm. That ship had been built in 1980 by Wartsila (yard number 309) at Turku, Finland as the VIKING SAGA for Rederi AB Sally, then part of the Viking Line consortium. She served the Stockholm to Helsinki overnight route until replaced by the OLYMPIA in 1986, then switched to a new role, cruising mainly from Helsinki. She was later rebuilt with a rather more streamlined forward superstructure. In her current incarnation, she cruised in the Baltic Sea for Sally Line until March 1994, when she ran aground on the approach to Helsinki. She went to La Spezia for repairs and while there her after decks were rebuilt. She was then chartered to Norwegian Cruise Line and renamed LEEWARD for Caribbean service; her first cruise departed in July 1995. At the end of that charter she was taken up by Star Cruises in 2000 and as the SUPERSTAR TAURUS operated for a while in the Far East. She moved to Silja Cruise in 2002 and offered short cruises in the Baltic as the SILJA OPERA. With the sale of Silja Line in 2006 to Tallink, the SILJA OPERA was surplus to requirements and was retained by Sea Containers. She subsequently moved to Tilbury, England for lay-up and was renamed OPERA. After the loss of the SEA DIAMOND, Louis needed a new ship quickly and the OPERA was just about all that was available. She was refitted and renamed CRISTAL, entering service in the summer of 2007. She was renamed LOUIS CRISTAL in March 2011, and generally operates from Piraeus in summer. During the winter of 2011/2012 she operated a new series of cruises based in Cuba. IMO 7827213

LOUIS OLYMPIA was the fourth ship to be delivered to the still relatively new Royal Caribbean Cruise Lines, as the SONG OF AMERICA. She was built by Wartsila (yard number 431) at Helsinki, Finland for service in the Caribbean Sea. She was named by opera singer Beverly Sills. Replaced by new tonnage she was sold to Airtours of the UK (marketed as Sun Cruises) and renamed as the SUNBIRD in 1999. Airtours later re-styled themselves as My Travel, but that did not stop the mounting losses in other sections of the company from almost pulling the whole business down. The cruise business was sold in 2004, with Louis Cruise Lines taking a number of ships, including the SUNBIRD. From 2005 she was chartered to Thomson Cruises as the THOMSON DESTINY, but in 2012 was 'swapped' for LOUIS MAJESTY (now THOMSON MAJESTY) and renamed LOUIS OLYMPIA.

THOMSON MAJESTY For details see under Thomson Cruises (TUI).

THOMSON SPIRIT This ship was purchased by Louis in 2008 having previously been chartered in and out. See under Thomson Cruises (TUI).

CELESTYAL CRUISES

The Company Celestyal Cruises is an operating name for Louis Cruise Lines' Piraeus-based cruises. The name came into use in September 2014. The ships to be operated under this brand are LOUIS CRISTAL and LOUIS OLYMPIA.

Area operated Cruises from Piraeus

CUBA CRUISE

The Company Cuba Cruise is a subsidiary operation with Canadian connections that uses the LOUIS CRISTAL for winter cruising around Cuba.

Website www.yourcubacruise.com

Area operated Cuba

LOUIS CRISTAL	25611gt	1980	21.0k	D2	960p	1200p	180c	158.9m	25.2m	5.6m	MT

LOUIS CRISTAL For details see Louis Cruises (above)

MAGNA CARTA STEAMSHIP COMPANY

The Company Magna Carta Steamship Company is a British registered operator of coastal, canal and lake cruises around Scotland, formed in 1999. The company also previously operated the SPIRIT OF CHARTWELL on the River Thames.

Address 136 Hamilton Terrace, London NW6 9UX

Telephone +44 207 372 2077 **Fax** +44 207 604 3634

Website www.magnacarta.bz

Area operated Scotland

LORD OF THE GLENS	729gt	1985	18.0k	D2	54p	54p	18c	45.0m	10.5m	3.2m	GB

LORD OF THE GLENS was built in Greece as the VICTORIA. She was renamed VICTORIA II in 1999 and took her current name in 2000, following a major refit. She is a near sister to the NATIONAL GEOGRAPHIC ISLANDER. IMO 8966470

MAJESTIC CRUISE LINES

The Company Majestic Cruise Lines is an American owned company operating the FREEWINDS on behalf of the International Association of Scientologists.

Address 118 North Fort Harrison Avenue, Clearwater, Florida 33755-4013, United States of America

Telephone +1 727 445 4309

Website www.freewinds.org

Area operated Caribbean

FREEWINDS	9780gt	1968	20.0k	D2	468p	500p	170c	134.3m	19.9m	5.5m	PA

FREEWINDS was built by Wartsila (yard number 1161) at Turku, Finland as the BOHEME for Wallenius Lines for charter to Commodore Cruise Lines for Caribbean cruising. She was sold to Sally Shipping in 1981 and passed to Sally subsidiary Hanseatic Caribbean Shipping later that year. In 1986

Louis Cruises' **Louis Olympia** off Rhodes *(William Mayes)*

Magna Carta Steamship Company's **Lord of the Glens** at Fort Augustus *(Peter Godliman)*

Majestic Cruise Line's **Freewinds** at Aruba *(Rick Frendt)*

she was acquired by the International Association of Scientologists and registered under the ownership of San Donato Properties Corporation and renamed FREEWINDS. She is operated by Majestic Cruise Lines for scientologist members. IMO 6810811

MAJESTIC INTERNATIONAL CRUISES

The Company Majestic International Cruises is a cruise ship-owning company that does not operate ships for its own account. The company was founded in the late 1980s and has also owned the OCEAN EXPLORER I (1998-2004) and the OCEAN MONARCH (2002-2007). The company's OCEAN COUNTESS was lost by fire while undergoing refit in 2013.

Address 4 Zissimopoulou Street, 16674 Glyfada, Athens, Greece

Telephone +30 210 8912600 **Fax** +30 210 8912615

Website www.majesticcruises.gr

Area operated Does not operate for its own account

OCEAN MAJESTY	10417gt	1966	20.0k	D2	500p	613p	235c	130.6m	19.2m	5.4m	PT

OCEAN MAJESTY was built by Union Naval de Levante (yard number 93) in Valencia, Spain as the car ferry JUAN MARCH for Spain's state carrier, Compania Trasmediterranea. She was one of a series of four ships designed for both the overnight Barcelona to Palma, Majorca run and the longer route from Barcelona to the Canary Islands. She was sold in 1985 to Sol Maritime Services of Limassol, Cyprus. She was renamed SOL CHRISTIANA and placed on a new service linking Piraeus with Crete, Rhodes, Cyprus and Israel. The service was not a success and she was sold to another Cypriot operator, renamed KYPROS STAR and set to work as a ferry serving Rhodes, Cyprus and Egypt from Piraeus. In 1988 she operated for Italy's Adriatica and sailed between Brindisi in Italy and Patras in Greece. Between 1989 and 1994 the ship underwent a total transformation, emerging as the cruise ship OCEAN MAJESTY for Majestic International Cruises. She was initially chartered to Epirotiki Line as the OLYMPIC and again for the following year as the HOMERIC. For 1995 the ship was sub-chartered to Page & Moy Holidays for a number of cruises. Subsequently she made regular appearances in the Page & Moy cruise programme, but 2009 was her last season. She was chartered to Turkish operator, Apex Tour for use in the Eastern Mediterranean and the Black Sea during 2010 and 2011, but is now operated by Hansa Touristik. IMO 6602898

MANO MARITIME

The Company Mano Maritime is a company within the Mano Holdings Group, an Israeli private company in the maritime and leisure sectors. Mordechai Mano founded Mano Maritime in 1945. The company's third passenger ship, THE JASMINE, was sold for service as a ferry in the Red Sea in 2006. She became a cruise ship again as EASYCRUISE LIFE and is now the OCEAN LIFE. In 2009 the company acquired MSC's RHAPSODY.

Address 2 Pal-Yam Avenue, PO Box 1400, Haifa 33031 Israel

Telephone +972 4 860 6666 **Fax** +972 4 866 7666

Website www.mano.co.il

Area operated Eastern Mediterranean and Black Sea

GOLDEN IRIS	16852gt	1977	18.5k	D2	800p	1000p	350c	163.6m	22.8m	6.0m	PA
ROYAL IRIS	14717gt	1971	18.0k	D2	720p	1000p	330c	142.1m	21.9m	5.5m	PA

GOLDEN IRIS was built for Cunard as the CUNARD PRINCESS (launched as the CUNARD CONQUEST) by Burmeister & Wain (yard number 859) in Copenhagen, Denmark, for service in the Caribbean Sea. She was acquired by Mediterranean Shipping Cruises in 1995 and renamed RHAPSODY. In 2006 her registry was changed from Italy to Panama on transfer from MSC Crociere to fellow MSC subsidiary, Gramerco International. Following her return from South Africa in the spring of 2009, she was sold to Mano Maritime and renamed GOLDEN IRIS. IMO 7358573

ROYAL IRIS began life as the EAGLE for Southern Ferries, a company owned by the Peninsular and Oriental Steam Navigation Company. She was built by Dubigeon-Normandie (yard number 123) at Nantes, France as a car ferry for service between Southampton, Lisbon and Tangiers. In December 1975 she was sold to Nouvelle Compagnie de Paquebots, Marseilles for service in the Mediterranean Sea as the AZUR. In early 1982 she underwent conversion to become a pure cruise ship and she

Mano Cruises' *Golden Iris* off Larnaca *(Rick Frendt)*

Mano Cruises' *Royal Iris* off Rhodes *(William Mayes)*

Mira Cruise's *Mira 1* as *Fuji Maru* *(Jonathan Boonzaier)*

continued to serve her owners until sold to Chandris Lines in 1987, at which time she was renamed as THE AZUR. In 1995 she became the first ship in the new fleet of Festival Cruises, but was not officially renamed, although she carried the name AZUR for some time. When Festival Cruises failed in early 2004, she was laid up at Gibraltar and briefly renamed ELOISE prior to being acquired by Golden Cruises for operation by Mano Maritime. She was renamed ROYAL IRIS in late 2004, and underwent a refit at the Perama shipyard in Greece. IMO 7032997

METROPOLITAN TOURING (ETICA)

The Company Metropolitan Touring, founded in 1953, is one of Ecuador's leading travel companies and operator of expedition cruise ships within the Galapagos Islands. Space on most sailings is block-booked by various US and European tour operators.

Address Avenida De Las Palmeras N45-74 and De Las Orquideas, Quito, Ecuador

Telephone +593 2 298 8200 **Fax** +593 2 334 1250

Website www.metropolitan-touring.com

Area operated Galapagos Islands

ISABELA II	‡1025gt	1979	12.0k	D2	40p	40p	24c	53.7m	11.6m	3.4m	EC
LA PINTA	1438gt	1983	12.0k	D2	32p	48p	24c	63.0m	12.0m	3.2m	EC
SANTA CRUZ	1602gt	1979	13.0k	D2	90p	90p	50c	72.3m	11.8m	3.2m	EC

ISABELA II was built by Halter Marine (yard number 848) at Patterson, Louisiana, USA as the offshore supply ship CINDY BRILEY. In 1985 she became the CARL B DOWNS and took her present name in 1988 when she passed to ETICA. She was converted in the same year for use as a cruise ship in the Galapagos Islands. IMO 7914535

LA PINTA was built by Astilleros Construcciones (yard number 175) at Vigo, Spain as the ferry CITANIA for local service around Vigo. She subsequently became the SEA TRAVELLER II, then the SEA LINER before reverting to her original name in 1992. Three years later she was the SUN JO 1, for an Israeli controlled Florida based company. She became ETICA's PINTA I in 2007 following a major reconstruction in Peru, and was renamed as LA PINTA in 2009. IMO 8112897

SANTA CRUZ was built by Astilleros y Talleres Celaya (yard number 178) at Bilbao, Spain as the SANTA CRUZ for ETICA. She underwent a major reconstruction in Chile in 1998. IMO 7811721

MIRA CRUISE

The Company Mira Cruise is a Japanese cruise line that was established in 2014. The FUJI MARU was acquired from Nippon Charter Cruise and will enter service in 2015 as a floating commercial hospital where passengers can undergo medical treatments while enjoying a cruise.

Area operated Not yet operating

| MIRA 1 | 23235gt | 1989 | 20.0k | D2 | 364p | 603p | 135c | 167.0m | 24.0m | 6.6m | PA |

MIRA 1 was Japan's largest cruise ship when completed as the FUJI MARU in 1989 by Mitsubishi Heavy Industries (yard number 1177) at Kobe, Japan for Mitsui OSK Passenger Lines. She has operated mainly on charter cruises, under the Nippon Charter Cruises organisation, a joint venture between Mitsui OSK and Japan Cruise Lines, within Asia and the Pacific Ocean. In 2013 she was sold to Mira Cruise and is currently undergoing refit at Tsuneishi Heavy Industries. She is expected to enter service in April 2015. IMO 8700474

MITSUI OSK PASSENGER LINES

The Company Mitsui OSK Lines is one of the world's largest shipping companies, with a fleet of more than 500 ships under the control of its group companies. The cruise business is operated by Mitsui OSK Passenger Lines, or MOPAS for short, and also by Nippon Charter Cruise, a joint venture between Mitsui OSK and Japan Cruise Line. Nippon Charter Cruise is recorded as the registered owner of the FUJI MARU. Mitsui OSK was formed in 1964 with the merger of Mitsui Steamship Company (de-merged from its parent in 1942) and the long-established (1884) OSK Line. A further reorganisation took place in 1999 when Navix Line was absorbed into the group. The various elements that make up Mitsui OSK today have been carrying passengers since 1868. The NIPPON MARU's near sister, the FUJI MARU was sold in 2013.

Address 9-13 Akasaka 1-Chome, Minato-ku, Sankaido Building, 107 8532 Tokyo, Japan

Telephone +81 3 5114 5247 **Fax** +81 3 5114 5270

Website www.nipponmaru.jp

Area operated Asia and worldwide for Japanese speaking passengers

| NIPPON MARU | 22472gt | 1990 | 18.0k | D2 | 368p | 607p | 160c | 166.6m | 23.6m | 6.6m | JP |

NIPPON MARU is a product of the Kobe, Japan shipyard of Mitsubishi Heavy Industries (yard number 1188), and carries one of the most prestigious names in Japanese passenger shipping. The ship operates a mixture of cruises ranging from short domestic voyages of a few days to three-month round the world cruises. In December 2009 she underwent a major refit, during which 18 balconies were added. IMO 8817631

MONARCA DISCOVERY CRUISES

The Company Monarca Discovery Cruises is a trading name of Cruceros de Aventura Monarca del Pacifico SA, a Mexican company.

Address Av. Ano de Juarez 205, Iztapalpa, Mexico DF 09070 Mexico

Telephone +52 555 685 7030 **Fax** +52 555 686 7006

Website www.monarcacruises.com

Area operated Mexico

| PACIFIC MONARCH | 336gt | 1971 | 11.0k | D1 | 40p | 40p | 17c | 41.1m | 8.5m | 2.3m | US |

PACIFIC MONARCH was built by Blount Marine Corporation, Warren, Rhode Island as the NEW SHOREHAM I. As built she was 38.1 metres long. She later became the GLACIER BAY EXPLORER and was acquired by Cruise West in 2000 and renamed SPIRIT OF GLACIER BAY. In 2006 she became Adventure Cruise Lines' PACIFIC MONARCH, following refurbishment. The ship was acquired by her current owner in 2011 and has undergone an extensive refit. IMO 8963739

MSC CROCIERE

The Company MSC Crociere is an Italian subsidiary of the Mediterranean Shipping Company of Geneva, Switzerland; the world's largest privately owned shipping business. What is today MSC was established in 1969 by Captain Gianluigi Aponte from Sorrento as Aponte Shipping Company. Entry into the cruise market came eighteen years later with the acquisition of what was left of Lauro Line. The business, operating a single ship, the ACHILLE LAURO, was restyled as Star Lauro, but following her loss in 1994, the cruise operation was renamed during the following year as Mediterranean Shipping Cruises. In 1989 the company acquired the former Matson liner MONTEREY, which remained in service until 2006. The next acquisition was the ENRICO COSTA, in 1994, which was operated until 2000 as the SYMPHONY. In the following year the RHAPSODY, formerly the CUNARD PRINCESS arrived. In spring 2009, following her return from South Africa, the RHAPSODY was sold to Mano Cruises. MSC also operates one of the largest fleets of containerships worldwide and local ferries in Italy; a total of more than 420 ships, owned and chartered. The order with STX St Nazaire for two Musica class ships was converted in 2009 into an order for a single Fantasia class ship. MSC acquired South African travel company Starlight Cruises in 2011. The four smallest ships will be lengthened by Fincantieri in 2014/15, providing space for an additional 200 cabins on each ship.

Address Via Agostino Depretis 31, Naples 80133, Italy

Telephone +39 081 794 2111 **Fax** +39 081 794 2707

Website www.msccrociere.com and www.msccruises.co.uk

Area operated Mediterranean and Caribbean Seas, South Africa and South America

MSC ARMONIA	58625gt	2001	21.0k	DEP2	1554p	2065p	765c	251.2m	28.8m	6.9m	PA
MSC DIVINA	139072gt	2012	23.0k	DE2	3502p	3959p	1388c	333.3m	37.9m	8.7m	PA
MSC FANTASIA	137936gt	2008	23.0k	DE2	3274p	4363p	1370c	333.3m	37.9m	8.7m	PA
MSC LIRICA	59058gt	2003	20.8k	DEP2	1560p	2065p	732c	251.0m	28.8m	6.6m	PA
MSC MAGNIFICA	92128gt	2010	22.0k	DEP2	2518p	3013p	1038c	293.0m	32.2m	7.9m	PA
MSC MUSICA	92409gt	2006	22.0k	DEP2	2550p	3013p	1014c	293.0m	32.2m	7.9m	PA

MSC Cruises' **MSC Preziosa** in Marseille *(William Mayes)*

MSC Cruises' **MSC Armonia** off Kotor *(William Mayes)*

MSC Cruises' **MSC Fantasia** leaving Palermo *(William Mayes)*

MSC OPERA	59058gt	2004	20.8k	DEP2	1712p	2199p	728c	251.2m	28.8m	6.8m	PA
MSC ORCHESTRA	92409gt	2007	22.0k	DEP2	2550p	3013p	1054c	293.0m	32.2m	7.9m	PA
MSC POESIA	92627gt	2008	22.0k	DEP2	2550p	3013p	1039c	293.0m	32.2m	7.9m	PA
MSC PREZIOSA	139072gt	2012	23.0k	DE2	3502p	3959p	1388c	333.3m	37.9m	8.7m	PA
MSC SINFONIA	58625gt	2002	21.0k	DEP2	1554p	2065p	765c	251.0m	28.8m	6.8m	PA
MSC SPLENDIDA	137936gt	2009	23.0k	DE2	3247p	3882c	1370c	333.3m	37.9m	8.7m	PA

MSC ARMONIA began as the second new building for Festival Cruises as the EUROPEAN VISION. She was built by Chantiers de l'Atlantique (yard number V31) at St Nazaire, France. Festival Cruises failed in early 2004 and Mediterranean Shipping Cruises quickly snapped up the ship, renaming her MSC ARMONIA. IMO 9210141

MSC DIVINA was built by STX Europe (formerly Aker Yards and before that Chantiers de l'Atlantique), (yard number U32) at St Nazaire, France. The ship was originally going to be named MSC FAVOLOSA. She was named by Sophia Loren in Marseille on 26 May 2012. In 2014 the ship spent a season cruising from Florida. IMO 9585285

MSC FANTASIA is the first of a pair of massive ships for MSC, built by Aker Yards (yard number A33) at St Nazaire France. Sophia Loren christened the ship in Naples in December 2008. IMO 9359791

MSC LIRICA was built by Chantiers de l'Atlantique (yard number K32) at St Nazaire, France for Mediterranean Shipping Cruises. She was named by Sophia Loren. IMO 9246102

MSC MAGNIFICA was built by STX Europe at St Nazaire (yard number T32). She was named by Sophia Loren in Hamburg on 6 March 2010. IMO 9387085

MSC MUSICA is the first of a trio of ships built by Chantiers de l'Atlantique (yard number Q32), and delivered in 2006. She is another of the company's ships to have been named by Sophia Loren. IMO 9320087

MSC OPERA, a sister to MSC LIRICA, was delivered by Chantiers de l'Atlantique (yard number L32) in 2004 and named by Sophia Loren. IMO 9250464

MSC ORCHESTRA, a sister to the MSC MUSICA was built by Chantiers de l'Atlantique (yard number R32), named by Sophia Loren and delivered in 2007. MSC ORCHESTRA will be positioned in the Far East in 2015. IMO 9320099

MSC POESIA is the third in a series of six ships, built by Aker Yards (yard number S32) at St Nazaire, France. She was named in Dover by Sophia Loren. IMO 9387073

MSC PREZIOSA was ordered from STX Europe (yard number X32) at St Nazaire, France by Libya's General National Maritime Transport Company and was expected to be named PHOENICIA. The design of the ship is similar to that of MSC's MSC FANTASIA. In view of the troubles in Libya, the shipbuilder cancelled the contract and eventually sold the ship to MSC Cruises to be completed as the MSC PREZIOSA. IMO 9595321

MSC SINFONIA was built by Chantiers de l'Atlantique (yard number X31) at St Nazaire, France as the EUROPEAN STARS for Festival Cruises. She was originally advertised to carry the name EUROPEAN DREAM. When Festival Cruises failed, the ship was laid up for some time before being acquired by Mediterranean Shipping Cruises and refitted as the MSC SINFONIA for service beginning in the spring of 2005. IMO 9210153

MSC SPLENDIDA was built by STX Europe (yard number B33) at St Nazaire. She was named by Sophia Loren in Barcelona in July 2009. IMO 9359806

Cruise ships on order

NEWBUILD 1	c168000gt	2017	k		4500p	5700p	1536c	315.0m	43.0m	m	PA
NEWBUILD 2	c168000gt	2019	k		4500p	5700p	1536c	315.0m	43.0m	m	PA
NEWBUILD 3	c154000gt	2017	k		4140p	5300p	1413c	323.0m	41.0m	m	PA
NEWBUILD 4	c154000gt	2018	k		4140p	5300p	1413c	323.0m	41.0m	m	PA

NEWBUILD 1 and **2** are on order with STX at St Nazaire. At the time of writing this order had only got as far as being a letter of intent, but there was an option for a further pair of ships.

NEWBUILD 3 and **4** are the new so-called Seaside class ships on order with Fincantieri. There is an option for a third ship. IMO 9745366 and 9745378

NOBLE CALEDONIA

The Company Noble Caledonia is a British operator of exploration, expedition and educational tours and cruises. The company was founded in 1991 and has operated the ISLAND SKY on long-term seasonal charter for many years. In 2010 the company acquired the ship. The company also sells space on numerous other small ships, both ocean and river, worldwide.

Address 2 Chester Close, Belgravia, London SW1X 7BE, England

Telephone +44 207 752 0000 **Fax** +44 207 245 0388

Website www.noble-caledonia.co.uk

Area operated Worldwide

CALEDONIAN SKY	4200gt	1991	15.5k	D2	100p	100p	71c	90.6m	15.3m	3.6m	BS
ISLAND SKY	4200gt	1992	15.5k	D2	116p	116p	72c	90.6m	15.3m	4.1m	BS
QUEST	1268gt	1992	13.0k	D1	50p	60p	20c	49.6m	11.0m	3.4m	BS

CALEDONIAN SKY was built for Renaissance Cruises as the RENAISSANCE SIX by Nuovi Cantieri Apuania (yard number 1145) at Marina di Carrara, Italy as one of a series of eight small luxury cruise ships. She was sold to Sun Cruises of Singapore in 1998, when replaced by impressive new tonnage, and renamed as the SUN VIVA 2. Following the loss of the SUN VISTA that company was taken over by Star Cruises and she was renamed MEGASTAR CAPRICORN in 2000. She was soon sold on, and her purchaser, Hebridean Island Cruises had her refitted, reducing her passenger capacity from 112 to 80, thus producing the exclusive and luxurious HEBRIDEAN SPIRIT in 2001. Troubled economic times forced her sale in April 2009, shortly before Hebridean International Cruises went into administration. She was renamed SUNRISE in April 2009 for a new career as a charter yacht. That phase was short-lived as she was chartered by Noble Caledonia to operate as the CALEDONIAN SKY from 2012. IMO 8802870

ISLAND SKY was built by Nuovi Cantieri Apuania (yard number 1147) at Marina di Carrara in Italy as the RENAISSANCE EIGHT for Renaissance Cruises. She remained with the company until it filed for bankruptcy in the autumn of 2001, following which she was renamed as the RENAI II and laid up. She became the SKY in 2003 and was renamed ISLAND SKY in 2004 when acquired by Mauritius Island Cruises. ISLAND SKY and her sister the ISLAND SUN (now the CORINTHIAN II of Travel Dynamics International) were acquired by Danish container operator Clipper Group from Mauritius Island Cruises, which has now ceased trading. Noble Caledonia chartered the ISLAND SKY from 2004 from Clipper Group of Denmark, but acquired the ship in 2009. IMO 8802894

QUEST was built as the SAQQIT ITTUK for Greenland Government owner KNI Piilersvisoq as a coastal passenger liner for 150 passengers by the Orskov Shipyard (yard number 157) at Frederikshavn, Denmark. She was renamed as DISKO II in 2004 and converted into an expedition cruise ship by Hotell and Fartyginredning of Gothenburg, Sweden, although the work took place in Tallinn, Estonia. The works included the installation of 26 new outside cabins, and a new observation lounge. When she re-entered service, it was under charter to the German tour operator, Norden Tours, for whom she undertook summer Greenland coastal cruises. She was acquired by Clipper Group in 2007, further refurbished, including the addition of sponsons and upgraded lifeboats, and renamed QUEST. She operates for a variety of expedition cruise companies. IMO 8913904

NOMADS OF THE SEAS

The Company Nomads of the Seas is a Chilean company, founded in 2006 by Andres Ergas, offering expedition cruises.

Address 5A Piso, 4446, Las Condes, Chile

Telephone +56 2 2414 4690 **Fax** +56 2 206 1450

Website www.nomads.cl

Area operated Chile

ATMOSPHERE	695gt	2006		k	D2	28p	28p	32c	45.7m	10.0m	2.8m	CL

ATMOSPHERE was built by Astilleros y Servicios Navales (yard number 147) at Valdivia, Chile for Transportes Y Turismo Austral. IMO 9401001

MSC Cruises' **MSC Musica** at St. Lucia *(Rick Frendt)*

Noble Caledonia's **Caledonian Sky** in Sydney *(Alf Sims)*

Noble Caledonia's **Island Sky** in Istanbul *(William Mayes)*

NORDISK CRUISE LINE

The Company Nordic Cruise Line is a new company, an offshoot of Nordisk Faergefart, set up to operate the BRAHE on short international cruises from Denmark. However it appears that this may not happen as the ship is no longer certified for international voyages.

Website www.nordiskcruiseline.dk

Area operated Denmark

BRAHE	1105gt	1943	12.0k	D2	90p	110p	24c	56.5m	10.1m	2.8m	FI

BRAHE For details see under Saimaa Travel.

NORTH STAR CRUISES

The Company North Star Cruises was established in 1987. The new ship TRUE NORTH replaced a 1999-built ship of the same name, and is equipped with a Bell 407 helicopter.

Address PO Box 654, Broome 6725, Western Australia

Telephone +61 8 9192 1829

Website www.northstarcruises.com.au

Area operated Australia North West coast, and to Papua New Guinea

TRUE NORTH	776gt	2005	13.0k	D2	36p	36p	20c	49.9m	10.0m	2.2m	AU

TRUE NORTH was built by Image Marine Pty Ltd (yard number 287) in Fremantle, Western Australia. IMO 9308651

NORWEGIAN CRUISE LINE (NCL)

The Company The origins of Norwegian Cruise Line date from 1966 when the Norwegian Klosters Rederi ordered a car ferry from a Bergen shipyard to fill what was perceived as a gap in the ferry market, a route from Southern England to Spain. Due to external difficulties the route was quickly abandoned and alternative work was sought for the 11,000 ton SUNWARD. Under the Norwegian Caribbean Line banner she was placed in a new cruise service to the Caribbean, based in Miami, Florida. Such was the success that a second, slightly larger, vessel was ordered, the STARWARD, and then another, the SKYWARD. Two further ships were ordered in 1970 from an Italian yard, but after the first (the SOUTHWARD) was delivered the building cost of the second ship escalated dramatically and the company abandoned her. She was subsequently completed as P&O's SPIRIT OF LONDON. In 1979 the Klosters company acquired the long laid-up transatlantic liner FRANCE and after a major refit she became the world's largest cruise ship – the NORWAY. Further expansion occurred in 1984 with the acquisition by Klosters of another Norwegian owned company, Royal Viking Line, together with its three luxury ships. That company ran for a while as a separate entity, but by 1991 its earlier ships had been absorbed into Norwegian Caribbean Line and Royal Viking Line was left with just two new ships, both of which were eventually sold to units of the now Carnival Group. Royal Cruise Line together with its one remaining ship, the CROWN ODYSSEY, joined the group in 1990. Transfers to that fleet over the next four years included two of the original Royal Viking trio, together with the last ever RV ship, the ROYAL VIKING QUEEN. More new ships came on stream during the 1990's and in a restyling the company adopted the title Norwegian Cruise Line. Following a battle for the company between Carnival Holdings and Star Cruises, the protagonists agreed to take split ownership of Norwegian Cruise Line and its then subsidiary, Orient Lines, in the ratio of 40 to 60. Subsequently Carnival withdrew and control passed to Star Cruises in 2000. During the period that Star Cruises wholly owned NCL several of Star's new-buildings were allocated to the company, and two of NCL's smaller ships went in the opposite direction. In 2007 Star Cruises sold 50% of Norwegian Cruise Line (together with control) to Apollo Management. NCL America was a US based former subsidiary of Star Cruises specifically set up to operate US registered and crewed ships in the Hawaiian Islands. Passenger numbers did not meet expectations, leading to the PRIDE OF HAWAI'I being withdrawn from service and repositioned to Europe for 2008. In late 2008 NCL America became wholly owned by Apollo Group, following the withdrawal by Star Cruises, and the PRIDE OF ALOHA was returned to Star. NCL America has now been absorbed into the mainstream NCL operation. Subsequently, NCL was listed on NASDAQ, with 12% of the share capital being traded. A further public offering was made in 2014 so at the time of writing the remaining major holdings were Genting Group (Star Cruises owners) 27.7%, Apollo Management 19.9% and TPG Capital 7.8%. In September 2014 NCL acquired Prestige Cruise

Holdings from Apollo Management.

Address 7665 Corporate Centre Drive, Miami, Florida 33126, United States of America

Telephone +1 305 436 4000 **Fax** +1 305 436 4120

Website www.ncl.com

Areas Operated North America, Caribbean Sea, South America, Europe and Hawai'i

NORWEGIAN BREAKAWAY	145655gt	2013	21.0k	DEP2	4020p	p	1595c	324.0m	39.7m	8.6m	BS
NORWEGIAN DAWN	92250gt	2002	23.0k	DEP2	2338p	2683p	1071c	294.1m	32.2m	8.2m	BS
NORWEGIAN EPIC	155873gt	2010	20.0k	DE2	4100p	5186p	1753c	329.5m	40.2m	8.7m	BS
NORWEGIAN GEM	93530gt	2007	23.0k	DEP2	2382p	2750p	1100c	294.1m	32.2m	8.2m	BS
NORWEGIAN GETAWAY	145655gt	2014	21.0k	DEP2	4020p	p	1595c	324.0m	39.7m	8.6m	BS
NORWEGIAN JADE	93558gt	2006	23.0k	DEP2	2388p	2750p	1067c	294.1m	32.2m	8.6m	BS
NORWEGIAN JEWEL	93502gt	2005	23.0k	DEP2	2374p	2750p	1101c	294.1m	32.2m	8.2m	BS
NORWEGIAN PEARL	93530gt	2007	23.0k	DE2	2384p	2750p	1101c	294.1m	32.2m	8.2m	BS
NORWEGIAN SKY	77104gt	1999	20.0k	DEP2	2002p	2450p	919c	258.7m	32.3m	8.0m	BS
NORWEGIAN SPIRIT	75338gt	1998	23.0k	DE2	2000p	2975p	959c	268.6m	32.2m	7.9m	BS
NORWEGIAN STAR	91740gt	2001	23.0k	DEP2	2346p	2683p	1060c	294.1m	32.2m	8.0m	BS
NORWEGIAN SUN	78309gt	2001	21.0k	DE2	1936p	2400p	940c	258.6m	32.3m	7.6m	BS
PRIDE OF AMERICA	80439gt	2005	20.5k	DEP2	2138p	2300p	941c	281.3m	32.2m	8.0m	US

NORWEGIAN BREAKAWAY was completed by Meyer at Papenburg (yard number 678), although part of the hull was built at Meyer's Rostock yard. Her godmothers were members of the Rockettes from the Radio City Music Hall. For 2014 she is based year-round in New York. IMO 9606912

NORWEGIAN DAWN was ordered for Star Cruises from Jos. L. Meyer (yard number 649) at Papenburg, Germany as the SUPERSTAR SCORPIO but allocated to Norwegian Cruise Line while under construction. She was named by actress Kim Cattrall. The ship's area of operation is principally the Caribbean and the US East Coast, although in 2009 and 2010 she undertook a number of cruises from New York to Bermuda during the summer. The ship underwent a major refit in May 2011. The NORWEGIAN DAWN is owned by Star Cruises. IMO 9195169

NORWEGIAN EPIC was ordered from Aker Yards (Yard number C33) at St Nazaire, France. She is one of a pair of ships ordered, with an option of a third. However, in the autumn of 2008 the order for the second ship was cancelled and the option for a third will not be exercised. She was delivered in 2010 and was christened in New York by country music artist Reba McEntire on 3 July. The NORWEGIAN EPIC operates in Europe in the summer and the Caribbean in winter. IMO 9410569

NORWEGIAN GEM was built by Meyer Werft (yard number 670) and following her naming in New York by Cindy Cardella in December 2007 was positioned to the US East Coast. She operates from New York to Bermuda and on the US East Coast and Caribbean Sea. IMO 9355733

NORWEGIAN GETAWAY was built by Meyer Werft (yard number 692). The ship was christened in Miami on 7 February 2014 by the Miami Dolphins Cheerleaders. The NORWEGIAN GETAWAY is based full-time in the Caribbean. IMO 9606924

NORWEGIAN JADE was built by Meyer Werft (yard number 668) at Papenburg, Germany as the PRIDE OF HAWAI'I for NCL America. With passenger numbers on her Hawaii services not meeting expectations, following a refit in Cadiz she was moved to Europe in 2008 under the name NORWEGIAN JADE, and for 2009 cruised from Southampton in the summer. She is now based in Europe in summer and the Caribbean in winter. IMO 9304057

NORWEGIAN JEWEL commenced her career with three cruises from Dover, England following delivery from Jos. L. Meyer (yard number 667) at Papenburg, Germany. She then operated a series of cruises on the East Coast of North America before positioning to the Caribbean where she was christened by Melania Trump in Miami. She now cruises in the Caribbean Sea, in Alaska and on the US East Coast. IMO 9304045

NORWEGIAN PEARL was built by Meyer Werft (yard number 669) at Papenburg, Germany. She was named by American talk show host Rosie O'Donnell and now operates in the Caribbean and Alaska. IMO 9342281

NORWEGIAN SKY was laid down for Costa Crociere in 1996 as the COSTA OLYMPIA by Bremer Vulkan (yard number 108) at Vegesack, Germany but not completed due to the bankruptcy of the shipyard.

NCL's **Norwegian Breakaway** off Calshot *(William Mayes)*

NCL's **Norwegian Dawn** at San Juan *(Rick Frendt)*

NCL's **Norwegian Epic** at St Thomas *(Rick Frendt)*

NCL's **Norwegian Gem** in New York *(Claudia Frendt)*

NCL's **Norwegian Sky** at Freeport *(Rick Frendt)*

NCL's **Norwegian Spirit** in Istanbul *(William Mayes)*

The partially built hull was acquired by Norwegian Cruise Line and moved to Lloydwerft at Bremerhaven, Germany to be completed as the NORWEGIAN SKY. She was renamed as the PRIDE OF ALOHA following the partial sinking of the still incomplete PRIDE OF AMERICA in the shipyard at Bremerhaven, and entered service for NCL America in the Hawaiian Islands. Following a disappointing market performance the PRIDE OF HAWAI'I was withdrawn, followed soon after by the PRIDE OF ALOHA, which went back to Norwegian Cruise Line as the NORWEGIAN SKY. She now operates 3- and 4- day Bahamas trips from Florida. IMO 9128532

NORWEGIAN SPIRIT was built by Meyer Werft (yard number 646) at Papenburg, Germany as the SUPERSTAR LEO, the first new ship for Star Cruises. She was transferred to Norwegian Cruise Line in 2004 and renamed NORWEGIAN SPIRIT. She is a sister to the SUPERSTAR VIRGO. Until April 2012 she was based in New Orleans and then moved to the Mediterranean. She now alternates between Europe and the Caribbean. The NORWEGIAN SPIRIT is owned by Star Cruises. IMO 9141065

NORWEGIAN STAR was laid down as the SUPERSTAR LIBRA by Meyer Werft (yard number 648) at Papenburg, Germany for Star Cruises, but switched to subsidiary Norwegian Cruise Line before completion. She currently cruises in Europe and the Caribbean, and is owned by Star Cruises. IMO 9195157

NORWEGIAN SUN's hull was built by Aker MTW (yard number 005) at Wismar, Germany and she was completed by Lloydwerft (yard number 109) at Bremerhaven, Germany. She currently operates in Alaska and the Caribbean Sea. IMO 9218131

PRIDE OF AMERICA was ordered by the new United States Lines (part of the American Classic Voyages grouping) from the Ingalls Shipbuilding Yard (yard number 7671) at Pascagoula, Mississippi, USA as one of a pair of what were to be the first ocean passenger ships to be constructed in a US shipyard for more than 40 years. As in other histories in this book, the events of September 11, 2001 had a devastating effect on American Classic Voyages and the company filed for bankruptcy. Norwegian Cruise Line later purchased the one almost complete hull and the parts for the second ship and had the hull towed to Bremerhaven, arriving in December 2002, where the ship was to have been completed for the Hawaiian cruise market. The ship was lengthened by 25 metres at this time. While being completed, the PRIDE OF AMERICA as she was now named, was partially sunk during a storm on 14 January 2004. The shipyard subsequently filed for bankruptcy and it is thought that what little there was of the second ship has now been scrapped or incorporated into another ship. As an 'American built' and US flagged ship she is able to operate in the Hawaii Islands without the need to call at a foreign port. Her godmother was Elaine Chao, then US Secretary of Labour. IMO 9209221

Cruise ships on order

NORWEGIAN BLISS	c164600gt	2017	24.0k	DEP2	4200p	p	c	324.6m	41.4m	8.3m	BS
NORWEGIAN ESCAPE	c164600gt	2015	24.0k	DEP2	4200p	p	c	324.6m	41.4m	8.3m	BS
NEWBUILD 3	c164600gt	2018	24.0k	DEP2	4200p	p	c	324.6m	41.4m	8.3m	BS
NEWBUILD 4	c164600gt	2019	24.0k	DEP2	4200p	p	c	324.6m	41.4m	8.3m	BS

NORWEGIAN BLISS and **NORWEGIAN ESCAPE** are so called Breakaway Plus ships ordered from the Meyer Shipyard ay Papenburg (yard numbers 694 and 693). IMO 9677076 and 9703796

NEWBUILD 3 and **4** are further units of the Breakaway Plus class. IMO 9751509 and 9751511

PRESTIGE CRUISE HOLDINGS

The Company Prestige Cruise Holdings was set up by Apollo Management, a New York-based investment group, in 2007 to hold the group's interests in its premier and luxury cruise businesses. Oceania Cruises was acquired in February 2007 and during 2008 Regent Seven Seas Cruises was purchased from Carlson. In September 2014 an agreement was reached for NCL to acquire Prestige Cruise Holdings.

OCEANIA CRUISES

The Company Oceania Cruises was founded in 2002 by cruise industry veterans Joe Watters and Frank Del Rio. Renaissance Cruises collapsed in September 2001 and all of its ships were laid up, many of them at Gibraltar. Subsequently they were all acquired by Cruiseinvest, an investment company connected with the ship builder, as that organisation still had financial commitments. Oceania Cruises subsequently entered into charters for the R ONE, R TWO and R FIVE, introducing them one at a time. In 2006 the company purchased the three ships. In February 2007 private equity

NCL's **Norwegian Star** off Cozumel *(Rick Frendt)*

NCL's **Norwegian Sun** at Ketchikan *(Rick Frendt)*

NCL's **Pride of America** *(Rick Frendt)*

Oceania Cruises' *Insignia* at Dubrovnik *(William Mayes)*

Oceania Cruises' *Marina* off Dikili *(William Mayes)*

Regent's *Seven Seas Mariner* in Venice *(Philip Hall)*

firm Apollo Management acquired a majority stake in the company. Shortly afterwards two new ship orders were announced. When the INSIGNIA returned from her charter to Hapag-Lloyd in spring 2014, she and her two sisters were given a major upgrade to bring them more in line with the new ships. At the time of writing it was expected that an order for two further ships of the MARINA class would be placed with Fincantieri.

Address Suite 308, 8300 North West 33rd Street, Doral, Florida 33122-1940 United States of America

Telephone +1 305 514 2300

Website www.oceaniacruises.com and www.oceaniacruises.co.uk

Area operated Europe, South America and the Caribbean Sea, the Far East and China

INSIGNIA	30277gt	1998	20.0k	DE2	684p	684p	400c	181.0m	25.5m	5.9m	MH
MARINA	66084gt	2011	20.0k	DE2	1250p	1250p	800c	239.3m	32.2m	7.6m	MH
NAUTICA	30277gt	2000	20.0k	DE2	684p	684p	400c	181.0m	25.5m	5.9m	MH
REGATTA	30277gt	1998	20.0k	DE2	684p	684p	400c	181.0m	25.5m	5.9m	MH
RIVIERA	66172gt	2012	20.0k	DE2	1252p	1252p	780c	251.5m	32.2m	7.0m	MH

INSIGNIA was the first of the second generation cruise ships built for Renaissance Cruises by Chantiers de l'Atlantique (yard number H31) at St Nazaire, France as the rather unimaginatively named R ONE. This series of eight ships was decorated in the elegant style of the Edwardian ocean liners. INSIGNIA, christened in Monte Carlo by Virginia Watters, entered service for Oceania Cruises in 2004. The INSIGNIA was chartered to Hapag-Lloyd from spring 2012 for two years as the COLUMBUS 2, but returned to the Oceania fleet in March 2014. IMO 9156462

MARINA was the first of a pair of ships ordered in 2007 from the Fincantieri Shipyard (yard number 6194) at Sestri near Genoa. She was floated out on 26 February 2010 and delivered at the beginning of 2011. She was named in Miami by US chat show host Mary Hart on 5 February. IMO 9438066

NAUTICA was built as the R FIVE, the first member of the second quartet of ships for Renaissance Cruises by Chantiers de l'Atlantique (yard number P31) at St Nazaire, France. She operated for Pullmantur as the BLUE DREAM in 2004, although not officially renamed. NAUTICA began sailing for Oceania Cruises in 2005 and was christened in Istanbul by Miami philanthropist and civic leader Fana Holtz. IMO 9200938

REGATTA was built by Chantiers de l'Atlantique (yard number I31) at St Nazaire, France as the R TWO for Renaissance Cruises. REGATTA entered service for Oceania Cruises in 2003, and was christened in Barcelona by Marcia Del Rio. IMO 9156474

RIVIERA was ordered from Fincantieri in March 2007 and was built at the Sestri yard (yard number 6195) in Genoa. IMO 9438078

REGENT SEVEN SEAS CRUISES

The Company Regent Seven Seas Cruises, formerly Radisson Seven Seas Cruises, was a complicated structure of organisations, partly a joint venture between the US leisure group Carlson (owners of Radisson) and Vlassov (owners of V Ships of Monaco). The company's origins go back to 1992, when Carlson set up a new subsidiary, Diamond Cruise Line, later Radisson Diamond Cruises, to operate the RADISSON DIAMOND. The company later took over Seven Seas Cruises, with its single ship the SONG OF FLOWER, changing its name at that time to Radisson Seven Seas Cruises, and later took on the lease of the PAUL GAUGUIN. The V Ships joint venture began in 1999 with the delivery of the SEVEN SEAS NAVIGATOR. The company was renamed as Regent Seven Seas Cruises in 2006. In 2008 the company was acquired by Apollo Management and placed in its Prestige Cruises division.

Address Suite 100, 8300 NW 33rd Street, Doral, Florida 33122-1940, United States of America

Telephone +1 954 776 6123

Website www.rssc.com

Areas operated Worldwide

SEVEN SEAS MARINER	48075gt	2001	20.0k	DEP2	700p	780p	447c	216.0m	28.8m	7.0m	BS
SEVEN SEAS NAVIGATOR	28803gt	1999	19.5k	D2	490p	542p	324c	170.6m	24.0m	7.3m	BS
SEVEN SEAS VOYAGER	42363gt	2003	20.0k	DEP2	700p	769p	445c	206.5m	28.8m	7.1m	BS

SEVEN SEAS MARINER was built by Chantiers de l'Atlantique (yard number K31) at St Nazaire, France for Radisson Seven Seas Cruises, with a hull based on that of Festival Cruises' MISTRAL. IMO 9210139

SEVEN SEAS NAVIGATOR's hull was built in St Petersburg, Russia by Admiralteyskiy Sudostroitelnyy Zavod (yard number 02510). It was intended that she would be the Ukrainian research vessel AKADEMIK NICOLAY PILYUGIN. Unfinished, the hull was purchased by V-Ships (renamed BLUE SEA) and transferred to the Mariotti shipyard at Genoa for completion as the SEVEN SEAS NAVIGATOR. IMO 9064126

SEVEN SEAS VOYAGER's hull was built by Cantieri Nav. Visentini at Donada, Italy under sub-contract to T. Mariotti of Genoa (yard number MAR001), who completed the construction of the ship. The ship was christened in Monaco in the presence of His Serene Highness Prince Albert II by Barbara Carlson Gage. IMO 9247144

Cruise ship on order

SEVEN SEAS EXPLORER	c67000gt	2016	20.0k	DE2	750p	750p	460c	223.0m	32.0m	7.1m	BS

SEVEN SEAS EXPLORER was ordered from Fincantieri in 2013 and will be built at the Sestri shipyard. Construction commenced in July 2014. IMO 9703150

NYK CRUISES

The Company Nippon Yusen Kaisha (NYK) was formed in 1885 with the merger of the Mitsubishi Mail Steamship Company and Kyodo Unyu Kaisha, creating a fleet of 58 ships. Over the ensuing years the company developed an impressive network of liner services that eventually encompassed the whole world. It was not until 1929, however, that the now familiar twin red stripes on a white background was adopted as the company's new funnel marking. NYK emerged from the Second World War with 37 ships and gradually began to re-establish itself, initially in Japanese domestic service, and from 1950 in international trades, although now in freight rather than passengers. The merger in 1964 with Mitsubishi Shipping Company, created a new NYK Group, owning a total of 87 ships. Four years later the company began to containerise its cargo services, and in 1969 NYK disposed of its coastal and domestic operations to concentrate on its liner shipping business. In 1989 Crystal Cruises was established, and in the same year NYK began operating the expedition ship FRONTIER SPIRIT. NYK today operates a fleet of around 800 ships around the world. The company operates a single ship in the Japanese domestic market.

Address The Landmark Tower Yokohama, 2-1, Minatamirai 2-chome, Nishi-ku, Yokohama 220-8147, Japan

Website www.asukacruise.co.jp

Area operated Japan and worldwide

ASUKA II	50142gt	1990	21.0k	DE2	872p	960p	470c	240.9m	29.6m	7.8m	JP

ASUKA II was the first ship for the newly formed Crystal Cruises. She was built by Mitsubishi Heavy Industries (yard number 2100) at Nagasaki, Japan, as the CRYSTAL HARMONY and was christened by Mary Tyler Moore. She was transferred to parent company NYK in December 2005 as the ASUKA II, to replace the ASUKA, which had been sold. Asuka was the capital city of Japan in the 6th century. IMO 8806204

CRYSTAL CRUISES

The Company Crystal Cruises was established by NYK in 1989 as a luxury cruise operator geared to the US market. It would appear that the increase in capacity created with the arrival of the CRYSTAL SERENITY in 2003 was not matched by the increase in passengers, as the company's first ship, the CRYSTAL HARMONY, was transferred to Crystal's parent company at the end of 2005.

Address 11755 Wiltshire Boulevard, Suite 900, Los Angeles, California 90025, United States of America

Telephone +1 310 785 9300

Website www.crystalcruises.com

Area operated Worldwide

Regent's *Seven Seas Navigator* at St. Maarten *(Rick Frendt)*

Regent's *Seven Seas Voyager* in Istanbul *(William Mayes)*

NYK Cruises' *Asuka II* in Sydney *(Alf Sims)*

Crystal Cruises' **Crystal Serenity** off Monte Carlo *(Rick Frendt)*

Crystal Cruises' **Crystal Symphony** at St Thomas *(Rick Frendt)*

Ocean Adventures' **Eclipse** *(company picture)*

CRYSTAL SERENITY	68870gt	2003	22.0k	DEP2	1080p	1140p	635c	250.0m	32.2m	7.6m	BS
CRYSTAL SYMPHONY	51044gt	1995	22.0k	DE2	940p	940p	545c	238.0m	30.2m	7.6m	BS

CRYSTAL SERENITY was built by Chantiers de l'Atlantique (yard number H32) at St Nazaire, France, and christened by Dame Julie Andrews in Southampton. IMO 9243667

CRYSTAL SYMPHONY was built by Kvaerner Masa Yards (yard number 1323) at Turku, Finland. Her godmother is Angela Lansbury. IMO 9066667

OCEAN ADVENTURES

The Company Ocean Adventures SA is an Ecuador registered company, established in 2001.

Address Avenida Republica de El Salvador N36-84 Naciones Unidas, Edificio Quilate 9th Floor, Quito, Ecuador

Telephone +593 2 2466301 **Fax** +593 2 2463681

Website www.oagalapagos.com

Area operated Galapagos Islands

ECLIPSE	1610gt	1998	12.0k	D2	48p	48p	31c	64.0m	12.5m	3.3m	EC

ECLIPSE was built by Astilleros Construcciones (yard number 176) at Vigo, Spain as the ferry CAMELIA. The hull was launched in 1982 but spent many years uncompleted at the shipyard. Later she is thought to have become the AGEAN SEA II and was acquired by Ocean Adventures in 1998, following which she was converted for cruising and renamed ECLIPSE. IMO 8978954

OCEAN DREAM CRUISE

The Company Ocean Dream Cruise is a Thai registered company.

Address 8/44 Moo 6, North Pattaya Road, Pattaya Nua, Chonburi, 20150 Thailand

Website www.oceandreamcruise.com

Area operated Weekend cruises to Cambodia from Pattaya, Thailand

OCEAN DREAM	17042gt	1972	17.5k	D2	840p	1040p	c	163.3m	22.8m	5.6m	TG

OCEAN DREAM was the first new passenger ship to be bought by the Peninsular & Oriental Steam Navigation Company since the CANBERRA of 1961, and that company's first purpose built cruise ship, although she had not been ordered by P&O, but acquired off the stocks. She was laid down as one of a pair of ships for Kloster's Norwegian Caribbean Cruise Line by Cantieri Navale del Tirreno e Riuniti shipyard (yard number 290) at Riva Trigoso in Italy. Her sister was delivered as the SOUTHWARD (now Caspi Cruises RIO), but due to escalating costs the order for this ship was cancelled. She was to have been named SEAWARD, but was eventually launched for P&O as the SPIRIT OF LONDON. She was initially employed on the US West Coast along with the 1954-built ARCADIA. When P&O acquired Princess Cruises in 1974, the SPIRIT OF LONDON was transferred to that operation and renamed SUN PRINCESS. By 1989 she was the baby of the fleet and no longer fitted in with the larger ships, so was sold to Premier Cruise Line who renamed her STARSHIP MAJESTIC. In 1995 she was chartered to CTC Lines for cruising from the UK and from Australia, and renamed SOUTHERN CROSS. CTC Lines ceased trading in 1997 and the ship was sold to Festival Cruises, becoming the FLAMENCO. After Festival failed in 2004, she was quickly acquired by Elysian Cruises (Ravenscroft Shipping) and renamed NEW FLAMENCO. She commenced a charter with Travelplan in the spring of 2004. In 2007 she was acquired by Club Cruise, renamed FLAMENCO I, and fixed on a charter for use as an accommodation ship for miners in New Caledonia. In November 2008 Club Cruise defaulted on its loans and subsequently the ship was sold at auction in Singapore for US$ 3.4 million, against the $ 26 million that Club Cruise paid for the ship two years earlier. She did not enter service with her new owner and remained in lay up at Port Klang until sold in October 2010 for breaking at Alang. However, due to a dispute between the owners and the breakers she remains at Port Klang. Late in 2011 she was purchased by Chinese interests and renamed OCEAN DREAM. She currently operates occasional short cruises to Cambodia. IMO 7211517

OCEAN STAR CRUISES

The Company Ocean Star Cruises is a trading name of Corporacion de Cruceros Nacionales SA de CV, a company created in 2010 by the Mexican Government and private investors to promote tourism in Mexico. The ship does not appear to be operating at the time of writing.

Address Tamarindos 100, Bosque de Alisios 102, Col Bosque de las Lomas, 05120 Mexico City, Mexico

Telephone +52 55 5081 6020

Website www.oceanstar.com.mx

Area operated Mexico (not currently operating)

OCEAN STAR PACIFIC	23149gt	1971	21.0k	D2	1040p	1160p	400c	193.3m	24.0m	6.7m	PA

OCEAN STAR PACIFIC was the second ship in the founding fleet of the new Royal Caribbean Cruise Line when delivered. She was built by Wartsila (yard number 393) in Helsinki, Finland as the NORDIC PRINCE for year-round service in the Caribbean Sea. In 1980 she returned to her builder to have a new 26m mid section inserted, increasing her passenger capacity from 714 to 1194. By 1994 she had served out her useful life with Royal Caribbean and was sold to Airtours, one of the UK's largest package holiday operators. She was placed into service as the CAROUSEL under the Sun Cruises banner. Airtours pulled out of cruising in late 2004 and Louis Cruise Lines acquired the ship and renamed her AQUAMARINE. In 2007 she was chartered to Transocean Tours and operated as the ARIELLE. Transocean Tours used this ship to operate a number of cruises from the UK in 2007. In 2008 Transocean Tours had the use of the MARCO POLO so did not need the ARIELLE, which returned to Louis and reverted to her previous name, AQUAMARINE. She ran on short cruises from Piraeus in the summer, but in late 2009 inaugurated Louis Cruise Lines' new (short-lived) Indian programme, based at Kochi. In 2010 she was sold to Corporacion de Cruceros (trading as Ocean Star Cruises) of Mexico and renamed OCEAN STAR PACIFIC. Following a major refit, she entered service on 10 April 2011 and, five days later, was disabled by an engine room fire. She was repaired and put back into service. IMO 7027411

OCEANWIDE EXPEDITIONS

The Company Oceanwide Expeditions is a Netherlands based operator of expedition cruises to the Polar Regions. The company also markets space on other ships.

Address Bellamypark 9, 4381 CG Vlissingen, The Netherlands

Telephone +31 118 410 410

Website www.oceanwide-expeditions.com

Area operated Arctic and Antarctic regions and the Atlantic islands

ORTELIUS	4575gt	1989	14.3k	D1	106p	116p	47c	91.2m	17.2m	5.3m	CY
PLANCIUS	3434gt	1976	10.0k	DE3	106p	116p	45c	89.3m	14.4m	4.9m	NL

ORTELIUS was built by Stocznia im. Komuny Paryskiej (yard number B961/03) at Gdynia, Poland for Glavmorneft, as one of six similar vessels. The MARINA TSVETAYEVA is owned by Morskaya Kompaniya Sakhalin-Kurily, and is thought to operate for that company when not in service with Poseidon, for whom she is marketed as the MARINA SVETAEVA. The ship was also marketed by Aurora Expeditions from 2007 until about 2010. The ship was sold to Oceanwide Expeditions in September 2011 and entered service as the ORTELIUS after a major refit. Abraham Ortelius (1527-1598) was a Flemish cartographer and geographer and is generally thought to have produced the first world atlas. IMO 8509181

PLANCIUS was built as the TYDEMAN, an oceanographic research vessel for the Royal Dutch Navy by the De Mervede shipyard (yard number 612) at Hardinxveld, in the Netherlands. She was decommissioned in 2004, purchased by Oceanwide Expeditions in 2006 and converted for adventure cruising. Her transformation was completed by October 2009. Petrus Plancius (1552-1622) was a Dutch astronomer and cartographer. IMO 7432044

ONE OCEAN EXPEDITIONS

The Company One Ocean Expeditions is a Canadian business.

Telephone +351 962 721 836

Website www.oneoceanexpeditions.com

Area operated Arctic, Antarctic, Norway and Canada

AKADEMIK IOFFE	6450gt	1989	14.5k	D2	96p	96p	63c	117.0m	18.3m	6.1m	RU
AKADEMIK SERGEY VAVILOV	6344gt	1988	14.5k	D2	92p	92p	63c	117.0m	18.3m	6.1m	RU

AKADEMIK IOFFE was, until recently, operated by Peregrine Adventures under the marketing name PEREGRINE MARINER. She is owned by the Shirskov Oceanological Institute of Kaliningrad, and was built by the Hollming Shipyard (yard number 266) at Rauma, Finland for the Russian Academy of Sciences. The ship was designed for research into long distance submarine acoustics. She was transferred to her current owner in 1993. In 1995 she operated for Marine Expeditions under the marketing name MARINE ADVENTURER, but was not officially renamed. From 2011 she operated for One Ocean Expeditions and is sometimes marketed as the ONE OCEAN NAVIGATOR. Abraham Ioffe (1880-1960) was a nuclear physicist with the Russian Academy of Sciences. IMO 8507731

AKADEMIK SERGEY VAVILOV was built by the Hollming Shipyard (yard number 265) at Rauma, Finland for the Russian Academy of Sciences. She was operated by Peregrine Tours under the marketing name PEREGRINE VOYAGER, although not officially renamed. She was transferred to the Shirskov Oceanological Institute of Kaliningrad in 1993. Her owners, under the trading style Poseidon Arctic Expeditions, may also operate the ship. She is currently operating for One Ocean Expeditions under the marketing name ONE OCEAN VOYAGER. Sergey Vavilov was a Russian botanist who lived from 1887 to 1943. IMO 8507729

PACIFIC BLUE CRUISES

The Company Pacific Blue Cruises Ltd is a company formed in 2011, which previously traded as Vanuatu Cruises.

Address PO Box 709, Port Vila, Vanuatu

Website www.vanuatu.travel.com

Area operated Vanuatu

LYCIANDA	‡385gt	1984	12.0k	D2	44p	60p	16c	39.5m	7.8m	1.8m	FJ

LYCIANDA was built for Blue Lagoon Cruises by Industrial & Marine Engineering (yard number 31) at Suva, Fiji. This ship was acquired by her current owner in 2011. IMO 8401987

PANDAW RIVER CRUISES

The Company The Irrawaddy Flotilla Company was established by Scottish merchants in 1865. By the 1920s the company was running more than 650 vessels on the rivers of Burma and had become the largest privately owned fleet of ships in the world. In 1942 the entire fleet was scuttled as an act of denial when the Japanese invaded the country. The company became operational again at the end of the Second World War, but in 1948 after the British had left Burma the company handed over its fleet to the Inland Water Transport Board. The Irrawaddy Flotilla Company name was revived in 1995 by historian Paul Strachan when he restored the 1947-built PANDAW. Pandaw River Cruises took the concept further and now operate five new ships on the rivers of Myanmar, Borneo, Vietnam and Cambodia. The ships are in the style of classic colonial steamers. Six smaller ships with a passenger capacity of 20 have recently been introduced.

Address 7500 Beach Road 14-314/315 The Plaza, Singapore 199591

Telephone +44 203 287 6113 (UK sales office)

Website www.pandaw.com

Area operated Myanmar, Borneo, Vietnam and Cambodia

BASSAC PANDAW	gt	2012	D2	10.0k	60p	60p	28c	50.9m	10.2m	1.5m	MM
INDOCHINE PANDAW	gt	2008	D2	10.0k	60p	60p	28c	55.0m	10.0m	0.9m	VN

Ocean Star Cruises' ***Ocean Star Pacific*** at Curacao *(Rick Frendt)*

Pacific Blue Cruises' ***Lycianda*** at Port Vila *(David Robinson)*

Pandaw River Cruises' ***Orient Pandaw*** *(company picture)*

MEEKONG PANDAW	gt	2003	D2	10.0k	64p	64p	28c	60.0m	11.0m	1.5m	MM
ORIENT PANDAW	gt	2008	D2	10.0k	60p	60p	28c	55.0m	10.0m	0.9m	VN
PANDAW II	gt	2001	D2	10.0k	48p	48p	28c	55.0m	10.0m	0.9m	MM
TONLE PANDAW	gt	2002	D2	10.0k	66p	66p	28c	55.0m	10.0m	0.9m	MM

INDOCHINE PANDAW and **ORIENT PANDAW** were built in Saigon. The other ships were built locally in Myanmar.

PASSAT KREUZFAHRTEN

The Company Passat Kreuzfahrten was established in 2011 and is based in Hamburg. The company ceased trading in September 2014 after the DELPHIN's owner took the ship back for its own use, thought to be as an accommodation vessel in India.

Address Ueberseeallee 3, 20457 Hamburg, Germany

Website www.passatkrezfahrten.de

Area operated

| DELPHIN | 16214gt | 1975 | 21.0k | D2 | 474p | 554p | 230c | 156.3m | 21.8m | 6.2m | BS |

DELPHIN was built by the Wartsila Shipyard (yard number 1212) at Turku in Finland as the BYELORUSSIYA for the Black Sea Shipping Company of the Soviet Union. On the break-up of the Eastern Bloc the company became Ukrainian. In October 1992 she was seriously damaged when she fell over in a dry dock in Singapore. She was towed to Bremerhaven, where she arrived in May 1993. In December of that year she was renamed KAZAKHSTAN II, but her operators faced severe financial difficulties resulting in the arrest of ships and the eventual collapse of the company. In 1995 she was sold to Lady Lou Shipping, a Cypriot registered but German controlled company. Her ownership was passed to Dolphin Maritime in 1998, another company within the same group and she was renamed DELPHIN. She operated for Hansa Kreuzfahrten on year round charter, in the Caribbean in winter, the Mediterranean and Atlantic Isles in the shoulder seasons and in Northern Europe and Scandinavia in summer. The ship was reported to have been sold to an unknown Caribbean based owner (possibly Royal Zante Cruises) in late 2006, but this never happened. Hansa Kreuzfahrten filed for bankruptcy in late 2010 and the ship was arrested in Venice. After more than a year laid up the ship was bought by Vishal Cruises of Mauritius and chartered to the new Passat Kreuzfahrten. IMO 7347536

PAUL GAUGUIN CRUISES

The Company Paul Gauguin Shipping, the owner of the PAUL GAUGUIN, had a long term arrangement with Regent Seven Seas Cruises to market the ship. That arrangement came to an end in 2010 and Paul Gauguin Cruises was sold by Grand Circle Corporation of Boston to Pacific Beachcomber, an operator of resorts in French Polynesia.

Address 11100 Main Street, Suite 300, Bellevue, WA 98004, United States of America

Telephone +1 425 440 6171 **Fax** +1 425 440 6186

Website www.pgcruises.com

Area operated French Polynesia and the South Pacific, South East Asia and Europe

| PAUL GAUGUIN | 19170gt | 1997 | 18.0k | DE2 | 320p | 332p | 217c | 156.0m | 22.0m | 5.2m | BS |
| TERE MOANA | 3504gt | 1998 | 14.0k | D2 | 88p | 88p | 66c | 100.3m | 13.1m | 3.0m | BS |

PAUL GAUGUIN was built by Chantiers de l'Atlantique (yard number G31) at St Nazaire, France for Services et Transports – Tahiti. She was to have been named TAHITI NUI, but was built with her current name. She was christened by Carole Poylo, in the presence of Maria Gauguin, granddaughter of the famous painter. Initially hotel services were to be provided by Radisson Seven Seas Cruises, but the company then operated the ship under lease. The ship was sold to a consortium incorporating the respective owners of Grand Circle Travel and Vantage Travel (both based in Boston, Massachusetts) in 2005, but the ship continued to be operated by RSSC in conjunction with that organization on her French Polynesian itineraries until 2010. She continues to cruise in the same area for her new owners. Paul Gauguin (1848-1903) was one of the leading French painters of the post impressionist period. From 1891 until his death he lived in French Polynesia. IMO 9111319

TERE MOANA, the sleek, yacht-like luxury cruise ship was built by Alstom Leroux Naval (yard number

625) at St Malo, France for Compagnie des Isles du Ponant as the LE LEVANT, named after one of the islands off the coast of Provence, France. She has undertaken a number of charters, including one to Classic Cruises International. She began to operate for Paul Gauguin Cruises in 2012 as the TERE MOANA. IMO 9159830

PHOENIX REISEN

The Company Phoenix Reisen is a German privately owned tour and travel company, founded by Johannes Zurnieden. Until withdrawn in November 2008, the company's longest serving ship was the MAXIM GORKIY. The company also operated the ALEXANDER VON HUMBOLDT (now MINERVA) and the ALEXANDER VON HUMBOLDT II (now VOYAGER) on charter for a number of years.

Address Pfalzer Strasse 14, 53111 Bonn, Germany

Telephone +49 228 9260 0

Website www.phoenixreisen.com

Area operated Europe and South America and world cruises

ALBATROS	28518gt	1973	18.5k	D2	850p	850p	340c	205.5m	25.2m	7.5m	BS
AMADEA	29008gt	1991	18.0k	D2	600p	600p	250c	192.8m	24.7m	6.6m	BS
ARTANIA	44656gt	1984	18.0k	D2	1200p	1200p	420c	230.6m	29.2m	7.8m	BM

ALBATROS has had a long and varied career. She was built by Wartsila (yard number 397) at Helsinki, Finland as the ROYAL VIKING SEA, the final member of the trio of luxurious first generation vessels for the new Royal Viking Line. She was lengthened in 1983 in Bremerhaven, but just a year later both she and her owners were acquired by Kloster Cruise (Norwegian Cruise Line). Royal Viking Line continued to operate as a separate entity for some time. In 1991 the ship was transferred within the group to Royal Cruise Line and renamed ROYAL ODYSSEY. Later, while NCL was experiencing financial difficulties, the ship was sold to Actinor and chartered back. In 1997 she was renamed NORWEGIAN STAR and chartered to a new company, Norwegian Capricorn Line, in which Norwegian Cruise Line had an interest. Norwegian Capricorn Line used the ship for cruises from Australia, but was not entirely successful. She passed to Star Holdings in 1999, and in 2001 she was operated by Star Cruises as the NORWEGIAN STAR 1, but did not stay in the Far East for long as, following a charter to Crown Investments for cruising on the Chinese coast, she moved to the Mediterranean Sea as the CROWN, serving the Spanish market. By now Club Cruise of the Netherlands owned her. Phoenix Reisen managed to charter the ship at relatively short notice in 2004 to replace the previous ALBATROS, which had suffered mechanical failure and was considered beyond economic repair. From spring 2004 she has sailed as the ALBATROS. Club Cruise of The Netherlands acquired her in 2006, on the strength of the Phoenix Reisen charter. Club Cruise went into administration in late 2008, but Phoenix Reisen now appears to own the ship through one of its group companies. IMO 7304314

AMADEA was built by Mitsubishi Heavy Industries (yard number 2050) at Nagasaki, Japan as the ASUKA for operation by NYK in the deluxe sector of the Japanese cruise market. The ASUKA became Phoenix Reisen's fourth ship, AMADEA, in March 2006 when she was replaced in the NYK fleet by the CRYSTAL HARMONY (renamed ASUKA II) in December 2005. The AMADEA is managed by V-Ships. IMO 8913162

ARTANIA was the first purpose built cruise ship to be ordered by the P&O Group. She was built by Wartsila (yard number 464) at Helsinki, Finland as the ROYAL PRINCESS and delivered in late 1984. Initially used on US based itineraries for Princess Cruises, she also undertook trips around South America, and in later years spent the summer in European waters. In a major redeployment within the British division of Carnival she was transferred to P&O Cruises in spring 2005 as the ARTEMIS. She cruised from Southampton for much of the year, but in winter incorporated a long voyage to exotic destinations into her itinerary. In the autumn of 2009 she was sold to a German company, formed to acquire the ship for operation by Phoenix Reisen as the ARTANIA. She entered service with Phoenix Reisen in May 2011 and is managed by V-Ships of Monaco. The name Artania is thought to relate to a mythical kingdom in ancient Russia. The ARTANIA is scheduled to be re-engined in the autumn of 2014. IMO 8201480

Passat Kreuzfahrten's *Delphin* at Pembroke Dock *(David Trevor-Jones)*

Paul Gauguin Cruises' *Paul Gauguin* in Tahiti *(Rick Frendt)*

Paul Gauguin Cruises' *Tere Moana* in Istanbul *(William Mayes)*

Phoenix Reisen's *Albatros* (Kelvin Holmes)

Phoenix Reisen's *Amadea* off Helgoland (William Mayes)

Phoenix Reisen's *Artania* off Bremerhaven (William Mayes)

PLANTOURS & PARTNER

The Company Plantours and Partner GmbH is a German cruise operator, long-term charterer of the VISTAMAR, and operator of European river cruises. In late 2006 Venice-based Ligabue acquired the company. The charter of the VISTAMAR ended in early 2012 and from June 2012 the company has operated the former C. COLUMBUS, trading as the HAMBURG.

Address Obernstrasse 76, D28195 Bremen, Germany

Telephone +49 421 173690 **Fax** +49 421 1736935

Website www.plantours-partner.de

Area operated Amazon, Western Europe, Scandinavia, Mediterranean, round Africa

HAMBURG	15067gt	1997	18.5k	D2	420p	420p	170c	145.0m	21.5m	5.1m	BS

HAMBURG was built as the C. COLUMBUS at the Wismar, Germany yard of MTW Schiffswerft (yard number 451) for Columbus Conti 1 Kreuzfahrt for operation by Hapag-Lloyd. She cruised in Northern Europe, the Great Lakes and Round the World in 2007. Hapag-Lloyd's charter, which was due to run until 2013, was terminated early (Hapag-Lloyd replaced her with Oceania's INSIGNIA, renamed COLUMBUS 2) and the ship was quickly chartered by Plantours & Partner to operate from 2012 as the HAMBURG. IMO 9138329

PLEIN CAP CROISIERES

The Company Plein Cap Croisieres is a trading style of French company, Marina Cruises, founded in 1997. The company has operated the ADRIANA, latterly the ADRIANA III for a number of years, but in 2011 operated the VISTAMAR for two short seasons and in 2012 was expected to operate the ship on a full time basis. However, the ship was sold to Abou Merhi Lines of Beirut. In 2014 the company is not operating its own ship, but is offering cruises on two German ships, the HAMBURG and the FTI BERLIN.

Address 251 route de La Colle, 06270 Villeneuve Loubet, France

Telephone +33 4 9320 2120 **Fax** +33 4 9373 7001

Website www.plein-cap.com

Area operated Mediterranean, Red Sea, Indian Ocean, Black Sea and Scandinavia

POLAR QUEST EXPEDITIONS

The Company Polar Quest is a Swedish operator of expedition cruises. In addition to the ships listed here, the company markets space on a large number of major polar exploration ships.

Address Stora Nygatan 29, PO Box 180, 40123 Gothenburg, Sweden

Telephone +46 31 333 1730 **Fax** +46 31 333 1731

Website www.polar-quest.com

Area operated with these ships, Spitzbergen

QUEST	1268gt	1992	13.0k	D1	52p	60p	20c	49.6m	11.0m	3.4m	BS
STOCKHOLM	383gt	1953	10.5k	D1	12p	12p	c	37.8m	8.8m	3.2m	SE

QUEST For details see under Noble Caledonia.

STOCKHOLM was built by Helsingborgs Varf AB at Helsingborg for SNMA as the STOCKHOLM. She was renamed STOCKHOLM AV GOTEBORG in 1997 and converted for cruising in 1999 with just six cabins, all with private facilities. She is marketed as the STOCKHOLM. IMO 8226612

POMOR-TUR

The Company Pomor-Tur is a Russian travel and tour operator. The company was founded in 1994 and has operated the NIKOLAI GOGOL on the Dvina River since 1999.

Address ul Resurrection 99, Archangel, 163071 Russia

Telephone +7 8182 203320 **Fax** +7 8182 202720

Website www.pomor-tur.ru

Area operated River cruises from Archangel

NIKOLAI GOGOL		gt	1911	10.0k		53p	53p	c	70.7m	14.0m	1.4m	RU

NIKOLAI GOGOL was built by Sormovskoy at Nizhny Novgorod in 1911 for the Northern Shipping Company as a paddle steamer. She was completely renovated between 1994 and 1996 and has recently undergone a further major refit. She has a 360hp triple expansion engine.

PONANT CRUISES

The Company Ponant Cruises (formerly Compagnie des Iles du Ponant) was established in 1988 by Phillipe Videau and others, and raised the required capital by subscription to purchase and operate the luxury yacht LE PONANT. The company also became a tour agency, but later bought out the other investors to own the ship outright. The purchase of LE LEVANT was financed in the same way and that ship currently has 280 shareholders. In 2003, in conjunction with French tour operator Tapis Rouge Croisieres, the SONG OF FLOWER was acquired from Radisson Seven Seas Cruises and renamed LE DIAMANT. She is operated by Compagnie des Iles du Diamant, a joint venture between 'Ponant' and Tapis Rouge. French container shipping line CMA-CGM was the majority shareholder in the company, holding 70% of the stock. The Iles du Ponant are a group of islands off the northern and western coasts of Brittany, France. Bridgepoint Capital, a UK venture capital group acquired Ponant Cruises in September 2012.

Address 408 Avenue du Prado, F13008 Marseilles, France

Telephone +33 488 666400

Website www.ponant.com

Area operated Worldwide

L'AUSTRAL	10944gt	2011	16.0k	DE2	264p	264p	139c	142.0m	18.0m	4.6m	FR
LE BOREAL	10944gt	2010	16.0k	DE2	264p	264p	139c	142.0m	18.0m	4.6m	FR
LE PONANT	1189gt	1991	14.0k	SD1	56p	64p	32c	84.3m	11.9m	4.0m	FR
LE SOLEAL	10992gt	2013	16.0k	DE2	264p	264p	139c	142.1m	18.0m	4.7m	FR

L'AUSTRAL was built by Fincantieri (yard number 6193) at Ancona, Italy. She was originally planned for delivery in October 2010, but the owner delayed this until March 2011. IMO 9502518

LE BOREAL is the lead ship in a pair (later a quartet) of modern, sleek, yacht-like vessels built by Fincantieri (yard number 6192) at Ancona, Italy. She was delivered in June 2010. IMO 9502506

LE PONANT was built by Societe Francaise Construction Navales (yard number 863) at Villeneuv-la-Garenne, France. In early April 2008 pirates seized the ship and its crew of 30 off the coast of Somalia as the vessel was re-positioning to the Mediterranean Sea without passengers. The ship and crew were released a week later after a ransom was thought to have been paid. The ship's usual areas of operation are the Mediterranean Sea and the Indian Ocean. IMO 8914219

LE SOLEAL is the third ship in the LE BOREAL series built by Fincantieri (yard number 6229) at Ancona. IMO 9641675

Cruise ship on order

LE LYRIAL	10992gt	2015	16.0k	DE2	244p	244p	139c	142.1m	18.0m	4.7m	FR

LE LYRIAL is on order from Fincantieri (yard number 6230) at Ancona. IMO 9704130

PORTUSCALE CRUISES

The Company Portuscale Cruises is a new Portuguese company formed to acquire and operate four ships from the administration of Classic International Cruises. All of Classic's ships were under arrest in the autumn of 2012 and on 20 December the company was put into liquidation. Portuscale acquired four of the five ships and are expected to follow the pattern set by Classic International Cruises and both operate their own programme and charter ships out to other operators. A total of more that €20 million has been invested in the refurbishment of the ships by Portuscale Cruises, a part of the leisure and industrial portfolio of Rui Alegre. All of the ships are registered in Madeira.

Address Rua Ivens 44, 3 Andar, 1200-227 Lisbon, Portugal

Plantours & Partner's **Hamburg** at Alesund *(William Mayes)*

Ponant Cruises' **L'Austral** off Rovinj, Croatia *(William Mayes)*

Ponant Cruises' **Le Ponant** at Monte Carlo *(Rick Frendt)*

Portuscale Cruises' *Funchal* off Falmouth *(William Mayes)*

Portuscale Cruises' *Azores* *(company picture)*

Portuscale Cruises' *Porto* in Lisbon *(Bill Lawes)*

Telephone +351 213 463 015 **Fax** +351210 496 058

Website www.portuscalecruises.pt

Area operated Worldwide, often under charter

AZORES	16144gt	1948	16.5k	D2	552p	659p	185c	160.0m	21.0m	7.6m	PT
FUNCHAL	9563gt	1961	17.0k	D2	469p	598p	155c	152.7m	19.0m	6.3m	PT
LISBOA	16531gt	1955	17.0k	D2	568p	707p	240c	162.4m	21.3m	7.6m	PT
PORTO	5888gt	1965	16.0k	D2	320p	376p	150c	116.8m	16.5m	5.3m	PT

AZORES was built as the transatlantic liner STOCKHOLM for Swedish America Line by the Gotaverken shipyard (yard number 611) in Gothenburg, Sweden. In 1956, while on her regular service between Gothenburg and New York, she famously collided with and sank the Italia Line flagship ANDREA DORIA. After repair by the Bethlehem Steel shipyard in Brooklyn the STOCKHOLM re-entered service on her Atlantic route. In 1960 Swedish America Line sold her to VEB Deutsche Seereederei for use by the East German Free Trades Union organisation, which renamed her VOLKERFREUNDSCHAFT. She operated cruises for East German workers until sold on in 1985 to Neptunus Rex Enterprises of Panama. She was renamed VOLKER and laid up at Southampton. She became the FRIDTJOF NANSEN in late 1986 and was moved to Oslo for use as a refugee accommodation ship. Star Lauro acquired the ship in 1989 and intended to have her refurbished and renamed SURRIENTO. In the event, she was laid up in Genoa, renamed ITALIA I and later sold to Nina Compagnia di Navigazione for whom the refit was eventually completed, transforming her appearance. She was then renamed ITALIA PRIMA and later operated cruises from Havana, Cuba as the VALTUR PRIMA. From 2001 she was laid up at Havana, until chartered by Festival Cruises in late 2003 and renamed CARIBE, but Festival collapsed shortly afterwards and the ship remained unused until taken on a ten-year bareboat charter by Classic International Cruises in 2004 and renamed ATHENA after a refit in Lisbon. She was to have replaced the PRINCESS DANAE, allowing that ship to go for an extended overhaul, but the amount of work required to bring her up to standard was greater than expected, thus delaying her entry into service. Following her refit she operated two cruises under charter in the German market. She then operated for part of the year for British travel company, Travelscope, until that arrangement was abruptly terminated in March 2007. Travelscope subsequently collapsed in early 2008. The ATHENA was due to spend the summer of 2009 with Mediterranean Classic Cruises in the Eastern Mediterranean, but she was instead chartered to Phoenix Reisen as a temporary replacement for the ALEXANDER VON HUMBOLDT, which had been arrested. The ATHENA then headed back to Australia for another season based there for Classic International. In 2010 she operated Page & Moy's last cruises. During the summer of 2011 the ATHENA sailed from Gothenburg, Sweden, and in the winter of 2011/12 she returned to Australia with a line voyage each way (from Civitavecchia, returning to Portsmouth) and cruises from Fremantle and Adelaide. After a major refit in Marseille, in 2014 she was chartered by Portuscale to Ambiente Kreuzfahrten, but the season was not successful and the charter was terminated early. From January 2015 she joins the Cruise & Maritime Voyages fleet on charter. IMO 5383304

FUNCHAL was the last of the Portuguese liners, and arguably the most attractive. She was built in Denmark, at the Helsingor Shipyard (yard number 353) for Empressa Insulana de Navegacao of Lisbon, a mini liner, for the almost local service from Lisbon to Madeira, the Azores and the Canary Islands. As built she had two Parsons steam turbines, which gave her a service speed of 20 knots. She was occasionally used as the Portuguese Presidential Yacht, and undertook voyages in that role as far afield as Brazil. She suffered recurring engine problems and in 1972 her machinery was replaced by diesel engines during a major refit in Amsterdam. Her owner, along with the other Portuguese liner operators, faced severe financial crisis and was merged in 1974 with Companhia Colonial to form Companhia Portuguesa de Transportes Maritimos. By now, the FUNCHAL was used almost exclusively for cruising and undertook a number of charters. Her owner was wound up in 1985 and the FUNCHAL was sold to Great Warwick of Panama, managed by Arcalia Shipping. She was subsequently operated by Arcalia Shipping under its own name. In late 2007 and early 2009 the ship underwent a phased major refit in order to enable her to carry on sailing beyond 2010. Her final upgrade began during the winter of 2010/11 and was not completed until March 2012. The FUNCHAL had been earmarked as the ship for Metropolis Tur for 2011, but that company took the PRINCESS DAPHNE instead. Portuscale completed the refit and the FUNCHAL is now operated in the Portuguese, British and Swedish markets by the company. Funchal is the capital of the Portuguese island of Madeira. IMO 5124162

LISBOA began life as the Port Line cargo ship, PORT MELBOURNE, built by Harland & Wolff (yard number 1483) at Belfast, Northern Ireland, for the company's liner service from London to Australia. By 1971 Port Line was owned by Cunard Line, so when the latter company was acquired by Trafalgar House Investments, the less profitable routes, including that operated by the PORT MELBOURNE, were discontinued. She was sold along with her sister ship, the PORT SYDNEY, to Greek ship owner J C Karras. The PORT MELBOURNE was renamed THERISOS EXPRESS and was earmarked for conversion into a car ferry. That project never materialised and she was eventually renamed DANAE and converted into a luxury cruise ship. She began her new career in 1977, and two years later was chartered to Costa Line, along with her sister, now named DAPHNE. In 1984 Costa Line purchased the ships. In 1990 the sisters were transferred to a joint venture company, Prestige Cruises, in which Costa had a 50% stake. Costa later regained full control, but in 1991, while undergoing a refit the ship caught fire and was subsequently declared a constructive total loss due to the damage caused by smoke, and water from the ship's sprinklers. Renamed ANAR, she was towed to Piraeus, where she was fully refurbished under the name STARLIGHT PRINCESS. She did not operate under that name, but was chartered to the Swedish Baltic Line as the BALTICA. She subsequently undertook further charters to Northern European operators before being sold to Waybell Cruises in 1996 for use by Classic International Cruises as the PRINCESS DANAE. She was completely refitted at that time. During 2006 the ship went through a major refurbishment. She operated a series of cruises for Travelscope in the summer of 2007. During 2011/12 she was operated by the French company NDS Voyages, an associate of Classic International. As LISBOA for Portuscale, she has not yet secured any charters but had been expected to operate in the French market. IMO 5282483

PORTO was built by Brodogradiliste Uljanik (yard number 248) at Pula, in what was then Yugoslavia, as the ISTRA for Jadrolinija. She operated initially on a 14-day itinerary from Venice to the far Eastern Mediterranean. She was sold to Caravella Shipping of the Ukraine in 1991 and renamed as the ASTRA. In 1996 she passed to Goring Shipping, another Ukraine owner, who renamed her ASTRA I. Constellation Cruise Holdings, a company within the Arcalia Shipping group, acquired her in 1999 and renamed her ARION for use by Classic International Cruises. She underwent a major reconstruction in Lisbon in 2000, costing some $15 million. ARION operated a number of Adriatic and Black Sea cruises for Classic International Cruises in 2011. The ship was renamed PORTO on acquisition by Portuscale Cruises. IMO 6419057

POSEIDON ARCTIC VOYAGES

The Company Poseidon Arctic Voyages is a British expedition cruise company. The company also sells space on other major expedition ships such as the SEA EXPLORER in 2014/2015.

Address 9 Perseverance Works, Kingsland Road, London E2 8DD

Telephone +44 870 068 9142 **Fax** +44 870 068 8265

Website www.northpolevoyages.com

Area operated Antarctic and Arctic, Kamchatka and Sakhalin

50 LET POBEDY	23439gt	2007	21.4k	NST3	128p	128p	140c	159.6m	28.0m	11.0m	RU
SEA SPIRIT	4200gt	1991	14.5k	D2	112p	112p	94c	90.4m	15.3m	4.0m	BS

50 LET POBEDY For details see under Quark Expeditions (TUI).

SEA SPIRIT was built at the Italian Marina di Carrara yard of Nuovi Cantieri Apuania (yard number 1144) as the RENAISSANCE FIVE for Renaissance Cruises. Sold in 1997 to Sun Viva, she was renamed as the SUN VIVA. When Star Cruises acquired that company in 2000 she became the MEGASTAR SAGITTARIUS, but was quickly sold to Cruise West and renamed SPIRIT OF OCEANUS. In 2010 this ship began a unique world cruise which was to have lasted for 335 days. The tour was terminated early and the ship was sold to Clipper Group, who renamed her SEA SPIRIT and almost immediately chartered her to Quark Expeditions. The ship appears to be operating for Poseidon from October 2015. IMO 8802868

QUASAR EXPEDITIONS

The Company Quasar Nautica has been operating cruise yachts in the Galapagos Islands since the mid 1980's. The company also operates the 18-passenger GRACE.

Address Jose Jusseiu N41-28y, Alonso de Torres, Quito, Ecuador

Telephone +593 2 244 6996 **Fax** +593 2 225 9305

Website www.galapagosexpeditions.com

Area operated Galapagos Islands

EVOLUTION	654gt	1970	10.0k	D1	32p	32p	18c	58.5m	8.9m	3.2m	EC

EVOLUTION was built by KK Kanasashi Kosen (yard number 986) at Shimitzu, Japan as the fishing vessel WAKACHIBA MARU. In 1980 she became the YUWA MARU and was converted into the cruise ship EVOLUTION in 2004. IMO 7122326

REAL JOURNEYS

The Company Real Journeys is a New Zealand tour operator and cruise ship owner, founded in the early 1950's by Les and Olive Hutchins. Real journeys also owns and operates the 1912-built coal-fired steamer TSS EARNSHAW on Lake Wakapitu, and the 12-berth FRIENDSHIP. The ships listed here were previously operated by Fiordland Travel, a business acquired by Real Journeys in 1966.

Address PO Box 1, Corner Town Centre and Mokonui Streets, Te Anua 9640, New Zealand

Telephone +64 3 249 6000

Website www.realjourneys.co.nz

Area operated The fjords of New Zealand

FIORDLAND NAVIGATOR	693gt	2001	11.0k	D1	52p	70p	9c	38.2m	10.0m	m	NZ
MILFORD MARINER	693gt	2000	11.0k	D2	60p	60p	10c	38.2m	10.0m	m	NZ
MILFORD WANDERER	258gt	1992	9.5k	D1	61p	61p	5c	28.5m	8.4m	m	NZ

All three ships were built by J K Stevenson Ltd at Invercargill, New Zealand. IMO 8975641, 8975653 and 8975665

RESIDENSEA

The Company Residensea is the company formed to operate THE WORLD. The concept for THE WORLD, the first luxury apartment ship, was that of Knut Kloster Jr, son of the founder of Kloster Cruise (now Norwegian Cruise Line). The original plans were for a ship of twice the size of THE WORLD, but these were scaled back before construction once it became apparent that it would be difficult to sell on the scale originally envisaged. Some apartments are available for rent on a cruise basis.

Address 14471 Miramar Parkway, Suite 401, Miramar, Florida 33027, United States of America

Telephone +1 954 416 3644 **Fax** +1 954 431 7151

Website www.aboardtheworld.com

Area operated Worldwide

THE WORLD	43188gt	2002	19.0k	D2	330p	657p	250c	196.4m	29.2m	6.9m	BS

THE WORLD is one of that select number of ships where the hull was built in one yard and the ship completed elsewhere. The hull was constructed at Bruce's Shipyard (yard number 247) in Landskrona, Sweden and towed to the Fosen Yard at Rissa, Norway for completion. The ship was originally to have been about 80,000 tons, but insufficient interest had been generated by a crucial stage in the planning, so the size was scaled back. The ship features 106 two- and three-bedroom apartments, 19 one- and two-bedroom studio apartments and 40 studios. IMO 9219331

RIVAGES DU MONDE

The Company Rivages du Monde is a French travel and tour operator, specialising in cruises and founded in 2001. The company will be operating St Lawrence cruises under its own name and Mediterranean cruises under the Taaj Croisieres name, a company that Rivages du Monde acquired in April 2014. However, Taaj Croisieres was put into liquidation on 29 July 2014.

Address 29 rue des Pyramides, 75001 Paris, France

Telephone +33 1 58 36 08 36

Website www.rivagesdumonde.fr

Residensea's *The World* at Split *(Martin Grant)*

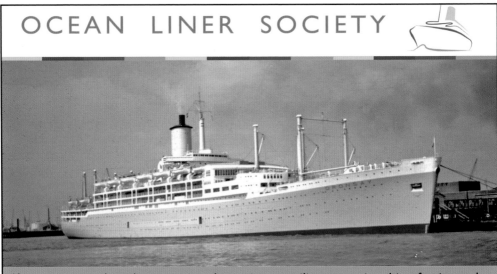

Area operated St Lawrence Seaway, Canada

SAINT LAURENT PRESTIGE	4954gt	2001	10.0k	DP2	226p	226p	74c	91.4m	15.2m	3.8m	BS

SAINT LAURENT PRESTIGE For details see SEA VOYAGER under Clipper Group.

TAAJ CROISIERES

The Company Taaj Croisiers in a French travel operator. In 2014 the company took space on the COSTA CLASSICA, but for 2015 will be chartering the LOUIS AURA for a number of cruises between April and July. The company was formed in 1988 and entered the ocean cruise business in 2011. Other Costa ships, including the COSTA VOYAGER have been used in earlier years. Taaj Croisieres went into liquidation on 29 July 2014.

Telephone +33 1 56 03 56 40

Area operated Mediterranean and Northern Europe

LOUIS AURA		15781gt	1968	20.0k	D2	658p	912p	329c	160.1m	22.8m	6.7m	MT

LOUIS AURA For details see under Louis Cruises.

ROYAL CARIBBEAN CRUISES LIMITED

The Company The early history of Royal Caribbean Cruises Limited (RCCL) can be found under Royal Caribbean International. The cruise ship operator within the group was renamed as Royal Caribbean International in 1997, the same year that the Celebrity Cruises business was acquired, with the new Royal Caribbean Cruise Lines becoming the holding company for the operating entities. In late 2001 a proposed joint venture operation with P&O Princess Cruises was close to becoming a reality before Carnival Corporation stepped in with its own bid for the P&O companies. During the following year the Island Cruises joint venture with British tour operator, First Choice was established. That venture closed in 2009. In summer 2006 Royal Caribbean Cruises' bid for Pullmantur, Spain's largest cruise operator and a major player in that country's tour industry, was accepted by owners, Marsans Group, and the European interest further expanded with the introduction of Croisieres de France in 2008. The Pullmantur acquisition also allowed the extraction of the mis-placed former Renaissance ships from the Spanish company and the establishment of Azamara Cruises. Royal Caribbean's way into the German market is through the joint venture TUI Cruises, established in conjunction with Germany's TUI AG. These developments, coupled with RCI ships based in the UK and the Mediterranean give RCCL a very strong, and easily expandable base in four of Europe's most important markets. Royal Caribbean is the second largest of the world's cruise ship groups. In 2012 Royal Caribbean group ships carried around 4.4 million passengers, up approximately 10% from 2008. In 2014 Pullmantur's non-ship-related activities were sold.

Address 1050 Caribbean Way, Miami, Florida 33132-2096 United States of America

Telephone +1 305 539 6000

AZAMARA CLUB CRUISES

The Company Azamara Cruises was created on May 4, 2007. Originally intended for Celebrity Cruises' Xpeditions brand, the two former Renaissance Cruises ships, transferred from Pullmantur Cruises, started the new venture, which is positioned between Premium and Luxury. Royal Caribbean Cruises Limited had previously been interested in acquiring Oceania Cruises (the operator of three similar ships), but that particular avenue of expansion was not encouraged. Azamara Cruises is operated as a subsidiary of Celebrity Cruises. In late 2009 the company was restyled as Azamara Club Cruises. Azamara roughly translates from Latin as blue sea.

Address 1050 Caribbean Way, Miami, Florida 33132-2096, United States of America

Telephone +1 305 341 0206

Website www.azamaraclubcruises.com

Areas operated Caribbean Sea, Europe, South America and Antarctica, Asia and world cruises

AZAMARA JOURNEY	30277gt	2000	18.5k	DE2	694p	686p	408c	181.0m	25.5m	6.0m	MT
AZAMARA QUEST	30277gt	2000	18.0k	DE2	694p	694p	376c	181.0m	25.5m	6.0m	MT

AZAMARA JOURNEY was marketed while under charter to Pullmantur Cruises in 2003-4 as the BLUE

STAR, but not officially renamed from R SIX. She was built by Ateliers et Chantiers de l'Atlantique (yard number Q31) at St Nazaire, France as the R SIX, one of a series of eight elegantly furnished ships for Renaissance Cruises. Following the collapse of that company in 2001 she, along with many of her sisters, was laid up in Gibraltar. The ships were auctioned and acquired by Cruiseinvest, an offshoot of her builders, who still had a significant financial interest in the ships. Pullmantur eventually chartered her. In 2005 she was acquired by Pullmantur and renamed BLUE DREAM. She spent her first winter operating on the Brazilian coast for tour operator CVC, before returning to Europe for the summer. Pullmantur was acquired by Royal Caribbean in 2006 and one of the first moves was to take this ship for the Celebrity Expeditions brand, in an exchange with Celebrity's ZENITH. She was intended to take the name CELEBRITY JOURNEY for her new owner, but just before she entered service following a major refit she was switched to new brand Azamara Cruises as the AZAMARA JOURNEY. IMO 9200940

AZAMARA QUEST was built as the R SEVEN by Chantiers de l'Atlantique (yard number X31) at St Nazaire, France for Renaissance Cruises. Following the failure of that company she was laid up off Gibraltar before being sold to Cruiseinvest, a company associated with her builders, part of the Alstom Group. She was subsequently chartered by Delphin Seereisen and renamed DELPHIN RENAISSANCE. In 2006 she was purchased by Pullmantur and renamed BLUE MOON. In October 2007 she transferred to Azamara Cruises as the second ship for this new company and was named the AMAZARA QUEST. It was originally intended that this ship would join her sister (above) as the CELEBRITY QUEST in the Celebrity Expeditions fleet. IMO 9210218

CELEBRITY CRUISES

The Company Celebrity Cruises was founded in 1989 as a joint venture between Greek shipping company Chandris Group and bulk shipping company Overseas Shipholding Group, as an up market cruise operation to complement its existing passenger operations, which were generally at the lower end of the market. Chandris gradually disposed of its own fleet and concentrated on a small number of high quality ships within the Celebrity brand. The first ship was the former Italian transatlantic liner GALILEO GALILEI, which entered service after a massive refit in 1990 as the MERIDIAN. The second ship, HORIZON, was also the first new-build for the company, and began a relationship with the shipbuilder Jos. L. Meyer which would produce another four ships over the next seven years. Celebrity Cruises became part of the Royal Caribbean Cruises Limited group in 1997, although at the time Carnival Corporation had also made an offer for the company. In 2004 the company acquired the small expedition ship XPEDITION to expand its range of cruises to include the Galapagos Islands. For 2005, in a further expansion, Celebrity teamed up with Quark Expeditions to offer a cruise from Ottawa to the Arctic, and in 2006 the Antarctic from Ushuaia aboard the Russian icebreaker KAPITAN KHLEBNIKOV. In 2007 the Celebrity Expeditions sub-brand was going to be further expanded with the transfer of two of the former Renaissance ships from fellow subsidiary Pullmantur Cruises. However, in a change of plan these ships became the start-up vessels for Azamara cruises. Unfortunately, Celebrity Cruises seems to be the latest in a long line of cruise companies that thinks it necessary to put its corporate name into its ships' names.

Address 1050 Caribbean Way, Miami, Florida 33132-2096, United States of America

Telephone +1 305 539 6000 **Fax** +1 305 406 8630

Website www.celebritycruises.com

Areas operated Caribbean Sea, Alaska, Mexican Riviera, East Coast USA, Europe

CELEBRITY CENTURY	72458gt	1995	21.5k	D2	1814p	2156p	858c	246.5m	32.2m	7.8m	MT
CELEBRITY CONSTELLATION	90940gt	2002	24.0k	GEP2	2170p	2449p	999c	294.0m	32.2m	8.2m	MT
CELEBRITY ECLIPSE	121878gt	2010	22.0k	DEP2	2852p	3145p	1271c	315.0m	36.8m	8.3m	MT
CELEBRITY EQUINOX	121878gt	2009	22.0k	DEP2	2850p	3145p	1250c	315.0m	36.8m	8.3m	MT
CELEBRITY INFINITY	90940gt	2001	24.0k	GEP2	2170p	2579p	999c	294.0m	32.2m	8.2m	MT
CELEBRITY MILLENNIUM	90963gt	2000	24.0k	GEP2	2138p	2449p	999c	294.0m	32.2m	8.2m	MT
CELEBRITY REFLECTION	125366gt	2012	22.0k	DEP2	3046p	3609p	1250c	315.0m	36.8m	8.3m	MT
CELEBRITY SILHOUETTE	122210gt	2011	22.0k	DEP2	2850p	3179p	1250c	315.0m	36.8m	8.3m	MT
CELEBRITY SOLSTICE	121878gt	2008	22.0k	DEP2	2883p	3145p	1250c	315.0m	36.8m	8.3m	MT
CELEBRITY SUMMIT	90940gt	2001	24.0k	GEP2	2158p	2449p	999c	294.0m	32.2m	8.2m	MT
XPEDITION	2842gt	2001	15.0k	D1	98p	98p	56c	88.5m	14.0m	3.6m	EC

CELEBRITY CENTURY For details see CTrip (below).

Azamara Club Cruises' *Azamara Quest* off Kotor *(William Mayes)*

Celebrity Cruises' *Celebrity Century* off Villefranche *(Richard Mayes)*

Celebrity Cruises' *Celebrity Constellation* at Lanzarote *(William Mayes)*

CELEBRITY CONSTELLATION was built by Chantiers de l'Atlantique (yard number U31) at St Nazaire, France as the CONSTELLATION. She was renamed in 2007. Itineraries for 2015 centre on the Mediterranean and Black Seas and the Caribbean. IMO 9192399

CELEBRITY ECLIPSE is the third ship in the series of five built by Jos. L. Meyer (yard number 677) at Papenburg, Germany. She entered service in the spring of 2010 and her first work was to rescue Britons stranded in Spain by the Icelandic ash cloud. She now operates from Southampton during the summer and in the Caribbean Sea in winter. IMO 9404314

CELEBRITY EQUINOX was built by Jos. L. Meyer (yard number 676) at Papenburg, Germany. She was named in Southampton by Nina Barough, founder of the British breast cancer charity Walk The Walk. She operates in Europe in the summer and in the Caribbean Sea in winter. IMO 9372456

CELEBRITY INFINITY, built as the INFINITY, is the second of the Millennium class ships to come from Chantiers de l'Atlantique (yard number S31) at St Nazaire, France. She had the Celebrity prefix added to her name in 2007. Her itineraries include Alaska, West Coast USA, South America and the Caribbean. IMO 9189421

CELEBRITY MILLENNIUM is the lead ship in a series of four built by Chantiers de l'Atlantique (yard number R31) at St Nazaire, France. She suffered serious problems with her pod propulsion system before delivery, as the MILLENNIUM, and had to be dry-docked for repairs subsequently. The MILLENNIUM's speciality restaurant has some of the original walnut panels from the White Star Line's Atlantic liner OLYMPIC, built in 1911. She was renamed CELEBRITY MILLENIUM in 2008 and currently operates in Alaska and South East Asia. IMO 9189419

CELEBRITY REFLECTION was built by Jos. L. Meyer at Papenburg, Germany (yard number 679) as the final member of the Solstice class, although slightly larger than her sisters. She was named on 1 December 2012 by Jovanka Goronjic, Megan Mathie, Helen O'Connell and Rosey Rodriguez, all Celebrity employees. Her itineraries are Caribbean and Mediterranean based. IMO 9506459

CELEBRITY SILHOUETTE is the fourth ship in the Solstice class, built by Jos. L. Meyer (yard number 679) at Papenburg in Germany. She was delivered in July 2011 and named in Hamburg by Michelle Morgan. The ship's areas of operation are the Caribbean Sea and Europe. IMO 9451094

CELEBRITY SOLSTICE was built by Jos. L. Meyer (yard number 675) at Papenburg, Germany as the lead ship in the Solstice class. She was named in Fort Lauderdale by ocean scientist, Professor Sharon Smith. After completing her summer 2011 European season she moved to the Caribbean and now operates Alaska and Australasian cruises. IMO 9362530

CELEBRITY SUMMIT was built by Chantiers de l'Atlantique (yard number T31) at St Nazaire, France as the SUMMIT, and was renamed with the Celebrity prefix in 2008. She cruises from the US East Coast and in the Caribbean Sea, including many round trips from New York (Cape Liberty) to Bermuda. IMO 9192387

XPEDITION was built by Schiffswerft U Maschinenfabrik Cassens (yard number 228) at Emden in Germany as the SUN BAY for Sun Bay Shipping, by whom she is still owned. Celebrity chartered her from Islas Galapagos Turismo in 2004 to commence a programme of cruises in the Galapagos Islands. She is marketed as the CELEBRITY XPEDITION. IMO 9228368

CROISIERES DE FRANCE

The Company Croisieres de France is a subsidiary of Royal Caribbean Cruise Lines aimed at developing the French cruise market, and was established in August 2007, although cruises did not commence until May 2008, using the BLEU DE FRANCE (now SAGA SAPPHIRE). The company, which is part of Pullmantur, operates the HORIZON and the ZENITH in 2014, with the CELEBRITY CENTURY due to replace the latter in 2015. That will now not happen and the ZENITH will be retained.

Address 8 rue du Dahomy, 75011 Paris, France

Telephone +33 1737 75400

Website www.cdfcroisieresdefrance.com

Area operated Mediterranean Sea in summer and Caribbean Sea in winter

HORIZON	47427gt	1990	21.4k	D2	1442p	1828p	620c	208.0m	29.0m	7.4m	MT
ZENITH	47413gt	1992	17.0k	D2	1442p	1776p	620c	208.0m	29.0m	7.2m	MT

HORIZON was Celebrity's first new ship and was built by Jos. L. Meyer (yard number 619) at

Celebrity Cruises' *Celebrity Silhouette* off Kotor *(William Mayes)*

Croisieres de France's *Horizon* at Calais *(Philippe Brebant)*

Pullmantur's *Empress* at Cherbourg *(Philippe Brebant)*

Pullmantur's **Sovereign** in Barcelona *(Rick Frendt)*

Royal Caribbean's **Adventure of the Seas** in Barcelona *(William Mayes)*

Royal Caribbean's **Enchantment of the Seas** at Nassau *(Rick Frendt)*

Papenburg, Germany. When delivered in 1990 as the HORIZON, she was the largest ship to have been completely built in a building hall. She generally operated in the Caribbean and on the East Coast of the USA and Canada in her last years with Celebrity. In autumn 2005 she transferred within the group to Island Cruises with the new name ISLAND STAR. For her first winter with her new owner she operated in Brazil and in summer 2006 moved to the Mediterranean to serve the UK market. Island Cruises was closed in spring 2009 and the ship transferred to Pullmantur. From early summer 2009 she took up a new service and was to be based in Acapulco year-round as the PACIFIC DREAM. That did not work out as anticipated and she quickly came back to Europe to operate in the Mediterranean, being renamed HORIZON in 2010. She transferred to Croisieres de France in spring 2012 after a major refit. IMO 8807088

ZENITH was delivered to Celebrity Cruises two years after the HORIZON by the Papenburg yard of Jos. L. Meyer (yard number 620). In 2007 she was transferred from Celebrity Cruises to fellow Royal Caribbean subsidiary Pullmantur Cruises in a ship swap involving the BLUE DREAM. She began her service with Pullmantur on Adriatic itineraries, but she was moved to Croisieres de France in 2014. IMO 8918136.

CTRIP

The Company CTrip is a major Chinese travel business which has entered into an agreement with Royal Caribbean Cruise Lines to buy the CELEBRITY CENTURY and mange the ship in a joint venture with Royal Caribbean. The ship, which was destined for Crosieres de France, will be handed over at the conclusion of her current programme, in March 2015.

Address 99 Fu Quan Road, Shanghai 200335, Peoples Republic of China

Website www.ctrip.com

Area operated China

CELEBRITY CENTURY	72458gt	1995	21.5k	D2	1808p	2156p	858c	246.5m	32.2m	7.8m	MT

CELEBRITY CENTURY is the lead ship of a trio of ships (the others were GALAXY and MERCURY, both now with TUI Cruises as MEIN SCHIFF 1 & 2) built by Jos. L. Meyer (yard number 637) at Papenburg, Germany as the CENTURY. Her maiden voyage in 1995 was from Southampton to New York. Her refit in 2006 included the addition of three decks of balconies, resulting in an increase in gross tonnage from 70,606 to 72,458. She was renamed two years later as CELEBRITY CENTURY. In 2015 she will tranfer to Croisieres de France as a replacement for the ZENITH. IMO 9072446

PULLMANTUR CRUISES

The Company Pullmantur, formerly part of the Marsans Group, is a large Spanish tour company operating its own small airline, cruise line and tour business. The company was established in 1971, but only entered the cruise business with the establishment of Pullmantur Cruises in 2000. Pullmantur has a total staff of more than 2,000, and in the few years since the cruise division was formed, has taken almost 50% of the Spanish cruise market. During the early part of 2006 the entire fleet, with the exception of PACIFIC was re-flagged to Malta. The company passed to Royal Caribbean Cruises Limited in 2006. Following the takeover Royal Caribbean took the two R ships for Celebrity Expeditions and replaced them by transferring the ZENITH and, in 2008, the EMPRESS OF THE SEAS. Two ships were acquired from P&O Cruises Australia, and with the departure of HOLIDAY DREAM (currently SAGA SAPPHIRE), the SOVEREIGN arrived. In a surprise move the OCEANIC was sold at short notice to Panamanian Interests for onward charter to the Peaceboat Organisation.

Address Calle Mahonia 2 , 28043 Madrid, Spain

Telephone +34 902 095512

Website www.pullmanturcruises.com

Area operated Mediterranean, Northern Europe, Caribbean, Mexico and South America

EMPRESS	48563gt	1990	17.0k	D2	1590p	2020p	645c	210.8m	30.7m	7.1m	MT
MONARCH	73937gt	1991	21.0k	D2	2390p	2744p	856c	268.3m	32.2m	7.5m	MT
SOVEREIGN	73529gt	1987	19.0k	D2	2324p	2852p	825c	268.3m	32.2m	7.5m	MT

EMPRESS was ordered from Chantiers de l'Atlantique (yard number G29) at St Nazaire in France in

1987 by Admiral Cruises as their FUTURE SEAS. Admiral Cruises was merged with Royal Caribbean the following year and the ship was delivered as the NORDIC EMPRESS and employed on shorter Caribbean cruises. In 2004 she was refitted and subsequently renamed EMPRESS OF THE SEAS by Gloria Estefan. In 2007 she operated Caribbean cruises as well as a new series of Bermuda cruises from Philadelphia. In spring 2008, the ship was transferred to Pullmantur Cruises as the EMPRESS. In 2011 the EMPRESS sails in Northern Europe and in the Mediterranean. IMO 8716899

MONARCH is one of a trio of ships built by Chantiers de l'Atlantique (yard number A30) at St Nazaire, France, for Royal Caribbean International and was named by actress Lauren Bacall. In later years she operated cruises to the Bahamas from Port Canaveral, Florida. In 2013 she was transferred to Pullmantur and renamed MONARCH. She continues to operate exclusively in the Caribbean. IMO 8819500

SOVEREIGN is the lead ship of a trio built by Chantiers de l'Atlantique (yard number A29) at St Nazaire, France. When delivered to Royal Caribbean Cruise Lines, as the SOVEREIGN OF THE SEAS, she was the world's largest cruise ship. She was named by Rosalynn Carter, wife of former US president, Jimmy Carter. She was transferred to Pullmantur Cruises in November 2008, and, as the SOVEREIGN, from 2009 took over the weekly Mediterranean Breezes itinerary based at Barcelona, made popular by the OCEANIC. IMO 8512281

ROYAL CARIBBEAN INTERNATIONAL

The Company Royal Caribbean Cruise Line was founded by Anders Wilhelmsen & Co and I M Skaugen & Co in 1969 (and later joined by Gotaas Larsen) to take a part of the fledgling Caribbean cruise trade. The first ship, the SONG OF NORWAY, was delivered during the following year. During the next two years, two further new ships were introduced. By the end of the 1970's the ships were too small for the market they were serving, and two of them were stretched by means of a new mid-section approximately 26 metres in length. A fourth ship, the 37,000-ton SONG OF AMERICA was introduced in 1982. By 1988 Anders Wilhelmsen & Co had bought out the other partners, but later entered into a new agreement with other parties in order to raise finance for new-buildings. In the same year, Royal Caribbean merged with Admiral Cruise Line. When delivered in 1988, the 73,000-ton SOVEREIGN OF THE SEAS was the world's largest cruise ship. In 1993 Royal Caribbean became a public company, with a listing on the New York Stock Exchange, although a major block of stock was retained by Anders Wilhelmsen & Co. The company became Royal Caribbean International in 1997, to better reflect its global operations. By 1998 the three original ships with which the company had laid its foundations had found new homes, and Royal Caribbean was in the middle of a massive building programme. With the entry into service in 1999 of the VOYAGER OF THE SEAS (137,000 tons), the company once again operated the largest cruise ship in the world. This class of ship has subsequently been eclipsed by the massive ships of the 'Freedom' class, which in turn are dwarfed by the 225,000 gross ton OASIS OF THE SEAS and ALLURE OF THE SEAS. The MAJESTY OF THE SEAS is earmarked for transfer to Pullmantur in due course. With five new ships on order, Royal Caribbean is in the process of expanding significantly.

Address 1050 Caribbean Way, Miami, Florida 33132-2096, United States of America

Telephone +1 305 539 6000

Website www.royalcaribbean.com

Areas operated Caribbean Sea, East Coast North America, Alaska, China and Europe

ADVENTURE OF THE SEAS	137276gt	2001	23.7k	DEP3	3114p	3807p	1185c	311.0m	38.6m	8.6m	BS
ALLURE OF THE SEAS	225282gt	2010	22.0k	DEP3	5400p	6318p	2354c	361.0m	47.0m	9.3m	BS
BRILLIANCE OF THE SEAS	90090gt	2002	24.0k	GEP2	2142p	2543p	848c	293.2m	32.2m	8.1m	BS
ENCHANTMENT OF THE SEAS	82910gt	1997	22.0k	DE2	2252p	2730p	852c	301.4m	32.2m	7.8m	BS
EXPLORER OF THE SEAS	137308gt	2000	23.7k	DEP3	3114p	3840p	1185c	311.0m	38.6m	8.6m	BS
FREEDOM OF THE SEAS	154407gt	2006	22.5k	DEP3	3634p	4375p	1360c	338.8m	38.6m	8.8m	BS
GRANDEUR OF THE SEAS	73817gt	1996	22.0k	DE2	1992p	2406p	760c	279.1m	32.2m	7.6m	BS
INDEPENDENCE OF THE SEAS	154407gt	2008	22.0k	DEP3	3600p	4375p	1360c	339.0m	38.6m	8.5m	BS
JEWEL OF THE SEAS	90090gt	2004	24.0k	GEP2	2112p	2502p	859c	293.2m	32.2m	8.1m	BS
LEGEND OF THE SEAS	69472gt	1995	24.0k	DE2	1804p	2074p	726c	264.3m	32.0m	7.3m	BS
LIBERTY OF THE SEAS	154407gt	2007	22.5k	DEP3	3600p	4375p	1360c	338.8m	38.6m	8.8m	BS
MAJESTY OF THE SEAS	74077gt	1992	21.0k	D2	2350p	2767p	912c	268.3m	32.2m	7.5m	BS
MARINER OF THE SEAS	138279gt	2003	23.7k	DEP3	3114p	3807p	1185c	311.0m	38.6m	8.6m	BS

Royal Caribbean's *Grandeur of the Seas* in Marseille *(William Mayes)*

Royal Caribbean's *Independence of the Seas* at Ajaccio *(William Mayes)*

Royal Caribbean's *Legend of the Seas* in Barcelona *(William Mayes)*

NAVIGATOR OF THE SEAS	138570gt	2002	23.7k	DEP3	3114p	3807p	1214c	311.0m	38.6m	8.6m	BS
OASIS OF THE SEAS	225282gt	2009	22.0k	DEP3	5400p	6360p	2394c	361.0m	47.0m	9.3m	BS
RADIANCE OF THE SEAS	90090gt	2001	24.0k	GEP2	2143p	2466p	894c	293.2m	32.2m	8.1m	BS
RHAPSODY OF THE SEAS	78878gt	1997	22.0k	DE2	1998p	2416p	759c	279.0m	32.2m	7.8m	BS
SERENADE OF THE SEAS	90090gt	2003	24.0k	GEP2	2146p	2476p	884c	293.2m	32.2m	8.1m	BS
SPLENDOUR OF THE SEAS	69472gt	1996	24.0k	DE2	1830p	2074p	761c	264.3m	32.0m	7.3m	BS
VISION OF THE SEAS	78717gt	1998	22.0k	DE2	2050p	2514p	742c	279.0m	32.2m	7.8m	BS
VOYAGER OF THE SEAS	137276gt	1999	23.7k	DEP3	3114p	3840p	1176c	311.1m	38.6m	8.6m	BS

ADVENTURE OF THE SEAS was built by Kvaerner Masa Yards (yard number 1346) at Turku, Finland as the third and final unit of the original requirement for three Eagle Class ships. Subsequently two further ships were ordered. ADVENTURE OF THE SEAS generally operates Southern Caribbean cruises from San Juan, but now spends the summers in Europe. In 2015 she will cruise from Southampton. Her godparents were four members of the New York Fire Department - Tara Stackpole, Kevin Hannafin, Margaret McDonnell and Richard Lucas. IMO 9167227

ALLURE OF THE SEAS was built by STX (yard number 1364) at Turku, Finland. She was named in Port Everglades on 29 November 2010 by Shrek cartoon character Princess Fiona. The ALLURE OF THE SEAS undertakes 7-night Eastern and Western Caribbean cruises from Fort Lauderdale, but for the summer of 2015 will be based in Barcelona. IMO 9383948

BRILLIANCE OF THE SEAS is the second ship in a four ship series under construction by Jos. L. Meyer (yard number 656) at Papenburg, Germany. She was named by Marilyn Ofer. The BRILLIANCE OF THE SEAS is currently scheduled to cruise in Europe, the Caribbean and to Canada and New England, from New York. IMO 9195200

ENCHANTMENT OF THE SEAS is one of a pair of ships built by Kvaerner Masa Yards (yard number 493) at Helsinki, Finland. During 2005 she was lengthened by the Keppel Verolme Shipyard in Rotterdam by means of the insertion of a 22-metre mid section, increasing her tonnage to 80,700 and adding a further 151 cabins. She generally operates short cruises from Port Canaveral. Her godmother is Coleen Fain, wife of the CEO. IMO 9111802

EXPLORER OF THE SEAS, named by Jackie Joyner-Kersee, is the second of the Eagle Class ships built by Kvaerner Masa Yards (yard number 1345) at Turku, Finland. The EXPLORER OF THE SEAS is now deployed in the Caribbean, Europe and South Pacific, including Australia. IMO 9161728

FREEDOM OF THE SEAS is the first of the Ultra-Voyager class ships, and when delivered in 2006, took the title of the world's largest passenger ship. She was built by Aker Finnyards at Turku, Finland (yard number 1352), and currently alternates east and west Caribbean itineraries. Her godmother was Katherine Louise Calder, foster mother to over 400 children. IMO 9304033

GRANDEUR OF THE SEAS is one of a pair of ships built by Kvaerner Masa Yards (yard number 492) at Helsinki, Finland. Named by Aviva Ofer, she operates in Europe and the Caribbean. IMO 9102978

INDEPENDENCE OF THE SEAS is the last of the so-called Ultra-Voyager class ships constructed by Aker Finnyards (yard number 1354) at Turku, Finland. She was named at Southampton on 30 April 2008 by Sir Steven Redgrave and spent her first two seasons based at Southampton. She returned for the summers of 2010 and 2011, spending the winters in the Caribbean, but until 2014 was based in Southampton year round. She moves back to the Caribbean in the autumn of 2014. IMO 9349681

JEWEL OF THE SEAS was built by Jos. L. Meyer (yard number 658) at Papenburg, Germany. Kathy Mellor, 2004 National Teacher of the Year, was her godmother. The JEWEL OF THE SEAS currently cruises in Alaska and the Caribbean. IMO 9228356

LEGEND OF THE SEAS is the lead ship of a pair built by Chantiers de l'Atlantique (yard number A31) at St Nazaire, France. Her current areas of operation include Europe, the Far East, Australasia, Canada and the Caribbean. Cindy Pritzker, wife of board member Jay Pritzker, named her. IMO 9070620.

LIBERTY OF THE SEAS was built by Aker Finnyards at Turku, Finland (yard number 1353). When her 2014 Mediterranean season finishes she will move to the Caribbean, based at Fort Lauderdale, then to Cape Liberty for Canada and New England cruises. At the end of 2015 she will be based at Galveston, Texas. Her godmother was Donnalea Madeley. IMO 9330032

MAJESTY OF THE SEAS is the final member of a trio built by Chantiers de l'Atlantique (yard number B30) at St Nazaire, France. She was named by Her Majesty Queen Sonja of Norway. She operates short

Royal Caribbean's *Majesty of the Seas* at Coco Cay *(Rick Frendt)*

Royal Caribbean's *Navigator of the Seas* in Istanbul *(William Mayes)*

Royal Caribbean's *Oasis of the Seas* *(Richard Mayes)*

Bahamas and Caribbean cruises from Miami, Florida. IMO 8819512

MARINER OF THE SEAS is the fifth and (for the time being) final unit in the Eagle Class and was built by Kvaerner Masa Yards (yard number 1348) at Turku, Finland. The MARINER OF THE SEAS was named by Jean Driscoll, Olympian and Paralympian, and is currently employed in the Far East, based in Singapore and Shanghai. IMO 9227510

NAVIGATOR OF THE SEAS was laid down by Kvaerner Masa Yards (yard number 1347) at Turku, Finland as the JOURNEY OF THE SEAS, but was renamed during construction. Her godmother is tennis player Steffi Graf. The NAVIGATOR OF THE SEAS is currently based in Galveston for Caribbean cruises but will move to Fort Lauderdale later in 2015. IMO 9227508

OASIS OF THE SEAS was built by STX (yard number 1363) at Turku, Finland under the name Project Genesis. Together with her sister ship they are the most expensive passenger ships ever built, with an estimated price tag of $1.1 billion each, and are expected to be the largest passenger ships in service for some years. When delivered in late 2009 the OASIS OF THE SEAS was immediately based in Fort Lauderdale, operating 7-night Eastern and Western Caribbean itineraries. She returned to Europe for a series of short cruises in 2014, prior to being dry-docked in Rotterdam. At her naming ceremony on 1 December 2009 she had seven godmothers, including Gloria Estefan. IMO 9383936

RADIANCE OF THE SEAS is the company's first gas turbine powered ship and was built by Jos. L. Meyer (yard number 655) at Papenburg, Germany. She currently operates in Alaska and the Pacific, including Australia and is the lead ship in a series of four Panamax vessels. She was named by Margot Pritzker, wife of board member Thomas Pritzker. IMO 9195195

RHAPSODY OF THE SEAS was built by Chantiers de l'Atlantique (yard number E31) at St Nazaire, France as the first ship of another pair (the other one being VISION OF THE SEAS). Named by Bodil Wilhelmsen. The RHAPSODY OF THE SEAS is scheduled to operate in Alaska, Hawaii, Australia, the Far East and Europe over the next two years. IMO 9116864

SERENADE OF THE SEAS was built by Jos. L. Meyer (yard number 657) at Papenburg, Germany. When her 2014 Mediterranean season finishes she will spend the winter cruising to the Caribbean from New Orleans before returning to Northern Europe in the spring of 2015. She was named by Whoopi Goldberg. IMO 9228344

SPLENDOUR OF THE SEAS is the second ship of the first pair built by Chantiers de l'Atlantique (yard number B31) at St Nazaire, France. At the end of her 2014 Mediterranean season she will winter in South America before returning to the Mediterranean. In the winter of 2015 she will be based in Dubai. Her godmother is Lise Wilhelmsen. IMO 9070632

VISION OF THE SEAS was built as the second ship of the second pair by Chantiers de l'Atlantique (yard number F31) at St Nazaire, France. She currently operates in the Caribbean and the Mediterranean and was named by Helen Stephan, wife of Royal Caribbean's founder and vice-chairman, Edwin Stephan. IMO 9116876

VOYAGER OF THE SEAS was built by Kvaerner Masa Yards (yard number 1344) at Turku, Finland as the lead ship in the Eagle Class of (initially three and later five) massive vessels. The VOYAGER OF THE SEAS became the largest passenger ship ever built when she entered service in the autumn of 1999. Her godmother is Katarina Witt. VOYAGER OF THE SEAS is now based in Australia and China. IMO 9161716

Cruise ships on order

QUANTUM OF THE SEAS	c167800gt	2014	22.0k	DEP2	4180p	4905p	1500c	348.0m	41.0m	8.5m	BS
ANTHEM OF THE SEAS	c167800gt	2015	22.0k	DEP2	4180p	4905p	1500c	348.0m	41.0m	8.5m	BS
OVATION OF THE SEAS	c167800gt	2016	22.0k	DEP2	4180p	4905p	1500c	348.0m	41.0m	8.5m	BS
OASIS CLASS NO 3	c225000gt	2016	23.0k	DEP2	5400p	6400p	2200c	361.0m	47.0m	9.3m	BS
OASIS CLASS NO 4	c225000gt	2018	23.0k	DEP2	5400p	6400p	2200c	361.0m	47.0m	9.3m	BS

QUANTUM OF THE SEAS is on order with Meyer Werft (yard number 697) at Papenburg, Germany and will be delivered in October 2014. She will be named by Kristin Chenoweth and initially based in New York before being repositioned to China in May 2015. IMO 9549463

ANTHEM OF THE SEAS is the second ship in the Quantum Class, under construction by Meyer Werft (yard number 698). She will spend her first summer based in Southampton before repositioning to New York. IMO 9656101

Royal Caribbean's *Quantum of the Seas* at the Papenburg shipyard *(William Mayes)*

Royal Caribbean's *Serenade of the Seas* in the Sea of Marmara *(William Mayes)*

Royal Caribbean's *Vision of the Seas* *(Bill Lawes)*

OVATION OF THE SEAS is on order with Meyer Werft (yard number 699). IMO 9697753

OASIS CLASS NO 3 is under construction at STX France (yard number A34) St Nazaire. IMO 9682875

OASIS CLASS NO 4 is on order at STX France. IMO 9744001

TUI CRUISES

The Company A Royal Caribbean and TUI Group joint venture. See under TUI AG.

RUNNING ON WAVES

The Company Running on Waves is a Russian company.

Address Derbenerskey Embankment, 115114 Moscow, Russia

Telephone +7 495 228 1908

Website www.88parsec.com

Area operated Eastern Mediterranean, Black Sea and charters

RUNNING ON WAVES	634gt	2011	18.0k	SD1	36p	45p	22c	64.0m	9.0m	3.2m	MT

RUNNING ON WAVES was built by Odys Stocznia (yard number SV 64) at Gdansk, Poland as a three-masted barquentine. IMO 9589205

SAGA GROUP

The Company Saga Holidays and Saga Shipping are subsidiaries of the British financial services and holiday group Saga Group Limited. Sidney de Haan bought his first seaside hotel, in Folkestone, Kent in 1948. Three years later he operated his first holiday for retired people, thus establishing the business that was to become Saga. Initially, the company only catered for the over 60s, but this was subsequently relaxed to include anyone over the age of 50. In 1984 Roger de Haan (Sidney's son) took control of the business. The Saga Group was sold by its founding family in October 2004 to private equity firm Charterhouse. Subsequently Charterhouse and the private equity owners of the AA merged their interests under the Acromas umbrella. In 2014 a public share offering was made and a minority holding is now traded on the London Stock Exchange. The company also operated the Spirit of Adventure brand until November 2013 when it was closed and its single ship transferred to Saga Cruises.

SAGA CRUISES

The Company Although the company had been selling cruises on other operators' ships for many years, it was not until 1997 that the company introduced its first owned ship, the SAGA ROSE (previously Norwegian America Line's SAGAFJORD). Prior to that, however, the company had undertaken many whole ship charters from as early as 1978, when Epirotiki Lines' ATLAS was used. Other vessels were used from time to time, including the RUSS in 1992. Saga cruises are only sold to the over 50's, and are not generally sold through travel agents. The time for expansion came and the company introduced the SAGA PEARL (now Swan Hellenic's MINERVA) on summer charter in 2003 and 2004. Late in 2003 the company purchased the CARONIA from Cunard Line, with delivery scheduled for late 2004, when she was renamed SAGA RUBY. The SAGA ROSE was retired at the end of 2009 and was replaced by the SAGA PEARL II. That ship was replaced in turn by the SAGA SAPPHIRE in 2012, becoming the QUEST FOR ADVENTURE. However, in late 2013 she reverted to the name SAGA PEARL II in anticipation of the withdrawal of the SAGA RUBY. The SAGA RUBY had an unfortunate end to her Saga career, breaking down on two of her three final cruises.

Address The Saga Building, Enbrook Park, Folkestone, Kent, CT20 3SE, England

Telephone +44 1303 771964 **Fax** +44 1303 771243

Website www.saga.co.uk

Area operated Europe, North Atlantic and Caribbean

SAGA PEARL II	18627gt	1981	18.0k	D2	446p	446p	252c	164.3m	22.6m	6.1m	MT
SAGA SAPPHIRE	37049gt	1981	21.0k	D2	706p	706p	415c	199.6m	28.5m	8.4m	MT

Running on Waves at Kos *(William Mayes)*

Saga Cruises' ***Saga Pearl II*** anchored off Geiranger *(William Mayes)*

Saga Cruises' ***Saga Sapphire*** in Magdalena Bay, Spitzbergen *(William Mayes)*

SAGA PEARL II was built by Howaldtswerke-Deutsche Werft (yard number 165) at Hamburg, Germany as the ASTOR (laid down as the HAMMONIA) for Hadag Cruise Line. In 1984 she was acquired by the South African Marine Corporation of Cape Town for a new liner service between Southampton and Cape Town and for off-season cruising. It became apparent very early that the ship's engines were not powerful enough to maintain the required liner schedule and she was sold in August 1985 to VEB Deutfracht Seereederei of East Germany. She was refitted in Hamburg and as the ARKONA became the replacement for the VOLKERFREUNDSCHAFT (now Classic International Cruises' ATHENA). She was on a 10-year charter from Astoria Shipping to Transocean Tours, thought to be due to expire in 2012, as the ASTORIA. Club Cruise of The Netherlands acquired her in March 2007, but the charter remained in place. It would appear that Transocean Tours had agreed to an early termination of the charter as the ASTORIA was to be sold to Saga Group at the end of her 2008/9 world cruise. In the event, just a week before that cruise was due to start, during a routine overhaul, serious machinery problems were noticed, thus forcing the cancellation of the cruise. Within a week Club Cruise was in administration. Saga had previously agreed to purchase the ship for its Spirit of Adventure brand, later diverting the ship to Saga Cruises. However, with the bankruptcy of Club Cruise, Saga's acquisition of the ship was delayed by several months, and she remained under arrest in Barcelona. Subsequently, Saga secured the ship at an auction in Gibraltar, and after a major refit in Swansea, estimated at £20 million, she entered service in March 2010 as the SAGA PEARL II. In May 2012 she transferred to Spirit of Adventure as the QUEST FOR ADVENTURE, but came back to the Saga fleet in 2013 as the SAGA PEARL II. IMO 8000214

SAGA SAPPHIRE was built by Bremer Vulkan (yard number 1001) at Vegesack, Germany for Hapag-Lloyd of Bremen as the EUROPA. She was widely acclaimed as the most luxurious ship afloat, but after 17 years of worldwide cruising she was sold to Star Cruises, but retained for a further year until the new EUROPA was delivered. She was possibly renamed MEGASTAR ASIA for a very short time, but soon had the name SUPERSTAR EUROPE for cruising the waters of Southeast Asia. In February 2000 she became the SUPERSTAR ARIES and was due to transfer to the Orient Lines fleet in the spring of 2003 as the OCEAN VOYAGER, but following a general downturn in business, was retained within the Star Cruises fleet. She was sold to Pullmantur in 2003 and renamed HOLIDAY DREAM in March 2004. Her Caribbean winter cruises were also marketed by Brazilian tour operator CVC, but with the acquisition of Pullmantur by American based Royal Caribbean, her Cuba calls ceased. In early 2008 she was transferred from Pullmantur to Croisieres de France and after refit in Barcelona was renamed BLEU DE FRANCE. She was acquired by Saga in 2010, and chartered back to Pullmantur until late 2011. Following a major refit by Fincantieri in Palermo she entered service in March 2012 as the SAGA SAPPHIRE, but immediately ran into mechanical problems causing the maiden cruise to be curtailed and the following one to be cancelled. IMO 7822457

SAGA HOLIDAYS

The Company Saga Holidays offers a wide range of holidays throughout the world, including some small ship cruising on the Croatian coast.

Address Enbrook Park, Folkestone, Kent, CT20 3SE, England

Telephone +44 1303 771964 **Fax** +44 1303 771243

Website www.saga.co.uk

Area operated Croatian coast

DALMATIA		gt	2011	8.5k	D2	38p	42p	c	37.0m	7.6m	m	HR
EMANUEL	306gt	2006	9.5k	D1	36p	36p	c	37.6m	7.0m	m	HR
LIBERTY		gt	2011	9.0k	D2	40p	40p	7c	45.0m	9.0m	m	HR
VAPOR	197gt	2005	10.0k	D1	36p	40p	c	33.0m	7.6m	m	HR

All of the above ships were built locally in Croatia and are marketed by Katarina Line when not being used by Saga.

SAIL WINDJAMMER

The Company Sail Windjammer is a relative newcomer operating a single former Windjammer Barefoot Cruises ship.

Telephone +1 888 972 9745

Website www.sailwindjammer.com

Area operated Grenada

MANDALAY	420gt	1923	7.0k	SD1	58p	58p	25c	61.6m	10.0m	4.9m	TZ

MANDALAY is a barquentine, which was built for E F Hutton by Burmeister & Wain (yard number 323) in Copenhagen, Denmark and named HUSSAR. She was acquired by George Vetlesen and Maude Monell in 1935 and renamed as the VELMA. After war service with the United States she was acquired by Columbia University for operation as a research ship from about 1953. Windjammer Barefoot Cruises acquired her in 1983, when she was renamed MANDALAY. On the demise of that company in 2008 she was purchased by her Angermeyer Cruises and refitted for service in the Galapagos Islands. It is unclear if this service ever operated and she was acquired by her current owner. The MANDALAY is probably the only cruise ship to be registered in Zanzibar. IMO 7738383

SAIMAA TRAVEL

The Company Saimaa Travel is a Finnish travel agency, which acquired the BRAHE in 2010. The BRAHE has been chartered to Nordisk Cruise Line, a company associated with the owners of Saimaa Travel, for two years.

Address Kipparinkatu 1, FI 51300 Lappeenranta, Finland

Telephone +358 5 5410 100 **Fax** +358 5 5410 140

Website www.saimaatravel.fi

Area operated Coasts and inland waterways of Southern Finland

BRAHE	1105gt	1943	12.0k	D2	90p	110p	24c	56.5m	10.1m	2.8m	FI

BRAHE was built in 1943 by the Pullman Standard Car Manufacturing Company of Chicago, Illinois, USA as the US warship PCE 830, later BEC 4. Subsequently she became the British naval ship HMS KILCHERNAN. She was sold to Norwegian owners and rebuilt as the coastal passenger ferry SUNNHORDLAND. She began cruising as the KRISTINA BRAHE for Fagerlines on the coasts and lakes of Finland in 1975, passing to Kristina Cruises in 1985. Saimaa Travel acquired the ship in 2010 and renamed her BRAHE. Peter Brahe was at one time the Regent of Finland. IMO 5345065

SALAMIS CRUISE LINES

The Company Salamis Cruise Lines is a Cypriot private sector company within the Salamis Tours (Holdings) Group (established in 1959), which is publicly quoted on the Cyprus Stock Exchange. The company previously operated the most regular service on long ferry routes in the Eastern Mediterranean. However, the political violence in the state of Israel and the occupied territories of Palestine caused this service to cease in 2002. The company's ro-ro passenger ferry has been variously laid up and chartered to other Mediterranean operators, but was sold in 2005. Salamis Lines has operated short cruises from Cyprus for a number of years, and also owns two ro-ro freighters.

Address Salamis House, 1 G. Katsounotos Street, PO Box 50531, 3607 Lemesos, Cyprus

Telephone +357 2586 0000 **Fax** +357 2537 4437

Website www.salamiscruiselines.com

Area operated Short cruises from Cyprus to Israel and the Greek Islands

SALAMIS FILOXENIA	15402gt	1975	22.0k	D2	510p	800p	216c	156.3m	21.8m	5.9m	CY

SALAMIS FILOXENIA was owned by Club Cruise of The Netherlands' subsidiary Maritime & Leasing Ltd and operated on year-round charter for Travelscope until the beginning of 2008. She was built by Wartsila (yard number 1213) at Turku, Finland as the GRUZIYA, one of a series of five ro-ro passenger vessels for the Black Sea Shipping Company of Odessa, and was immediately chartered to the German tour operator, TUI. She subsequently operated for a number of charterers until the early 1990's when, following the break-up of the Soviet Union, the Black Sea Shipping Company was in financial difficulties. In 1994 the ship was chartered to the United States Military Sealift Command. In the following year BLASCO, as her owners had become, renamed her as the ODESSA SKY. In 1998 she was converted at Bremerhaven for use as the casino ship CLUB CRUISE 1, and was later renamed simply as CLUB 1. She was acquired by Club Cruise in 1999, converted back to a normal cruise ship and renamed as the VAN GOGH. Her first charter in 2000 was to Nouvelles Frontieres, but in recent years she became a regular with Travelscope. On the failure of Travelscope, Club Cruise tried to

Sail Windjammer's **Mandalay** *(Chris Mason)*

Salamis Cruise Lines' **Salamis Filoxenia** at Syros *(Rick Frendt)*

Sea Cloud Cruises' **Sea Cloud II** at Le Havre *(Philippe Brebant)*

operate the ship under the trading name of Van Gogh Cruises, but this was unsuccessful and the ship eventually operated under charter to Metropolis Tur of Russia in 2008. She was laid up at Piraeus until sold at auction to Salamis Lines. She was renamed SALAMIS FILOXENIA and replaced the 1962-built SALAMIS GLORY in 2010. Filoxenia translates as hospitality. IMO 7359400

SEA CLOUD CRUISES

The Company Sea Cloud Cruises, founded in 1979, is a subsidiary of the German Hansa Truehand Group, a business with interests in ship management, engineering and consultancy. The company also currently operates a single river cruise ship on the waterways of Europe, having recently disposed of the other vessel. The remaining ship, RIVER CLOUD II has also been sold for delivery at the end of 2014.

Address An der Alster 9, D20099 Hamburg, Germany

Telephone +49 403 095 250 **Fax** +49 403 095 9222

Website www.seacloud.com

Area operated Worldwide

SEA CLOUD	2532gt	1931	12.0k	SD2	64p	64p	60c	109.7m	14.6m	4.9m	MT
SEA CLOUD II	3849gt	2000	14.0k	SD2	94p	94p	65c	117.0m	16.0m	5.3m	MT

SEA CLOUD was built by the Krupp Shipyard in Kiel, Germany as the HUSSAR, the largest sailing yacht ever built, for E F Hutton, a wealthy New York businessman. After their divorce in 1935, Hutton handed the ship over to his former wife (who had actually designed the vessel) and she renamed her SEA CLOUD. Following the entry of the United States into the Second World War, the SEA CLOUD was taken up for military service, principally around the Azores and Southern Greenland. She was equipped with weaponry and also served as a weather station under the name IX-99. The ship was returned to her owners at the end of the war, and after a refit lasting four years she re-emerged as good as new. The SEA CLOUD was sold in 1955, becoming the presidential yacht of the Dominican Republic, and renamed ANGELITA. Following the assassination of the president in 1961, she was renamed again, becoming the PATRIA. Five years later, she was back in American hands as the ANTARNA for Operation Sea Cruises. She was subsequently laid up at Colon for eight years before being bought by her German owners and renamed again as the SEA CLOUD. She was refitted in Kiel, and entered service as a sail cruise ship in 1979. Her current owners acquired her in 1994. During late 2010 and early 2011 the ship was upgraded to comply with the 2010 SOLAS requirements and she re-entered service in May 2011. IMO 8843446

SEA CLOUD II was built by Astilleros Gondan (yard number 405) at Castropol, Spain for operation by Sea Cloud Cruises. IMO 9171292

Cruise ship on order

SEA CLOUD HUSSAR	4228gt	2014	14.0k	SDE2	136p	136p	90c	135.7m	17.2m	5.6m	MT

SEA CLOUD HUSSAR is under construction by Factoria de Naval Marin (yard number 158) at Marin, near Vigo, Spain and is expected to become the largest full-rigged passenger tall ship ever built if she eventually enters service. There have been long delays in the construction process. IMO 9483712

SEADREAM YACHT CLUB

The Company Seadream Yacht Club, a Norwegian registered company, was founded in August 2001 by Atle Brynestad (the founder of Seabourn) and Larry Pimentel (former President of Cunard-Seabourn). Pimentel retired in January 2009. The company operates two luxury yacht-type vessels.

Address 601 Brickell Key Drive, Suite 1050, Miami, Florida 33131, United States of America

Telephone +1 305 631 6100 **Fax** +1 305 631 6110

Website www.seadream.com

Area operated Mediterranean Sea in summer, Caribbean Sea in winter

SEADREAM I	4333gt	1984	17.5k	D2	112p	112p	95c	104.8m	14.5m	4.3m	BS
SEADREAM II	4333gt	1985	17.5k	D2	112p	112p	95c	104.8m	14.5m	4.3m	BS

SEADREAM I and **SEADREAM II** were built as the SEA GODDESS I and SEA GODDESS II by Wartsila (yard numbers 466 and 467) at Helsinki, Finland for Sea Goddess Cruises of Norway (Norske Cruise) as luxury yacht style vessels. Following a disastrous year for the company in 1986, Cunard Line took the two ships on a twelve-year charter. Cunard continued to market the ships as Sea Goddesses. Following the acquisition of Cunard by Carnival Corporation in 1998, the ships were transferred to Carnival's luxury cruise line, Seabourn, and renamed as SEABOURN GODDESS I and II. In 2001 they were both sold to a new company, Seadream Yacht Club and renamed SEADREAM I and SEADREAM II. IMO 8203438 and 8203440

SERENISSIMA CRUISES

The Company Serenissima Cruises was formed to acquire and bring the ANDREA back into service. It is a trading name of Russian river cruise operator Volga Cruises. One of the lead charterers is Noble Caledonia.

Website www.msserenissima.com

Area operated Generally chartered out

SERENISSIMA	1960	2598gt	17.5k	D2	107p	107p	40c	87.4m	13.3m	4.9m	SV

SERENISSIMA was built by AS Trondheims Mek. Verksted (yard number 244) at Trondheim, Norway as the HARALD JARL for Det Nordenfjeldske Dampskibsselskab (NFDS) for service on the Norwegian Coastal Express (Hurtigruten). In 1989 she passed to another Hurtigruten operator, TFDS. She continued to operate in this service until sold in 2002 to Elegant Cruises and refitted for use as a luxury expedition cruise ship. She was renamed ANDREA, after the granddaughter of the company's president. Elegant Cruises was declared bankrupt in 2009 and the ship spent some years under arrest in Croatia before being purchased by her current owner. The refurbishment to meet current SOLAS requirements (started by Elegant Cruises) was completed and as SERENISSIMA she re-entered service in the spring of 2013. IMO 5142657

SILVERSEA CRUISES

The Company Silversea Cruises, created by the Lefebvre family of Rome debuted in 1994 with its first ship, the SILVER CLOUD. A recent innovation has been to provide personalised voyages allowing embarkation and disembarkation at almost any port, providing a minimum of five nights is spent aboard. In a diversification, the company entered the soft expedition market in 2008 with the introduction of the PRINCE ALBERT II. Eventually, the option on a sister to the SILVER SPIRIT was not exercised. Galapagos operator Canordos and its single ship was acquired in 2012 and as the SILVER GALAPAGOS the ship joined the fleet in September 2013.

Address Head Office Gildo Pastor Centre, 7 rue de Gabian, 98000 Monte Carlo, Monaco

European office: Level 3, The Asticas Building, 21 Palmer Street, London, SW1H 0AH, England

Telephone +377 9770 2424 **Fax** +377 9770 2428

+44 844 251 0837 **Fax** +44 844 770 9060

Website www.silversea.com

Areas operated Worldwide

SILVER CLOUD	16927gt	1994	20.0k	D2	296p	296p	222c	155.8m	21.4m	5.3m	BS
SILVER DISCOVERER	5218gt	1989	18.0k	D2	120p	120p	96c	103.0m	15.4m	4.3m	BS
SILVER EXPLORER	6130gt	1989	14.0k	D2	132p	132p	117c	108.1m	15.6m	4.4m	BS
SILVER GALAPAGOS	4077gt	1990	14.5k	D2	100p	100p	75c	88.3m	15.3m	4.0m	EC
SILVER SHADOW	28258gt	2000	20.5k	D2	382p	382p	302c	182.0m	24.8m	6.0m	BS
SILVER SPIRIT	36009gt	2009	20.3k	D2	540p	540p	376c	195.8m	26.6m	6.3m	BS
SILVER WHISPER	28258gt	2001	20.5k	D2	382p	388p	302c	182.0m	24.8m	6.0m	BS
SILVER WIND	17235gt	1995	20.0k	D2	298p	298p	222c	155.8m	21.4m	5.3m	BS

SILVER CLOUD and **SILVER WIND** were built by Cantieri Navali Visentini (yard numbers 775 and 776) at Donada, Italy and completed by Esercizio at Viareggio, Italy. The SILVER WIND underwent a major refurbishment in the autumn of 2008. IMO 8903923 and 8903935

SILVER DISCOVERER was built by Nippon Kokan KK (yard number 112) at Tsu, Japan as the OCEANIC GRACE for Oceanic Cruises. In 1997 she was renamed as the OCEANIC ODYSSEY for Spice Island Cruises, but lasted less than a year with that organisation, being sold in 1998 and becoming the

Sea Cloud Cruises' *Sea Cloud* off Nice *(William Mayes)*

Seadream Yacht Club's *Seadream I* off Cannes *(William Mayes)*

Serenissima Cruises' *Serenissima* in Venice *(William Mayes)*

Silversea's *Silver Explorer* off Honfleur *(Philippe Brebant)*

Silversea's *Silver Spirit* at San Juan *(Rick Frendt)*

Silversea's *Silver Whisper* at Bequia *(Rick Frendt)*

CLIPPER ODYSSEY for Clipper Cruise Line. When First Choice Holidays acquired Clipper Cruise Line, the CLIPPER ODYSSEY was not required and was sold to Clipper Group, from whom she is seasonally chartered by Abercrombie & Kent and Noble Caledonia, amongst others. In 2008 she was chartered to Zegrahm Expedition (TUI) for five years. In 2013 she was taken on charter by Silversea, refitted and renamed SILVER DISCOVERER. Her christening by Elda Turco Bulgherini, professor of law at the University of Rome, took place in March 2014 in Singapore. IMO 8800195

SILVER EXPLORER was built by Rauma Repola (yard number 304) at Rauma, Finland as the DELFIN CLIPPER for Delfin Cruises. Following the failure of Delfin she was repossessed by her builder and later renamed SALLY CLIPPER in 1990 for a charter to Sally Line for Baltic cruising. In 1992 she became the BALTIC CLIPPER and later that year was renamed again, becoming the DELFIN STAR for gambling cruises from Hong Kong and Singapore. She was sold to the Samsung Shipyard in South Korea in 1997 and renamed DREAM 21. She was subsequently renamed WORLD DISCOVERER in 2002 when sold to Discoverer Reederei (the owner of Society Expeditions). Society Expeditions ceased trading in June 2004. She was subsequently repossessed by the Sembawang Shipyard, which was owed substantial sums in respect of her conversion, and remained laid up in Singapore. She was reported to have been sold to Chikara Shipping early in 2007, but that transaction was never completed. Subsequently she was acquired by Silversea and after a major refit has emerged as the soft expedition ship PRINCE ALBERT II. She was renamed in Monte Carlo in the presence of HSH Prince Albert II. Early in 2011 she was renamed again, becoming the SILVER EXPLORER. IMO 8806747

SILVER GALAPAGOS was built by Cantieri Navali Ferrari (yard number 45) at La Spezia, Italy as the RENAISSANCE THREE for Renaissance Cruises. She was purchased by Canodros in 1997, as a replacement for the GALAPAGOS EXPLORER. Canodros and the ship were acquired by Silversea in 2012 and after refit and renaming as SILVER GALAPAGOS she entered service in September 2013. IMO 8708660

SILVER SHADOW and **SILVER WHISPER** were built by Cantieri Navali Visentini (yard numbers 981 and 982) at Donada, Italy and completed by T. Mariotti at Genoa, Italy. IMO 9192167 and 9192179

SILVER SPIRIT was ordered from Fincantieri (yard number 6178) in March 2007 and was completed at the Ancona yard. She enterered service on 23 December 2009 and was named in Port Everglades by Silia Lefebvre on 21 January 2010. IMO 9437866

SKORPIOS TOURS

The Company Naviera & Turismo Skorpios is a Chilean private sector business, founded in 1976 by Constantino Kochifas Caracamo, a businessman and shipowner from Southern Chile. The first cruises to the San Rafael Glacier utilized the small cargo ship MIMI, with a capacity for 12 passengers. The company's next ship, SKORPIOS I, operated from 1978 to 2008.

Address Augusto Leguia Norte 118, Las Condes, Santiago, Chile

Telephone +56 2 477 1900 **Fax** +56 2 232 2269

Website www.skorpios.cl

Area operated Chilean Patagonia

SKORPIOS II	1263gt	1988	12.0k	D1	130p	160p	34c	70.0m	10.0m	2.9m	CL
SKORPIOS III	1597gt	1995	14.0k	D1	100p	125p	34c	69.0m	10.0m	3.3m	CL

SKORPIOS II was built by Kochifas (yard number 1) at Puerto Montt in Chile. She was launched in 1981, but not completed until 1988. IMO 8006397

SKORPIOS III was built by Kochifas Shipyard (yard number 2) at Puerto Montt, Chile. IMO 9143908

ST LAWRENCE CRUISE LINES

The Company St Lawrence Cruise Lines, a Canadian business, was founded by Robert Clark in 1981.

Address Suite 200, 253 Ontario Street, Kingston, Ontario, K7L 2Z4 Canada

Telephone +1 613 549 8091 **Fax** +1 613 549 8410

Website www.stlawrencecruiselines.com

Area operated The St Lawrence and Ottawa Rivers in Canada

CANADIAN EMPRESS	463gt	1981	10.0k	DE2	64p	66p	13c	32.9m	9.2m	1.5m	CA

CANADIAN EMPRESS was built for the company in Canada.

STAR CLIPPERS

The Company Star Clippers was founded by Swedish entrepreneur Mikael Krafft in 1991. Fred. Olsen Travel is the United Kingdom agent for Star Clippers. Until the recent economic downturn, the company was planning to build a new ship for delivery in 2010. However, the 7,400 gross ton, 296-passenger ship has been deferred for the time being.

Address Clipper Palace, 4 rue de la Turbie, 98000 Monte Carlo, Monaco

Telephone +377 9797 8400 **Fax** +377 9797 8401

Website www.starclippers.com

Area operated Caribbean Sea, French Polynesia and the Far East, all three ships operate in the Mediterranean Sea in summer

ROYAL CLIPPER	4425gt	2000	13.5k	SD1	227p	227p	105c	132.7m	16.0m	5.7m	MT
STAR CLIPPER	2298gt	1992	12.0k	SD1	170p	170p	75c	111.6m	15.0m	5.5m	MT
STAR FLYER	2298gt	1991	12.0k	SD1	170p	170p	75c	111.6m	15.0m	5.5m	MT

ROYAL CLIPPER, inspired by the legendary tall ship, PREUSSEN of 1902, is the only 5-masted full-rigged ship built since that time. Her 42 sails require a crew of 20 just to handle the canvas. She was built by Stocznia Gdansk (yard number B811/01) at Gdansk, Poland, and was launched as the GWAREK in 1991 for Zaglebie Gdanska S A. Her hull lay incomplete at Gdansk until purchased by White Star Clippers in 1998. At that time her owners contracted with Cenal Shipyard to lengthen the hull by 23 metres, and this hull was then delivered to the de Merwede shipyard in The Netherlands for fitting out in April 1999. She had originally been fitted with Sulzer-Cegielski engines, but these were replaced with Caterpillar diesels. She was completed and delivered as the ROYAL CLIPPER in July 2000. She cruises in the Caribbean and Mediterranean Seas. IMO 8712178

STAR CLIPPER and **STAR FLYER** were built by Scheepswerf van Langerbrugge (yard numbers 2184 and 2183) at Ghent, Belgium. The STAR FLYER was actually launched as the STAR CLIPPER, but following a complaint by American owner Clipper Cruise Line, the name was changed. Star Clippers subsequently won the US court case and called the second ship STAR CLIPPER. The STAR FLYER operated in Northern Europe for the first time in 2012, and also, along with her sister, cruises in the Mediterranean and Caribbean Seas. IMO 8915445 and 8915433

TRAVEL DYNAMICS INTERNATIONAL

The Company Travel Dynamics International, formerly known as Classical Cruises, is an operator of high calibre educational programmes on small ships and was founded in the 1970's. The company operated the CLELIA II, CORINTHIAN and CALLISTO. Now the company no longer appears to operate any vessels for its own account but offers space on other ships, including three of those operated by Grand Circle Cruise Line.

Address 132 East 70th Street, New York, NY 10021-5007, United States of America

Telephone +1 212 517 7555 **Fax** +1 212 774 1560

Website www.traveldynamics.com

EXPLORER MARITIME CRUISES

The Company Explorer Maritime Cruises is a trading name of Travel Dynamics International.

Address 132 East 70th Street, New York, NY 10021-5007, United States of America

Telephone +1 212 517 7555 **Fax** +1 212 774 1560

Area operated East Coast USA and Canada and the Great Lakes

YORKTOWN	2354gt	1988	10.0k	D2	138p	138p	42c	78.3m	12.2m	3.8m	US

YORKTOWN was built in 1988 by First Coast Shipbuilding Inc, at Green Cove Springs, Florida, USA as the YORKTOWN CLIPPER for Clipper Cruise Line. Cruise West acquired her in 2006 and later renamed

Silversea's **Silver Wind** arriving at Lanzarote *(William Mayes)*

Star Clippers' **Royal Clipper** off Piran, Slovenia *(William Mayes)*

Star Clippers' **Star Flyer** in Hamburg *(William Mayes)*

her as the SPIRIT OF YORKTOWN. Following a period of lay up in Seattle after the collapse of Cruise West she was acquired by Travel Dynamics and renamed YORKTOWN. Unfortunately, the ship has suffered from serious mechanical problems and the current season's cruises have been cancelled and the ship is laid up. IMO 8949472

TUI AG

The Group TUI AG, of Germany, is the largest tourism and service group in the world, employing more than 80,000 people in over 500 companies throughout the world. TUI and Carnival Corporation agreed to set up a joint venture company in Germany, of which Aida Cruises would be a building block. However, the proposed deal failed to get regulatory approval and instead TUI formed a joint venture with Royal Caribbean Cruise Lines, TUI Cruises. The first ship to be allocated to this new operation was the former Celebrity Cruises' GALAXY. TUI AG merged with UK based First Choice Holidays in 2007 to form TUI Travel plc, in which TUI had a 51% stake. At that time Thomson Cruises was transferred from TUI AG to the new UK business, bringing the English speaking brands together. TUI Travel plc became wholly owned by TUI AG in 2014. TUI AG still holds a significant stake in containership owner Hapag-Lloyd.

Address Karl-Weichert-Allee 4, 30625 Hanover, Germany

Telephone +49 511 56600 **Fax** +49 511 5661901

Website www.tui-group.com

HAPAG LLOYD CRUISES

The Company Hapag-Lloyd Cruises is part of the giant German shipping group Hapag-Lloyd, itself part of the travel and leisure group TUI. Hapag-Lloyd was formed in 1970 on the amalgamation of Hamburg America Line and Norddeutscher Lloyd. The former had been established in 1847 by a group of Hamburg ship owners and businessmen. The North German Lloyd company was formed ten years later. At the outbreak of the First World War, Hamburg America Line (Hapag) was one of the world's largest shipping companies, with a fleet of 175 ships, including some magnificent transatlantic liners. NDL had 135 ships at this time, and both companies effectively lost all of them. Hapag re-entered the passenger shipping market in 1923 with the liner ALBERT BALLIN, and during the following year NDL introduced the COLUMBUS, the largest and fastest ship in the German fleet. By 1926, Hapag was once again a major ship owner with a fleet of 118 vessels. NDL's BREMEN took the Blue Riband of the North Atlantic in 1929. The Second World War saw the loss of both fleets for the second time, following which NDL concentrated on passenger trades and Hapag on cargo services. The Preussag Group acquired a controlling interest in Hapag-Lloyd in 1997, and five years later acquired the minority interests to become the sole shareholder. In 1998 Hapag-Lloyd acquired a majority shareholding in the major German travel group Touristik Union International. In 2001 Preussag re-branded its tourist businesses as World of TUI. Until 2009 Hapag-Lloyd operated an impressive fleet of large containerships, but then disposed of a majority interest in that business. With the arrival of the EUROPA 2 it is clear that the company intends to maintain its position at the top of the German market.

Address Ballindamm 25, 20095 Hamburg, Germany

Telephone +49 40 3070 3070

Website www.hl-cruises.com

Area operated Worldwide

BREMEN	6752gt	1990	15.0k	D2	155p	164p	100c	111.5m	17.0m	4.6m	BS
EUROPA	28890gt	1999	21.0k	DEP2	400p	400p	285c	198.6m	24.0m	6.1m	BS
EUROPA 2	42830gt	2013	18.0k	DEP2	500p	500p	370c	225.3m	26.7m	6.3m	MT
HANSEATIC	8378gt	1991	16.0k	D2	175p	184p	125c	122.7m	18.0m	4.8m	BS

BREMEN began life as the FRONTIER SPIRIT, an expedition ship for Japan's NYK Line. She was built by Mitsubishi Heavy Industries (yard Number 1182) at Kobe in Japan. She has been used by Hapag-Lloyd as the expedition cruise ship BREMEN since 1993. In 2005 she was to have been chartered to a new business under the name Expedition Leaders in order to promote dual language (German and English) cruises, but that arrangement never materialised. Her programme includes Antarctica, Greenland and Northern Europe. The city of Bremen in Germany, after which this ship is named, has a history going back more than 1,200 years, and played a major role in the Hanseatic League. IMO 8907424

Hapag-Lloyd's **Bremen** in Helsinki *(William Mayes)*

Hapag-Lloyd's **Europa 2** off Rovinj, Croatia *(William Mayes)*

Hapag-Lloyd's **Europa** off Santorini *(Rick Frendt)*

TUI Cruises' *Mein Schiff 2* in Hamburg *(William Mayes)*

TUI Cruises' *Mein Schiff 3* at Kotor *(William Mayes)*

Quark Expeditions' *Ocean Nova* at Longyearbyen *(William Mayes)*

EUROPA was built by Kvaerner Masa Yards (yard number 495) in Helsinki, Finland as a replacement for an earlier, and unusually, larger ship of the same name. IMO 9183855

EUROPA 2 was built by the STX France yard (yard number H33) at St Nazaire and delivered in 2013. IMO 9616230

HANSEATIC was built by Rauma Yards (yard number 306) at Rauma in Finland in 1991 as the SOCIETY ADVENTURER for Society Expeditions. However, once completed she was laid up in the shipyard until March 1993, when she was chartered by Hanseatic Tours and given the name HANSEATIC. Hanseatic Tours was acquired by Hapag-Lloyd in 1996. The HANSEATIC operates in Antarctica and Greenland, with positioning and other voyages in between. The Hanseatic League was a mercantile league of German and Baltic cities, which began to emerge in the 1240's and which seems to have ceased to have importance in 1669, although never officially dissolved. Hamburg, Lubeck and Bremen are still known as Hanseatic Cities. IMO 9000168

TUI CRUISES

The Company TUI Cruises is a German Joint Venture between Royal Caribbean Cruise Lines and TUI AG, established in 2008. The company commenced operating in spring 2009. In addition to the ships listed the company holds options for a further pair, to be named MEIN SCHIFF 7 and MEIN SCHIFF 8 for delivery in 2018 and 2019.

Address Anckelmannsplatz 1, 20537 Hamburg, Germany

Telephone +49 40 286 677168 **Fax** +49 40 286 677103

Website www.tuicruises.com

Area Operated Caribbean, Baltic and Mediterranean Seas and Norway

MEIN SCHIFF 1	76998gt	1996	21.5k	D2	1924p	2232p	780c	263.9m	32.2m	7.7m	MT
MEIN SCHIFF 2	77302gt	1997	21.5k	D2	1912p	2229p	780c	263.9m	32.2m	7.7m	MT
MEIN SCHIFF 3	99526gt	2014	21.7k	DEP2	2506p	2790p	1000c	293.2m	35.8m	8.0m	MT

MEIN SCHIFF 1 is the second member of a trio of ships built by Jos. L. Meyer (yard number 638) at Papenburg, Germany for Celebrity Cruises as the GALAXY. Renamed CELEBRITY GALAXY in 2008, in spring 2009 she was transferred to TUI Cruises, the new Royal Caribbean/TUI German joint venture, to become the company's first ship and after a refit in Bremerhaven was renamed MEIN SCHIFF. In anticipation of the arrival of a second ship she was renamed as MEIN SCHIFF 1 in November 2010. IMO 9106297

MEIN SCHIFF 2 is the third and final member of the trio of ships built by Jos. L. Meyer (yard number 639) at Papenburg, Germany for Celebrity Cruises. She entered service in 1997 as the MERCURY and was renamed in 2008 as the CELEBRITY MERCURY. She was transferred to TUI Cruises to begin operating for that company in 2011, when she was renamed MEIN SCHIFF 2 by Olympic fencing champion Anja Fichtel. IMO 9106302

MEIN SCHIFF 3 is the company's first new ship and was built by STX Finland (yard number 1383) at Turku. She was delivered in June 2014, named by Helene Fischer, and spends her first season in the Mediterranean. IMO 9641730

Cruise ship on order

MEIN SCHIFF 4	c99500gt	2015	21.7k	DEP2	2506p	2790p	1000c	293.2m	35.8m	8.0m	MT
MEIN SCHIFF 5	c99500gt	2016	21.7k	DEP2	2506p	2790p	1000c	293.2m	35.8m	8.0m	MT
MEIN SCHIFF 6	c99500gt	2017	21.7k	DEP2	2506p	2790p	1000c	293.2m	35.8m	8.0m	MT

MEIN SCHIFF 4 is under construction by STX Finland (yard number 1384). IMO 9678408

MEIN SCHIFF 5 and **6** were ordered from Meyer Finland in August 2014. IMO 9753193 and 9753208

TUI TRAVEL

The Company The Adventure Fleet, formerly First Choice Expedition Cruising, was part of First Choice Holidays, a leading British-based international leisure travel group. First Choice was, until the spring of 2009, a partner with Royal Caribbean Cruises Limited in Island Cruises (see under RCCL). In 2007 First Choice holidays merged with TUI AG to form TUI Travel plc. TUI AG held 51% of the new company, with the remainder in the hands of the former shareholders of First Choice. First Choice Expedition

Cruising was formed in 2006 by the amalgamation of Australian-based Peregrine Adventures and Intrav's Clipper Cruise Line. In May 2007 the company acquired Quark Expeditions, and during the spring of 2008 reorganised the expedition cruise business under the name The Adventure Fleet. The Clipper Cruise Line name was discontinued and the CLIPPER ODYSSEY returned to her owner. The Adventure Fleet name has now been dropped and Quark Expeditions is the dominant brand. TUI AG acquired the remaining shares in TUI Travel plc in 2014.

Website www.tuitravelplc.com

QUARK EXPEDITIONS

The Company Founded by Lars Wikander and Mike McDowell, Quark Expeditions began taking travellers to far-flung destinations in 1991 with a voyage aboard the SOVIETSKIY SOYUZ to the North Pole. The KAPITAN KHLEBNIKOV was first used in the following year, and has remained a favourite ever since. Quark Expeditions became part of TUI in 2007. Other expedition operators also market many of the ships and Quark Expeditions also sell voyages on other vessels. OCEAN ENDEAVOUR has been chartered for the southern summer of 2015.

Address 93 Pilgrim Park, Suite 1, Waterbury, VT 05676, United States of America

Telephone +1 203 803 2888 **Fax** +1 203 857 0422

Website www.quarkexpeditions.com

Area operated Arctic (July and August), Antarctic (November to March)

50 LET POBEDY	23439gt	2007	21.4k	NST3	128p	128p	140c	159.6m	28.0m	11.0m	RU
OCEAN DIAMOND	8282gt	1974	16.0k	D2	172p	226p	120c	124.2m	16.0m	4.9m	BS
OCEAN ENDEAVOUR	12907gt	1982	17.5k	D2	198p	198p	c	137.1m	21.0m	5.8m	MH
OCEAN NOVA	2183gt	1992	12.0k	D1	73p	73p	38c	72.8m	11.3m	3.7m	BS
SEA ADVENTURER	4376gt	1975	14.0k	D2	122p	122p	72c	100.0m	16.2m	4.7m	BS
SEA EXPLORER	4200gt	1991	15.5k	D2	114p	114p	70c	90.3m	15.3m	4.0m	MH
SEA SPIRIT	4200gt	1991	14.5k	D2	112p	112p	94c	90.4m	15.3m	4.0m	BS

50 LET POBEDY was built by the Baltijskiy Zavod shipyard (yard number 1705) in St Petersburg, Russia for the Murmansk Shipping Company. Her keel was laid in 1989 and she was launched in 1993, but not completed until 2007. She was originally to have been named URAL, and has a 5-metre wide stainless steel ice belt hull capable of breaking ice up to 2.5 metres thick. She is a nuclear powered icebreaker, whose name translates as 50 Years of Victory; this is the name under which she is marketed. IMO 9152959

OCEAN DIAMOND was built by Kristiansands Mekaniske Verksted (yard number 220) at Kristiansand, Norway, one of a pair of ro-ro freighters, as the BEGONIA (although she was launched as the FERNHILL) for Oslo ship owners, Fearney & Eger. These ships were immediately transferred to an associated Dutch company. Fearney & Eger reacquired the BEGONIA in 1985 and sent her to the Lloyd Werft yard at Bremerhaven; here she was converted into the exploration cruise ship EXPLORER STARSHIP. On completion she was chartered to Exploration Cruise Line and served initially in the Caribbean and later on the US West Coast and in Alaska. Exploration Cruise Line filed for bankruptcy in 1988 and eventually Fearney & Eger were able to recover their ship. She was soon sold to Seven Seas Cruise Line, a new company set up by the Japanese Kawasaki Kisen Kaisha Line and the Norwegian Skaugen concern. Following a refit that converted her to a luxury 214-passenger ship, she entered service from Singapore as the SONG OF FLOWER in February 1990. During the next five years she cruised in most of the then popular cruising areas, but in 1995 the operation was merged with Radisson Diamond Cruises, although her owners retained the ship for a further two years before she was sold to the new Radisson Seven Seas Cruises. No longer in keeping with the remainder of the fleet, she passed to her current operator in 2003 and following a major refit emerged as LE DIAMANT. In 2012 the ship was sold and was renamed by managers FleetPro Ocean as the OCEAN DIAMOND and then chartered to Quark Expeditions. IMO 7325629

OCEAN ENDEAVOUR For details see under Adventure Canada.

OCEAN NOVA was built by the Orskov Shipyard (yard number 159) in Frederikshavn, Denmark for the KNI Pilersvisoq, a Greenland Government company, as the SARPIK ITTUK, a coastal passenger liner. In February 2000 she was lengthened by 23 metres at Stocznia Remontowa, Gdansk, Poland. She was acquired by Nova Cruising and converted for use as a cruise ship in 2006. She is managed by International Shipping Partners of Miami and chartered to Quark Expeditions under the name OCEAN NOVA. IMO 8913916

Quark Expeditions' *Sea Adventurer* *(Mark Oelbaum)*

Thomson Cruises' *Island Escape* at Toulon *(Rick Frendt)*

Thomson Cruises' *Thomson Dream* in Barcelona *(Rick Frendt)*

SEA ADVENTURER was built by Brodogradiliste Titovo (yard number 408) at Kraljevica in what was then Yugoslavia as the ALLA TARASOVA, one of a series of eight ships for Murmansk Shipping for coastal passenger service. Among her surviving sisters are the LYUBOV ORLOVA and the MARIYA YERMOLOVA. In 1997 she was rebuilt as the cruise ship CLIPPER ADVENTURER for Clipper Cruise Line. Clipper Cruise Line was acquired by First Choice Travel and the ship was surplus to requirements so was sold to Clipper Group and chartered back on a limited basis. She then operated on a number of seasonal charters to expedition cruise companies, most noticeably Quark Expeditions. While operating for Adventure Canada in August 2010 she ran onto an uncharted rock in the Arctic. She was refloated and repaired, and then bareboat chartered with purchase options to Albatros Travel Group. That purchase never occurred so she has continued to operate in the charter market. She was renamed SEA ADVENTURER in October 2012. IMO 7391422

SEA EXPLORER was built as the RENAISSANCE SEVEN by Nuovi Cantieri Apuania (yard number 1146) at Marina di Carrara, Italy for Renaissance Cruises. She became the REGINA RENAISSANCE in 1992, reverting to her original name in 1998. Sold in 2001 she was renamed as the RENAI I. In 2003 she became the SUN, and in the following year was renamed as the ISLAND SUN. She was then owned by Mauritius Island Cruises, but was sold in 2005 along with her sister the ISLAND SKY (now operated by Noble Caledonia) to the Danish Clipper Group. Mauritius Island Cruises has now ceased to trade. The ship was renamed CORINTHIAN II and following a refit in Piraeus was chartered to Travel Dynamics for service in the Mediterranean Sea and beyond. She subsequently passed to Clipper Group, was renamed SEA EXPLORER and operates for Quark Expeditions. IMO 8802882

SEA SPIRIT was built at the Italian Marina di Carrara yard of Nuovi Cantieri Apuania (yard number 1144) as the RENAISSANCE FIVE for Renaissance Cruises. Sold in 1997 to Sun Viva, she was renamed as the SUN VIVA. When Star Cruises acquired that company in 2000 she became the MEGASTAR SAGITTARIUS, but was quickly sold to Cruise West and renamed SPIRIT OF OCEANUS. In 2010 this ship began a unique world cruise which was to have lasted for 335 days. The tour was terminated early and the ship was sold to Clipper Group, who renamed her SEA SPIRIT and almost immediately chartered her to Quark Expeditions. IMO 8802868

THOMSON CRUISES

The Company Thomson Holidays, the long established British package holiday company began offering cruises on other companies ships in the late 1960's, but by 1973 the company was chartering ships on a long-term basis. The first such vessels were the CALYPSO, formerly Shaw Savill & Albion's SOUTHERN CROSS and the rather smaller ITHACA that had been built for Zim Israel as the ZION. Lord Thomson founded the company in 1965, with the purchase of Universal Sky Tours, Britannia Airways and Riviera Holidays. By 1974 Thomson was the largest of the UK package tour operators. Thomson withdrew from the charter market in the early 1980's, but later re-entered the market with the ISLAND BREEZE, THE EMERALD and THE TOPAZ. Thomson Travel Group was floated on the London Stock Exchange by the Thomson Group in 1999, and in the following year was acquired by the German Preussag Group. In 2001 Preussag re-branded its tourist business as World of TUI, encompassing 66 brands within the group. In 2007, Thomson Travel Group became part of TUI Travel plc on the merger of TUI AG and First Choice Holidays.

Address Wigmore House, Wigmore Lane, Luton, LU2 9EX, England

Telephone +44 1582 399970

Website www.thomson.co.uk

Area operated Scandinavia, Mediterranean, Atlantic Islands, Caribbean and the Red Sea

ISLAND ESCAPE	40171gt	1982	18.0k	D2	1536p	1741p	540c	185.2m	27.0m	6.8m	BS
THOMSON CELEBRATION	33933gt	1984	18.0k	D2	1254p	1374p	520c	214.7m	27.2m	7.5m	MT
THOMSON DREAM	54763gt	1986	22.5k	D2	1506p	1773p	600c	243.2m	29.7m	6.5m	MT
THOMSON MAJESTY	41662gt	1992	21.0k	D2	1462p	1800p	600c	207.3m	27.6m	5.8m	MT
THOMSON SPIRIT	33930gt	1983	18.0k	D2	1254p	1374p	520c	214.7m	27.2m	7.5m	MT

ISLAND ESCAPE was built by Dubigeon-Normandie (yard number 164) at Nantes, France for The United Steamship Company (Bahamas) Ltd, a DFDS of Copenhagen subsidiary, as the SCANDINAVIA to operate in the cruise ferry service between New York and the Bahamas for Scandinavia World Voyages. After disappointing results she was transferred to DFDS and put into service on its capital cities car ferry route between Copenhagen and Oslo in 1984. Later that year she was sold to Sundance Cruises of Nassau, Bahamas and after a refit entered service as the STARDANCER in spring 1985. In

Thomson Cruises' **Thomson Majesty** in Corfu *(William Mayes)*

Thomson Cruises' **Thomson Spirit** at Zeebrugge *(William Mayes)*

Un-Cruise Adventures' **Safari Endeavour** at Juneau *(Rick Frendt)*

the summer months she operated from Vancouver to Alaska and in winter from Los Angeles to Puerto Vallarta. In 1990 she was sold to Royal Caribbean Cruise Line, renamed VIKING SERENADE and put into service on the West Coast of the USA. During a major refit in 1991 by Southwest Marine in San Diego, California, passenger cabins replaced her car decks. She continued to operate for Royal Caribbean until being transferred to a new joint venture with British tour operator First Choice in spring 2002. Renamed as the ISLAND ESCAPE, her itineraries for the newly formed Island Cruises included the Mediterranean in summer and South America in winter. Island Cruises ceased trading in spring 2009 and the company's ships were dispersed to the partners in the joint venture. The ISLAND ESCAPE joined the Thomson fleet and continues to offer a casual style of cruising in the western Mediterranean and around the Canary Islands. The ship operates from Palma between March and October and is laid up over the winter. IMO 8002597

THOMSON CELEBRATION is one of a pair of cruise ships ordered by Holland America Line from Chantiers de l'Atlantique (yard number X27) at St Nazaire, France in 1980. She was delivered as the NOORDAM in March 1984 and sailed on her maiden voyage from Le Havre, France to Tampa, Florida on 8 April. She subsequently cruised to Alaska in the summer and to Mexico in the winter. In later years she often spent the summer in Europe. In late 2004 she was chartered by Holland America Line to Thomson Cruises and renamed the THOMSON CELEBRATION. She was acquired by TUI in 2010. Her debut season featured ex-UK cruises in the summer, after which she was based in the Canary Islands. She now uses Marmaris in Turkey as her summer base, and operates in the Caribbean in winter. IMO 8027298

THOMSON DREAM was built for Home Lines by Jos. L. Meyer (yard number 610) at Papenburg, Germany and delivered in 1986 as the HOMERIC. She operated for Home Lines on their summer service between New York and Hamilton, Bermuda, but spent her winters cruising in the Caribbean. Home Lines was acquired by Holland America Line in 1988 and on 2 November the HOMERIC was renamed WESTERDAM. Her duties were now split between the Caribbean (winter) and Alaska cruises from Vancouver (summer). In October 1989 the ship was returned to her builders to have a 39.6 metre mid section inserted, resuming service in March 1990 and subsequently being re-registered to the Dutch flag in 1996. She was transferred to Costa Crociere during 2002 and renamed COSTA EUROPA. During a refit in 2007 the area over the bridge that was previously a cinema was converted into six grand suites with oval balconies. From April 2010 she is chartered to Thomson Cruises as the THOMSON DREAM for a period of ten years. After a first season, during which she was subject to some criticism, she underwent a seven-week refit at Blohm & Voss in Hamburg, which is also thought to have included the replacement of the main engine blocks. The ship is based in Palma during the summer and in the winter operates a programme in the Caribbean. IMO 8407735

THOMSON MAJESTY was laid down for Birka Line of Mariehamn, Aland Islands by Wartsila (yard number 1312) at Turku, Finland. She was to have been named BIRKA QUEEN. Following the failure of Wartsila, the ship was completed by Kvaerner Masa Yards for Majesty Cruise Line as the ROYAL MAJESTY and made her maiden voyage from Southampton to New York in July 1992. She was 32,396 tons and 173.5 metres long as built and subsequently operated for Dolphin Cruise Line. She passed to Norwegian Cruise Line in 1997 and was renamed NORWEGIAN MAJESTY. In 1999 she was lengthened by 33.8 metres by Lloydwerft at Bremerhaven, Germany by means of a new mid-section constructed by Aker MTW at Wismar, Germany. She was sold to Louis Cruise Lines in 2008, but continued to operate on Caribbean itineraries for NCL until delivered to Louis in late 2009, at which time she was renamed LOUIS MAJESTY for Western Mediterranean itineraries. In 2012 she was swapped with THOMSON DESTINY (now LOUIS OLYMPIA) and renamed THOMSON MAJESTY. She is currently based in Corfu in the summer and in the Canary Islands in the winter. IMO 8814744

THOMSON SPIRIT was built by Chantiers de l'Atlantique (yard number V27) at St Nazaire, France as the first of a pair of ships of fairly revolutionary appearance for Holland America Line. She was delivered as the NIEUW AMSTERDAM in 1983. In 2000 she was sold to American Hawaii Cruises (part of American Classic Voyages) for use in the Hawaiian Islands as the PATRIOT. Following the September 11 terrorist attacks in 2001, the company collapsed and the ship was repossessed by Holland America Line and laid up. She was chartered to Louis Cruise Lines in May 2002 and renamed SPIRIT. In May 2003 she was sub-chartered to Thomson Cruises, as the THOMSON SPIRIT. During the spring of 2007 she operated for Louis Cruise Lines as the SPIRIT, and spent a further two weeks deputizing for the ill-fated SEA DIAMOND. Louis Cruise Lines acquired the ship in 2008. She now operates in Northern Europe for Thomson, but often undertakes cruises for Louis before and after her main season. For the summer of 2012 the THOMSON SPIRIT re-introduced Thomson's ex-UK cruise programme, but in 2015 Thomson will again not be operating from UK ports. The THOMSON SPIRIT will be based in the Eastern Mediterranean for the summer of 2015. She only operates for Thomson during the summer period. IMO 8024014

ZEGRAHM EXPEDITIONS

The Company Zegrahm Expeditions is a Seattle-based expedition cruise and holiday company, formed in 1990, that had the CLIPPER ODYSSEY on a five-year charter from Clipper Group. The company also charters and sells space on other expedition ships. Zegrahm Expeditions was acquired by TUI plc in July 2009 and may be incorporated into Quark Expeditions in due course. Cruises on other operators' expedition ships are also offered. The company is not currently operating any ships for its own account.

Address 192 Nickerson Street, Suite 200, Seattle, Washington State, 98109, United States of America

Telephone +1 206 285 4000 **Fax** +1 206 285 5037

Website www.zegrahm.com

TURISMO NUEVO MUNDO

The Company Turismo Nuevo Mundo is a major Chilean tour operator, which now appears to be operating Antarctic Shipping Corporation's ANTARCTIC DREAM. That company was founded in Chile in 2002 by a group of former naval officers.

Address Turismo Nuevo Mundo Building, Muelle Prat s/n, Valparaiso, Chile

Telephone +56 32 225 3817

Website www.turismonuevomundo.com

Area operated Antarctica and Patagonia, and Spitzbergen

ANTARCTIC DREAM	2180gt	1959	10.0k	D3	80p	80p	40c	82.0m	11.9m	4.6m	HN

ANTARCTIC DREAM was built by Haarlemsche Scheepsbouw (yard number 552) at Haarlem in the Netherlands as the PILOTO PARDO for the Chilean Navy. In 1998 she was sold to Paoa Naviera and renamed as the HOTU MATUA. She joined her current owner, Dreamright Investment, in 2003 and adopted the name ANTARCTIC DREAM for her new cruise services. Since 2009 a range of Spitzbergen itineraries have been offered during the summer. The ship is now operated by Turismo Nuevo Mundo. IMO 5278432

UN-CRUISE ADVENTURES

The Company Dan Blanchard, former CEO of American Safari Cruises, formed Inner Sea Discoveries early in 2009 and acquired the assets of American Safari Cruises, which had been established in 2007. The company later purchased two of the vessels from the long-defunct Glacier Bay Cruiseline and following refurbishment they entered service in May 2011. The company re-branded itself as Un-Cruise Adventures in 2012 and absorbed the fleet of American Safari Cruises.

Address 3826 18th Avenue W, Seattle, WA98119, United States of America

Telephone +1 206 284 0300 **Fax** +1 206 283 9322

Website www.un-cruise.com

Area operated Alaska, California, Mexico and Hawaii

SAFARI ENDEAVOUR	1425gt	1983	13.0k	D2	102p	107p	28c	66.1m	11.3m	2.6m	US
SAFARI EXPLORER	695gt	1998	10.0k	D2	36p	40p	16c	45.7m	11.6m	m	US
SAFARI VOYAGER	1195gt	1983	9.0k	D2	64p	64p	29c	51.9m	11.0m	m	CO
S S LEGACY	1472gt	1984	13.0k	D1	96p	99p	26c	58.5m	12.2m	2.9m	US
WILDERNESS ADVENTURER	c500gt	1983	10.0k	D1	60p	60p	20c	47.5m	11.6m	m	US
WILDERNESS DISCOVERER	‡683gt	1992	10.0k	D2	76p	76p	24c	51.5m	11.9m	m	US
WILDERNESS EXPLORER	910gt	1976	13.0k	D2	84p	84p	21c	51.8m	11.0m	2.1m	US

SAFARI ENDEAVOUR was built by Jeffboat Inc (yard number 82-2542) at Jeffersonville, Indiana, USA as the NEWPORT CLIPPER. She later became SEASPIRIT and took the name SPIRIT OF ENDEAVOUR in 1993 when acquired by Cruise West. Following the failure of that company in 2009 she was laid up in Seattle until acquired by American Safari Cruises in the summer of 2011 and renamed SAFARI ENDEAVOUR. IMO 8963698

Un-Cruise Adventures' **SS Legacy** at Seattle *(Theodore W Scull)*

Un-Cruise Adventures' **Wilderness Discoverer** at Ketchikan *(Rick Frendt)*

Variety Cruises' **Galileo** at Santorini *(William Mayes)*

SAFARI EXPLORER was built by Freeport Shipbuilding and Marine Repair (yard number 151) at Freeport, Florida as the research and survey vessel RAPTURE. She was converted for cruising in 2001, and was acquired by her current owner in 2008 and renamed SAFARI EXPLORER. IMO 8964654

SAFARI VOYAGER was built by the Chesapeake Marine Railway Company in Baltimore, USA as the AMERICA. She later became the TEMPTRESS VOYAGER and took her current name in 2002 when acquired by Voyager Holdings. She operated for Lindblad in Baja California, Costa Rica and Nicaragua. The ship was acquired by Colombia Ecotourism in 2010 without a change of name. She was acquired in 2013 by Un-Cruise Adventures and after renovation was renamed as SAFARI VOYAGER. IMO 8963753

SS LEGACY was built by Bender Shipbuilding & Repair Company (yard number 140) at Mobile, Alabama, USA as the PILGRIM BELLE. On sale to Cruise West (West Travel) in 1984 she became the COLONIAL EXPLORER, and in 1988 was renamed again as VICTORIAN EMPRESS. In 1993 she became SPIRIT OF 98 and was employed on the Columbia and Snake Rivers. Cruise West ceased trading in September 2010 and the ship was laid up until acquired by American Safari Cruises and renamed SAFARI LEGACY. She was renamed SS LEGACY in 2012. IMO 8963703

WILDERNESS ADVENTURER was built by Blount Marine Corporation (yard number 250) at Warren, Rhode Island, USA as the CARIBBEAN PRINCE for American Canadian Caribbean Line. Glacier Bay Cruiseline purchased her in 1997 and she was renamed WILDERNESS ADVENTURER. Glacier Bay Cruiseline ceased trading in 2005 and the ships were laid up. WILDERNESS ADVENTURER was acquired by Inner Sea Discoveries in 2010 and following refurbishment entered service in May 2011. IMO 8978667

WILDERNESS DISCOVERER was built by Blount Marine Corporation (yard number 280) at Warren, Rhode Island, USA as the MAYAN PRINCE for American Canadian Caribbean Line. She was acquired by Glacier Bay Cruiseline in 1998 and renamed WILDERNESS DISCOVERER. New operator Inner Sea Discoveries bought the ship in 2010; she had been laid up since the demise of Glacier Bay Cruiseline in 2005. IMO 8859689

WILDERNESS EXPLORER was built by the Eastern Shipbuilding Corporation (yard number 1) at Boothbay Harbor, Maine, USA as the COLUMBIA. However, when launched she had the name INDEPENDENCE. She was operated by American Cruise Lines until acquired by Cruise West in 2000 and renamed as the SPIRIT OF DISCOVERY. Cruise West ceased trading in September 2010 and the fleet was laid up. Inner Sea Discoveries acquired the ship in September 2011 and renamed her WILDERNESS EXPLORER. IMO 7641413

UNKNOWN CHINESE OPERATOR

JIA RI	7717gt	1986	16.0k	D2	400p	400p	200c	120.0m	18.8m	5.2m	CN

JIA RI was built at the Xingang Shipyard in China as the coastal passenger/cargo vessel BAI LING. She was converted into the cruise ship JIA RI by Guangzhou Wenchong Shipyard in 1998, and has since operated short cruises in Chinese waters. Until recently she has been in use by her owner, Shanghai Wan Bang Cruise Company, which is a subsidiary of the Shenzhen Zhongda Cruise Company. She was then chartered to Shanghai Inter-Continents Cruiser Management Company for operation between Beihai in China and Halong Bay in Vietnam as the GLOBETROT PRINCESS. She was sold in December 2013 and renamed JIA RI. IMO 9028029

VARIETY CRUISES formerly ZEUS GROUP

The Company Variety Cruises is an operating name for Zeus Group. The Zeus Group is a Greek company whose origins can be traced back to the founding of D Venetopoulos Travel and Tourism in 1949 by Diogenis Venetopoulos. In 1966 the company was renamed as Zeus Tours and two years later began offering small ship cruises using the chartered yacht ELEFTHERIOS. In 1973 the company's first owned vessel, the NIKI, a converted wooden cargo vessel joined the fleet. Today the Zeus Group operates under the brand Variety Cruises. In 2006 the business of Variety Yachting was established as the owner/manager of small motor yachts, too small to warrant inclusion in this book.

Address 214-216 Syngrou Avenue, 17672 Athens, Greece

Telephone +30 210 691 9191 **Fax** +30 210 699 8484

Website www.varietycruises.com

Area operated Aegean Ionian and Red Seas

GALILEO	480gt	1995	11.0k	SD2	52p	55p	17c	48.0m	10.0m	2.9m	GR
HARMONY G	498gt	2001	11.0k	D2	44p	46p	17c	53.9m	7.1m	3.7m	GR
HARMONY V	693gt	1985	12.0k	D2	50p	52p	16c	55.0m	8.2m	3.0m	GR
PAN ORAMA	674gt	1991	11.0k	SD2	50p	54p	18c	53.3m	12.0m	3.0m	GR
PAN ORAMA II	498gt	2004	10.0k	SD1	50p	55p	18c	50.0m	11.0m	4.3m	GR
PEGASUS	730gt	1990	10.0k	D2	46p	51p	17c	45.0m	11.0m	3.0m	GR
VARIETY VOYAGER	1593gt	2012	14.0k	D2	72p	72p	28c	68.0m	11.5m	3.5m	GR

GALILEO was built by Fratsis G Shipyard (yard number 470) at Perama, Greece as a three-masted yacht for the Zeus Group. IMO 8986286

HARMONY G was built by N Savvas Shipyard at Eleusis in Greece. IMO 8984989

HARMONY V was built by Dentas Gemi Insaat ve Onarim Sanayii (yard number 34) in Istanbul, Turkey as the TURA for Goksel Denizcilik. She was renamed TURQUAZ in 2000. She became DIOGENIS V later the same year. She underwent a rebuild in 2009 and was renamed HARMONY V. IMO 8620853

PAN ORAMA was built by N Kastrinos (yard number 23) at Perama, Greece as a three-masted yacht for the Zeus Group. IMO 8928260

PAN ORAMA II was built by Koutalis Kostergias in Piraeus as the PANTHEON. She was renamed PAN ORAMA II in 2012. IMO 9325453

PEGASUS was built by L Glynos in Greece as the DOUBLE FORCE. She was renamed PEGASUS in 2002 and acquired by Zeus Group in 2006. IMO 8936841

VARIETY VOYAGER was completed as the HARMONY A by Emmanouil Psarros shipyard (yard number 08013) in Piraeus. IMO 9657090

VIKING LINE

The Company Today's Viking Line is the sole remaining company from the consortium that formed the original Viking Line in 1959, when the VIKING began sailing between Finland, the Aland Islands and Sweden. That company was Vikinglinjen AB, established by Aland Island sea captain Gunnar Eklund. The company joined forces with Rederi AB Slite and Alandfarjan AB (later SF Line) to form the joint marketing company Oy Viking Line AB in 1966. Vikinglinjen AB (then part of Rederi AB Sally) left the consortium in 1988 and Rederi AB Slite was put into liquidation by the banks in 1993, leaving just SF Line, which restyled itself as Viking Line in 1995. Viking Line is one of the two major ferry companies operating overnight services between Stockholm, Sweden and Helsinki and Turku, both Finland.

Address Norragatan 4, AX 22100 Mariehamn, Aland Islands, Finland

Telephone +358 18 26211 **Fax** +358 18 26116

Website www.vikingline.fi

Area operated 24 hour cruises from Stockholm, Sweden

VIKING CINDERELLA	46398gt	1989	22.0k	D2	1828p	2766p	224c	190.9m	29.0m	6.6m	SE

VIKING CINDERELLA was built by the Wartsila shipyard (yard number 1302) in Turku, Finland as the CINDERELLA for the SF Line of Finland, part of the Viking Line consortium. She was initially employed on the overnight intercity route between Stockholm and Helsinki, providing a tandem sailing on alternate nights. She also provided some cruise sailings from Helsinki to Tallinn. From 1993 she became the principal vessel on the Stockholm to Helsinki service, running opposite the MARIELLA. With the arrival of the GABRIELLA, she switched to full time cruising, initially from Helsinki, but latterly from Stockholm. She was renamed VIKING CINDERELLA in 2003. The VIKING CINDERELLA has a large vehicle deck, which allows passengers to park their cars on the ship while on the 24-hour cruise to Mariehamn. IMO 8719188

Variety Cruises' *Pan Orama* at Corfu *(William Mayes)*

Viking Line's *Viking Cinderella* in Stockholm *(William Mayes)*

Viking Ocean Cruises' *Viking Star* *(Fincantieri)*

Voyages to Antiquity's ***Aegean Odyssey*** at Rhodes *(Clive Harvey)*

Windstar Cruises' ***Star Pride*** in Istanbul *(William Mayes)*

Windstar Cruises' ***Wind Star*** off Kusadasi *(Martin Grant)*

VIKING OCEAN CRUISES

The Company Viking Ocean Cruises is a start up ocean cruise operator that is part of the hugely successful Viking River Cruises, now operating a fleet of 53 vessels. The company's first two ships were ordered from Fincantieri in April 2012. The order was later increased to four ships with options for two more. Viking River Cruises was established in 1997

Address Scharferweg 18, 4057 Basel, Switzerland

Website www.vikingcruises.co.uk/oceans

Area operated Mediterranean and Northern Europe

Cruise ships on order

VIKING STAR	c47800gt	2015	k	DE2	930p	930p	c	227.2m	28.8m	6.3m	MT
VIKING SEA	c47800gt	2016	k	DE2	930p	930p	c	227.2m	28.8m	6.3m	MT
VIKING SUN	c47800gt	2016	k	DE2	930p	930p	c	227.2m	28.8m	6.3m	MT
NEWBUILD 4	c47800gt	2017	k	DE2	930p	930p	c	227.2m	28.8m	6.3m	MT

VIKING STAR and **VIKING SEA** are the first two ships ordered from Fincantieri (yard numbers 6236 and 6237) at the Marghera shipyard in Venice. The VIKING STAR was floated out on 24 June 2014. IMO 9650418 and 9650420

VIKING SUN and **NEWBUILD 4** are the second pair of ships ordered from Fincantieri. IMO 9725421 and 9725433

VOYAGES TO ANTIQUITY

The Company Voyages to Antiquity was established in 2009 by serial cruise company founder Gerry Herrod to operate the AEGEAN ODYSSEY on Eastern Mediterranean cultural cruise itineraries. Herrod had previously created Ocean Cruise Lines, Orient Lines and Discovery World Cruises.

Address 8 South Parade, Summertown, Oxford, OX2 7JL, United Kingdom

Telephone +44 1865 302 550

Website www.voyagestoantiquity.com

Area operated Mediterranean, Red Sea and Black Sea

AEGEAN ODYSSEY	12094gt	1973	18.0k	D2	378p	378p	c	140.5m	20.8m	6.6m	MT

AEGEAN ODYSSEY began life as the ro-ro cargo ship NARCIS of Zim Israel Navigation of Haifa. She was built by Santierul Naval Galatz (yard number 617) at Galatz, Romania. In 1985 she was acquired by Dolphin Hellas Shipping and renamed ALKYON. She was substantially refitted at Perama, Greece and re-delivered in 1988 as the AEGEAN DOLPHIN. During the following year she was renamed the DOLPHIN, but she reverted to her previous name in 1990. In 1996 she was renamed AEGEAN I and operated at least one cruise for Discovery Cruises. She also undertook a charter to Renaissance Cruises in that year. In 1998 she commenced cruising for Golden Star Cruises. Following an ownership dispute involving Louis Cruise Lines the ship was laid up in 2006. She was acquired by Gerry Herrod in 2008 and given a major refurbishment in Greece before entering service in 2010 as the AEGEAN ODYSSEY. She had a major refit towards the end of 2012 during which 18 new cabins were added. IMO 7225910

WINDSTAR CRUISES

The Company Windstar Cruises Inc. has its origins in the formation in 1984 of Windstar Sail Cruises Limited, a Bahamas registered company set up by Karl Gosta Andren to build and operate the first large commercial sailing vessels since the 1920's. The first two ships were ordered in October 1985 and a third shortly afterwards with an option for a fourth ship, never exercised. The WIND STAR was delivered in October 1986, followed six months later by the WIND SONG. Unfortunately, the company's marketing failed to generate the passenger volume required to fill their ships, so in June 1987 Holland America took on this role, at the same time acquiring a 50% stake in the company. The remaining 50% was purchased in September 1988 and although the company retained an outward appearance of independence, there was a certain amount of integration behind the scenes. In 1994 the head office was moved to Holland America's address in Seattle and the company name was changed to Windstar Cruises Inc. In early 2003 the WIND SONG, suffered an engine room fire and was declared a constructive total loss. She was subsequently scuttled. Windstar Cruises became part of Ambassadors International in early 2007, when it was acquired from Carnival Corporation. In mid 2009, the company took over the management of its vessels from V-Ships. As Ambassadors International began to feel the effects of recession it closed Majestic America Line (Delta Queen Steamboat Company and American West) and attempted to concentrate on Windstar. However in early 2011 Ambassadors International filed for Chapter 11 bankruptcy protection and subsequently sold Windstar to Xanterra Parks and Resorts. Early in 2013 the company announced the acquisition of the SEABOURN LEGEND, SEABOURN PRIDE and SEABOURN SPIRIT.

Address 2101 4th Avenue, Suite 210, Seattle, WA 98121, United States of America

Telephone +1 206 292 9606 **Fax** +1 206 340 0975

Website www.windstarcruises.com

Areas operated Mediterranean and Caribbean

STAR BREEZE	9975gt	1989	19.0k	D2	208p	212p	150c	133.8m	19.0m	5.2m	BS
STAR LEGEND	9961gt	1992	19.0k	D2	208p	212p	150c	135.0m	19.0m	5.2m	BS
STAR PRIDE	9975gt	1988	19.0k	D2	208p	212p	150c	133.8m	19.0m	5.2m	BS
WIND SPIRIT	5736gt	1988	14.0k	SD1	148p	168p	91c	134.2m	15.8m	4.1m	BS
WIND STAR	5703gt	1986	12.0k	SD1	148p	168p	91c	134.2m	15.5m	4.1m	BS
WIND SURF	14745gt	1989	12.0k	SDE2	308p	397p	178c	187.2m	20.0m	5.0m	BS

STAR BREEZE was the second ship to be delivered to Seabourn by Schichau Seebeckwerft (yard number 1070) at Bremerhaven in Germany, and christened by Aagot Brynestad. In November 2005 the SEABOURN SPIRIT became the first cruise ship to be attacked by pirates off the coast of Somalia. The SEABOURN SPIRIT has been sold to Windstar Cruises with delivery in spring 2015. She will be renamed STAR BREEZE. IMO 8807997

STAR LEGEND was to have been the third ship of the series for Seabourn Cruise Line. However, the company did not exercise the option, although Royal Viking Line effectively later took it up. She was delivered to that company by Schichau Seebeckwerft (yard number 1071), Bremerhaven as the ROYAL VIKING QUEEN in 1992. By this time the three original Royal Viking ships had left the company, so the fleet consisted of only this ship and the ROYAL VIKING SUN. She was renamed QUEEN ODYSSEY in 1994 and passed to Seabourn in 1996, becoming the SEABOURN LEGEND. She has been sold to Windstar Cruises with delivery in 2015, and will be renamed STAR LEGEND. IMO 9008598

STAR PRIDE was ordered from Schichau Seebeckwerft (yard number 1065) at Bremerhaven in Germany as the first of two luxurious mega-yachts by the newly formed Seabourn Cruise Line. She was christened as the SEABOURN PRIDE by Shirley Temple Black. The ship was sold to Windstar Cruises in 2013 with delivery in 2014 after which she became the STAR PRIDE in April 2014. IMO 8707343

WIND SPIRIT was built, along with her sisters the WIND STAR and the WIND SONG (lost in 2003), by Societe Nouvelle des Ateliers et Chantiers du Havre (yard number 272) at Le Havre, France, as a motorised sailing yacht capable of being schooner rigged. She is the fastest of the trio of ships built for the company. Wind assisted she can make 17 knots and has sailed predominantly in the Mediterranean and Caribbean. Clara van der Vorm, wife of the then chairman of Holland America Line, christened her. IMO 8603509

WIND STAR was delivered in late 1986 by Societe Nouvelle des Ateliers et Chantiers du Havre (yard number 269) and following a positioning cruise spent a season in French Polynesia. Her godmother was Louise Andren, the wife of the line's founder. She generally operates in the Caribbean and Mediterranean. IMO 8420878

WIND SURF was built by Societe Nouvelle des Ateliers et Chantiers du Havre (yard number 274) for Club Mediterranee SA (Club Med) of France. She was launched in 1988 as LA FAYETTE but was delivered in the following year as the CLUB MED 1, and registered in Fort de France, Martinique, thus qualifying her for French state subsidies. Wind assisted she is capable of making 14 knots. She operated in the Caribbean and Mediterranean as the CLUB MED 1 until June 1997 when she was bought by Windstar Cruises and renamed WIND SURF. Her operational areas remain unchanged. IMO 8700785

Windstar Cruises' **Wind Surf** at Rodney Bay St. Lucia *(Rick Frendt)*

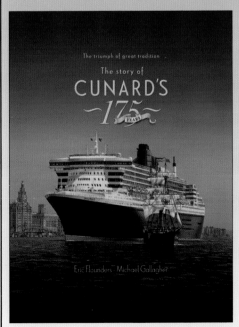

the **leading** *guide to the cruise industry*

section 2 Gambling Cruise Ships

GRAND CRUISES HOLDINGS

The Company Grand Cruises Holdings is part of the Hong Kong based Oceanic Group, set up to offer gambling cruises to nowhere from Singapore. She is usually anchored in International waters with gamblers shuttled to and fro by high speed ferry.

Website www.grandcruises.com.sg

Area operated

OCEAN GRAND	30413gt	1991	D2 21.8k	1600p	1600p	c	192.9m	29.4m	6.8m	PA

OCEAN GRAND was built by IHI (yard number 3012) in Tokyo as the ro-ro ferry FERRY LAVENDER for Shin Nihonkai Ferry Company. She was chartered by Agoudimos Lines in 2004 for service in the Adriatic as IONIAN KING. In 2011 she became the OCEAN ROSE and has now been chartered for three years for her new service, for which much of the car deck was converted for passenger use. She is owned by the Japanese theme park Ten Huis Bosch. IMO 9006629

JIMEI GROUP

The Company The Jimei Group is a Hong Kong registered company that operates in the casino cruise trade. The ship is registered to Sky High Fortune Maritime.

Address 1 B Hyde Center, 221 Gloucester Road, Wan Chai, Hong Kong, Peoples Republic of China

Telephone +852 2730 2000 **Fax**: + 852 2730 2488

Website www.jimei.com.hk

Area operated Gambling cruises from Hong Kong

JI MEI	9878gt	1966	21.0k	D2	412p	614p	c	140.8m	20.0m	5.8m	PA

JI MEI was built by Kieler Howaldtswerke (yard number 1190) as the Jahre Line ferry PRINSESSE RAGNHILD for the Oslo, Norway – Kiel, Germany service. After brief stints as JALINA and AMATISTA, she was sold to Fujian Xiamen Shipping of China and renamed JIN JIANG in 1981. Used as a ferry between Hong Kong and Xiamen, her name was later changed to JI MEI. In 1998 she was withdrawn from service and chartered to the newly formed Jimei Group to operate in the casino trades. She was given an extensive internal rebuilding when the company bought her outright in 2000. She operates both day and overnight cruises from Hong Kong, as well as a monthly cruise along the Chinese coast. IMO 6604482

MAJESTIC STAR CASINO

The Company Majestic Star Casino is an Indiana casino operator, founded by Don Barden in 1993. Although this ship has never had overnight accommodation, she is included due to her size.

Address 1 Buffington Harbour Drive, Gary, Indiana 46406-3001, United States of America

Telephone +1 888 225 8259

Website www.majesticstar.com

Area operated Gambling cruises from Gary, Indiana

MAJESTIC STAR	12805gt	1997	k	DP4	400d		c	108.0m	23.1m	3.5m	US

MAJESTIC STAR was built by Atlantic Marine (yard number 234) at Jacksonville, Florida, USA. IMO 8642933

Grand Cruise Holdings' **Ocean Grand** at Singapore *(Mark M Amielanczyk)*

Jimei Group's **Ji Mei** in Hong Kong *(Mark M Amielanczyk)*

Metropolis Cruise's **China Star** in Hong Kong *(Jonathan Boonzaier)*

METROPOLIS CRUISE

The Company Metropolis Cruise is a subsidiary of Hong Kong registered Hopewin Ship Management Limited.

Address Shop 5C1, Star House, 3 Salisbury Road, Tsim Sha Tsui, Kowloon, Hong Kong, Peoples Republic of China

Telephone +852 2736 8236

Website www.metropolis-cruise.com

Area operated Hong Kong

CHINA STAR	20295gt	1992	12.5k	D2	354p	354p	206c	131.2m	32.0m	8.4m	BS
METROPOLIS	17261gt	1972	18.7k	D2	761p	1000p	130c	155.0m	22.8m	6.0m	JM
ORIENTAL DRAGON	18455gt	1972	18.0k	D2	500p	500p	400c	168.4m	24.0m	6.3m	PA
STARRY METROPOLIS	15791gt	1976	21.0k	D2	500p	500p	200c	156.3m	21.8m	5.9m	JM

CHINA STAR was built by Finnyards (yard number 310) at Rauma, Finland as the RADISSON DIAMOND for Diamond Cruise Line. Conceived for a conference/seminar/incentive tours market, she had greater success as a cruise ship. She is still the only SWATH (Small Waterplane Area Twin Hull) cruise vessel. Her owners merged later with Seven Seas Cruises to become Radisson Seven Seas Cruises. She was sold to Asia Cruiser Club in early 2005 with delivery in June, at the end of her time with Radisson Seven Seas Cruises, for use as the gambling ship OMAR STAR in the Hong Kong casino cruise trade. In October 2005 she was renamed as the ASIA STAR. When the ship moved to Singapore she traded as Ben's Entertainment City. In June 2010 her operator became Treasure Ocean Limited, a British Virgin Islands company. She is now at least marketed by Metropolis Cruise as the CHINA STAR. IMO 9008407

METROPOLIS was built in Shimizu, Japan by K K Kanashasi Zosensho (yard number 1008) as the car and freight ferry SHIRETOKO MARU for Nippon Enkai Ferry KK of Tokyo. She was sold to Minoan Lines of Greece in 1988 and completely rebuilt as the passenger and car ferry N KAZANTZAKIS. China Golden Development Holdings purchased her in 2001, renamed her MING FAI PRINCESS and rebuilt her into a cruise ship with numerous gambling facilities. Initially she operated between Hainan Island in China and Halong Bay in Vietnam. In January 2007 she was renamed METROPOLIS, without a change of owner. Her current operator is styled as Metropolis Cruise Limited and she only operates from Hong Kong. IMO 7215161

ORIENTAL DRAGON was built as the SUN VIKING for the Wilhelmsen Group for its new joint venture, Royal Caribbean Cruise Lines, by Wartsila (yard number 394) at Helsinki, Finland as one of a trio of revolutionary new Caribbean cruise ships. She was the only one of the three ships not to be lengthened in 1978-80. Her ownership was officially transferred to Royal Caribbean in 1991. In 1994 she was sold to Star Cruises and renamed SUPERSTAR SAGITTARIUS for a new career cruising in South East Asia. In 1998 she was purchased by Hyundai Merchant Marine of Seoul, South Korea and began offering short cruises as the HYUNDAI PONGNAE. This venture was relatively unsuccessful and after a period of lay-up and brief service in China as the PONGNAE, she was sold to Kong Way of Hong Kong. Renamed OMAR III, she was marketed under the Asia Cruiser Club banner from Hong Kong. She then moved to Asia Cruise International in Singapore, initially under charter. She was acquired by the company in June 2007 and renamed LONG JIE. Following the opening of shore-based casinos in Singapore the company ceased trading and the ship was sold to Capital Dragon Global Holding of Hong Kong in March 2011 for conversion back to a conventional cruise ship. She was subsequently renamed ORIENTAL DRAGON. She has been acquired by Hopewin Ship Management and is now back in Hong Kong. IMO 7125861

STARRY METROPOLIS was built by Wartsila (yard number 1223) at Turku, Finland as the Russian cruise ferry KARELIYA. She was one of a class of five similar vessels and operated for many years under charter to London-based CTC cruises as the KARELIYA and later under the name LEONID BREZHNEV. After the break up of the Soviet Union she was renamed as the KARELIYA by the Black Sea Shipping Company. In 1998 she was sold to Kaalbye Shipping and renamed OLVIA. She was chartered to various cruise operators, and later operated for Peaceboat. She was sold to Wide Asia in early 2005, and entered the Hong Kong casino cruise trade in September as the CT NEPTUNE. She was later renamed as the NEPTUNE. She was renamed as STARRY METROPOLIS in 2011 when acquired by Hopewin Ship Management. IMO 7359498

Metropolis Cruise's **Oriental Dragon** in Hong Kong *(Jonathan Boonzaier)*

New Century's **Amusement World** at Penang *(Jonathan Boonzaier)*

New Century's **Leisure World** off Singapore *(Jonathan Boonzaier)*

NEW CENTURY CRUISE LINE

The Company New Century Cruise Lines is a Singapore-based casino cruise operator, founded in 1993 by Singaporean Albert Ng. From 2004 the company has been managed by Universal Shipmanagement, part of New Century Group.

Address 50 Tanah Merah Ferry Road, Singapore, 498833

Telephone +65 6214 2822

Website www.nctoursonline.com

Area operated Singapore and Malaysia

| AMUSEMENT WORLD | 12764gt | 1967 | 18.0k | D2 | 635p | 635p | c | 141.2m | 22.5m | 5.5m | PW |
| LEISURE WORLD | 15653gt | 1969 | 16.0k | D2 | 580p | 850p | c | 160.3m | 22.8m | 6.3m | PW |

NOTE: New Century ships carry a significant number of day cruise passengers who do not occupy cabins. Their numbers are not factored into above statistics. Furthermore, the ships have very large casino staffs. Some of these occupy passenger cabins, while others commute to the ships by ferry on a daily basis.

AMUSEMENT WORLD was built as Swedish Lloyd's ferry PATRICIA for service between the UK and Spain, by AB Lindholmens Varv (yard number 1095) in Gothenburg, Sweden. She was sold to Stena Line and became STENA OCEANICA in 1978. Since then she has sailed for numerous operators in a variety of roles under the names STENA SAGA, LION QUEEN, CROWN PRINCESS VICTORIA, PACIFIC STAR and SUN FIESTA. She was sold to New Century in 1997, and operated briefly as PUTRI BINTANG before becoming the casino ship AMUSEMENT WORLD. She operates mainly out of Penang in Malaysia. IMO 6620773

LEISURE WORLD was built by AG Weser Werk Seebeck (yard number 942) at Bremerhaven, Germany as the SKYWARD for Klosters Rederi, Oslo (Norwegian Caribbean Cruise Line) for cruising in the Caribbean Sea. She was sold for Asian cruising in 1991 as the SHANGRI-LA WORLD and during the following year became the ASEAN WORLD. Later in 1992 she was renamed as the FANTASY WORLD, then in 1993 as the CONTINENTAL WORLD. Later in 1993 she became the LEISURE WORLD for gambling cruises. She continues to operate in this trade and is usually anchored in international waters off Singapore, with gamblers shuttled to and fro by high speed ferry. IMO 6921828

SKYWILL MANAGEMENT

The Company Skywill Management is a Hong Kong company established in 2013.

Address Room 1407, 7th Floor Nan Fung Tower, 173 Des Voeux Road Central, Hong Kong, Peoples Republic of China

Area operated Hong Kong

| NEW IMPERIAL STAR | 12586gt | 1980 | 20.0k | D2 | 333p | 528p | c | 137.1m | 21.0m | 5.3m | SV |

NEW IMPERIAL STAR was built by Stocznia Szczecinska (yard number B492/01) at Szczecin, Poland as the DMITRIY SHOSTAKOVICH for the Black Sea Shipping Company of the Soviet Union. Following the collapse of that company she passed through a number of owners between 1996 and 2000, when she was rebuilt at the Remontowa Shipyard in Gdansk, Poland and later acquired by Macro Maritime, a Liberian registered company, and renamed PALOMA for Columbus Leisure Line. She was renamed PALOMA I in 2003 when acquired by D&P Cruises, an Italian company. Subsequently she undertook a number of charters, including that to Hansa Kreuzfahrten for whom she operated in the Mediterranean and Northern Europe. She was sold by D&P in February 2007 to Everis Capital Holdings for use as a gambling ship in Singapore and renamed ROYALE STAR. In 2010 she was laid up, after a brief stint operating from Penang, following the opening of casinos in Singapore. During 2013 the ship appears to have run some cruises from North Korea. In September 2013 she was acquired by Arising International Holdings and renamed NEW IMPERIAL STAR. IMO 7625794

SUCCESS CRUISES

The Company Success Cruises is now owned by Star Sail Investments, following the sale of the company and its single ship in 2014. It was previously owned by Success Universe Group and operates in the Hong Kong casino ship trade.

Address Suite 1601-2 & 8-10, 16th Floor, Great Eagle Centre, Wanchai, Hong Kong, Peoples Republic of China

Telephone +852 3107 1111

Website www.successcruises.com

Area operated Hong Kong

| REX FORTUNE | 9848gt | 1974 | 21.0k | D2 | 414p | 600p | 200c | 130.2m | 19.5m | 5.3m | BS |

REX FORTUNE was built by Helsingor Vaerft (yard number 404) at Helsingor, Denmark as the GOLDEN ODYSSEY for the new Royal Cruise Line of Greece. She initially operated cruises in the Mediterranean and later spent winter seasons in South America and the Caribbean Sea. From 1985 she began to spend her winters in South East Asia, and from the following year cruised in Alaskan waters in the summer. In 1989 Royal Cruise Line was sold to Norwegian Cruise Line and although there was little change to the operation, the GOLDEN ODYSSEY was re-flagged to the Bahamas. By 1994 she no longer fitted in with the rest of the fleet and was chartered to Mitsui-OSK Line. Later that year she was sold to Deutsche Seereederei, renamed ASTRA II and chartered to German tour operator Neckermann. She passed to Kong Wing (Asia Cruisers Club) in 2000 and was renamed as the OMAR II for gambling cruises from Hong Kong. She moved to Success Universe Group in 2004 and was renamed MACAU SUCCESS. In 2014 the operation was sold to Star Sail Investments and the ship was renamed REX FORTUNE. IMO 7346934.

Metropolis Cruise's **Starry Metropolis** in Hong Kong. *(Mark M Amielanczyk)*

Success Cruises' **Rex Fortune** as **Macau Success** in Hong Kong *(Mark M Amielanczyk)*

the **leading** *guide to the cruise industry*

section 3 Passenger ships in other transport roles

AMPHITRION YACHTING

The Company Amphitrion yachting is a Greek company. Zeus II operates conventional cruises while the other two vessels are available for charter.

Address Megalou Alexandrou 7, 16452 Argyroupolis, Greece

Telephone +30 210 411 2045

Website www.amphitrion-yachting.com

Area operated Greek islands

H&B I	gt	2001	9.0k	SD2	40p	40p	10c	44.0m	9.0m	3.8m	GR
H&B II	gt	2002	9.0k	SD2	40p	40p	10c	44.0m	9.0m	3.8m	GR
ZEUS II	gt	1942	12.0k	D2	32p	38p	9c	34.5m	5.8m	2.9m	GR

ARCTIC AND ANTARCTIC RESEARCH INSTITUTE

The Company Arctic and Antarctic Research Institute is a Russian state organisation.

Address 38 Bering Street, St Petersburg, 199397 Russia

Telephone +7 812 352 1520 **Fax** +7 812 352 2688

Website www.aari.nw.ru

Area operated Unknown

AKADEMIK TRYOSHNIKOV	12711gt	2012	16.0k	DE2	80p	80p	60c	133.5m	23.0m 13.5m	RU

AKADEMIK TRYOSHNIKOV was built for the Government of Russia's Arctic and Antarctic Research Institute by Admiralteyskiy Sudostroitelnny Zavod (yard number 2440) at Saint Petersburg, Russia. It is unlikely that this ship has been used for expedition cruises yet. IMO 9548536

ARTIKMORNEFTEGAZRAVEDKA

The Company Artikmorneftegazravedka is a Russian state-owned oil and gas exploration company, which appears to operate two passenger vessels in conjunction with its exploration activities.

Address Kolskiy Prospekt 1, 183032 Murmansk, Russia

Telephone +7 815 225 4647 **Fax** +7 815 28115

Website www.amngr.ru

Area operated Unknown

ANNA AKHMATOVA	4575gt	1988	14.3k	D1	150p	150p	34c	90.0m	17.2m	5.3m	RU
BORIS PASTERNAK	4575gt	1989	14.3k	D1	150p	150p	34c	90.0m	17.2m	5.3m	RU

ANNA AKHMATOVA was built by Stocznia im. Komuny Paryskiej (yard number B961/01) at Gdynia, Poland. Anna Akhmatova (1889-1966) was a Ukrainian born poet who found fame with her first poetry collections in 1912 and 1914, but was condemned by the Soviet authorities after the revolution. Following the death of Stalin in 1953 she came back into favour and is now regarded as one of the greatest Russian poets. The ANNA AKHMATOVA is currently laid up. IMO 8509167

BORIS PASTERNAK was built by Stocznia im. Komuny Paryskiej (yard number B961/02) at Gdynia, Poland. Boris Pasternak (1890-1960) was the author of Doctor Zhivago, for which he won the 1958 Nobel Prize for Literature, although he was not allowed to receive it. IMO 8509179

ATOMFLOT

The Company Atomflot (Federal State Enterprise Unitary Atomflot) is a Russian Government controlled company. In August 2008 the management of Russia's nuclear powered icebreakers and support vessels was transferred to Atomflot. This company also controls the ROSSIYA, TAYMIR and VATGACH none of which appear to have carried passengers.

Address 183017 Murmansk, Russia

Telephone +7 815 255 3355 **Fax** +7 815 255 3300

Website www.rosatomflot.ru

Area operated Unknown

50 LET POBEDY	23439gt	2007	21.4k	NST3	128p	128p	140c	159.6m	28.0m	11.0m	RU
SOVETSKIY SOYUZ	20646gt	1989	21.0k	NST3	106p	114p	48c	150.0m	30.0m	11.0m	RU
YAMAL	20646gt	1992	21.0k	NST3	100p	100p	130c	150.0m	30.0m	11.0m	RU

50 LET POBEDY for details see under Quark Expeditions.

SOVETSKIY SOYUZ was built by Baltiyskiy Zavod (yard number 703) at Leningrad, Russia for the Murmansk Shipping Company. Her name commemorates the Soviet Soyuz space programme. This ship is no longer operating as a passenger ship. IMO 8838582

YAMAL was built by the Baltic Shipbuilding and Engineering Works (yard number 704) at St Petersburg, Russia as the nuclear powered icebreaker YAMAL for the Murmansk Shipping Company. The Yamal peninsula in Siberia is home to the Nenets, reindeer herders who have occupied the region for more than 1,000 years. She has operated charters for Quark expeditions for a number of years, but does not appear to be in passenger service in 2011. IMO 9077549

BLUE DREAM SHIPPING

The Company Blue Dream Shipping is a trading name of Loral Ltd, a Turkish-owned Greek registered company founded in 2005 to acquire the TDI KARADENIZ from Turkish Maritime Lines as part of the Turkish Government privatisation scheme.

Address 94 Poseidonos Avenue, Glyfada, 16675 Athens, Greece

Area operated Not currently operating as the ship is being refitted.

DREAM	4326gt	1997	16.8k	D2	46p	46p	62c	106.0m	15.8m	3.9m	MT

DREAM was built by the Halic Shipyard (yard number 303) in Istanbul, Turkey as the overnight passenger vessel and cruise ship TDI KARADENIZ for Turkish Maritime Lines. Latterly she has operated summer cruising seasons in the Eastern Mediterranean. As part of the Turkish Government's privatisation policy, the ship was sold to her current owner in early 2005. The ship remained laid up, although there was the intention to convert her into a cruise ship with the name DREAM. The most current information available suggests that the ship is actually being converted into a private yacht and that she will be named POSEIDONOS. IMO 9005871

CHINA SHIPPING GROUP

The Company China Shipping Group was formed in 1997 with merger of Trans Shanghai, Trans Dalian, Trans Guanghzou, China Shipping International Marine and Zhong Jiao Marine Industry, all Chinese Government controlled companies. China Shipping Group operates more that 450 ships in total, including some smaller passenger vessels on which details are not available. Chinese domestic operators rarely keep Lloyds Register updated on the status of their vessels, and it is therefore likely that some of the ships listed here have already been scrapped.

Address 5th Floor, Shipping Tower, 700 Daming Donglu, Shanghai 200080, Peoples Republic of China

Telephone +86 216 596 6666 **Fax** +86 216 596 6219

Website www.cnshipping.com

Area operated Unknown, but likely to be Chinese coastal

TIAN YUN	‡5500gt	1984	16.5k	D2	948b	d	c	120.0m	17.0m	5.8m	CN
XIANG XUE LAN	16071gt	1996	20.0k	D1	244p	392p	95c	150.5m	24.0m	7.2m	PA

| XIN YU JIN XIANG | 12304gt | 1995 | 20.0k | D2 | 190p | 348p | 93c | 148.2m | 22.7m | 6.1m | CN |

TIAN YUN was built by the Xingang Shipyard (Yard number 248) at Tianjin, China. IMO 8311871

XIANG XUE LAN was built by MTW Schiffswerft (yard number 162) at Wismar, Germany. She operates a passenger and container service between China and South Korea. She was transferred from China Shipping Passenger Liner in 2008. IMO 9086904

XIN YU JIN XIANG was built by De Merwede (yard number 667) at Hardinxveld in the Netherlands as the YU JIN XIANG for China Shipping container Lines. She was transferred to China Shipping in 2008 and renamed. She is currently operated by COSCO Dalian Manning Co-operative. IMO 9110810

CHINA SHIPPING CONTAINER LINES

The Company China Shipping Container Lines is a Chinese Government owned company operating a fleet of around 150 ships. The ships listed here have a high passenger capacity and operate short sea passenger and cargo services across the Yellow Sea.

Address 450 Fushan Lu, Pudong Xinqu, Shanghai 200122, Peoples Republic of China

Telephone +86 216 596 6105

Website www.cscl.com.cn

Area operated China to South Korea

| ARAFURA LILY | 12304gt | 1996 | 20.0k | D2 | 190p | 348p | 95c | 148.2m | 22.7m | 6.1m | PA |
| ZI YU LAN | 16071gt | 1995 | 20.0k | D2 | 244p | 392p | 95c | 150.5m | 24.0m | 7.2m | CN |

ARAFURA LILY was built by the De Merwede Shipyard (yard number 668) in Hardinxveld, The Netherlands as the ZI DING XIANG for the Shanghai Hai Xing Shipping Company. She was renamed ARAFURA LILY for a charter in 1996 and appears not to have reverted to her original name. IMO 9110822

ZI YU LAN was built by MTW Schiffswerft (yard number 161) at Wismar, Germany. She is thought to have carried the name JAOKRAN for a short time in 2007. IMO 9086899

CHINA SHIPPING PASSENGER LINER

The Company China Shipping Passenger Liner was formed in 1997 with the merger of Dalian Marine Transport and Shanghai Shipping Passenger Company. Currently around 28 vessels of varying types are in operation. The ships shown here are all cargo/passenger vessels. Unfortunately information on these vessels is rather sketchy. It has been reported that this company is interested in entering the cruise market. Ships marked * are reported sold, but no other information is currently available.

Address 1 Minzhu Plaza, Zhongshonqu, 116001 Dalian, Peoples Republic of China

Telephone +86 411 8263 0160

Website www.cspl.com.cn

Area operated China coastal

CHANG BAI*	7670gt	1980	18.2k	D1	p	p	c	138.0m	17.6m	6.0m	CN
CHANG SHEN	‡5926gt	1979	18.2k	D2	p	850p	c	138.0m	17.6m	6.0m	CN
CHANG XIN	‡3857gt	1979	16.0k	D1	p	p	c	106.7m	15.8m	3.8m	CN
TIAN HE	‡5492gt	1983	k	D2	p	p	c	120.0m	17.0m	5.8m	CN
WANG XIN	‡3858gt	1984	16.0k	D2	p	p	c	106.7m	15.8m	3.8m	CN
WU TONG SHANG*	7160gt	1987	k	D2	p	p	c	120.0m	17.0m	5.8m	CN
XIN SHANG HAI YOU LUN	‡3857gt	1983	16.0k	D2	p	p	c	106.7m	15.8m	3.8m	CN

CHANG BAI and **CHANG SHEN** were built by the Hudong Shipyard in Shanghai, China. IMO 8425103 and 7741811

CHANG XIN was built by the Qiuxin Shipyard in Shanghai, China. IMO 8425177

TIAN HE was built by the Xingang Shipyard (yard number 239) at Tianjin, China. IMO 8311857

WANG XIN was built by the Qiuxin Shipyard in Shanghai, China. IMO 8833283

WU TONG SHANG was built by the Xingang Shipyard (yard number 250) at Tianjin, China as the XI

QUE. She was renamed WU TONG SHANG in 2005. IMO 8705371

XIN SHANG HAI YOU LUN was built by the Qiuxin Shipyard in Shanghai, China as the ZHAN XIN. She was renamed in 1998 and converted into a cruise ship. IMO 8831962

CHRISTINA LIMITED PARTNERSHIP

The Company The Christina Ltd Partnership is a Cook Islands company. The CHRISTINA O appears to be managed by Andrew Weir Yacht Management.

Website www.mychristinao.com

CHRISTINA O	1802gt	1943	19.0k	D2	36p	36p	32c	99.1m	11.1m	4.1m	PA

CHRISTINA O, the Onassis yacht for more than twenty years, began as the Canadian frigate STORMONT. She was built by Canadian Vickers Limited (yard number 167) at Montreal and was acquired by Aristotle Onassis in 1954, converted to a yacht and given the name CHRISTINA. In 1998 she was restored and is available for charter as the CHRISTINA O. At the time of writing she was reported to be laid up. IMO 8963818

COMPAGNIE POLYNESIENNE DE TRANSPORT MARITIME

The Company Compagnie Polynesienne de Transport Maritime is a French Polynesian registered company providing lifeline services to the Marquesas Islands. The ship listed here is the third vessel to be operated by the company, and the first one to be acquired new.

Address PO Box 220, 98713 Papeete, Tahiti, French Polynesia

Telephone +689 426242 **Fax** +689 434889

Website www.aranui.com

Area operated Passenger cargo service between Tahiti and the Marquesas, French Polynesia

ARANUI 3	7325gt	2002	15.0k	D1	208p	208p	c	117.0m	17.6m	5.5m	FR

ARANUI 3 was built by Societatia Comerciala Severnav (yard number 170) at Drobeta, Romania for the company's inter-island service in French Polynesia. Her crew is predominantly Marquesian. In addition to her passengers, she can carry up to 3,800 tons of general cargo. The ship's name means Great Highway in Maori, and perpetuates the name of the first ship purchased for this service from a New Zealand owner in 1959. IMO 9245354

Ship on Order

ARANUI 5	c7500gt	2015	15.0k	D2	300p	300p	c 126.0m	22.2m	5.2m	FR

ARANUI 5 is under construction at Huanghai Shipbuilding (yard number K19) at Rongchen. IMO 9677492

COTE D'AZUR SAS

The Company Societe Maritime Cote d'Azur SAS is a French company founded in 2009.

Addresss Boulevarde des Collines, RD559, 83120 Sainte-Maxine, France

Telephone +33 4 9455 7873 **Fax** +33 4 9455 7866

Area operated Charter yacht, area of operation unknown at time of writing

SALUZI	1739gt	2003	14.0k	D2	50p	50p	38c	69.1m	13.8m	2.1m	MT

SALUZI was built as one of a pair of small cruise ships for Bora Bora Cruises (now Nomade Yachting) by Austal Ships (yard number 173) at Fremantle, Western Australia as the TI'A MOANA. Nomade Yachting ran into financial difficulty in 2011 and this ship was sold and renamed SALUZI. IMO 9267522

DESGAGNES

The Company Desgagnes is a Canadian operator of small coastal cargo ships that also operates one passenger and cargo ship. The origins of the company go back to 1866, when Captain Zepherin Desgagnes started trading with the schooner MARY-ANN. Subsidiary Relais Nordik operates the

NORDIK EXPRESS.

Address 21 Marche-Champlain Street, Suite 100, Quebec, G1K 8Z8, Canada

Tel +1 418 692 5000 **Fax** +1 418 692 6044

Website www.desgagnes.com

Area operated St Lawrence, Canada

BELLA DESGAGNES	6655gt	2013	15.0k	DEP2	160b	381d	c	97.1m	19.3m	4.6m	CA
NORDIK EXPRESS	1749gt	1974	12.5k	D2	72b	196d	c	69.5m	13.4m	5.8m	CA

BELLA DESGAGNES was built by Brodogradiliste Kraljecica (yard number 555) at Kraljevica, Croatia and completed by Palumbo Spa of Naples following the bankrupcy of the former yard. She has a small ro-ro deck for 40 vehicles. IMO 9511519

NORDIK EXPRESS was built by the Todd Shipyard (yard number 61) at Seattle, USA as the offshore support vessel THERIOT OFFSHORE IV. She was renamed NORDIK EXPRESS in 1987 and began operating for her current owner in 1992. IMO 7391290

ECROLIGHT

The Company Ecrolight is an Australian company specialising in diving cruises and trading as Deep Sea Divers Den.

Address 319 Draper Street, Cairns, Queensland 4870, Australia

Tel +61 7 4046 7333 **Fax** +61 7 4031 1210

Website www.diversden.com.au

Area operated Diving cruises on the Queensland coast

OCEAN QUEST II	628gt	1988	12.0k	D2	26p	30p	16c	34.7m	15.0m	2.0m	AU

OCEAN QUEST II was built by SBF Engineering (yard number 36) at Fremantle, Western Australia as the catamaran cruiser MTS DISCOVERER for service in Papua, New Guinea. She was acquired by her current owner late in 2006, and was renamed as the OCEAN QUEST II. IMO 8717398

EDMISTON YACHT MANAGEMENT

The Company Edmiston Yacht Management is an Isle of Man registered company controlled from Monaco.

Address 27 Boulevard Albert 1er, 98000 Monte Carlo, Monaco

Telephone +377 9330 5444

Website www.edmiston.com

Area operated Does not operate for its own account. Vessels available for charter.

INDIAN EMPRESS	3176gt	2000	18.0k	D3	32p	32p	42c	95.0m	14.6m	4.5m	IM
LAUREN L	2942gt	2002	12.5k	D1	40p	40p	29c	88.5m	14.0m	3.6m	MT
MOONLIGHT II	2982gt	2004	18.0k	D2	36p	36p	38c	85.2m	14.0m	3.7m	MT

INDIAN EMPRESS was built by Southern African Shipyards (yard number Y950) and the hull was then taken to Oceanco Shipyards for completion. She entered service as the AL MIRQAB for Network Group. She became INDIAN EMPRESS in 2006. IMO 1006245

LAUREN L was built as the SUN BAY II by Schiffswerft u. Maschinenfabrik Cassens (yard number 235) at Emden in Germany for Sun Bay Shipping. She was renamed CORINTHIAN in 2002 and operated for Travel Dynamics International for a while. She was renamed CONSTELLATION in 2003 when sold to Mitridat Shipping, a subsidiary of Helios Shipping. She was acquired by her current owner (Constellation Shipping) in 2007 and renamed LAUREN L in 2008. IMO 9246827

MOONLIGHT II was built for Mediterranean Yachts as the ALYSIA by Neorion Shipyards (yard number 1102) at Syros, Greece. She was acquired by ADL Holdings (Alysia Shipping) in 2005. In 2010 she was renamed MOONLIGHT II under the ownership of SBK Marine Ltd. IMO 9288215

Christina Ltd Partnership's **Christina O** in London *(William Mayes)*

Cote D'Azur SAS' **Saluzi** *(Mark M Amielanczyk)*

CPTM's **Aranui 3** at Papeete *(Peter Plowman)*

ENKA INSAAT

The Company Enka Insaat ve Sanayi is a Turkish construction and engineering company, with a large number of major construction projects in Russia, the Caspian Sea area and Eastern Europe.

Address Enka Binasi 1, Balmumku Mah, Besiktas, 34349 Istanbul, Turkey

Telephone +90 212 376 1000 **Fax** +90 212 272 8869

Website www.enka.com

Area operated Accommodation ships

DICLE	967gt	1959	12.0k	D2	76p	80p	25c	56.0m	10.7m	3.1m	KZ
SAKARYA	732gt	1967	11.5k	D1	38p	38p	8c	49.9m	9.5m	3.3m	KZ

DICLE was built by Stord Verft (yard number 50) at Stord, Norway as the HARDANGERFJORD for the Norwegian coastal trade. In 1982 she was briefly renamed HARDANGERFJORD 1 to free up her previous name for a new ship. She was sold later that year becoming the FIRDA. In 1989 she passed to Brand and was renamed BRAND for expedition voyages. She was acquired by Dami Cruises and renamed DARLI in 2004, and following a major refit entered service on the beautiful Croatian coast. In April 2009, following a period of lay up, she was sold to Enka Insaat ve Sanayi of Turkey and renamed DICLE. IMO 5142750

SAKARYA was built by Cantieri Navali Felszegi (yard number 87) at Trieste, Italy as the Norwegian cargo ship TRILLINGEN. In 1971 she was renamed FLORNES and in 1992 passed to Danish owners who gave her the name SIKKER HAVN. In 2004 she was lengthened and converted for use as a cruise ship. She was acquired by her present owner in 2008 and renamed SAKARYA. IMO 6726711

FAR EAST RESEARCH INSTITUTE

The Company Far East Research Institute is a Russian state organisation. This organisation also owns the PROFESSOR KHROMOV (Heritage Expeditions – SPIRIT OF ENDERBY).

Address ul Fontannaya 24, Vladivostok, 690600 Russia

Telephone +7 423 222 4887

Website www.hydromet.com

Area operated Unknown

AKADEMIK SHOKALSKIY	1764gt	1982	14.0k	D1	54p	54p	23c	71.6m	12.8m	4.5m	RU
PROFESSOR MULTANOVSKIY	1753gt	1982	9.0k	D2	52p	52p	23c	71.6m	12.8m	4.5m	RU

AKADEMIK SHOKALSKIY was built by Oy Laivateollisuus Ab (yard number 343) at Turku, Finland for the Russian Hydrometeorological Institute. She was transferred to the Far Eastern Research Institute in 1994. She has operated for a number of expedition cruise companies, latterly Quark Expeditions. She joined Aurora Expeditions for 2011. Famously the ship became trapped in the Antarctic ice over Christmas and the New Year 2013/14. Her current useage could not be determined. Her name commemorates the Russian critic and novelist who lived from 1893 to 1984. IMO 8010336

PROFESSOR MULTANOVSKIY was built for the Government of Russia's Hydrometeorological Institute by Oy Laivateollisuus (yard number 346) at Turku, Finland. The ship is now operated by the Arctic and Antarctic Research Institute to whom she passed in 1994. She is named after Professor Boris Multanovskiy (1876-1946), an eminent meteorologist and polar researcher. Antarctica XXI operated the ship from November 2009 to January 2010. The ship did not appear to be in service during 2011, and during the following year was transferred to the Far East Research Institute. IMO 8010362

FAR EASTERN SHIPPING COMPANY

The Company The Far Eastern Shipping is a Russian owned company whose origins date to 1880, although the present company name was not used until 1935.

Address Morozava St 7a, 4th Floor, Vladivostok, 690065, Russia

Website www.fesco.ru

KAPITAN KHLEBNIKOV	12288gt	1981	18.7k	DE3	108p	112p	70c	129.4m	26.5m	8.5m	RU

Edmiston Yacht Management's *Lauren L* off Monte Carlo *(Tony Davis)*

Far Eastern Shipping Company's *Kapitan Khlebnikov (Bill Lawes)*

Gemi Kurtama Denizcilik's *Savarona* in the Bosphorus *(William Mayes)*

Hydrometeorological & Environmental's ***Professor Molchanov*** at Ushuaia *(Bill Lawes)*

IHH Insani Yardim Vakfi's ***Gazi M*** in Istanbul *(William Mayes)*

Indonesia Ministry of Sea Communications' ***Sabuk Nusantara 42*** *(Jonathan Boonzaier)*

KAPITAN KHLEBNIKOV was constructed by Wartsila (yard number 430) at Helsinki, Finland as an icebreaker for the Far Eastern Shipping Company of Vladivostok. She was converted for use as an expedition ship by Rickmer Lloyd at Bremerhaven in 1992, and operated on charter to Quark Expeditions for many years. The ship was withdrawn from the cruise market in March 2012 and resumed full time service as an icebreaker. IMO 7824417

FIRST HERITAGE MARINE

The Company First Heritage Marine is a Lebanese registered company offering the BLUE DAWN as a charter yacht. She is operated by Faros Shipping of the Cook Islands.

Address Highway Street, PO Box 215, Zahle, Lebanon

Telephone +961 8 869955

Website www.farosshipping.com

Area operated Charter yacht in the Mediterranean Sea

BLUE DAWN	896gt	1959	16.0k	D2	10p	10p	11c	62.1m	9.5m	3.3m	CK

BLUE DAWN was built by J. J. Sietas KG Schiffswerft GmbH & Co (yard number 452) in Hamburg, Germany as the ORANGE MOON for German owners. Still under the German flag, she was renamed TOM KYLE in 1961, HARLEKIN in 1977, SEALORD in 1984 and HARLEKIN I in 1985. She passed to her current owner in 2004, was renamed BLUE MOON and has been converted into a luxury yacht for the charter market. IMO 5364073

GEMI KURTARMA DENIZCILIK

The Company Gemi Kurtarma Denizcilik is a Turkish company, which has taken a 49-year charter on the Turkish Government-owned cruise yacht SAVARONA, expiring in 2038. The company charters the vessel out through charter brokers. At the time of writing there were proposals to take the ship out of passenger service and turn her into a museum.

Address Akarkent Sitesi 8, Cadde T21, No 2 Ist Villa KismiBeykoz, 34800 Istanbul, Turkey

Telephone +90 216 485 9070 **Fax** +90 216 485 9075

Website www.savarona.com.tr

Area operated Turkish coast but may not be operating currently

SAVARONA	4701gt	1931	18.0k	D2	34p	34p	55c	136.0m	17.5m	6.5m	TR

SAVARONA was built by Blohm & Voss in Hamburg, Germany for Mrs Emily Cadwallader (the grand-daughter of John Roebling, the builder of New York's Brooklyn Bridge) as the world's largest private yacht. The ship was sold to the Government of Turkey in 1938, and was briefly used as a presidential yacht for Kemal Ataturk, the by then ailing president and founder, in 1923, of the Turkish Nation. The ship was eventually converted for use as a training ship and renamed GUNES DIL. She was almost destroyed by fire in 1979, but following the placing of the charter to her current operator, was rebuilt and currently operates where required. She is named after a long-necked African black swan living in the Indian Ocean. IMO 5314810

GOVERNMENT OF INDONESIA (NAVY)

The Company The Indonesian Navy acquired two former passenger ferries from PT Pelni in 2005 for use as transport ships.

Area operated Indonesia

KRI TANJUNG FATAGAR	14501gt	1984	D2	20.0k	1741t		145c	144.8m	23.4m	5.9m	ID
KRI TANJUNG NUSANIVE	14501gt	1984	D2	20.0k	1572t		145c	144.8m	23.4m	5.9m	ID

KRI TANJUNG FATAGAR was built by Jos. L. Meyer (yard number 611) at Papenburg, Germany for PT Pelni as the passenger ferry RINJANI. She was transferred to the Indonesian Navy and renamed in 2005. Penant number 974. IMO 8303252

KRI TANJUNG NUSANIVE was built by Jos. L. Meyer (yard number 609) at Papenburg, Germany as the KAMBUNA for PT Pelni's overnight passenger services. She was transferred to the Indonesian Navy in 2005. Penant number 973. IMO 8209688

GOVERNMENT OF NEWFOUNDLAND AND LABRADOR

The Company The Government of Newfoundland and Labrador runs a fleet of nine vessels, most of which are cargo carriers. The ship listed here is the sole passenger/cargo ship in the fleet that is not a ro-ro. She is operated by Labrador Marine on behalf of the Government.

Address 440 Main Street, Lewisporte, Newfoundland, A0G 3A0, Canada

Telephone +1 709 535 6233

Area operated Newfoundland and Labrador coasts

| NORTHERN RANGER | 2556gt | 1986 | 14.0k | D1 | 46b | 86d | 34c | 71.9m | 15.6m | 4.2m | CA |

NORTHERN RANGER was built by Port Weller Dry Docks (yard number 75) at St Catherine's, Ontario, Canada. IMO 8512504

HAUMANA CRUISES

The Company Haumana Cruises is a trading name of Tahiti Cruises, a French Polynesian company. The company operates only charter and group cruises.

Address BP 9254, Motu Uta, 98713 Papeete, Tahiti

Telephone +689 500674 **Fax** +689 500672

Website www.tahiti-haumana-cruises.com

Areas operated Tahiti (group cruises and charters only)

| HAUMANA | 511gt | 1986 | 10.0k | D2 | 24p | 24p | 16c | 36.5m | 13.7m | 1.8m | FR |

HAUMANA was built by Precision Marine Holding (yard number 735) at Fremantle, Western Australia as the catamaran passenger ferry MOTIVE EXPLORER. In 1987 she became the KIMBERLEY EXPLORER and six years later took the name REEF TREK. She was converted to a cruise vessel in 1997 for Tahiti Cruises and renamed HAUMANA. Haumana translates as magical spirit. IMO 8611001

HYDROGRAPHIC RESEARCH INST. OF ST PETERSBURG

The Company The Hydrographic Research Institute of St Petersburg is a Russian state organisation. The ships listed here have operated expedition cruises in the Arctic and Antarctic for a number of years, latterly with Oceanwide Expeditions. Evidence suggests that they are not currently in use as cruise ships.

Address Prospekt Moskovskiy 12, St Petersburg 190031, Russia

| ALEKSEY MARYSHEV | 1698gt | 1990 | 12.5k | D1 | 46p | 46p | 20c | 66.0m | 12.8m | 3.5m | RU |
| GRIGORIY MIKHEYEV | 1729gt | 1990 | 12.5k | D1 | 46p | 46p | 20c | 66.0m | 12.8m | 3.5m | RU |

ALEKSEY MARYSHEV was built by the Holming Shipyard (yard number 287) at Rauma, Finland for the Hydrographic Research Institute of St Petersburg. Her name commemorates the former Captain of the Soviet High Fleet and hydrographer, Aleksey Vasiljevitsj Maryshev (1906-1981). The ship is currently laid up in St Petersburg. IMO 8909329

GRIGORIY MIKHEYEV is owned by the Hydrographic Research Institute of St Petersburg, Russia and was built by the Hollming Shipyard (yard number 288) at Rauma in Finland. IMO 8909331

HYDROMETEOROLOGICAL & ENVIRONMENTAL MONITORING

The Company This is a Russian Government institution.

Address ul Mayakovskogo 2, Archangel, 163020, Russia

Website www.sevmeteo.ru

| PROFESSOR MOLCHANOV | 1753gt | 1982 | 9.0k | D1 | 49p | 49p | 23c | 71.6m | 12.8m | 4.5m | RU |

PROFESSOR MOLCHANOV was built for the Government of Russia's Hydrometeorological Institute by Oy Laivateollisuus (yard number 344) at Turku, Finland. The ship passed to the Murmansk Territorial Hydrometeorological Institute in 1994. She operated mainly on charters to Quark Expeditions until about 2008. In 2011 she passed to her current owner and is probably in use as a research ship. Pavil

Alexandric Molchanov (1893-1930) was an eminent meteorologist who developed radio signals for weather balloons and was the first Soviet to captain a Zeppelin. IMO 8010348

IHH INSANI YARDIM VAKFI

The Organisation IHH Insani Yardim Vakfi (The Foundation for Human Rights and Freedoms and Humanitarian Relief, in English) is a Turkish based humanitarian organisation that came to attention when the MAVI MARMARA was attacked by Israeli forces while on an aid mission to Gaza in May 2010. The organisation had previously bought the ship from IDO for a nominal sum. The organisation also owned the general cargo ship GAZZE, which was broken up in 2011.

Address Buyul Caraman Cad., Taylasan Sok. No 3 Pk, 34230 Fatih, Istanbul, Turkey

Telephone +90 212 631 2121 **Fax** +90 212 621 7051

Website www.ihh.org.tr

Area operated Humanitarian aid voyages

GAZI M	4142gt	1994	15.0k	D2	150b	1500d	62c	93.0m	15.8m	3.9m	TR

GAZI M was built by Turkiye Gemi Sanayii A.S. (yard number 302) at the Halic (Golden Horn) shipyard in Istanbul, Turkey for the Turkish Maritime Lines Group as the MAVI MARMARA, although she was launched as the BEYDAGI. With the gradual disposal of Turkish Maritime Lines assets, she passed to IDO, Istanbul Sea Buses along with the Istanbul City Lines passenger and car ferry fleets. She was sold in 2010 to IHH and in May of that year was involved in a humanitarian aid convoy to Gaza, which was attacked by Israeli forces, during which nine of the MAVI MARMARA's complement were killed. The Israelis detained the ship and only returned her in December 2010. Her name translated as Blue Marmara, a reference to the sea through which she once operated. When spotted in Istanbul in June 2014, she had been renamed GAZI M. IMO 9005869

INDONESIA MINISTRY OF SEA COMMUNICATIONS

The Company Indonesia's Ministry of Sea Communications is a government organization responsible for providing essential passenger and cargo shipping services throughout the Indonesian archipelago. Passenger services are operated by subsidiary company PT PELNI. In addition, the Ministry has recently commisioned a fleet of smaller passenger/cargo vessels that it operates directly on routes to remote communities. The ships only carry a small number of passengers in individual cabins. The majority are housed in open dormitories equipped with bunk beds. Crew numbers are unknown.

Address Jalan Medan Merdeka Barat 8, Kel Gambir, Jakarta, 10110, Indonesia

Telephone +62 21 381 1308 **Fax** +62 21 381 1786

Website www.dephub.go.id

Area operated Indonesian local passenger services

SABUK NUSANTARA 27	784gt	2011	D2	11.0k	10b	244d		51.8m	10.4m	2.9m	ID
SABUK NUSANTARA 28	1158gt	2011	D2	12.0k	14b	376d		58.5m	12.0m	2.8m	ID
SABUK NUSANTARA 29	811gt	2012	D2	11.0k	10b	244d		51.8m	10.4m	2.9m	ID
SABUK NUSANTARA 30	1202gt	2011	D2	12.0k	16b	376d		62.8m	12.0m	2.7m	ID
SABUK NUSANTARA 31	1202gt	2011	D2	12.0k	16b	376d		62.8m	12.0m	2.7m	ID
SABUK NUSANTARA 32	1202gt	2011	D2	12.0k	16b	376d		62.8m	12.0m	2.7m	ID
SABUK NUSANTARA 33	1202gt	2013	D2	12.0k	16b	376d		62.8m	12.0m	2.7m	ID
SABUK NUSANTARA 34	1202gt	2013	D2	12.0k	16b	376d		62.8m	12.0m	2.7m	ID
SABUK NUSANTARA 37	1202gt	2014	D2	12.0k	16b	376d		62.8m	12.0m	2.7m	ID
SABUK NUSANTARA 38	1202gt	2013	D2	12.0k	16b	376d		62.8m	12.0m	2.7m	ID
SABUK NUSANTARA 39	1202gt	2014	D2	12.0k	16b	376d		62.8m	12.0m	2.7m	ID
SABUK NUSANTARA 40	1202gt	2014	D2	12.0k	16b	376d		62.8m	12.0m	2.7m	ID
SABUK NUSANTARA 41	1202gt	2014	D2	12.0k	16b	376d		62.8m	12.0m	2.7m	ID
SABUK NUSANTARA 42	1202gt	2014	D2	12.0k	16b	376d		62.8m	12.0m	2.7m	ID
SABUK NUSANTARA 43	2004gt	2014	D2	12.0k	20b	430d		68.5m	14.0m	2.9m	ID
SABUK NUSANTARA 44	2004gt	2014	D2	12.0k	20b	430d		68.5m	14.0m	2.9m	ID
SABUK NUSANTARA 48	2004gt	2014	D2	12.0k	20b	430d		68.5m	14.0m	2.9m	ID
SABUK NUSANTARA 49	2004gt	2014	D2	12.0k	20b	430d		68.5m	14.0m	2.9m	ID

PT Pelni's *Gunung Dempo* (Jonathan Boonzaier)

PT Pelni's *Labobar* (Jonathan Boonzaier)

PT Pelni's *Sinabung* (Bill Lawes)

The above ships were built at PT Daya Radar Utama in Tanjung Priok with the exception of SABUK NUSANTARA 29 and SABUK NUSANTARA 41, which were built by PT Mariana Bahagia in Palembang. IMO numbers and yard numbers: SABUK NUSANTARA 27, 9618458, 146; SABUK NUSANTARA 28, 9618460, 147; SABUK NUSANTARA 29, 9647136, 60; SABUK NUSANTARA 30, 9642746, 153; SABUK NUSANTARA 31, 9642758, 155; SABUK NUSANTARA 32, 9642760, 156; SABUK NUSANTARA 33, 9675028, 188; SABUK NUSANTARA 34, 9675016, 187; SABUK NUSANTARA 37, 9712149, 239; SABUK NUSANTARA 38, 9712797, 240; SABUK NUSANTARA 39, 9712802, 241; SABUK NUSANTARA 40, 9712814, 242; SABUK NUSANTARA 41, 9723021, 63; SABUK NUSANTARA 43, 9734044, 262; SABUK NUSANTARA 44, 9734056, 263; SABUK NUSANTARA 48, 9753894, 290; SABUK NUSANTARA 49, 9753909, 291.

PT PELNI

The Company PT PELNI (PT Pelayaran Nasional Indonesis) was established in 1952 as a direct competitor to the Dutch Koninklijke Paketvaart Maatshaappij, and eventually as the sole operator of passenger liner services within Indonesia. The company is state owned and serves more than 100 ports in 24 provinces of this 17,000-island nation. The company also operates some smaller vessels without overnight berths, and a number of ro-ro ferries. The relationship with the Meyer shipyard began in 1959, when five traditional passenger/cargo vessels were constructed for the company. That relationship was substantially strengthened following a shipping disaster off the Indonesian coast in 1981, after which the Government began a major modernisation programme for the PT PELNI fleet. In 2005 two of the early ships from this programme, the KAMBUNA and the RINJANI, both dating from 1984, were transferred to the Indonesian Navy.

Address Jalan Gajah Mada 14, Jakarta Pusat 10130, Indonesia

Telephone +62 21 633 4342 **Fax** +62 21 638 54130

Website www.pelni.co.id

Area operated Indonesian local passenger services

AWU	6041gt	1991	D2	14.0k	54b	915d	84c	99.8m	18.0m	4.2m	ID
BINAIYA	6022gt	1994	D2	15.0k	54b	915d	84c	100.0m	18.0m	4.2m	ID
BUKIT RAYA	6022gt	1994	D2	14.0k	54b	915d	84c	99.8m	18.0m	4.2m	ID
BUKIT SIGUNTANG	14643gt	1996	D2	20.3k	384b	1619d	147c	146.5m	23.4m	5.9m	ID
CIREMAI	14581gt	1993	D2	20.0k	420b	1553d	145c	146.5m	23.4m	5.9m	ID
DOBONSOLO	14581gt	1993	D2	20.0k	420b	1554d	145c	146.5m	23.4m	5.9m	ID
DORO LONDA	14685gt	2001	D2	22.4k	104b	2026d	147c	146.5m	23.4m	5.9m	ID
GUNUNG DEMPO	14017gt	2008	D2	17.0k	96b	1487d	141c	146.6m	23.4m	5.9m	ID
KELIMUTU	6022gt	1986	D2	14.0k	54b	866d	84c	99.8m	18.0m	4.2m	ID
KELUD	14665gt	1998	D2	22.4k	416b	1557d	157c	146.5m	23.4m	5.9m	ID
KERINCI	14501gt	1983	D2	20.0k	600b	996d	119c	144.8m	23.4m	5.9m	ID
LABOBAR	15136gt	2004	D2	22.4k	66b	3084d	161c	146.5m	23.4m	5.9m	ID
LAMBELU	14649gt	1997	D2	20.3k	384b	1619d	147c	146.5m	23.4m	5.9m	ID
LAWIT	6022gt	1986	D2	14.0k	54b	866d	84c	99.8m	18.0m	4.2m	ID
LEUSER	6041gt	1994	D2	15.0k	54b	916d	84c	99.8m	18.0m	4.2m	ID
NGGAPULU	14739gt	2002	D2	22.4k	104b	2026d	155c	145.6m	23.4m	5.9m	ID
PANGRANGO	2620gt	1995	D2	14.0k	44b	466d		68.5m	14.0m	2.9m	ID
SANGIANG	2620gt	1999	D2	14.0k	44b	466d		68.5m	14.0m	2.9m	ID
SINABUNG	14716gt	1997	D2	20.0k	1102b	804d	147c	146.5m	23.4m	5.9m	ID
SIRIMAU	6022gt	1991	D2	15.0k	54b	915d	84c	99.8m	18.0m	4.2m	ID
TATAMAILAU	6041gt	1990	D2	15.0k	54b	915d	84c	99.8m	18.0m	4.2m	ID
TIDAR	14501gt	1988	D2	20.0k	416b	1488d	145c	144.0m	23.4m	5.9m	ID
TILONGKABILA	6022gt	1995	D2	14.0k	54b	916d	84c	99.8m	18.0m	4.2m	ID
UMSINI	14501gt	1985	D2	20.0k	296b	1441d	119c	144.0m	23.4m	5.9m	ID
WILIS	2620gt	1999	D2	14.0k	44b	466d		68.5m	14.0m	2.9m	ID

All of the above ships were built by Jos. L. Meyer at Papenburg, Germany for PT Pelni, with the exception of the PANGRANGO and SANGIANG, which were assembled by PT PAL Shipyard in Surabaya, largely from parts produced by Jos. L. Meyer, and WILIS, which was built by PT PAL Shipyard.

IMO numbers and yard numbers:

AWU, 8915653, 630; BINAIYA, 9032161, 634; BUKIT RAYA, 9032173, 635; BUKIT SIGUNTANG, 9124536, 642; CIREMAI, 9032135, 631; DOBONSOLO, 9032147, 632; DORO LONDA, 9226487, 661; GUNUNG DEMPO, 9401324, 664; KELIMUTU, 8502341, 614; KELUD, 9139684, 645; KERINCI, 8209676, 608; LABOBAR, 9281542, 663; LAMBELU, 9124548, 643; LAWIT, 8502353, 615; LEUSER, 9032159, 633; NGGAPULU, 9226499, 662; PANGRANGO, 9072123, 121; SANGIANG, 9157208, 122; SINABUNG, 9139672, 644; SIRIMAU, 8915641, 629; TATAMAILAU, 8915639, 628; TIDAR, 8700292, 617; TILONGKABILA, 9102760, 641; UMSINI, 8303264, 612; WILIS, 9157210, 126.

CIREMAI and **DOBONSOLO** both underwent an extensive conversion in 2013 that saw a significant portion of the passenger accommodation removed and replaced by extra container capacity on deck, together with a large freight deck installed in the hull that is accessed via side ramps. The ships now accommodate approximately 950 passengers in cabin, dormitory and deck classes.

KERINCI was the first ship built for PELNI by Meyer Werft. The ship was retired from active service in 2013 and is currently laid up in Tanjung Priok pending disposal

ISTANBUL TECHNICAL UNIVERSITY

AKDENIZ	7864gt	1955	17.0k	D2	444p		144.3m	18.6m	6.2m	TR

AKDENIZ is the last surviving member of a series of beautifully proportioned coastal passenger cargo ships built for Turkish Maritime Lines in 1955/56 by A G Weser at Bremen (yard number 1293) in Germany. Her initial employment took her from Istanbul to Piraeus, Naples, Genoa, Marseilles and Barcelona. In later years she operated Turkish coastal services and cruises in the Mediterranean Sea and beyond. She was withdrawn from service in 1997 and transferred to the Technical University of Istanbul for use as an accommodation and cadet ship for the Turkish Maritime Academy. IMO 5006815

KOVALEVSKIY BIOLOGICAL INSTITUTE

The Company Kovalevskiy Biological Institute is a Government of the Republic of Ukraine controlled organisation.

Address Prospekt Nakhimova 2, 99011 Sevastopol, Krym, Ukraine

Telephone +380 692 544110 **Fax** +380 692 557813

Area operated It is not known if this ship is currently carrying passengers

PROFESSOR VODYANITSKIY	1498gt	1976	14.0k	D1	32p	p	c	68.9m	11.9m	4.2m	UA

PROFESSOR VODYANITSKIY was built by Oy Lavateollisuus (yard number 312) at Turku, Finland for the Ukraine Academy of Sciences, transferring to her current owner in 1994. It is not known if she currently operates passenger sailings. IMO 7406148

LINDOS MARITIME

The Company Lindos Maritime is a Greek Company, owned by the Greek Cypriot Haji-Ioannou family.

Address 16 Atki Moutsapoulou, 18535 Piraeus, Greece

Telephone +30 210 428 0451

Area operated Yacht available for charter

ESMERELDA	1002gt	1981	12.5k	D2	22p	22p	19c	61.5m	10.0m	4.5m	BS

ESMERELDA was built by Cantieri Navale Ugo Codecasa (yard number 38) at Viareggio, Italy as the MARIA ALEKSANDRA, although laid down as the TAOUEY. She later became the LUISELLA. She was renamed in about 2003 when acquired by Lindos Maritime. IMO 8979817

LUXURY YACHT CHARTER

The Company Luxury Yacht Charter Sdn Bhd is a Singapore company owned by Brian Chang, Chairman of Raffles Yacht, Singapore.

Address 11th Floor, Menara Berjaya, K2 Plaza, 179 Jalan Bukit Bintang, 55100 Kuala Lumpur, Malaysia

Area operated Charters from Singapore

| ASEAN LADY | 2385gt | 2004 | 14.0k | D2 | 22p | 22p | c | 88.1m | 21.3m | 3.5m | PA |

ASEAN LADY was built by Yantai Raffles Shipyard (yard number YPZ97-92) at Yantai, China. Her appearance is rather unusual as she has a large outrigger on one side. IMO 9303857

MAURITIUS SHIPPING

The Company Mauritius Shipping Corporation is part of Swiss controlled Societe de Gerance Maritime SA (SGM) and operates two cargo/passenger ships serving Mauritius, Rodriques, Reunion and Madagascar. The ships are managed and operated by MSC Coraline, a Mauritius Shipping Corporation subsidiary.

Address Suite 412, St James Court, St Denis Street, Port Louis, Mauritius

Telephone +230 208 5900 **Fax** +230 212 5176

Website www.mauritiusshipping.intnet.mu

Area operated Local services in the Indian Ocean from Mauritius

| MAURITIUS PRIDE | 5234gt | 1990 | 14.5k | D2 | 12b | 248d | 52c | 99.5m | 17.0m | 6.5m | MU |
| MAURITIUS TROCHETIA | 5492gt | 2001 | 14.5k | D2 | 108p | 108p | 37c | 107.9m | 17.5m | 6.2m | MU |

MAURITIUS PRIDE was built by the Husumer Shipyard (yard number 1505) at Husum, Germany for the company. The ship has been withdrawn from service and offered for sale. IMO 8906767

MAURITIUS TROCHETIA was built by the Hudong Shipyard (yard number H1260A) at Shanghai, China for the company. IMO 9225287

MERCY SHIPS

The Company Mercy Ships, a global charity, has operated hospital ships in developing nations since 1978. In the organisation's own words 'Following the example of Jesus, Mercy Ships brings hope and healing to the poor, mobilizing people and resources worldwide'. Don and Deyon Stephens founded the organisation in 1978, with the purchase of the VICTORIA (at a cost of $1m) being completed in October of that year. The ANASTASIS, as the VICTORIA was renamed, was then the world's largest non-government hospital ship. She was joined in 1994 by the CARIBBEAN MERCY and five years later by the AFRICA MERCY, which underwent an eight year refit as a hospital ship with six operating theatres and an 84-bed ward. The AFRICA MERCY took the title of the largest non-government hospital ship when she entered service in 2007. In late 2006 the CARIBBEAN MERCY was sold. In 2007, with the entry into service of the AFRICA MERCY, the ANASTASIS was sold for scrap.

Address PO Box 2020, Lindale, Texas 75771-2020, United States of America

Telephone +1 903 939 7000 **Fax** +1 903 882 0336

Website www.mercyships.org

Area operated Worldwide

| AFRICA MERCY | 16572gt | 1980 | 19.0k | D2 | | | | 152.0m | 22.8m | 6.0m | MT |

AFRICA MERCY was built by Helsingor Vaerft (yard number 418) at Helsingor, Denmark as one of a trio of Inter-City train ferries for Danske Statsbaner (DSB – Danish State Railways) for service between Korsor and Nyborg on the Great Belt. As the DRONNING INGRID she served until the opening of the Great Belt Bridge in 1997 and was then laid up at Nakskov, Denmark. She was purchased for Mercy Ships in 1999 and temporarily renamed INGRID. She took her current name, AFRICA MERCY, in 2000 and then underwent an 8-year conversion on the River Tyne in North East England. She entered service in April 2007, replacing the ANASTASIS. She underwent another major refit in Durban between September 2010 and February 2011. IMO 7803188

Ship on order

| NEWBUILD | c36000gt | 2017 | 12.0k | D2 | | | | 174.0m | 28.6m | m | MT |

NEWBUILD is under construction at the Tianjin Xingang Shipyard (yard number NB011-1) and will become the world's largest hospital ship on completion. The construction of the ship is being managed by Stena Ro-Ro. IMO 9726499

Istanbul University's *Akdeniz* *(Simon Olsen)*

Mauritius Shipping's *Mauritius Trochetia* *(Jonathan Boonzaier)*

Mercy Ships' *Africa Mercy* in Durban *(Trevor Jones)*

MORSKAYA KOMPANIYA SAKHALIN-KURILY

The Company Morskaya Kompaniya Sakhalin-Kurily is a Government of the Russian Federation controlled company.

Address ul Sovetskaya 103 A, Kholmsk, Sakhalinskaya Oblast, 694620 Russia

Area operated In the Sakhalin region of Eastern Russia, possibly carrying oil workers

IGOR FARKHUTDINOV	4575gt	1991	14.3k	D1	150p		p	c	90.0m	17.2m	5.3m	RU
POLARIS	2097gt	1968	13.0k	D1	76p	96p	36c	70.5m	15.5m	4.4m	RU

IGOR FARKHUTDINOV was built for Yuzhmorgeologiya as the research vessel NEVA by Stocznia im. Komuny Paryskiej (yard number B961/06) at Gdynia, Poland as the last of a series of six similar research vessels. She was renamed as the ADMIRAL LAZAREV in 1996 and passed to her current owner in 2003 when she took the name IGOR FARKHUTDINOV, honouring the former Governor of the Region of Sakhalin. IMO 8714384

POLARIS was built as the DISKO for the local services of KNI Service A/S within Greenland by Svendborg Skibsvaerft (yard number 122) at Svendborg, Denmark. Her owner was restyled as Arctic Umiaq Line in 1994. She was laid up at Nakskov, Denmark in 1999 and during the following year passed to Scandinavian Cruise Line for whom she was renamed SHEARWATER. Rebuilt at Fredericia in Denmark, she re-entered service later in 2000 cruising around Scotland and the Isles. In 2001 she was renamed as the BRAND POLARIS and two years later took the name VIKING POLARIS. She was acquired by the Murmansk Shipping Company and was renamed POLARIS at the end of 2004 and operated for a variety of expedition cruise companies. She was transferred to her current operator at the end of 2013. IMO 6807395

MURMANSK ADMINISTRATION

The Company The full title of this Russian Federation controlled organisation is the State Institution Murmansk Administration for Hydrometeorology and Environmental Monitoring.

Address ul Shmidta 23, Murmansk 183789, Russia

Telephone +7 8152 473726 **Fax** +7 8152 472406

Website www.kolgimet.ru

Area operated Ships chartered out

VIKTOR BUYNITSKIY	693gt	1986	12.8k	D1	30p	35p		c	49.9m	10.0m	3.6m	RU

VIKTOR BUYNITSKIY was built by the Valmet Shipyard (yard number 370) at Turku, Finland for the Murmansk Territorial Administration. Viktor Harlampievich Buynitskiy (1911-1980) was a renowned oceanographer. It is not thought that this ship is currently operating in a passenger-carrying capacity, but she was used in 2010 for a cruise for the Nansen and Amundsen Basins Observational System, part of the International Arctic Research Centre of the University of Alaska. The ship is currently listed as laid up. IMO 8422448

MURMANSK SHIPPING COMPANY

The Company The Murmansk Shipping Company was founded in 1939, but one of the most significant events in the company's history was the expedition by the icebreaker ARKTIKA in 1977 to the North Pole, making that ship the first surface vessel to reach the Pole. In 1993 the company was converted from a state-owned enterprise into a joint-stock company. Murmansk Shipping Company operates a fleet of ice-strengthened cargo ships and tankers and one conventional icebreaker.

Address 15 Kominterna Street, 183038 Murmansk, Russia

Telephone +7 8152 481049 **Fax** +7 8152 481148

Website www.msco.ru

Area operated The White Sea

KLAVDIYA YELANSKAYA	4329gt	1977	13.0k	D2	206p	224p	50c	100.0m	16.2m	4.6m	RU

KLAVDIYA YELANSKAYA is a passenger and cargo vessel offering a service from Murmansk. However, she does also offer occasional cruises. She was built by Brodogradiliste (yard number 416)

at Kraljevica in what was then Yugoslavia. The ship was used as a vantage point for journalists and relatives during the raising of the sunken Russian submarine KURSK in 2001. IMO 7422922

NOMADE YACHTING BORA BORA

The Company Nomade Yachting Bora Bora is a privately owned Tahitian company, founded in 2002 as Bora Bora Cruises and initially operating two luxury yachts, and several smaller day vessels in the islands of French Polynesia. Following financial difficulties one of yachts was sold. Until recently the company offered cruises on its vessels, but it now appears that the TU MOANA is only available for charters.

Telephone +1 866 202 2590

Website www.bora-bora-cruises.com

Area operated Tahiti and the Leeward Islands

| TU MOANA | 1697gt | 2003 | 14.0k | D2 | 50p | 50p | 38c | 69.1m | 13.8m | 2.1m | FR |

TU MOANA was built by Austal Ships (yard number 172) at Fremantle, Western Australia as one of a pair of ships for the company. The name means 'to stand upright in the sea' and comes from the Polynesian dialect of Tahiti. IMO 9267510

OCEAN ATLANTIC PARTNERS

The Company Ocean Atlantic Partners is a group of investors associated with FleetPro Ocean, who manage the ship.

| OCEAN ATLANTIC | 12798gt | 1986 | 22.0k | D2 | 236p | p | c | 139.5m | 21.0m | 5.8m | MH |

OCEAN ATLANTIC was built by Stocznia Szczecinska im A Warskiego (yard number B492/06) at Szczecin, Poland as the Russian passenger and vehicle ferry KONSTANTIN CHERNENKO. In 1988 she moved to the Far East Shipping Company and was renamed RUSS. She subsequently operated in a number of roles, including a charter to Saga in 1992. In 2010 she had a major internal rebuild for charter to S Continental as the SC ATLANTIC. Acquired in 2012 by associates of FleetPro Ocean, she was renamed OCEAN ATLANTIC and has just completed a charter as a wind farm construction accommodation ship for Areva in the North Sea. She is currently laid up. IMO 8325432

OGASAWARA KAIUN

The Company Ogasawara Kaiun Co Ltd is a Japanese company.

Address 8th Floor, Tamachi Sunny Place, 7-9 Shibaura 3-chome, Minato-ku, Tokyo 108-0014, Japan

Telephone +81 3 3451 5171 **Fax** +81 3 3541 4522

Website www.ogasawarakaiun.co.jp

Area operated Long distance Japanese domestic service from Tokyo

| OGASAWARA MARU | ‡6700gt | 1997 | 22.5k | D2 | 198b | 833d | 49c | 131.0m | 17.2m | 5.7m | JP |

OGASAWARA MARU was built by Mitsubishi Heavy Industries (yard number 1030) in Japan. She is a passenger and cargo vessel, serving the long route south from Tokyo to Bonin Island. IMO 9150353

OPERATION MOBILIZATION

The Company Operation Mobilization is a missionary organisation founded, by George Verwer, taking its floating bookshops to the ports of the world. The first ship, the UMANAC, was purchased from the Danish Government in 1970 and became the LOGOS. The DOULOS joined the fleet in 1977 and the LOGOS II was purchased as a replacement for the LOGOS, which was lost after running onto rocks in South America in 1988. With the arrival of the newly refitted LOGOS HOPE in 2008, the LOGOS II was sold for scrap. The DOULOS was found to be in a poor condition during dry-docking in Singapore in 2010 and was immediately taken out of service. She was subsequently sold to become a static exhibit.

Address Alte Neckarelzer Str. 2, D74821 Mosbach, Germany

Telephone +49 6261 92630

Website www.gbaships.org and www.omships.org

Morskaya Kompaniya Sakhalin-Kurily's **Polaris** in an earlier role *(Bill Lawes)*

Nomade Yachting's **Tu Moana** at Papeete *(Peter Plowman)*

Operation Mobilization's **Logos Hope** in Hamburg *(William Mayes Collection)*

Area operated Worldwide

LOGOS HOPE		12519gt	1973	22.0k	D2	500b			129.0m	20.8m	4.9m	MT

LOGOS HOPE was built by Werft Nobiskrug (yard number 678) at Rendsburg, Germany as the GUSTAV VASA for Saga Line's Baltic Sea car ferry services. In 1983 Smyril Line of the Faeroes bought her and she was renamed NORRONA for her long journeys between Denmark and Torshavn and Iceland. On the delivery of a new NORRONA she was renamed NORRONA 1 and laid up in Esbjerg, Denmark. OM acquired her in 2004 and after a spell in Malta she was moved to Trogir in Croatia to be refitted as the LOGOS HOPE. Her refit was completed early in 2008. IMO 7302914

PACIFIC SEAWAYS

The Company Pacific Seaways is a subsidiary of Care Offshore.

Address L'Oujonnet. PO Box 5, 1195 Bursinel, Switzerland

Area operated Still refitting

KAY		6273gt	1990		D1	150p	150p	c	90.0m	17.2m	5.3m	VC

KAY was built by Stocznia im. Komuny Paryskiej (yard number B961/05) at Gdynia, Poland as the VLADIMIR CHIVILIKHIN for Dalryba. She later passed to Vladivostok Trawling and in 1998 was registered as the KAY for Falkland Investments. Her current owner acquired her in 1999. She spent a number of years in Singapore and Bangkok being converted into a luxury yacht before being moved to Split in Croatia in November 2007. The conversion work was later halted due to financial problems and eventually the KAY arrived, still unfinished, in Valletta on 24 February 2014. IMO 8509208

PASCOAL AND FILHOS

The Company Pascoal and Filhos is a Portuguese food manufacturer, specialising in fish and fish products, established in 1937 and operating its own fishing boats. The company set up a new venture in about 2007 to rescue and operate, as exhibition ships, former fishing vessels under the title Maritime Cultural Tourism.

Address PO Box 12, Avenida dos Bacalhoeiros, Gafanha da Nazare, 3830-353 Ilhavo, Portugal

Telephone +351 34 390290 **Fax** +351 34 390299

Website www.pascoal.pt

ARGUS	430gt	1939	8.0k	SD1	112p	112p	45c	63.8m	9.9m	5.0m	PT
SANTA MARIA MANUELA	607gt	1937	9.0k	D1				63.7m	9.9m	m	PT

ARGUS was built by Scheepswerf de Haan & Oerlemans (yard number 206) at Heusden in The Netherlands as the ARGUS, one of the last of the fishing schooners of the Portuguese Grand Banks fleet. She moved to Windjammer Barefoot Cruises in 1976 and was renamed POLYNESIA I as a four-masted sailing cruise vessel. Including her bowsprit, she is 75.5 metres long. She carried the name OISEAU DE POLYNESIA for the 1984 season, but changed to POYNESIA in the following year. With the demise of Windjammer she was laid up and eventually acquired by Pascoal and Filhos in 2009 for restoration under the name ARGUS. IMO 5023564

SANTA MARIA MANUELA was built by Companhia Uniao Fabril (yard number 33) in Lisbon as the fishing vessel SANTA MARIA MANUELA. She was restored and converted between 1994 and 2007. IMO 5312628

PATRICIA VOYAGES

The Company Patricia Voyages is a marketing name of Trinity House, the General Lighthouse Authority for England, Wales and the Channel Islands. The PATRICIA is sold though Strand Travel, www.strandtravelltd.co.uk.

Address The Quay, Harwich, Essex, CO12 3JW, England

Telephone +44 1255 245034

Website www.trinityhouse.co.uk

Area operated Around the coasts of England and Wales

Pascoal and Filos' **Argus** as Windjammer Barefoot Cruises' **Polynesia** at Aruba *(Rick Frendt)*

Patricia Voyages' **Patricia** in Southampton *(William Mayes)*

Peaceboat Organisation's **Ocean Dream** at Le Havre *(Philippe Brebant)*

PATRICIA	2639gt	1982	14.0k	D2	12p	12p	c	86.3m	13.8m	4.4m	GB

PATRICIA was built by Henry Robb (yard number 530) at Leith, Scotland as the lighthouse and buoy tender PATRICIA for Trinity House. In recent years she has carried a small number of passengers on operational voyages. IMO 8003632

PEACEBOAT ORGANISATION

The Company Peace Boat is a Japan-based non-government and non-profit organisation, founded in 1983 by Kiyomi Tsujimot (a female student at the Waseda University in Tokyo) and others, that works to promote peace, human rights, equality, sustainable development and environmental protection. The Peaceboat used THE TOPAZ, for a number of years until she was replaced in 2008 by the CLIPPER PACIFIC. That ship suffered a number of mechanical problems and the charter was terminated part way through her first voyage, with the passengers being transferred to the hastily chartered MONA LISA. The OCEANIC joined in 2009 as a permanent replacement and commenced Peaceboat's 66th voyage in April 2009, but in 2011 she was replaced by another of Pullmantur's ships, the OCEAN DREAM.

Address B1 3-13-1 Takadanobaba, Shinjuku, Tokyo 169-0075 Japan

Telephone +81 3 3363 8047 **Fax** +81 3 3363 7562

Website www.peaceboat.org

Area operated Three world cruises plus shorter Asian voyages annually

OCEAN DREAM	35265gt	1981	21.0k	D2	1022p	1350p	550c	204.0m	26.3m	7.0m	PA

OCEAN DREAM was the first new cruise ship to be ordered by Carnival Cruise Lines. She was built by Aalborg Vaerft (yard number 234) of Aalborg, Denmark and delivered in December 1980 for service in the Caribbean as the TROPICALE. As the smallest unit in Carnival Cruise Lines' fleet in 2001, she was transferred to Costa Crociere and renamed the COSTA TROPICALE for service in the Mediterranean. In the autumn of 2005 she took up a new role within the group, being transferred to P&O Cruises (Australia) and renamed PACIFIC STAR by Sarah Davies, Miss World Australia 2004. For 2008 the PACIFIC STAR was due to spend a season home-ported in Singapore, but in the event was sold to Pullmantur Cruises and renamed OCEAN DREAM for service in the Caribbean and Pacific Coast Mexico. In 2011 she was sold to Maritime Holdings Group for charter to the Peaceboat Organisation. IMO 7915096

PEARL SHIPS

The Company Pearl Ships is a ship management company, formed in 2008 in the United Arab Emirates.

Website www.pearlships.com

DELMA	2990gt	2004	18.0k	D2	36p	36p	38c	85.2m	14.0m	3.7m	MT
TOPAZ	12532gt	2012	19.5k	DE2	64p	64p	c	147.2m	21.5m	5.7m	CI

DELMA was built by Neorion Shipyard (yard number 1101) at Syros, Greece as the ANNALIESSE. She was sold to Gulf Energy Maritime in 2007 and renamed DELMA. IMO 9288203

TOPAZ was built by Luerssen Werft (yard number 13677) at Bremen. IMO 9551454

PLATINUM YACHT MANAGEMENT

The Company Platinum Yachts is a Dubai based company that builds, converts and manages large super yachts owned by the Crown Prince of Dubai and his family. The company is part of Dubai World, the owner of the Peninsular and Oriental Steam Navigation Company and is also listed as the manager of the QUEEN ELIZABETH 2.

Address PO Box 261555, Dubai, United Arab Emirates

Telephone +971 4 884 4131 **Fax** +971 4 884 5331

Website www.platinumyachts.ae

CRUISEONE	4077gt	1990	15.5k	D2	p	p	c	88.3m	15.3m	4.0m	MT
DUBAI	12488gt	2006	25.0k	D2	p	p	88c	162.0m	22.0m	5.0m	AE

DUBAI MAGIC	388gt	2002	10.0k	D2	52p	52p	c	45.0m	10.0m	5.4m	AE
DUBAWI	4077gt	1989	14.0k	D2	44p	44p	71c	90.6m	15.3m	4.0m	AE

CRUISEONE was built by Cantieri Navale Ferrari (yard number 44) at La Spezia, Italy as the RENAISSANCE TWO, the second in a series of eight ships for the new Renaissance Cruises, a company in which the Norwegian ship owner Fearney & Eger was initially involved. She was sold in 1998 as new and larger ships were delivered, and became THE NEPTUNE for Malaysian owner Robert Tan, who chartered her to his Singaporean brother Alan Tan to operate under the Universal Cruises banner. She was briefly renamed as THE NEPTUNE 2 when sold to Owen Shipping. She was converted from her original luxury to a very basic ship carrying twice the number of passengers, in a Singapore shipyard, before entering service in the spring of 2005 for EasyCruise as the EASYCRUISEONE in the Western Mediterranean. EasyCruise replaced her with a larger ship in 2008 and she passed to the control of Platinum Yacht Management and was renamed CRUISE ONE. She is currently undergoing conversion. IMO 8708658

DUBAI had her hull constructed by Blohm & Voss (yard number 965) in Hamburg and was completed by Platinum Yachts (yard number 1) in Dubai. IMO 1006324

DUBAI MAGIC was built by Aegean Yachts (yard number 24) at Bodrum, Turkey as the GRAND MAGIC. She was acquired by Platinum Yachts in 2007 and renamed DUBAI MAGIC. IMO 9277864

DUBAWI was built as the RENAISSANCE; eventually the first ship in what became a series of eight for Renaissance Cruises by Cantieri Navale Ferrari (yard number 43) at La Spezia, Italy. Her career with the line was short-lived as she was placed on long term charter to casino cruise operator Universal Cruise Lines of Singapore two years later. Subsequently she was renamed THE MERCURY. She was laid up when Universal went bankrupt in 2002. Ownership then passed to a Malaysian company called Viking Lines, who continued to keep the ship in lay-up until she was sold to New Century at the beginning of 2004. She operated overnight casino cruises from Singapore and ports in Malaysia as the LEISURE WORLD I until sold in March 2007 to Dubai based Platinum Yacht Management and renamed DUBAWI for conversion into a luxury private yacht. This work was completed early in 2009. IMO 8708646

PREMIER BOATS

The Company Premier Boats is a Spanish company, formed in 2011.

Address Carrer de Benito Jeronimo Feijoo 07181, Portals Nous, Bealearic Islands, Spain.

Area operated Last seen laid up in Palma, Majorca

HARMONY II	686gt	1955	12.0k	D2	12p	12p	c	57.7m	8.7m	2.7m	VC

HARMONY II was built by the Brodogradiliste Uljanik shipyard (yard number 165) at Pula in Yugoslavia as the coastal passenger and cargo vessel MOSTAR (although launched as the OSIJEK) for the Yugoslavian state ferry operator, Jadranska Linjska Plovidba, the fore-runner of today's Jadrolinija. After a little over 10 years service she was sold to a Greek operator and converted into a day cruise ship under the name MELTEMI II. In 1983 she was sold to Epirotiki Lines and renamed APOLLO I, but continued her day cruise role. In 1987 she was renamed PRINCE ALBERT and came to the UK. Her use in the early years is somewhat hazy, but she was laid up at Tilbury for a number of years before being towed to Liverpool in 1999 where her lay-up continued. Plans to convert her for use as a Russian restaurant came to nothing. In 2002 she was sold to Pedley Furniture and towed to Ipswich where she was converted to become a floating furniture showroom. The original HARMONY (a sailing boat) was built by a team, including the company's founder, Neville Pedley, consisting of four members of Shoreditch Training College's diploma year, in 1951. In a change of plan a number of Mediterranean cruises were advertised on the HARMONY II in 2008, although it is unclear exactly who was operating the ship. She operated under the name Harmony Yacht Club and offers cruises, charters and conference facilities, but appears to have been sold to local interests in Majorca. IMO 5242627

Platinum Yacht Management's **Dubawi** in Cherbourg *(Philippe Brebant)*

Prima Management's **Lili Marleen** at Port Klang *(Mark M Amielanczyk)*

Private Sea Yachting's **Alexander** in Piraeus *(Rick Frendt)*

PRIMA MANAGEMENT

The Company Prima Management is part of the Halim Mazmin shipping and ship agency group of Malaysia.

Address 49 The Boulevard, Mid Valley City, Lingkaran Syed Putra, 59200 Kuala Lumpur, Malaysia

Telephone +60 3 2730 5000

Website www.halimazmin.com

Area operated Charter yachts - Malaysia

LILI MARLEEN	704gt	1994	8.5k	SD1	50p	54p	25c	76.0m	9.5m	2.9m	MY
PUTERI MAHSURI	794gt	1990	11.0k	SD1	36p	36p	20c	66.5m	10.5m	4.5m	MY

LILI MARLEEN was built by Elsflether Werft (yard number 417) at Elsfleth, Germany for Peter Deilmann Cruises. She was acquired by her current owner without a change of name in 2004, and is a three masted sailing ship. IMO 9086863

PUTERI MAHSURI was built by the De Merwede Shipyard (yard number 654) at Hardinxveld, Netherlands as the KANRIN MARU. She passed to her current owner in 2003 and was renamed PUTERI MAHSURI. IMO 8900696

PRIVATE SEA YACHTING

The Company Private Sea Yachting is a Greek yacht management company, formerly Sete Yachting, managing a number of small vessels in addition to the ships listed here.

Address 360 Syngrou Avenue, 17674 Athens, Greece

Telephone +60 3 2730 5000 **Fax** +60 3 2730 5151

Website www.privateseayachting.gr

Area operated Charter yachts

AL SALAMAH	12234gt	1999	17.0k	D2	40p	40p	96c	139.3m	23.5m	4.8m	KY
ALEXANDER	5933gt	1966	17.0k	D2	54p	54p	60c	122.0m	16.9m	5.8m	MT
TURAMA	8343gt	1990	15.0k	D2	52p	52p	60c	116.4m	17.0m	4.4m	MT

AL SALAMAH was built by Fr. Luerssen Werft at Bremen (yard number 13341) as the MIPOS. It appears that she was later owned by Saudi Arabia's Prince Sultan Bin Abdul Aziz, but her current ownership is somewhat obscure. IMO 1007043

ALEXANDER was built by Lubecker Flender Werke (yard number 558), at Lubeck in Germany as the REGINA MARIS, a small cruise ship for Lubeck Line of Germany. As built she had a small garage for about 40 cars. In 1976 she was sold to Canadian owners, who renamed her MERCATOR ONE. She did one season of Caribbean cruises before being arrested for non-payment of debts. She was laid up until late 1979, when she was sold to Peter Deilmann, and renamed FRANKFURT, although when she entered service as an upmarket ship in 1980 she had reverted to her original name. Sun World Cruises of St Louis chartered her in 1982 and used her for a series of cruises on the St Lawrence in Canada. Deilmann again used the REGINA MARIS for a short series of cruises in 1983, following which she was laid up. In October 1983 she was acquired by John S Latsis and then underwent a two-year refit at Bremerhaven, to emerge as the luxury yacht ALEXANDER (named after Latsis' grandson). IMO 6603012

TURAMA was built by Rauma (yard number 305) at Rauma in Finland for Delfin Cruises, an investment group from the Finnish Aland Islands, as the DELFIN CARAVELLE. Delivered in June 1990, the ship operated unsuccessfully until October, when the company ceased operations and the ship was returned to her builder. In 1991 she was chartered to Sally Line as the SALLY CARAVELLE to replace the burnt-out SALLY ALBATROS. At the end of 1991 she was chartered to Odessa Cruise Lines, renamed COLUMBUS CARAVELLE and sub-chartered to the German tour operator, Transocean Tours. In 1994 she moved to Singapore to become a gambling ship, marketed as the LIDO STAR, but her name was never officially changed. Following a lay-up in Singapore, she appears to have been renamed ERNEST HEMINGWAY, but was trading out of Hong Kong as the gambling ship CAPTAIN OMAR by January 2000. In 2004 she was bought by Greek owners, rebuilt as a luxury charter yacht and renamed the TURAMA. IMO 8907216

REDERIET SALTENS

The Company Rederiet Saltens, or the Saltens Shipowning Company was founded in 2008 to acquire and operate the GAMLE SALTEN.

Address Postboks 3, 8001 Bodo, Norway

Telephone +47 991 69551

Website www.gamlesalten.com

Area operated Stavanger

GAMLE SALTEN	630gt	1953	D1	13.0k	47p	p		c	53.2m	8.5m	3.6m	NO

GAMLE SALTEN was built by Trosvik Verksted (yard number 65) at Brevik, Norway as the SALTEN for the Salten Steamship Company for Norwegian coastal services. She became the school ship SJOKURS in 1967. She continued this role until 1995 when she was sold to Stavanger and Ryfylke Dampskipsselskap and renamed GAMLE SALTEN. Over the years she was restored. She was acquired by her current owner in 2008 and now operates cruises, trips and serves in a static role. IMO 5308067

RED SEA MANAGEMENT INTERNATIONAL

The Company Red Sea Management International manages the Saudi Royal Yacht PRINCE ABDUL AZIZ.

Address Room 113 Saudi Business Centre, Madina Road, Jeddah 21451, Saudi Arabia

PRINCE ABDUL AZIZ	4620gt	1984	D2	k	p	p		c	147.0m	18.3m	4.9m	SA

PRINCE ABDUL AZIZ was built by Helsingor Vaerft A/S (yard number 424) at Helsingor, Denmark and fitted out by Vosper Thorneycroft in Southampton. IMO 1003308

ROGALAND SJOASPIRANTSKOLE

The Company Rogaland Sjoaspirantskole (Rogaland Sea Recruit High School) is a maritime training institution, founded in 1949, run by the Young Seamen's Christian Society. The ship undertakes a small number of cruises each year in summer, usually to the north of Norway, but in 2014 includes UK ports and the Baltic.

Address Tommerodden, N4085 Hundvag, Norway

Telephone +47 5185 4860 **Fax** +47 5186 1885

Website www.gann.no

Area operated Norway

GANN	6257gt	1982	15.0k	D2	120s		36c	108.6m	16.5m	3.7m	NO

GANN was built by Aker Trondelag AS (yard number 827) at Trondheim, Norway as the so-called mid-generation Hurtigruten (coastal express) ship NARVIK. She passed to her current owner in February 2007, and took the name GANN, as a replacement for a smaller ship of the same name. During the Icelandic ash cloud crisis in 2010 she undertook at least two mercy dashes across the North Sea in a passenger carrying capacity. She is the sixth ship owned by the school to bear this name, which is thought to refer to the nearby Gandsfjord. IMO 8019344

ROSMORPORT

The Company Rosmorport is a Russian state controlled enterprise charged with the improvement of the management of Russia's seaports. It was set up in 2003.

Address Suschevskaya str 19, B7, 127055 Moscow, Russia

Telephone +7 495 626 1425 **Fax** +7 495 626 1239

Website www.rosmorport.ru

Area operated Not thought to be in use as a passenger ship

KAPITAN DRANITSYN	12919gt	1980	12.0k	DE3	100p	116p	60c	129.4m	26.5m	8.5m	RU

Red Sea Management International's *Prince Abdul Aziz* in Istanbul *(William Mayes)*

Rogaland Sjoaspirantskole's *Gann* in Oslo *(William Mayes)*

Semester at Sea's *Explorer* in Southampton Water *(Bill Lawes)*

KAPITAN DRANITSYN was built by Wartsila (yard number 429) at Helsinki, Finland for the Murmansk Shipping Company. In 1997 she rescued 128 passengers from the cruise ship HANSEATIC, which was in danger of sinking. She has featured in a number of expedition operators' programmes, and between 2007 and 2009 was chartered to a US oil company and based in Alaska. It is understood that she does not comply with the 2010 changes to SOLAS, and it seems that her last passenger service was a cruise for a Russian tour operator to Franz Josef Land in late 2010. IMO 7824405

SAMPO TOURS

The Company Sampo Tours operates day cruises on the icebreaker SAMPO between December and April.

Address Kauppakatu 16, 94100 Kemi, Finland

Telephone +358 16 258878 **Fax** +358 16 256361

Website www.sampotours.com

Area operated Day cruises in the Gulf of Bothnia, Finland

SAMPO		2630gt	1960	16.0k	D2	150d		16c	74.7m	17.4m	6.2m	FI

SAMPO was built by Wartsila (yard number 368) at Helsinki as an icebreaker. She was converted for use as a passenger ship in 1988 and carries 150 passengers on day cruises. IMO 5308938

SEA SWIFT

The Company Sea Swift is an Australian logistics company operating a single passenger and cargo vessel, several small landing craft type freight ships, tugs and barges.

Address 41-45 Tingira Street, Portsmith, Queensland 4870, Australia

Telephone +61 7 4035 1234 **Fax** +61 7 4035 1249

Website www.seaswift.com.au

Area operated Freight and passenger services from Cairns to Thursday Island

TRINITY BAY		1996	1594gt	D1	13.5k	50p	50p	13c	81.0m	15.0m	5.4m	AU

TRINITY BAY was built by the Far East Shipbuilding Company (yard number 374) at Geoje, South Korea as the dredger FASECO NO 103. She was only in service for a short time before being laid up. In 1998 Seaswift purchased the ship and had her converted to a container and general cargo carrier with a small amount of passenger accommodation. She was renamed TRINITY BAY. IMO 9149990

SEMESTER AT SEA

The Company The Institute for Shipboard Education or Semester at Sea, founded by Hong Kong shipping magnate C Y Tung, began operating in 1977 aboard the UNIVERSE in conjunction with the University of Colorado. In 1981 the relationship with the University of Pittsburgh, which was to last 25 years, began, using the same ship. She was scrapped in India in 1996 and replaced by the UNIVERSE EXPLORER, built in 1958 as Moore McCormack Lines' BRASIL. When she was sold for scrap in 2004 a fast modern ship, the EXPLORER, was acquired to continue the tradition of the 'university at sea'. These voyages are only available to students that can meet the entry requirements. Meals are served cafeteria style and the students are responsible for most of the housekeeping, leading to a requirement for fewer crew than might be expected on a ship of this size. The University of Virginia currently sponsors Semester at Sea.

Address 2410 Old Ivy Road, Charlottesville, VA 22903, United States of America

Telephone +1 800 854 0195 **Fax** +1 434 243 4076

Website www.semesteratsea.org

Area operated Three annual round the world voyages

EXPLORER		24318gt	2001	28.0k	D2	836s	836s	196c	180.4m	25.5m	7.3m	BS

EXPLORER was built by Blohm & Voss (yard number 962) in Hamburg, Germany, as the OLYMPIC EXPLORER for Royal Olympic Cruises. She was designed with a high speed to operate the company's new 'Three Continents in Seven Days' itinerary. Political unrest in the Middle East caused the abandonment of that programme and the ship was used on more mundane itineraries in the Mediterranean and Caribbean Seas. Ludicrously, after pressure from the Olympic organisation in the run-up to the Athens Olympic Games, the company re-styled itself as Royal Olympia Cruises and the ship was renamed OLYMPIA EXPLORER. The company within ROC that owned the ship filed for bankruptcy in 2003, later bringing down the whole group. She was laid up and later auctioned, being purchased by Stella Maritime and becoming the EXPLORER for Semester at Sea. IMO 9183518

SHIPPING CORPORATION OF INDIA

The Company The Shipping Corporation of India, an Indian Government controlled company, was formed in 1961 with the merger of the Eastern Steamship Corporation and the Western Steamship Corporation. The company currently controls about 100 ships including a number of smaller passenger vessels and some ro-ro ferries. SCI owns the HARSHA VARDHANA, which is chartered to the Andaman and Nicobar Administration. The other ships are owned by the latter organisation and managed by the Shipping Corporation of India. Additionally, a number of small ferries and ro-ros are owned by the Administration.

Address Shipping House, 245 Madam Cama Road, Mumbai 400-021, India

Telephone +91 22 220 27346 **Fax** +91 22 220 26905

Website www.shipindia.com

Area operated Indian Ocean, Andaman and Nicobar Islands

AKBAR	‡9539gt	1971	15.5k	D1	80b	1500d	c	149.4m	18.6m	7.7m	IN
CAMPBELL BAY	8402gt	2011	17.0k	D2	500p	p	c	125.0m	18.0m	4.5m	IN
HARSHA VARDHANA	9700gt	1974	17.0k	D1	753b	d	c	132.6m	21.5m	7.0m	IN
KAVARATTI	8763gt	2008	17.0k	D2	702b	d	c	118.0m	19.0m	5.3m	IN
NANCOWRY	14176gt	1992	15.5k	D2	300b	900d	119c	157.0m	20.1m	6.7m	IN
NICOBAR	14195gt	1991	15.5k	D2	300b	900d	119c	157.0m	20.1m	6.7m	IN
SENTINEL	2408gt	1982	12.0k	D2	b	d	c	81.3m	14.4m	4.1m	IN
SWARAJ DWEEP	14239gt	1999	16.0k	D2	300b	900d	119c	157.0m	20.1m	6.7m	IN

AKBAR was built by the Helsingor Shipyard (yard number 395) at Helsingor, Denmark. IMO 7116975

CAMPBELL BAY was built at ABG Shipyard (yard number 205) at Surat, India. IMO 9309124

HARSHA VARDHANA was built at the Magazon Dock (yard number 272) in Mumbai, India. IMO 7219026

KAVARATTI was built by the Hindustan Shipyard (yard number 11102) at Visakhapatnam, India. IMO 9238260

NANCOWRY was built in Szczecin, Poland by Stocznia Szczecinska (yard number B561/02). IMO 8606434

NICOBAR was built by Stocznia Szczecinska (yard number B561/01) in Szczecin, Poland. IMO 8606161

SENTINEL was built by the Mazagon Dock Shipyard (yard number 580) in Mumbai, India. IMO 8020159

SWARAJ DWEEP was built by the Hindustan Shipyard (yard number 11101) at Visakhapatnam, India. IMO 9101168

SOCIETA ITALIANA DI NAVIGAZIONE

The Company Societa Italiana di Navigazione is an Italian company.

Address Via Saverio Mercadante 32, 00198 Rome, Italy

Telephone +39 06 84 17000 **Fax** +39 06 85 344959

Website www.signoradelvento.com

Area operated Charter yacht Italian West coast, Sardinia and Corsica

SIGNORA DEL VENTO	818gt	1962	12.0k	D1	50p	54p	24c	50.0m	8.4m	3.0m	IT

SIGNORA DEL VENTO was built by Stocznia im Komuny Paryskiej (yard number B20/13) at Gdynia,

Shipping Corporation of India's **Kavaratti** *(Bill Lawes)*

Societa Italiana di Navigazione's **Signora Del Vento** in Civitavecchia *(Rick Frendt)*

Societe de Navigation des Australes' **Tuhaa Pae IV** at Papeete *(Peter Plowman)*

Poland as the trawler GOPLO. She was acquired by Kings Lake Shipping in 1993 and renamed PEACE. At some stage she was converted for use as a training ship, but in 2006 she was acquired by her current owner and converted for use as a cruise ship under the name SIGNORA DEL VENTO, entering service in 2008. IMO 5133589

SOCIETE DE NAVIGATION DES AUSTRALES

The Company Societe de Navigation des Australes is a company based in French Polynesia.

Address BP 1890, 98713 Papeete, Tahiti, French Polynesia

Area operated French Polynesia

TUHAA PAE IV	2346gt	2012	12.0k	D2	98p	98p	c	76.0m	13.6m		m	FR

TUHAA PAE IV was built by Colorado Shipyard Corporation at Cebu in The Philippines, under subcontract from Australia's Harwood Marine. The ship is a combination container and passenger/cargo vessel. IMO 9607473

SORLANDETS SEILENDE SKOLESKIBS

The Company Sorlandets Seilende Skoleskibs (Sorlandet Maritime Highschool) is the Norwegian operator of the training ship SJOKURS. The previous ship of this name has been acquired by Stavanger Municipality for preservation.

Address Kystveien 310, 4639 Kristiansand, Norway

Telephone +47 38 12 19 80 **Fax** +47 38 12 19 81

Area operated Norway as a training ship

Website www.sjoekurs.no

SJOKURS	2191gt	1956	14.0k	D1				81.3m	12.6m	4.5m	NO

SJOKURS was built as the Hurtigruten ship RAGNVALD JARL by Blohm & Voss (yard number 789) in Hamburg, Germany for NFDS. That business was absorbed into TFDS in 1989 and the ship was sold six years later to Rogaland Sea Recruit Highschool to become the maritime training ship GANN, although unconfirmed reports suggest that she carried the name SOUTHERN PRIDE for a short time. In early 2007 she passed to her current owner and was renamed SJOKURS as a replacement for a ship of the same name. IMO 5289247

SOUTH AFRICAN DEPT OF ENVIRONMENTAL AFFAIRS

The Company South African Department of Environmental Affairs is a South African Government department. It operates a polar research and passenger vessel.

Website www.environment.gov.za

Area operated Antarctica

S A AGULHAS II	12897gt	2012	14.0k	DE1	92p	100p	45c	134.0m	21.7m	7.7m	ZA

S A AGULHAS II was built by STX Finland shipyard (yard number 1369) at Rauma, Finland. She was launched on 22 July 2011 and named by Mrs Nosipho Ngcaba, Director General of the department. The ship entered service in April 2012. IMO 9577135

SOVEREIGN SEA HERMES

The Company Sovereign Sea Hermes is a Greek yacht refitting and management company.

Address 2A Areos Street, Vouliagmeni, 16671, Athens, Greece

Telephone +30 210 896 4460

Website www.sshmaritime.com

Area operated Mediterranean charter market

O'MEGA	1830gt	1985	14.0k	D2	30p	30p	21c	82.5m	11.6m	3.8m	GR

O'MEGA was built by Mitsubishi Heavy Industries (yard number 883) at Shimonoseki, Japan as the

TOSHIMA. She was renamed KIMA in 2001 and took her current name in 2004 when acquired by Omega Cruises and converted into a yacht. She passed to Prestige Yachting in 2008 and is managed by the associated Sovereign Sea Hermes. IMO 8503151

ST HELENA LINE

The Company Andrew Weir Shipping is the manager and operator of the RMS St Helena on behalf of St Helena Line. The RMS ST HELENA was managed from the outset by the Cornish business, Curnow Shipping. St Helena Line was formed in 1977 to fill the gap left when the Union Castle Mail Steamship Company ceased to operate passenger ships between the United Kingdom and South Africa (with regular calls at the island of St Helena). The first ST HELENA was a small former Canadian coastal passenger/cargo ship previously named the NORTHLAND PRINCE. She entered service in 1977 and continued until the new ST HELENA was delivered in 1990. During the Falklands War, the first ST HELENA was requisitioned for use as a mother ship for the minesweepers of the Royal Navy. Her temporary replacement was the former Blue Funnel passenger and cargo ship CENTAUR. In 2001 Curnow Shipping lost the contract to manage the ST HELENA to Andrew Weir Shipping. The island of St Helena, one of 13 remaining United Kingdom Overseas Territories, is currently having an airport built, which is due to open in February 2016, leading to the withdrawal of the RMS ST HELENA.

Address Andrew Weir Shipping Ltd, Dexter House, 2 Royal Mint Court, London, EC3N 4XX, England

Telephone +44 207 575 6480

Website rms-st-helena.com

Area operated South African and Namibian ports to St Helena, Ascension Island.

ST HELENA	6767gt	1990	14.5k	D2	98p	128p	56c	105.0m	19.2m	6.0m	GB

ST HELENA is the last British example of a true working passenger and cargo ship; ordered from the Aberdeen shipyard of Hall Russell (yard number 1000) in 1987, but completed by A&P Appledore in October 1990 after the collapse of the Scottish builder. She was built as a replacement for the former (smaller) ship of the same name to provide the lifeline service to the island of St Helena, once the staging post for the ships of the British East India Company. Following initial mechanical problems, she has served the Island well for the past 15 years. From 2005 her UK calls were limited to two each year with most voyages linking Cape Town to the island, but now she is based solely in Cape Town. She makes an annual call at the remote island of Tristan da Cunha. The ST HELENA is the sole remaining true Royal Mail Ship. IMO 8716306

STAD AMSTERDAM

The Company Rederij Clipper Stad Amsterdam is a Dutch company.

Address PO Box 12600, 1100AP Amsterdam, The Netherlands

Telephone +31 20 569 5839 **Fax** +31 20 569 1720

Website www.stadamsterdam.nl

Area operated Europe and Caribbean cruises and charters

STAD AMSTERDAM	723gt	2000	11.0k	SD1	28p	28p	30c	76.0m	10.5m	4.2m	NL

STAD AMSTERDAM is a three-masted square-rigged ship, built by Damen Oranjewerf (yard number 6900) in Amsterdam, The Netherlands. Her design is based on the AMSTERDAM of 1854. The ship was named by Mrs Rita Kok, wife of the former Prime Minister, Wim Kok, at Sail Amsterdam 2000. IMO 9185554

STATSRAAD LEHMKUHL

The Company Statsraad Lehmkuhl Foundation is a Norwegian organisation, founded in 1978, with the objective of preserving the working sailing ship STATSRAAD LEHMKUHL. The ship operates organised excursions and cruises and is also available for charter.

Address Skur 7, Bradbenken 2, 5003 Bergen, Norway

Telephone +47 55 30 17 00 **Fax** +47 55 30 17 01

Website www.lehmkuhl.no

Sorlandets Seilende Skoleskibs' *Sjokurs* in Oslofjord *(William Mayes)*

St Helena Line's *St Helena* at St Helena *(Alan Burkin)*

Stad Amsterdam at St. Maarten *(Rick Frendt)*

Statsraad Lehmkuhl in Bergen *(William Mayes)*

Stavanger Municipality's ***Sandnes*** in Stavanger *(William Mayes)*

Area operated Norway

STATSRAAD LEHMKUHL	1516gt	1914	11.0k	SD2	350d	150s	17c	84.6m	12.6m	5.2m	NO

STATSRAAD LEHMKUHL was built by Schiffswerke u Maschin Joh. C Tecklenborg (yard number 263) at Bremerhaven, Germany as the GROSSHERZOG FRIEDRICH AUGUST, a training ship for the German Merchant Marine. She was taken as reparations by the British in 1921 and two years later ended up in Bergen, where she was used as a sail training ship up to the outbreak of the Second World War. In 1940 she was seized by the Germans and between 1940 and 1945 she carried the name WESTWARTS. She can carry 350 day passengers or 150 trainees and her total length including the bowsprit is 98.0 metres. IMO 5339248

STAVANGER MUNICIPALITY

The Company Stavanger is a city on the west coast of Norway.

Address PO Box 407, N4002 Stavanger, Norway

Telephone +47 51 53 44 00 **Fax** +47 51 53 57 99

Website www.mssandnes.no

Area operated Tourist attraction at Stavanger, Norway

SANDNES	1432gt	1950	14.0k	D1	180p			67.6m	11.0m	4.8m	NO

SANDNES was built by Nylands Verksted (yard number 374) at Oslo, Norway as the passenger vessel SANDNES. She was renamed VIKINGFJORD in 1974 and was acquired by the Rogaland Sjoaspirantskole who renamed her GANN. She passed to Sorlandets Seilende Skoleskibs in 1995 and was renamed SJOKURS. When she was replaced in 2007 she was acquired by the Stavanger Municipality for use in promoting the city's maritime heritage, reverting to her original name, SANDNES. IMO 5310905

SULTANATE OF OMAN ROYAL YACHTS

The Company Royal Yachts is a Sultanate of Oman Government organisation.

Address Royal Court Affairs, PO Box 2769, Ruwi, Sultanate of Oman

Telephone +968 2473 3000 **Fax** +968 2474 0207

Website www.rca.gov.om

AL SAID	15850gt	2008	k	D2	p	p	c	155.0m	23.0m	5.5m	OM
LOALOAT AL BEHAR	4633gt	1982	18.0k	D2	p	p	c	103.8m	16.2m	4.7m	OM

AL SAID was built as the SUNFLOWER by Luerssen Werft (yard number 13644) in Bremen, Germany. She was delivered as the AL SAID. IMO 9463774

LOALOAT AL BEHAR was built by Cantieri Navale Picchioti (yard number 550) at Viareggio in Italy as the Oman Royal Yacht AL SAID. With the arrival of the new yacht in 2008 she was renamed LOALOAT AL BEHAR and is now operated by the Oman Department of Tourism. IMO 7980433

TALLSHIP COMPANY

The Company Tallship Company, formerly Rederij Tallship Artemis b.v., is a Dutch operator of tall ships that are available for day or longer charters.

Address Zevenhuizen 52, 8801 AW Franeker, The Netherlands

Telephone +31 517 342810 **Fax** +31 517 342808

Website www.tallship-company.com

Area Operated Mediterranean, North Sea and Baltic - charters

ANTIGUA	212gt	1957	9.0k	SD1	32p	32p	10c	49.5m	7.1m	2.9m	NL
ARTEMIS	321gt	1926	9.0k	SD1	28p	35p	14c	59.0m	7.0m	3.5m	NL
ATLANTIS	380gt	1905	9.0k	SD2	36p	36p	12c	42.5m	7.5m	3.8m	NL
ELIZABETH	200gt	1913	9.0k	SD1	35p	35p	10c	41.0m	6.9m	1.4m	NL
MARE FRISIUM	210gt	1916	9.0k	SD1	24p	38p	10c	49.5m	6.5m	2.2m	NL

ANTIGUA was built by Henry Scarr (yard number 750) at Hessle in England as the trawler ANTIGUA for Southard Trawlers. She later became a safety ship and was converted to a passenger vessel in 1997. She started operating for her current owner in 2006 and can carry up to 95 day passengers. She is a three-masted barquentine. IMO 5019800

ARTEMIS was built in 1926 by Nylands Verksted (yard number 281) in Oslo as the Danish whaling ship POLII. She was converted for use as a cargo ship in 1948 and renamed LISTER. Three years later she was lengthened. In 1966 she became the ARTEMIS and in 2000 was converted to become a three mast passenger sailing ship for the Frisian Sailing Company. Her present owner acquired her in 2006. She is a three-masted barque. IMO 5209699

ATLANTIS had her origins in the River Elbe where she served as the lightship ELBE 2 from the time that she was built by J H N Wichhorst (yard number 200) in Hamburg in 1905 until hit by the Danish freighter BANANA on 10 December 1974. She was laid up in Hamburg until 1979 and then served as a training ship for the Hamburg fire brigade from 1980 to 1983. Over the next two years she was converted into the three-masted barquentine ATLANTIS. Tallship Artemis acquired her in 2006. Her areas of operation are generally the Balearic Islands and the Cote d'Azur. She can carry up to 140 day passengers. IMO 8333635

ELIZABETH was built in 1913 as a Zeeland clipper. She can carry up to 60 day passengers when cruising in the Frisian Lakes, Waddensea and Ijsselmeer. She is a three-masted clipper.

MARE FRISIUM was built by N V Weerter Scheepsbouw (yard number 90) at Weert in The Netherlands as the Swedish fishing lugger PETRONELLA. She was lengthened in 1952 and converted for use as a cargo ship. In 1995 she was rebuilt as a three masted passenger topsail lugger and was renamed MARE FRISIUM in 1997. She can carry 90 day passengers. She is now a three-masted schooner. IMO 5344592

UKRAINE MARINE ECOLOGY RESEARCH CENTRE

The Company The Ukraine Marine Ecology Research Centre is a Government of the Republic of Ukraine owned organisation, established in 1994.

Address Frantsuzskiy Bulvar 89, 270009 Odessa, Ukraine

Telephone +380 482 636622 **Fax** +380 482 636741

Area operated Ukraine ports to Istanbul with passengers and cargo

SEVASTOPOL-I	2996gt	1967	16.0k	D2	100p	100p	c	97.1m	13.8m	5.2m	UA

SEVASTOPOL-I was built by Stocznia Szczecinska (yard number B88/02) at Szczecin, Poland as the MUSSON for the Government of Russia's Hydrometeorological Research Institute. She passed to Ukraine Marine Ecology and appears to operate a passenger and cargo service between Ukraine and Istanbul, Turkey. Her sister ship, the PASSAT may or may not carry passengers, but appears to operate cargo sailings from time to time around the Black Sea. A third ship of this type is the BRIZ. Sevastopol is a seaport city in the Crimea, a region of southern Ukraine. IMO 6904155

UNITED STATES TRAINING SHIPS

Websites www.csum.edu www.maritime.edu www.sunymaritime.edu www.mainemarite.edu

EMPIRE STATE	14557gt	1962	20.0k	STE1	684s		107c	172.2m	23.2m	9.6m	US
GOLDEN BEAR	12517gt	1989	20.0k	D1	300s		50c	152.1m	21.9m	9.3m	US
KENNEDY	13886gt	1967	19.0k	STE1	600s		110c	164.6m	23.2m	7.8m	US
STATE OF MAINE	12517gt	1990	20.0k	D1	258s		58c	152.4m	21.9m	9.1m	US

EMPIRE STATE was built by the Newport News Shipbuilding and Drydock Company (yard number 552) at Newport News, Virginia, USA as the OREGON of States Steamship Company, for Pacific trades. In 1977 she became Moore McCormac's MORMACTIDE and in 1989 was purchased for the New York Maritime Academy, converted by Bay Shipbuilding Corporation and renamed as the sixth EMPIRE STATE. IMO 5264510

GOLDEN BEAR is a cadet training ship attached to the California Maritime Academy, Vallejo, California. She was built by Bethlehem Steel (yard number 4667) at Sparrows Point, Maryland, USA as the hydrographic survey vessel USNS MAURY. She was converted for her current use in 1996 and renamed GOLDEN BEAR, the third ship to carry this name. IMO 8834407

KENNEDY was built by Avondale Shipyards (yard number 1069) at Avondale, Louisiana, USA as the freighter VELMA LYKES for Lykes Lines. She became CAPE BON in 1986 and five years later participated in Operation Desert Storm. In 2003 she was converted for use as a training ship for the Massachusetts Maritime Academy to replace the PATRIOT STATE, and was renamed ENTERPRISE in honour of the Academy's first training ship, which served from 1893 to 1909. In 2009 she was renamed KENNEDY. IMO 6621662

STATE OF MAINE is the second training ship of the Maine Maritime Academy and was built by Bethlehem Steel (yard number 4668) at Sparrows Point in Maryland as the fast oceanographic research vessel USNS TANNER. She was laid up in 1993 in the James River with engine problems. She was converted for use as a training ship between 1996 and 1997 and joined the academy in June 1997. She does not appear to have been renamed until 2000. IMO 8835217

VESTLAND CLASSIC

The Company Vestland Classic is an operating name for Vestland Marine, a Polish ship-management company, mainly dealing with offshore supply vessels, based in Gdynia.

Address Indre Nordhordland Dampbåtlag AS, Strandkaien 18, P O Box 3976, Sandviken, 5835 Bergen, Norway

Website www.vestlandclassic.com

Area operated Norwegian coast

NORDSTJERNEN	2191gt	1956	15.0k	D1	150b	140d	42c	80.8m	12.6m	4.5m	NO

NORDSTJERNEN was built by Blohm & Voss (yard number 787) in Hamburg, Germany as a replacement for a pre-war vessel of the same name for the Bergen Line. From 1994 she has operated the summer run from Tromso to Spitzbergen, acting as a relief Hurtigruten ship as required. In more recent years she has been based in Spitzbergen, although as a result of the charter of the FINNMARKEN to Chevron she resumed year-round Hurtigruten service. Her Hurtigruten service finished in March 2012 and she then had a season of Spitzbergen cruising before finishing in Bergen in September. She was refitted in Gdansk in 2013 and returned to Norway in July of that year. In 2014 she operated a short summer season on the Norwegian coast. Her name translates as North Star. IMO 5255777

VICTORY CHIMES

The Company The VICTORY CHIMES is owned by Captains Richard Files and Paul DeGaeta.

Address PO Box 1401, Rockland, ME04841, United States of America

Website www.victorychimes.com

Area operated Maine coast

VICTORY CHIMES		gt	1900	k		42p	54p	9c	m	m	m	US

VICTORY CHIMES was built by the Phillips Shipyard in Delaware as the schooner EDWIN & MAUDE. She was renamed VICTORY CHIMES in 1954. In 1987 she was purchased by Dominos Pizza and renamed DOMINO EFFECT and then underwent a three-year renovation. She was acquired by her current owners in 1990 and renamed.

VINTAGE CRUISES

The Company Vintage Cruises Ltd is a Portuguese registered company, owner of the SS DELPHINE. At the time of writing the ship is for sale at a price of 38 million Euro and has been laid up since 2010.

Address Salah H, 3 andar, Avenida Arriaga 30, 9000-064, Funchal, Madeira

Website www.ssdelphine.com

Area operated Mediterranean charters

SS DELPHINE	1961gt	1921	9.0k	SE2	24p	24p	21c	78.5m	10.8m	4.5m	PT

SS DELPHINE was built by the Great Lakes Engineering Works at River Rouge, Michigan, USA as the private yacht for Horace Dodge, one of the founders of the Dodge vehicle manufacturing business, and was named after his daughter. In 1926, while in New York, the DELPHINE caught fire and sank. She

Vintage Cruises' SS **Delphine** off Monte Carlo *(Tony Davis)*

WEM Lines' **RM Elegant** off Corfu *(Tony Davis)*

Yug Cargo's **Princessa Elena** in Istanbul *(Jonathan Boonzaier)*

was raised and restored, and in 1942 was acquired by the US Navy, becoming the USS DAUNTLESS, flagship of Admiral Ernest King. At the end of the Second World War, the Dodge family re-acquired the yacht and restored her again. From 1955 to 1967 she was permanently moored, but in that year she was donated to the People to People Health Foundation. In the following year she became the Lundeberg Maryland Steamship School and was renamed DAUNTLESS. In 1986 she was acquired by New York-based Travel Dynamics, with the idea of a full restoration for luxury cruising. That transformation never materialised, and three years later she was sold to Sun Sea Cruises with a similar plan. She was laid up in the Mediterranean until purchased by an investor who had her towed to Bruges, Belgium. The restoration took five years to complete, and in 2003, following a renaming by HRH Princess Stephanie of Monaco, the elegant SS DELPHINE entered service in the Mediterranean luxury yacht charter market. IMO 8971815

WEM LINES

The Company WEM Lines is a Greek ship owner and operator of general cargo ships and bulk carriers, founded in 1982. The RM ELEGANT is placed with brokers for charter.

Address 152 Kifisias Avenue and Sokhou Street, 11525 Athens, Greece

Telephone +30 210 672 7220 **Fax** +30 210 672 7221

Website www.wem.gr

Area operated Mediterranean Sea charters

RM ELEGANT	1541gt	2005	17.0k	D2	30p	30p	32c	72.4m	12.0m	3.4m	GR

RM ELEGANT was built by Kanellos Bros (yard number 586) at Perama, Greece for Marinic Marine Company, a subsidiary of WEM Lines. IMO 9334442

WINDWARD ISLES SAILING SHIP COMPANY

The Company Windward Isles Sailing Ship Company, a Canadian company, operates the PICTON CASTLE on round the world itineraries for square-rigger sail trainees, with or without experience.

Address PO Box 1076, 135 Bluenose Drive, Lunenburg, Nova Scotia, B0J 2C0, Canada

Telephone +1 902 634 9984 **Fax** +1 902 634 9985

Website www.picton-castle.com

Area operated Worldwide

PICTON CASTLE	284gt	1928	10.5k	D1	40p		12c	43.0m	7.2m	4.0m	CK

PICTON CASTLE was built by Cochrane & Sons (yard number 1031) at Selby in Yorkshire, England as the Swansea trawler PICTON CASTLE. In 1939 she was requisitioned for use as a minesweeper and given the HMS prefix. In 1955 she was renamed TETYS and two years later was converted into a cargo ship. In 1960 she became the UTSTRAUM, and in 1970 was renamed STEINFOREST. She became the BERGFOREST in 1973 and some years later is thought to have been converted for use as a dredger. She was given the name TURNSTEIN in 1981 and three years later was renamed as the DOLMAR. She was converted to a sail training ship in the late 1990's and renamed PICTON CASTLE. IMO 5375010

YWAM MEDICAL SHIPS

The Company YWAM Medical Ships is an Australian medical organisation working in Papua New Guinea.

Address 215 Walker Street, Townsville, Queensland, 4810, Australia

Website www.ywamships.org.au

Area operated Papua New Guinea

AMMARI	1520gt	1999	15.0k	D2	68p	p	c	60.0m	15.0m	2.1m	AU
PACIFIC LINK	282gt	1979	9.5k	D1	50p	p	c	36.9m	7.3m	3.2m	CK

AMMARI was built by Austal Ships (yard number 92) at Fremantle, Australia as the RIVAGE ST MARTIN for Rivages Croisieres. In 2005 she was acquired by Italian ferry operator Ustica Lines for cruising in the islands off Sicily as the AMMARI. She was sold on within a year to Fantasea Adventure

Cruises and in early 2007 was renamed FANTASEA AMMARI. In November 2012 she was renamed RIVERSIDE AMMARI. In 2014 she was acquired by YWAM Medical Ships for use as medical and training ship for Papua New Guinea and renamed AMMARI. IMO 9202429

PACIFIC LINK was built by the Hakodate Dock Company (yard number 700) in Hong Kong as the WAKASHIO MARU. In 1997 she was sold to New Zealand owners, becoming the BIZARRE. She took up her current name in 2001, and her current role in 2010, but is likely to be replaced by the AMMARI. IMO 7900340

YUG-KARGO

The Company Yug-Kargo is a Russian state controlled company.

Address Pereulok Vinogradnyy 8, Sochi 354068, Russia

Area operated Black Sea ports and Istanbul

PRINCESSA ELENA	2964gt	1991	13.0k	D1		p	200p		c	88.5m	13.6m	3.6m	SL

PRINCESSA ELENA was built by the Yichang Shipyard in China as the METANGULA for a Mozambique owner. She is thought to have been sold at auction in 2001 and may have been renamed REGINA ELENA. Yug-Kargo acquired her in 2002 and she became the PRINTSESSA YELENA, later westernised to PRINCESSA ELENA. IMO 8888824

ZANZIBAR SHIPPING

The Company Zanzibar Shipping is a Government of Tanzania owned company. The company also operates two small tankers.

Address Mizingani Road, PO Box 80, Zanzibar, Tanzania

Telephone +255 22 22787 **Fax** +255 22 22186

Area operated Between Zanzibar and Tanzania

MAENDELEO	‡1431gt	1980		D2	32b	422d		c	77.5m	12.2m	4.1m	TZ

MAENDELEO was built by Tsuneishi Shipbuilding Co (yard number OE80) at Numakuma, Japan IMO 7900974

Vestland Classic' **Nordstjernen** off Trondheim while operating for Hurtigruten *(Rick Frendt)*

the **leading** *guide to the cruise industry*

section 4 Passenger ships in static roles

ANDAMAN CLUB

The Company Andaman Club is a Thai operator of resort hotels and casinos.

Address 25th A Floor, Lumphini Tower, 1168/71 Pharamthi Road, Yannuawa, Bangkok 10120, Thailand

Telephone +66 2 5154 7558 **Fax** +66 2 5186 1885

Website www.andamanclub.com

Area operated Laid up NW of Phuket, Thailand

KONG OLAV	2637gt	1964	87.4m	13.3m	4.6m	TH

KONG OLAV was built by AS Bergens Mek. Verksted (yard number 433) at Bergen, Norway for DSDS, an operator on the Hurtigruten. That company became part of VDS in 1978. She was sold to Thai owners in 1997 and has since been laid up after plans to convert the ship into a floating hotel collapsed. There is doubt about the continued existence of this ship. IMO 6401206

ANEDIN HOSTEL

The Company Rederi AB Allandia (Anedin Linjen), is a Swedish company operating, until recently, a single overnight cruise ship between Stockholm and Mariehamn on the Finnish Aland Islands. The company, whose trading name is thought to be a Swedish version of Onedin Line – the title of a popular British television drama series of the 1970's about a 19th century ship owner – had begun running this service in that decade using the chartered ACHILLEUS. Ownership of the company passed through a number of hands over the years, including Sally Line and Effjohn International. The BIRGER JARL was taken out of service in the summer of 2013 and berthed at Gamle Stan in Stockholm as a hostel.

Address Skeppsbron13, Stockholm, Sweden

Telephone +46 8 684 10130

Website www.anedinhostel.com

Area operated

BIRGER JARL	3564gt	1953	15.0k	D1	340p	340p	110c	92.7m	14.2m	4.9m	SE

BIRGER JARL was built under that name by Finnboda Varf (yard number 351) in Stockholm, Sweden as a steam powered ferry for Stockholms Rederi AB Svea for service on the routes from Stockholm to Helsinki and Turku. By 1973, when she was sold to Bore Line subsidiary Jakob Lines, she had been wearing the corporate livery of the Silja Line consortium for a number of years. Her new owner set her to work in the north of the Gulf of Bothnia and renamed her as the BORE NORD. In the following summer she operated cruises for Bore Line between Turku and Visby, Gotland. She later served as an accommodation ship at Stavanger, Norway. Her next move was to Mini Carriers in 1977, for use on a new Baltic Sea service as the MINISEA; this service never materialised. In 1978 she was sold to the perhaps inappropriately named Caribbean Shipping Company of Panama as a replacement for the ACHILLEUS, referred to above. She began her new career on short cruises from Stockholm under the name BALTIC STAR and a little later was re-engined with diesels. In 2002, she reverted to her original name and from then was used mainly on 22 hour cruises to Mariehamn. Following the introduction of the 2010 SOLAS changes she was granted a temporary exemption for six months, which was then extended. In August 2011 the ship had a major internal refit in order to allow her to comply with the new requirements, but was taken out of service in June 2013. Birger Jarl is said to have been the founder, in about 1250, of what we now know as the city of Stockholm. IMO 5044893

Anedin Hostel's **Birger Jarl** in Stockholm *(William Mayes)*

Brazil Maru at Zhanjiang *(Tom Rinaldi)*

Cap San Diego at Bremerhaven *(William Mayes)*

AURORA AT PIER 38

Address Pier 38, San Francisco, CA 94102, United States of America

Area operated Floating entertainment venue in San Francisco

AURORA	2496gt	1955			89.5m	13.3m	3.8m

AURORA was built by Blohm & Voss (yard number 786) in Hamburg, Germany as the WAPPEN VON HAMBURG for the day cruise business from Hamburg and Cuxhaven to Helgoland and Hornum. She carried 1,600 passengers as built. In 1960 she was sold to Nomikos Lines of Greece, who had her refitted to carry 186 cruise passengers. She was renamed as the DELOS for cruising in the Greek Islands. In 1967 Westours acquired her for use as the Alaskan cruise ship POLAR STAR. In 1970 she passed to subsidiary company West Lines as the PACIFIC STAR. Only two years later she was sold to Xanadu Cruises and renamed as the XANADU. Eventually unable to compete, she was laid up in Vancouver in 1977. She was sold in the mid 1980's to become the exhibition and trade fair ship EXPEX. She moved to lay up off Los Angeles, but little was done to convert her for her new role. In 1991 she was acquired by Friendships, and renamed FAITHFUL for conversion to a mission ship. That never materialised and she was eventually seized and sold to James Mitchell, who intended to use her as a hospital ship, for which she was renamed XANADU 2. In September 2005 she was towed to Alameda, California where she was to be converted to a luxury yacht. Another failed project and she later moved to Rio Vista, where, after a long period laid up, she was restored and renovated. In 2010 with the new name AURORA she was towed to San Francisco to become a static attraction. The ship was given notice to move in September 2011 due to safety issues with the pier, but is believed to remain alongside. There are currently plans to re-develop the pier. IMO 5088227

BRAZIL MARU

Area operated Static in Zhanjiang, China

BRAZIL MARU	10216gt	1954	k	D2	156.0m	19.6m	8.7m

BRAZIL MARU was built by Mitsubishi Heavy Industries at Kobe, Japan for Osaka Shosen Kaisha for service between Japan and South America. In 1973 she became a static attraction at Toba, Japan. She was believed to have been broken up after being towed to China in 1996, but has recently been discovered in China, where she is still serving in a static role. IMO 5050866

CAP SAN DIEGO

The Company Cap San Diego Betriebsgesellschaft mbH is the operator of the museum and hotel ship CAP SAN DIEGO.

Address Uberseebrucke, D 20459 Hamburg, Germany

Telephone +49 40 36 42 09 **Fax** +49 40 36 25 28

Website www.capsandiego.de

Area operated Museum and hotel in Hamburg, Germany with occasional voyages along the River Elbe

CAP SAN DIEGO	9998gt	1962	k	D1	159.4m	21.5m	8.5m	DE

CAP SAN DIEGO was built by Deutsche Werft (yard number 785) in Hamburg for Hamburg Sudamerikanische Dampfschifffahrtsgesellschaft, more often referred to as Hamburg Sud. She was one of six sisters built for the trade between Hamburg and South American ports. With the onset of containerisation she was sold to the Spanish operator Ybarra in 1981 and in 1986 was renamed SANGRIA for her final voyage to the breakers. However, she was saved for the Free and Hanseatic City of Hamburg, returning to her home port on 31 October of that year. IMO 5060794

CAPTAIN JOHN'S

The Company Captain John's is the local name for the JADRAN, owned and operated by Toronto restaurateur John Letnik. The restaurant closed some years ago and the ship is likely to be scrapped.

Address 1 Queen's Quay West, Captain John's Pier, Toronto, Ontario, M5J 2H1, Canada

Telephone +1 416 363 6062 **Fax** +1 416 363 6065

Website www.captainjohns.ca

Area operated Static restaurant ship in Toronto, Canada

JADRAN	2564gt	1957	90.3m	13.0m	4.7m

JADRAN was built as the second member of a trio of coastal liners for the services of Jadrolinija along the coast of Yugoslavia. She was built by Brodogradiliste at Split to carry 200 berthed and 1,000 deck passengers. She also used to cruise in the off-season. In 1975 she was sold to her current owner and converted for use as a static restaurant ship. Her surviving sister, HERMES has recently been broken up. She is marketed as CAPTAIN JOHN'S.

C-BED FLOATING HOTELS

The Company C-Bed Floating Hotels is a Dutch company operating three ships as wind farm construction workers' accommodation vessels.

Address WTC Schipol Tower D, 4 th floor, Schipol Boulevard 219, 1118 BH Schipol, The Netherlands

Telephone +31 20 654 4030

Website www.c-bed.nl

Area operated Hotel ships for construction workers, currently off the coast of England

WIND AMBITION	13336gt	1974	18.5k	D2	80p	152.4m	20.0m	5.6m	GB
WIND PERFECTION	21161gt	1982	19.0k	D2	500p	153.4m	24.2m	5.8m	GB
WIND SOLUTION	8893gt	1969	17.0k	D2	150p	123.5m	19.6m	5.3m	GB

WIND AMBITION was built by Wartsila (yard number 1214) at Turku, Finland as the passenger and car ferry PRINSESSAN BIRGITA for the Swedish-owned Sessan Line. The company was later acquired by Stena Line and the ship became the STENA SCANDINAVICA, later shortened to SCANDINAVICA when she operated in the charter market. In 1990 she became Color Line's VENUS and operated from the northern UK to Norwegian ports. Following a ship swap with DFDS she became the KING OF SCANDINAVIA in 1994. She was sold in 2002 to operate for a German company providing a ferry service between southern Italy and Turkey, becoming the CESME. She moved to take up her current role as the WIND AMBITION in May 2010, after conversion at Fredericia in Denmark. IMO 7347548

WIND PERFECTION was built by AG Weser Seebeckwerft (yard number 1031) at Bremerhaven as the ferry OLAU BRITTANIA for Olau Line's service from Sheerness to Vlissingen. She later became Fred. Olsen's BAYARD for services between Norway and Denmark. She then operated for Color Line on similar routes as the CHRISTIAN IV. From 2010 to 2012 she was operated by Fastnet Line between Swansea and Cork, but after that route closed she was laid up until acquired for use as an accommodation ship and renamed WIND PERFECTION. IMO 8020642

WIND SOLUTION was built by Alborgs Vaerft (yard number 180) at Aalborg Denmark as the Sessan Line car ferry PRINSESSAN CHRISTINA. Stena Line subsequently acquired Sessan Line, but the ship was not renamed and continued on her Sweden to Denmark service. She was sold to JCE Safe in 1981 and was renamed SAFE CHRISTINA. Initially she was put out on charter, but when the company set up a rival Frederikshavn to Gothenburg service, Stena bought the ship back. She was renamed STENA NORDICA in 1983 and moved to Stena subsidiary Lion Ferry in 1985 as the EUROPAFARJAN I. During the following year she became the LION PRINCE. In 1999 she was sold to an Italian operator and renamed COMMODORE. She later moved to ENERMAR and operated from Genoa as the PALAU. She passed to her current owner in 2008 and after refit was renamed WIND SOLUTION. IMO 6918560

DELTA KING HOTEL

The Company Delta King Hotel operates the DELTA KING as a hotel in Sacramento.

Address 1000 Front Street, Old Sacramento, CA 95814, United States of America

Telephone +1 916 444 5464 **Fax** +1 916 444 5314

Website www.deltaking.com

Area operated Static hotel in Sacramento, USA

DELTA KING	‡3360gt	1927	86.9m	17.7m	m	US

DELTA KING was partially constructed by William Denny at Dumbarton in Scotland and the hull re-assembled and superstructure added at Stockton, California, for the overnight service between San

C-Bed's **Wind Ambition** *(Peter Therkildsen)*

Demar's **Enchanted Capri** off Havana *(Rick Frendt)*

Doulos in Singapore *(Mark M Amielanczyk)*

Francisco and Sacramento, entering service in 1927. She served as a troop carrier in San Francisco Bay during the Second World War, but was then mothballed by the US Navy. When the DELTA QUEEN was acquired for Mississippi service, the DELTA KING's engines were removed to provide spares for the former ship. Following a long period of inactivity, the derelict ship was acquired in 1984 and after a 5-year renovation opened in 1989 as the Delta King Hotel.

DELTA QUEEN HOTEL

The Company The DELTA QUEEN, withdrawn from service by Majestic America Line, has been temporarily located in Chattanooga as a hotel. It is understood that if SOLAS exemption can be acquired she may return to cruise service.

Address 100 River Street, Chattanooga, TN 37405, United States of America

Telephone +1 423 468 4500

Website www.deltaqueenhotel.net

Area operated Static hotel in Chattanooga, USA

DELTA QUEEN		‡3360gt	1927	10.0k	SR1	174p	174p		c	86.9m	17.7m		m	US

DELTA QUEEN was partially constructed by William Denny at Dumbarton in Scotland and the hull re-assembled and superstructure added at Stockton, California, for the overnight service between San Francisco and Sacramento and entered service in 1927. She served as a troop carrier in San Francisco Bay during the Second World War, but was then mothballed by the US Navy. Greene Line Steamers bought the DELTA QUEEN for $47,000 and boarded her up for her long journey to the Mississippi, via the Panama Canal. Following refurbishment she entered service in 1948 and has been an attraction on the Mississippi River ever since. However, in 2008 her owner, Majestic America Line filed for bankruptcy and the DELTA QUEEN, already under threat from an inability to have her SOLAS exemption extended, became a temporary hotel. She opened for business on 5 June 2009. Apparently the cold winter of 2013/14 caused burst pipes and the resulting damage has forced the closure of the hotel. IMO 8643327

DEMAR

The Company Demar is a Mexican Industrial company involved in the off-shore oil industry.

Address Puerto Industrial Pesquero, Col Pallas, Ciudad de Carmen, COM, Mexico

Website www.demar.com.mx

Area operated Accommodation and transport ship for offshore oil-workers in Mexico

ENCHANTED CAPRI		15410gt	1975	21.2k	D2	460p	650p	250c	156.2m	21.8m	5.9m		MX

ENCHANTED CAPRI was built as one of a series of five passenger/ro-ro vessels for the Black Sea Shipping Company by Wartsila (yard number 1221) at Turku, Finland as the AZERBAYDZHAN. She was chartered to CTC for UK cruising for several years. In 1991 she moved from the Soviet flag to that of Ukraine and five years later was renamed ARKADIYA for a charter to Royal Venture Cruises. During the following year she was chartered to Sea Escape under the name ISLAND HOLIDAY. From 1998 she operated for New Commodore Cruise Line as the ENCHANTED CAPRI. That business collapsed in 2000 and the ship was arrested in New Orleans. She subsequently sailed as a gambling ship from Florida before being chartered by her owner (Faraglioni) to Demar in 2003. She was purchased by Demar in late 2007 and is currently anchored off the Mexican coast about 65 nautical miles from Ciudad del Carmen. She is managed by ISP. IMO 7359474

DOULOS PHOS

The Company Singapore businessman Eric Saw acquired the DOULOS in March 2010. It is intended that the interior of the ship will be largely rebuilt to incorporate two decks of cabins, two large restaurants, a library, a museum and other facilities. It had been hoped that the ship would open in late 2011, but the Singapore authorities were reluctant to have the ship in town so in 2013 she was moved to Bitan Island in Indonesia. The intention is to open the ship where she now rests, although possibly dry berthed.

Website www.riverboat.com.sg

Area operated Static hotel, restaurant and Christian centre in Singapore

| DOULOS PHOS | 6818gt | 1914 | 13.0k | D1 | 414b | | 130.4m | 16.5m | 5.6m | MT |

DOULOS PHOS was built by the Newport News Shipbuilding and Dry Dock Company (yard number 176) as the cargo ship MEDINA for the US East Coast to Gulf of Mexico service of the Mallory Steamship Company. This unremarkable little ship survived both world wars and was sold in 1948 for conversion as an emigrant ship for the trade from Europe to Australia. Renamed as the ROMA she carried 287 first class passengers and almost 700 in tourist class. Costa Line purchased the ship in 1952 and she was rebuilt as that company's FRANCA C. Modern Fiat diesels replaced her coal-fired boilers and triple expansion steam engine. She ran between Italy and South America until 1959, following which she was used for cruising. Re-engined again in 1970, she cruised for a further seven years before, at the age of 63, she passed to Operation Mobilization and was renamed DOULOS for use as a Christian missionary ship and floating bookshop. After a remarkable 32 years service with Operation Mobilization, the ship failed her survey in Singapore in 2009 and it was thought that she would go for scrap. However, local Christian businessman Eric Saw acquired the ship, which has been renamed DOULOS PHOS, meaning servant light, for use as a static museum, restaurant and Christian centre in Singapore. When this project failed to materialise she was moved to a shipyard on the nearby Indonesian island of Batam, where it is planned to rebuild her as a floating resort for use at the nearby island of Bintan. IMO 5119105

EGYPTIAN GOVERNMENT

Area operated Egypt, as a static naval training ship

| EL HORRIYA | 4560gt | 1865 | 15.0k | ST3 | | 160c | 128.5m | 13.0m | 5.3m | EG |

EL HORRIYA was built by Samuda Brothers at Poplar on the River Thames, London as the paddle steamer MAHROUSSA, the Egyptian Royal Yacht. She was lengthened by about 12 metres in 1872 and again by a further 5 metres in 1905, at which time her paddle wheels were replaced by screw propulsion. She served as the Egyptian Royal Yacht until the abdication of King Farouk in 1951. She was taken over by the Egyptian Navy for use as a naval training ship, a role that she continues to play. IMO 8642816

HURTIGRUTE MUSEUM

Organisation The Hurtigrute Museum was established in 1999 to preserve the FINNMARKEN and material from the history of the Hurtigrute.

Address Richard With's Plass, 8450 Stokmarknes, Norway

Telephone +47 7611 8190 **Fax**: +47 7611 8191

Website www.hurtigrutemuseet.no

Area operated Static museum ship at Stokmarknes, Norway

| FINNMARKEN | 2188gt | 1956 | 16.0k | D1 | 131b | d | c | 81.3m | 12.6m | 4.5m | NO |

FINNMARKEN was built by Blohm & Voss (yard number 788) in Hamburg, Germany for Vesteraalens Dampskibsselskab. The ship had a major re-build in 1983. She remained in service for a further ten years on the Norwegian coast until replaced by the RICHARD WITH. IMO 5115240

KEEWATIN MARITIME MUSEUM

The Company The Keewatin Maritime Museum was established in 1967 in Douglas, Michigan. She was relocated in 2012.

Address 311 Talbot Street, PO Box 189, Port McNicoll, Ontario, L0K 1R0, Canada

Telephone +1 705 534 7070

Website www.sskeewatin.com

Area operated Static museum ship at Port McNicoll, Ontario, Canada

| KEEWATIN | 3856gt | 1907 | 14.0k | | | | | 107.0m | 13.3m | 4.9m | |

KEEWATIN was built by Fairfield Shipbuilding & Engineering at Govan in Scotland for the Canadian Pacific Railway for service on the Great Lakes. She sailed from Greenock to Montreal in September

1907 and was separated into two sections for her transit of the Welland Canal. She initially operated between Owen Sound, Port Arthur and Port William on Lake Superior, and was retired from service in 1967. The ship became a museum at Douglas, Michigan. In June 2012, having been acquired by Skyline International Developments, she returned to her home port of Port McNicoll, Ontario where she will be renovated and opened as a museum and event venue.

LAGOS YACHT HOTEL

The Company The Lagos Yacht Hotel is owned by the Lagos State Government, Lagos, Nigeria. Unfortunately little information was available as this edition went to press, but it seems that the vessel has disappeared.

Address 20 Marina, Lagos, Nigeria

Area operated Lagos, Nigeria static hotel

| THE YACHT HOTEL | 5756gt | 1997 | 0.0k | - | 200p | | 108.0m | 18.4m | 2.9m | |

THE YACHT HOTEL was built by Kvaerner Warnow (yard number 010) at Warnemunde, Germany for Sunborn International as the un-powered SUNBORN and was situated in London's Docklands. She was sold to her current owner in 2008 and went to Brazil for refit before taking her place on the Lagos waterfront. She is now THE YACHT HOTEL. IMO 8639950

LOGINN HOTEL

The Company Loginn Hotel is a waterfront hotel in Stockholm, Sweden.

Address Kajplats 16, Sodermalarstrand, Stockholm, Sweden

Telephone +46 8 442 4420 **Fax** +46 8 442 4421

Website www.loginn.se

Area operated Static hotel in Stockholm, Sweden

| KRONPRINSESSE MARTHA | 906gt | 1929 | | 58.6m | 9.5m | 4.2m | SE |

KRONPRINSESSE MARTHA was built for Stavanger Steamships for a Norwegian domestic service between Oslo and Bergen by Danziger Werft, Danzig as the KRONPRINSESSE MARTHA. In 1934 she saved 553 people from the sinking German luxury liner DRESDEN, off the Norwegian coast. Following the German occupation of Norway she was renamed RYFYLKE, reverting to her original name in 1945. Four years later her steam engine was replaced by a second-hand diesel engine, and she was rebuilt, increasing her length by 5 metres. Following a sinking in 1956, she was completely rebuilt with a rather more modern appearance. She ceased operating along the Norwegian coast in 1974 and for a short time became a static hotel ship at Stavanger, Norway. At the end of that year she was sold for use as a hotel ship in Sweden and renamed KOSTER. Following a major refurbishment in 1979 she became the SPORT ROVER for West Indies activity cruises. Her owners were declared bankrupt in the following year and she eventually returned to Europe and served for some years as a static casino ship in The Netherlands. In 1987 she was purchased by Magellan Cruises and went to Falmouth, England to be refitted for service in the Caribbean, for which she was to have been renamed CROWN PRINCESS MARTHA. That venture never materialised and in 1990 she reverted to her original name. In 1998 she became the EMERALD SEA but reverted to KRONPRINSESSE MARTHA in 2001 when she moved back to Sweden to become a hotel ship again. IMO 5197028

LYDIA

Address Avenue de la Grande Plage, Le Barcares, Languedoc-Roussillon 66420 France

Area operated Static spa and night club at Le Barcares on the French Mediterranean coast

| LYDIA | 2696gt | 1931 | | 91.1m | 13.5m | 4.8m | |

LYDIA was built by Burmeister & Wain in Copenhagen, Denmark for the Adelaide Steamship Company as the MOONTA for Australian coastal work from Adelaide. She carried 140 passengers. In 1955 she was acquired by Hellenic Mediterranean Lines for service between Marseilles, Greece and the Eastern Mediterranean. For her new role she took the name LYDIA. She was sold to French owners in 1967 and following her engine removal she was permanently moored in a basin at Le Barcares for use as a hotel, nightclub and casino, as part of a larger leisure complex.

Egyptian Government's **El Horriya** at Alexandria *(William Mayes)*

NYK **Hikawa Maru** at Yokohama *(Tom Rinaldi)*

Oasia at Gibraltar *(Tony Davis)*

NYK HIKAWA MARU

The Company The Hikawa Maru is owned by NYK Line and the City of Yokohama. She has recently been given a major refurbishment.

Address Yamashita-cho, Naka-ku, Yokohama 231-0023, Japan

Area operated Museum Ship at Yokohama, Japan

HIKAWA MARU	11622gt	1930	17.0k	D2				163.3m	20.1m	m	JP

HIKAWA MARU was built by the Yokohama Dock Company (yard number 177) for NYK Line of Japan for service between Japan and the west coast of the USA. In 1941 she became a Japanese Navy hospital ship, and was the only large Japanese liner not sunk during the Second World War. She was seized by the USA in 1945 and put into service transporting US personnel between the USA and Japan. She returned to Japan in 1947 and operated more mundane sailings than those for which she had been built. However, she resumed her Pacific passenger sailings in 1954, following a full refit. She was withdrawn in 1960 and refitted as a youth hostel. She has subsequently served various static roles, including latterly that of a museum ship. The hostel closed in 1973, but she continued to operate as a museum. By 2006 the ship was owned by Hikawa Maru Marine Tower Inc, but that company folded at the end of that year and the ship passed to NYK and the City of Yokohama. NYK restored the ship and she re-opened in April 2008.

OASIA HOTEL

The Company Millennium View Ltd is the registered owner of the OASIA, which in due course will become a hotel in Yangon, Myanmar. At the time of writing the ship was anchored off the coast of Thailand.

Address Yone Phyu Lay Building, 5th Floor Room 5C, 119-121 Anawrahta Road, Yangon, Myanmar

Telephone +95 1901 0589

Website www.oasia-yangon.com

Area operated

OASIA	24492gt	1973	18.0k	D2	661p	661p	380c	191.1m	25.0m	8.2m	MT

OASIA was delivered in 1973 by Swan Hunter (yard number 39) at Wallsend on Tyne, England as the VISTAFJORD for Den Norske Amerikalinje A/S (Norwegian America Line) and was thus the last passenger liner to be built in the United Kingdom. She was initially employed on line voyages between Oslo and New York, and worldwide cruising. By 1980 she was used exclusively for cruising and was transferred along with her sister the SAGAFJORD to Norwegian American Cruises A/S, but retained her Oslo registry. In 1983 the two ships, together with the Norwegian American Cruises name, were sold to Cunard Line and continued to trade under their existing names. Already by then in Cunard colours, the VISTAFJORD was renamed CARONIA following a major refit in 1999. She was the third Cunarder to carry this name, in a short-lived revival of the 'names ending in 'ia' theme'. CARONIA was based in Southampton for cruises from the United Kingdom to Europe and further afield, but in 2004 was sold to Saga Shipping with delivery in November of that year. Following a major refit in Malta, costing some £17 million, she took up service as the SAGA RUBY with her new owner early in 2005. In June 2010 she moved from the UK flag to that of Malta. She finished her service with Saga in January 2014 and after a refit in Gibraltar she sailed to Thailand under the name OASIA. IMO 7214715

OTANTIK GEMI OTEL

The Company Otantik is a small Turkish hotel operator with a hotel in Bursa and a café in the Marmara University at Istanbul.

Address Guzelyali Yat Limani Ici, Mudanya, Bursa, Turkey

Telephone +90 224 554 4300 **Fax** +90 224 554 4334

Website www.otantikotel.com

Area operated Hotel ship at Mudanya, on the Asian shore of the Sea of Marmara, north of Bursa

TURAN EMEKSIZ	780gt	1961	k		44p	44p		69.9m	13.6m	3.9m	TR

TURAN EMEKSIZ was built by Fairfields (yard number 810) on the River Clyde in 1961 as one of a series of steam reciprocating ferries for Turkish Maritime Lines Istanbul City Lines operation. She remained in service until 2004 after which she was laid up before being sold for conversion into a hotel. She now has 22 double rooms, including two massive suites, one at each end of the main deck. Turan Emeksiz was a student at Istanbul University who died during demonstrations in 1960. IMO 5370967

QE2 ENTERPRISES

The Company QE2 Enterprises is a UAE registered Government owned company, part of the Nakheel Hotels Group, formed in 2008 to operate the Nakheel-owned QUEEN ELIZABETH 2. It was intended that eventually the ship would become a hotel, conference centre and museum at Nakheel's Palm Jumeirah development project, but with the global economic slowdown conversion plans were put on hold. Later plans called for the ship to be refitted in China to become a floating Hotel in South East Asia. At the time of writing the QUEEN ELIZABETH 2 was laid up, but apparently being well maintained.

Address PO Box 17777, Dubai, United Arab Emirates

Telephone +971 4 390 3333 **Fax** +971 4 390 3314

Website www.nakheel.com

Area operated Dubai as a static hotel and tourist attraction

QUEEN ELIZABETH 2	70327gt	1969	28.5k	DE2	1778p	1778p	921c	293.5m	32.0m	9.9m	VU

QUEEN ELIZABETH 2 was launched in 1967 by HM Queen Elizabeth II. The ship's builders, Upper Clyde Shipbuilders (yard number 736), delivered her in December 1968, but a number of problems caused the curtailment of her inaugural cruise and the ship was returned to the shipyard. She eventually commenced her maiden voyage in May 1969, sporting a revolutionary single thin black funnel with white casing. In 1982 she served as a British troopship during the Falklands War and following her refit she emerged with a light grey hull and traditional Cunard funnel colours. This hull colour lasted for only a short time and she soon reverted to a traditional black hull. In October 1986 she was sent to the Lloyd Werft shipyard at Bremerhaven, Germany for a six-month refit that included the replacement of her sometimes-troublesome steam turbines with a new diesel-electric propulsion system. When she was re-delivered in April 1987 she had a much more substantial funnel. During her 39 years of service with Cunard she provided the traveller with a regular transatlantic service, undertook numerous cruises in Europe and from the United States of America, and completed many round-the-world cruises. From 2004 she was UK based, but still did annual world cruises and occasional transatlantic crossings. In September 2005, she became the longest serving Cunarder ever. Her sale for $100 million was announced in the summer of 2007 and she sailed on her final Cunard voyage on 11 November 2008. Despite impressive and somewhat controversial plans for the ship, economic circumstances have intervened and the ship remains laid up in Dubai. IMO 6725418

RIVER HOSTEL TURKU

The Company The River Hostel Turku is operated by Oy S/S Borea Ab, a Finnish registered company.

Address Aurajoki, Linnankatu 72, Turku 20100, Finland

Telephone +358 40 6892541

Website www.turkutouring.fi/en/s/river-hostel-turku_

Area operated Static hotel and museum in Turku, Finland

BORE	4295gt	1960	14.5k	D1	238p			99.8m	15.3m	5.5m	FI

BORE was built by AB Oskarshamns Varv (yard number 353) at Oskarshamn in Sweden as the steamship BORE for Bore Line's Baltic Sea services. She was the last steamship to be built for service in Scandinavia. Bore Line was part of the Silja Line consortium. In 1977 she began a summer ferry service across the top of the Gulf of Bothnia as the BOREA for Bore Line subsidiary, Jakob Line. In 1984 she was sold to Ab Helsingfors Steamship Company of Helsinki and chartered to Oy Aura Line Ab of Turku for ferry service between Turku and Stockholm. Aura Line failed in the same year and the ship was laid up. In the following year she was sold to the Vanderbilt Steamship Company of Vancouver and was to have been renamed VANDERBILT. However, the sale fell through and she continued in lay-

Otantik Otel's ***Turan Emeksiz*** at Mudanya *(Richard Mayes)*

Queen Elizabeth 2 at Dubai *(Jonathan Boonzaier)*

RMS ***Queen Mary*** at Long Beach *(Rick Frendt)*

up. Kristina Cruises acquired her in 1987 and she was immediately re-engined with diesels and following refurbishment was set to work cruising in the Baltic Sea as the KRISTINA REGINA. She later had two very substantial interior refits to bring her up to a high standard. In 2010 she was retired from active service and sold for use as a hotel ship in Turku, for which role she reverted to her original name. IMO 5048485

RMS QUEEN MARY HOTEL & CONVENTION CENTRE

The Company In February 1993 RMS Foundation inc was granted a lease by the City of Long Beach to operate the ship for five years, extended in 1995 to twenty years. Delaware North Companies, the former owner of the Delta Queen Steamboat Company, took over control of the QUEEN MARY in October 2009.

Address 1126 Queens Highway, Long Beach, California 90802, United States of America

Telephone +1 877 342 0738 (tours) 0742 (hotel)

Website www.queenmary.com

Area operated Static hotel and exhibition centre at Long Beach, California, USA

QUEEN MARY	‡81237gt	1936	28.5k	ST4				310.7m	36.0m	12.0m	US

QUEEN MARY was first conceived in the late 1920's as Cunard planned its next generation of express Atlantic liners. The order was placed with John Brown & Company, Clydebank, Scotland for what was known as yard number 534 on May 28, 1930. Construction began in December of that year, but within twelve months work had stopped due to The Depression. Eventually, the British Government was prepared to make a loan to allow the completion of the ship, on condition that Cunard and White Star Line were merged. The Government held a 'Golden Share' in order to prevent the company being acquired by foreign interests. Cunard White Star Limited was formed on January 1, 1934 and work on the partially completed ship resumed in April. The QUEEN MARY was launched by Her Majesty Queen Mary on September 26, 1934 and was handed over to Cunard White Star on May 12, 1936. On her sixth round trip she won the coveted Blue Riband from the NORMANDIE, but that ship took it back in 1937. In 1938 the QUEEN MARY regained the title and then held it for fourteen years until she lost it to the UNITED STATES in 1952. She saw impressive war service as a troop transport, carrying up to 10,000 troops at a time. She returned to peacetime transatlantic service in 1946 and continued until September 1967. She was sold to the City of Long Beach for use as a hotel ship and tourist attraction. The City spent a fortune renovating the ship, but her location, some distance from the main waterfront left her somewhat isolated. In 1988 the giant Walt Disney Corporation acquired the company that then held the lease on the ship. Disney disowned the ship in 1991 and her management moved into other hands. The current leaseholder, Queen's Seaport Development, filed for Chapter 11 protection in early 2005 due to falling income. The operation of the ship by RMS Foundation was not affected by this. Management was later taken over by Delaware North Companies in October 2009. IMO 5287938

ROYAL YACHT BRITANNIA TRUST

The Company The Royal Yacht Britannia Trust was formed in 1998 to operate and preserve the last British Royal Yacht, the BRITANNIA, which was withdrawn from service soon after the Labour Government came to power in the United Kingdom in 1997. In the summer of 2014 the trust acquired the former Northern Lighthouse Board tender FINGAL, which was built in 1964 and which had been laid up in the River Fal for many years under the name WINDSOR CASTLE. This ship will be converted into a boutique hotel and is expected to open in 2016.

Address Ocean Terminal, Ocean Drive, Leith, Edinburgh, EH6 6JJ, United Kingdom

Telephone +44 1315 555566 **Fax** +44 1315 558835

Website www.royalyachtbritannia.co.uk

Area operated Static exhibit at Leith

BRITANNIA	5769gt	1954	25.0k	STE2	p	p	c	125.6m	16.6m	5.2m	GB

BRITANNIA was built by John Brown (Clydebank) Ltd (yard number 691) on Clydebank, Scotland as what was probably the last British Royal Yacht. She was decommissioned at the end of 1997 and arrived in Leith in May 1998. IMO 8635306

SAHARA INDIA PARIWAR

The Company Sahara India Pariwar is an Indian industrial and commercial group with interests in the hotel and leisure sectors. The group also has a strong presence in housing, media, IT, food and power generation. It is thought that the MELODY was acquired for conversion into a floating hotel.

Website www.sahara.in

Area operated unknown

QING		35143gt	1982	23.5k	D2	1064p	1250p	530c	204.8m	27.4m	7.8m	PA

QING, formerly Home Lines' second new ship, the ATLANTIC, was built by Construction Navales & Industrielles de la Mediterranee (yard number 1432) at La Seyne, France and initially operated between New York and Bermuda. Home Lines was sold to Holland America Line in 1988, but the ATLANTIC was not included in the deal. She went instead to Premier Cruise Line, and after a refit in Bremerhaven she emerged as the Caribbean cruise ship STARSHIP ATLANTIC. In 1997 she was sold to Mediterranean Shipping Company and renamed MELODY. Following summer 2011 service in the Mediterranean, she moved to South Africa for the winter, where she is marketed by Starlight Cruises. The MELODY did not operate in 2013 and was sold in November to Sahara India Pariwar and renamed QING. IMO 7902295

SAVANNAH (UNITED STATES MARITIME ADMINISTRATION)

Website www.nssavannah.net or www.ns-savannah.org (N S Savannah Association)

Ship location Pier 13 Canton Marine Terminal, 4601 Newgate Avenue, Baltimore, MD21224, United States of America

SAVANNAH		15585gt	1962	k		p	p	c	168.6m	23.8m	9.0m	US

SAVANNAH was built for the United States Department of Commerce by the New York Shipbuilding Corporation (yard number 529) at Camden, New Jersey, USA as the world's first nuclear powered merchant ship. Her keel was laid in 1957 and she was launched on 21 July 1959. She cost $47 million to build, including $28 million for the nuclear reactor and fuel core. Following a series of demonstration and experimental voyages she entered commercial service in 1964 mainly between US ports and the Mediterranean. From 1965 she ceased to carry passengers. In 1972 she was laid up at Savannah. From 1981 to 1994 she was a museum ship at Charleston, South Carolina but has subsequently been laid up in the James River. The ship is currently berthed at Baltimore, Maryland and has undergone a considerable amount of maintenance. It is hoped that eventually she will become a permanent museum. IMO 5314793

SEA WORLD LTD

The Company Sea World Ltd is a Hong Kong-Chinese joint venture operating this ship as a static hotel in Shekou, China.

Area operated Static hotel ship at Shekou, near Shenzhen, Peoples Republic of China

MINGHUA		14225gt	1962		500p		168.8m	21.8m	6.6m	CN

MINGHUA was built by Chantiers de l'Atlantique (yard number M21) at St Nazaire, France as the four-class passenger liner ANCERVILLE for Paquet Lines and operated between Marseilles and ports in French West Africa. In 1970 she was transferred to Nouvelle Compagnie de Paquebots of Marseilles. She was sold to the China Ocean Shipping Company of Guangzhou in 1973 and used on trades between China and East Africa, as the MINGHUA, carrying mainly railway construction workers and technicians. She was laid up in 1977, but returned to service in 1979 on charters to several Australian interests, who used her for South Pacific cruises out of Sydney. This lasted until February 1983, when she returned to China for lay-up. In 1984 she was sold to a newly formed Hong Kong-Chinese joint venture company called Sea World Ltd, which converted her into a floating hotel in Shekou, near Shenzhen. Nearby land reclamation projects resulted in the sea surrounding the ship being filled in, leaving the ship marooned in the middle of a park, several hundred metres from the sea. The ship was recently given an extensive renovation and continues to serve as a restaurant, entertainment and banqueting facility, marketed as SEA WORLD. IMO 5015957

Royal Yacht *Britannia* at Leith *(Rick Frendt)*

Seaworld's *Minghua* at Shenzhen *(Tom Rinaldi)*

SS *Rotterdam* in Rotterdam *(William Mayes)*

SS GREAT BRITAIN TRUST

The Company The SS Great Britain Trust was established in 1970 to rescue and preserve the ship. The restoration programme was finally completed in 2005.

Address Great Western Dockyard, Gas Ferry Road, Bristol BS1 6TY, England

Telephone +44 1179 260680

Website www.ssgreatbritain.org

Area operated Static museum ship in Bristol, England

GREAT BRITAIN	3270gt	1843	k		m	m	m

GREAT BRITAIN was built in the Great Western Dockyard, Bristol (where she now resides) in 1843. Designed by the great Isambard Kingdom Brunel for the Great Western Steamship Company, she made her maiden transatlantic crossing in July 1845 in a record time of 14 days. Initially intended to be a paddle steamer, she was completed with a single 16 foot diameter iron screw. When launched in 1843 she was by far the largest ship in the world and could carry 252 passengers with a crew of 130. Although technologically successful, the venture was something of a financial failure, and her Atlantic days finished in 1846 after a serious grounding off the coast of Northern Ireland. Between 1852 and 1876 she served the route to Australia via the Cape as an emigrant carrier. Refitted to carry 750 passengers, she had a new engine and sails. A brief interlude in 1855/6 saw her in use as a troopship in the Crimean War. Between 1882 and 1886 she served purely as a sailing ship and it was during a sailing in 1886 carrying Welsh coal to San Francisco that she was forced to take shelter in Port Stanley in the Falkland Islands. Uneconomical to repair, she became a coal and wool hulk. By 1937 she was taking in water and was beached. In 1970 she was salvaged and brought back to Bristol for preservation.

SS MILWAUKEE CLIPPER PRESERVATION

The Company SS Milwaukee Clipper Preservation Inc was established in 1997 to rescue and preserve the ship.

Address PO Box 1370, Muskegon, Michigan 49443, United States of America

Telephone +1 231 683 1590

Website www.milwaukeeclipper.com

Area operated Static museum ship at 2098 Lakeshore Drive, Muskegon

MILWAUKEE CLIPPER	4272gt	1905	k	SR1	350p	350p	c	110.0m	13.7m	m	US

MILWAUKEE CLIPPER was built in Cleveland, Ohio by the American Shipbuilding Company (yard number 423) for the Anchor Line (Erie & Western Transportation Company), as the JUNIATA for Great Lakes service. She carried 350 passengers between Buffalo, New York and Duluth, Minnesota. She was withdrawn in 1937 following the introduction of new safety regulations, on account of her wooden superstructure. Sand Products Corporation of Muskegon acquired the ship in 1940 and she was rebuilt by the Manitowoc Shipbuilding Company with a new streamlined steel superstructure. She was renamed MILWAUKEE CLIPPER and in 1941 began service between Milwaukee and Muskegon, which continued until 1970. She was sold in 1977, renamed SS CLIPPER and moved to Chicago, where she operated as a static museum and convention ship. In 1990 she moved to Hammond, Indiana and was renamed MILWAUKEE CLIPPER. She returned to Muskegon under her present owner in 1997. IMO 5235375

SS ROTTERDAM

The Company The SS ROTTERDAM was owned by the Dutch company Rederij De Rotterdam BV, a consortium originally consisting of the housing company Woonbron and the investment company Eurobalance. In 2006 Eurobalance pulled out of the venture, and in 2008, on the instruction of the Dutch Minister for Housing, Woonbron was required to give up its involvement after a massive overspend on the conversion project. That 80% shareholding was eventually sold to Westcord Hotel, the owner of the nearby Hotel New York in a deal that was finalised in July 2013.

Address 3e Katendrechtse Hoofd 25, 3072 AM, Rotterdam, The Netherlands

Telephone +31 10 297 3090 (hotel)

Website www.ssrotterdam.com

Area operated Static hotel and conference centre in Rotterdam

ROTTERDAM	39674gt	1959	21.5k	ST2		228.2m	28.7m	9.0m	NL

ROTTERDAM was built by the Rotterdam Dry Dock Company (yard number 300) in Rotterdam, The Netherlands, and launched by Her Majesty Queen Juliana, as the flagship for Holland America Line's transatlantic service, and running mate to the NIEUW AMSTERDAM. In later years she was used exclusively as a cruise ship. Carnival acquired Holland America Line in 1988, and the ROTTERDAM continued to serve her new owners, developing a very loyal following. In 1997, she no longer met SOLAS requirements and was withdrawn from service, but quickly snapped-up by Premier Cruise Lines, upgraded and renamed REMBRANDT. She was later going to be renamed BIG RED BOAT IV, but the outcry led to her keeping her name. Premier Cruise Lines failed in 2000 and the REMBRANDT was laid up. She was eventually acquired by Dutch interests with a view to returning her to Rotterdam as a static exhibit and hotel ship. The REMBRANDT was towed to Gibraltar in 2004 for some preliminary work, including asbestos removal, to be carried out. She was renamed ROTTERDAM in 2004. Her then owner, SS Rotterdam B V was declared bankrupt, and as the ship had been the security for loans made by the Port Authority of Rotterdam, ownership passed to the latter. Following attention at a shipyard in Cadiz, she was towed to Gdansk, Poland in the autumn of 2005 for the final restoration work to be completed. A dispute over the asbestos remaining on board led to the ship being removed from Polish waters in summer 2006 to Wilhelmshaven, where the work was completed. The ROTTERDAM returned to the city of Rotterdam on 4 August 2008 and after many delays finally opened for business on 15 February 2010. IMO 5301019

STF A F CHAPMAN

The Company STF A F Chapman is a hostel ship in Stockholm.

Address Flaggmansvagen 8, 11149 Stockholm, Sweden

Telephone +46 8 463 2266 **Fax** +46 8 611 7155

Website www.stfchapman.com

Area operated Hostel ship in Stockholm

A F CHAPMAN	‡1425gt	1888			136p	71.1m	11.4m	3.7m	SE

A F CHAPMAN was built by the Whitehaven Shipbuilding Company (yard number 65) in Whitehaven, England as the DUNBOYNE for Charles E Martin & Co of Dublin, Ireland. In 1915 she was renamed G D KENNEDY by Norwegian owners and took her current name in 1923 when she was acquired by Swedish owners. During the Second World War she served as a barracks in Stockholm and was acquired by the City of Stockholm in 1947. She served as a youth hostel in Stockholm from about 1949. The ship was closed for major renovation from autumn 2005 but has now re-opened. IMO 8639924

SUNBORN INTERNATIONAL

The Company Sunborn Hotels is a Finnish company operating hotels in Finland, Germany and England. The operation included two yacht hotels, until the vessel based in London's Docklands was sold to Nigerian owners in 2008. The company won a contract to operate a yacht hotel in Port Forum, Barcelona. This venture was supposed to open in 2011, but the date has been moving forward for some time and at the time of writing had still not opened. Another floating hotel is planned for London. The Gibraltar hotel opened in early 2014.

Address Juhana Herttuan Puistokatu 23, FI 21100 Naantali, Finland

Telephone +358 244 56251 **Fax** +358 244 54520

Website www.sunborn.com

Area operated Naantali, Finland and Gibraltar static hotel

SUNBORN GIBRALTAR	c15000gt	2013	0.0k	-	378p	142.0m	21.0m	3.8m	NL
SUNBORN PRINCESS	7264gt	2002	0.0k	-	280p	119.0m	18.4m	2.9m	FI

SUNBORN GIBRALTAR was built in Malaysia by Boustead Naval Shipyard (yard number 24). IMO 9475272

STF A F **Chapman** in Stockholm *(William Mayes)*

Sunborn Gibraltar *(Tony Davis)*

SUNBORN PRINCESS was built by Kvaerner Warnow (yard number 404) at Warnemunde, Germany for Sunborn International and is currently in use as a hotel at Naantali, Finland. IMO 8971833

TIANJIN TANGGU STATE-OWNED ASSETS INV & MAN CO

Area operated Static in Tianjin, China

ORIENT PRINCESS	10298gt	1967	21.5k	D2	301p	488p	240c	150.3m	21.0m	6.6m	CN

ORIENT PRINCESS was built by Chantiers de l'Atlantique (yard number N23) at St Nazaire, France as the passenger cargo ship YAO HUA for the China Ocean Shipping Co of Guangzhou. Initially used on the trade between China and East Africa, she was converted into a cruise ship in the late 1970s and often chartered to US-based cruise operators. In 1986 she was sold to Hong Kong-based buyers, Main Fortune Ltd, and used for overnight casino cruises out of Hong Kong as the ORIENT PRINCESS. These continued until 2002, when the vessel was auctioned in Guangzhou. The ship was then sold to Chinese interests who plan to use her as a static attraction in Tianjin, where she currently operates as a floating karaoke lounge and restaurant. IMO 6708109

VERONICA HOTEL

The Company Veronica Hotel is owned by Daewoo Shipbuilding and Marine Engineering, one of the largest ship builders in the world. The hotel is situated in Duqm, Oman but seems to have closed in 2013.

Address PO Box 629, Postcode 115, Madinat Qaboos, Mucat, Oman

Telephone +968 252 12331

Website www.veronicaduqm.com

Area operated Hotel ship in Oman

VERONICA	28891gt	1966	21.5k	D2	728p			201.2m	26.5m	8.6m	BS

VERONICA was built by John Brown & Co (Clydebank) Ltd (yard number 728) on the River Clyde in Scotland, as the immensely elegant KUNGSHOLM for Swedish America Line's service from Gothenburg to New York. As that trade declined she switched to cruising and was subsequently sold to Flagship Cruises. In 1978 she was acquired by the Peninsular and Oriental Steam Navigation Company and after a drastic conversion, which included the loss of most of the forward funnel, entered service as the SEA PRINCESS. She initially replaced the ARCADIA in February 1979 in the Australian market, where she remained until 1982. She was then transferred to the British market, where she remained until 1986, operating alongside the CANBERRA. She then served Princess Cruises for five years before returning to the United Kingdom in 1991. She was renamed VICTORIA in March 1995, and at the end of 2002 was sold to the Greek controlled Leonardo Shipping and renamed MONA LISA for long-term charter to Holiday Kreuzfahrten to serve the growing German cruise demand. In September 2006 the operator was declared bankrupt and the MONA LISA was returned to her owner. Subsequently she was chartered for use as an accommodation ship at the 2006 Asian Games in Doha. She was registered as owned by Leonardo Shipping, a subsidiary of Kyma Ship Management. In early 2007 she was taken on a two x eight-month charter (with an option for a third term) as THE SCHOLAR SHIP, a university at sea, supported by Royal Caribbean Cruise Line. It therefore seemed logical that she should use the remainder of the year with Pullmantur Cruises, for which service she was renamed OCEANIC II. Following the loss of the SEA DIAMOND, the OCEANIC II was chartered to Louis Cruise Lines for one or two cruises, prior to taking up her Pullmantur duties. The OCEANIC II, under the guise THE SCHOLAR SHIP, completed her first two voyages, but due to lack of funding was unable to take the second year's programme. During the summer of 2008 she was chartered to Lord Nelson Seereisen, reviving the name MONA LISA, and was employed in a similar way in 2009 and 2010. However, while laid up for the winter 2008/9 she was hastily reactivated to take over the role of The Peaceboat, following a string of mechanical problems with the CLIPPER PACIFIC. Although moves were afoot to preserve her in Gothenburg, as with so many of these proposed rescues, nothing came of it and the ship was sold to Daewoo SME Oman when her 2010 summer charter to Lord Nelson Seereisen finished. She was refitted as the hotel ship VERONICA. IMO 6512354

WORLD OCEAN MUSEUM

Address Peter the Great Embankment 1, Kaliningrad, Russia

Website www.world-ocean.ru

Area operated Museum ship in Kaliningrad, Russia

VITYAZ		3248gt	1939	14.0k	D2	70p	70p	66c	109.4m	14.6m	5.9m	RU

VITYAZ was built by Deschimag Werk (yard number 614) at Bremerhaven as the passenger and cargo ship MARS for the Neptune Shipping Company. During the Second World War she was used as a hospital ship. In 1945 she became the EMPIRE FORTH for the British Ministry of Transport and in the following year was given to Russia, converted to a research ship and renamed EQUATOR. Subsequently she was renamed as the ADMIRAL MAKAROV and in 1949 she took the name that she has held ever since. Her research career came to and end in 1979 and she remained laid up until 1990, when it was decided that she should be preserved. The renovation was completed in 1994. IMO 5382609

LATE NEWS

Portuguese local excursion and river cruise operator Douro Azul has purchased the abandoned new-build ferry ATLANTIDA from her builder for conversion into an ocean cruise ship.

The ANTARCTIC DREAM is now apparently operating for Sinbad Navigation as a floating armoury for security teams for ships transiting the northern part of the Indian Ocean.

All Leisure Group's DISCOVERY has been sold for breaking and at the time of writing was making her final voyage under the name AMEN.

OCEAN STAR PACIFIC has been renamed PACIFIC and re-flagged to St Kitts & Nevis, possibly in anticipation of her final voyage.

PT Pelni's KERINCI has been sold for possible use as an accommodation ship.

Jimei Group has pulled out of the Hong Kong casino ship trade and the JI MEI has been sold to undisclosed Chinese interests.

Metropolis Cruise's METROPOLIS has been laid up after mechanical problems.

Hurtigruten has chartered NORDSTJERNEN for a summer season of Spitzbergen cruises in 2015.

The owners of Deilmann Cruise's DEUTSCHLAND filed for bankruptcy on 30 October 2014. It was hoped that a reconstruction could be completed in time for the ship's 2015 world cruise.

Cruise & Maritime Voyages acquire the GRAND HOLIDAY. The vessel will trade as from 2015 as MAGELLAN.

the **leading** *guide to the cruise industry*
section 5 Passenger ships unlikely to see further service

7107 ISLANDS CRUISE (built 1968 gross tonnage 5,113) was built as the Spanish car and passenger ferry VICENTE PUCHOL by Union Naval de Levante (yard number 101) at Valencia, Spain. She was delivered to Compania Trasmediterranea in December 1968. In 1987 she was sold to Attica Shipping of Greece, converted to a cruise ship and renamed ARCADIA. She was renamed ANGELINA LAURO for a single season in 1990 for a charter to Starlauro (now MSC), but reverted to ARCADIA during the following year. In 1997 she passed to Golden Sun Cruises of Greece without a change of name, but was re-acquired by Attica Shipping in 2000. In 2001 she was chartered to Great Lakes Cruises, but following a voyage to the Great Lakes from Europe, her charterers encountered difficulties and were forced to abandon their programme of cruises in the lakes. She was laid up in Montreal for 15 months before being sold at auction to Anaconda Maritime. She was renamed CARIBIC STAR and was to have been chartered to Megawest Cruises of Australia in 2004 for Pacific cruising as the TROPICAL ISLANDER, but that transaction failed to materialise. It then appeared that she may have been destined for World Yacht Club as a condominium ship, but that never happened. In May 2005 she was acquired by Danish company C&C Marine (Coco Explorer Cruises) and put into service in the Philippines. However, she was not successful and within a short time was laid up for sale. Taiwanese company Inluck International Cruise Group announced its purchase of the vessel in 2006, and its intention to rename her ASIA AND PACIFIC STAR. However this transaction was never completed. She was renamed 7107 ISLANDS CRUISE by the company of the same name, based in the Philippines, in April 2009, but was seized by the Philippines Customs Bureau in June 2009 for alleged failure to pay approximately $400,000 in import duty. The ship remains laid up and is now thought unlikely to re-enter service. IMO 6816970

AMBASSADOR II (built 1970 gross tonnage 11,940) had her first incarnation as the PRINZ OBERON. Built for Sweden's Lion Ferry by Nobiskrug Werft (yard number 663) at Rendsburg, Germany, she entered service on charter to Prinzenlinien on its Bremerhaven, Germany to Harwich, England service. She was sold to her operator in 1978 and continued to serve her North Sea route. Following the closure of the service she undertook a number of charters before becoming Transnordic Line's NORDIC SUN. In 1986 she was renamed CRUISE MUHIBAH for cruising service from Malaysia. She came back to Europe three years later and joined B & I Line in Dublin as the MUNSTER for Irish Sea ferry service. She was sold to New Olympic Ferries of Greece and renamed AMBASSADOR in 1993, but was re-sold within a year to EPA Invest of Limassol, renamed AMBASSADOR II, and put onto the charter market. Over the next three years she undertook a number of charters in the Mediterranean and Baltic Seas. In 1997 she passed to International Shipping Partners of Monrovia and spent almost two years being converted for use as a casino ship by A&P Appledore in England. She began what is likely to be the last phase of her career as a casino ship for Sterling Casino Lines in June 1999. In 2008 Sterling Casino Lines ceased trading and the ship was laid up at Orange, Texas. IMO 7011515

BAYKAL (built 1962 gross tonnage 5,230) was built for the Far East Shipping Company and last reported in Vladivostok around 2002. However she is reported by Lloyds Register to have been broken up in 1998 in Vietnam, before the above sighting. IMO 5401352

BERAKAH (built 1970 gross tonnage 1,716) was built by American Marine Corporation (yard number 1052) at New Orleans, Louisiana, USA as the FORCE TIDE. She was renamed NORPAC II in 1987, PACIFIC WARRIOR in 1992 and on transfer to Cruceros de Sur (Temptress Voyages) in 1995, TEMPTRESS EXPLORER. In 2001 ownership passed to Transamerica Ship Holding, and in May of the following year she was renamed PACIFIC EXPLORER. Cruise West had previously been marketing voyages on the TEMPTRESS EXPLORER. Cruise West ceased trading in September 2010 and the ship was laid up. She was renamed BERAKAH in 2013. IMO 7047136

BETA (built 1962 gross tonnage 5,230) was built as the AFGHANISTAN and last reported laid up in Novorossiysk.

CALEDONIA (built 1947 gross tonnage 955) was built by Cook, Welton and Gemmell (yard number 779) of Beverley, England as the trawler AKUREY for Canadian owners. She subsequently bore the names PETREL and PETREL V. She was converted to a square-rigged barquentine in 1977. In 2000 she passed to Canadian Sailing Expeditions and was renamed CAPE HARRISON. She was renamed again, this time as the CALEDONIA, in 2002. The owning company closed in November 2009. Her owners are now Caterpillar Financial Services. IMO 5007508

CALLISTO (built 1963 gross tonnage 499) was built as the MARINA by D W Kremer Sohn (yard number 1104) at Elmshorn in Germany. She became the ILLYRIA II in 1985 and was renamed CALLISTO in 2000 by Blue Sea Shipping Line. She had been operated under charter by Travel Dynamics International for several years, but now appears to be laid up. Callisto was the daughter of Lycaon, and was associated with Artemis, the goddess of the hunt in Greek Mythology. IMO 5416553

CAPTAIN COOK'S EXPLORER (built 1979 gross tonnage 1,160) was built as the MURRAY EXPLORER. She operated occasional overnight and weekend cruises from Sydney for Captain Cook Cruises. When the Australian business was taken over by Sealink this ship was no longer required and was sold to Harwood Marine. She is currently laid up but may be converted for use as an accommodation ship.

CARIB VACATIONER (built 1971 gross tonnage ‡2,430) was launched by De Merwede (yard number 601) at Hardinxveld in The Netherlands as the KIELER FORDE. She was completed as the cargo vessel CRAIGAVON, but reverted to her launch name in 1972. She became the NASSAU later in 1972, being slightly renamed as NASSAU I in 1978. Two years later she became NASSAU again. She was converted in 1982, and operated until 1986 as the very budget cruise ship VACATIONER. She was sold in 1986 and renamed CARIB VACATIONER. It is thought that she was renamed CORAL PRINCESS in 1992, and it appears that she may have been laid up at Curacao since 1998. IMO 7038214

COLUMBIA QUEEN (built 2000 gross tonnage ‡1,599) was built for the Delta Queen Steamboat Company at the time that it was part of American Classic Voyages. The ship was built by the Leevac Shipyard (yard number 311) at Jennings, Louisiana, USA. When the American Classic Voyages group collapsed in 2001, the ship was laid up and not reactivated until 2005, when put into service by Great American River Journeys. That operation ceased after a single season and the ship was laid up again. She was acquired by Majestic America Line in October 2006 and soon afterwards commenced a series of cruises in the Northwest Rivers. Following the failure of Majestic America Line, she was laid up at Portland, Oregon, where she remains. IMO 8643303

GAGE (built 1944 gross tonnage 7,612) was built in 1944 by Oregon Shipbuilding Corporation (yard number 118) in Portland, Oregon as a Haskell class attack transport. She is laid up as part of the US Reserve Fleet in the James River, and is named after Gage County, Nebraska.

ISLAND BREEZE (built 1967 gross tonnage ‡4,595) was built by Helsingor Skibsvaerft og Maskinbyggeri (yard number 381) at Helsingor, Denmark as the ro-ro freight ferry STAFFORD for DFDS for service between England and Denmark. In 1984 she was renamed DANA GLORIA, and later that year was sold to Tzamar Voyage and renamed VOYAGER. In 1985 she was converted to a passenger and car ferry and later sold to Cross Med Maritime Co to run from Patras, Greece to Brindisi, Italy as the MONACO for Euroferries. Three years later she was renamed SITIA for service between Piraeus and the island of Crete. In 1990 she was converted at the Avlis Shipyard at Chalkis, Greece, into a casino and cruise ship. At this time she had about 50 luxury cabins installed. During the next year she began running low cost cruises from Miami as the TROPIC STAR. In 1993 she was renamed PACIFIC STAR and began to operate day cruises from San Diego, USA to Ensenda, Mexico for Starlite Cruises. Following arrest over non-payment of bills, this service ceased and the ship returned to Greece in 1995 for lay-up under the name AEGEO STAR. She was finally sold at auction in 1997 to Fortune Ship Investments and renamed NEW YORK FORTUNE 1. In 2002 she was renamed as the ATLANTIS and during the following year started operating day cruises between the Greek islands of Crete and Santorini. She was laid up in 2005 and it was thought unlikely that she would see further service. However, although remaining laid-up she was renamed ISLAND BREEZE in 2007. IMO 6708252

JUPITER (built 1975 gross tonnage 20,804) was built by Dubigeon-Normandie (yard number 142) at Nantes, France for Silja Line's Sweden to Finland ferry services as the WELLAMO. Replaced by a larger ship in 1981 she was sold to DFDS, becoming the DANA GLORIA for operation between Copenhagen and Oslo, a role that she performed for many years. In 1984 she was chartered back to Silja Line as the SVEA CORONA for a few months. In 1988 she was lengthened by 22 metres by Jos. L. Meyer at Papenburg, Germany, returning to service between Copenhagen and Oslo as the KING OF SCANDINAVIA. In 1994 she formed part of a ship swap when exchanged with Color Line for the VENUS and some cash. She then operated as the JUPITER between Newcastle and various Norwegian ports

Polar Star at Ushuaia *(Rick Frendt)*

Captain Cook's **Explorer** in Sydney *(Rick Frendt)*

Island Breeze as **Atlantis** at Santorini *(Rick Frendt)*

Mariya Yermolova in Istanbul *(Rick Frendt)*

Monet in Nice *(Martin Grant)*

until the route and ship were sold to Fjord Line in 1998. She was replaced by a larger ship in 2006 and sold to a Singapore registered owner. Between 2007 and 2008 she was converted for use as a casino ship at Guangzhou, China. In 2008 it was planned to charter her to a Vietnamese travel company, but that failed to materialise. The ship did eventually manage a few cruises, but was laid up in December 2008 at Sihanoukville, Cambodia. She was sold in April 2010 to an undisclosed Asian owner and moved to Vietnam. She remains laid up at Nha Trang. IMO 7360186

LO SHAN (built 1974 gross tonnage 2,151) was built by Niigata Engineering (yard number 1233) at Niigata, Japan as the LO SHAN for Shun Tak Holding. She is currently laid up. IMO 7355052

MABUHAY SUNSHINE (built 1983 gross tonnage 7,262) was built for Oshima Unyu KK by Mitsubishi Heavy Industries (yard number 858) at Shimonoseki in Japan as the cruise ship SUNSHINE FUJI for domestic Japanese cruises. She was sold to Mabuhay Holiday Cruises of the Philippines in 1995 and rebuilt as the MABUHAY SUNSHINE, re-entering service on cruises out of Manila in 1996. The venture did not prove successful and the ship has been laid up for sale in Cebu since 1998. IMO 8300561

MAN GYONG BONG (built 1971 gross tonnage ‡3,317) was built by the Chongjin Shipyard in North Korea as a passenger cargo ship. She operated an irregular service between North Korea and Japan but was reported sold to unknown owners in 2007. Continued existence in doubt. IMO 7111406

MARIA KOSMAS (built 1977 gross tonnage ‡3,344) was built by the HMA Naval Dockyard at Melbourne, Australia as the oceanographic research vessel HMAS COOK. Following grounding in 1990 she was withdrawn from service. In 1993 she was sold to Greek interests and renamed MARIA KOSMAS for conversion to a cruise ship. She was laid up again in 1996 and in 2002 towed to Dubai. Her current use and whereabouts are unknown. IMO 8872784

MARIYA YERMOLOVA (built 1974 gross tonnage 4,364) was one of a series of eight ships built by Brodogradiliste Titovo (yard number 406) at Kraljevica, in what was then Yugoslavia, for the Murmansk Shipping Company. Other vessels were delivered to other Russian operating companies. Latterly the ship operated for Novoships in the Black Sea, but was reported to be the start up ship for new operator Caspian Cruises. It seems that the ship did not sail in this new role and she remains laid up. Mariya Yermolova was a Russian actress. IMO 7367524

MONET (built 1970 gross tonnage 1,453) was built as the YUSHAR for Northern Shipping by the Georgi Dimitrov Shipyard (yard number 903) in Varna, Bulgaria. She became the STELLA DALMATIAE in 1997 for Dalmacija Cruise Line and was renamed as the MONET in 1998 for Danaco, following a conversion by the Brodoremont Shipyard in Croatia. She subsequently passed to Ocean Winds in 2001 and Westwind Enterprises in 2003. She was operated by Jadropov International and marketed by Elegant Cruises. During 2009 Elegant Cruises was declared bankrupt and the ship remains under arrest in Croatia. Frenchman Claude Monet was one of the greatest impressionist painters. During early 2014 the ship's ownership changed so she may be about to be reactivated, or go for scrap. IMO 7045803

NIKOLAYEVSK (built 1962 gross tonnage 5,230) last reported laid up in Sochi, Russia.

OCEAN JEWEL OF ST PETERSBURG (built 1982 gross tonnage 12,602) was built as the MIKHAIL SUSLOV by Stocznia Szczecinska (yard number B492/04) at Szczecin, Poland as one of a series of ships built for the Black Sea Shipping Company. She was laid down as the VASILIY SOLOVYEV SEDOY. In 1989 she was renamed PYOTR PERVVY for conversion for use as an eye hospital. In 1997 she was renamed as the PETR PERVVY. In 2000 all of the passenger cabins and some crew cabins were removed, leaving just 26 cabins for officers. In 2001 she became the OCEAN EMPRESS for Oasis Shipmanagement. She was acquired by Titan Cruise Lines in 2003 and renamed OCEAN JEWEL OF ST PETERSBURG. From February 2006 she was laid up at the naval port of Bani, close to San Domingo in the Dominican Republic, and has remained there ever since. Her continued existence is in doubt. IMO 7625823

PACIFIC AURORA (built 1962 gross tonnage 1,183) was built by the Collingwood Shipyard (yard number 175) at Collingwood, Ontario, Canada as the passenger/cargo vessel TAVERNER for Marine Atlantic. She was acquired by British Columbia Discovery Voyages in 1997 and had been undergoing conversion for several years, before being sold on to Marine Growth Ventures in 2007 for use as a timeshare vessel on the Canadian Coast. The ship's ownership was registered as Marine Growth Canada. Following that company's bankruptcy, title in the ship was vested in secured creditor Greystone Business Credit II. It is not thought that the ship is operational. IMO 5353983

POLAR STAR (built 1969 gross tonnage 4,998) was built by Wartsila (yard number 389) at Helsinki,

Finland as the icebreaker NJORD for the Swedish Maritime Administration. Karlsen Shipping acquired her in 2000, converted her for use as an expedition ship and renamed her POLAR STAR operating for Polar Star Expeditions. On 31 January 2011 the ship struck submerged rocks in Antarctica and was later sent to Las Palmas in the Canary Islands for repair. She was subsequently reported to have been arrested and remains there at the time of writing. Polar Star Expeditions subsequently filed for bankruptcy. IMO 6905745

POLYNESIAN PRINCESS (built 1959 gross tonnage 977) was built by Brodogradiliste Titovo (yard number 361) at Kraljevica in Yugoslavia for the state ferry operator Jadrolinija as the OPATIJA. In 1968 she was acquired by the Government of Kiribati and was renamed NINIKORIA. In 1975 she became the TERAAKA, and is thought to have been renamed POLYNESIAN PRINCESS more recently. She is laid up in Ensenda, Mexico. IMO 5263853

PRINCE (built 1962 gross tonnage 5,145) was built by the Finnboda Shipyard (yard number 375) at Stockholm, Sweden as the SVEA JARL for Silja Line's (Rederi AB Svea) Baltic ferry services. In 1976 she was sold to rival consortium Viking Line (Rederi AB Slite) for use as the cruise ship APOLLO III on the lucrative 24-hour cruise service from Stockholm to Mariehamn in the Aland Islands. With the arrival of the new ATHENA in 1989 she was no longer required, and was sold to Thai owners to become the ANDAMAN PRINCESS. In the summer of 2006 she was sold to Advent Systems, of Tortola, British Virgin Islands, and renamed PRINCE for her final voyage. It was thought that she was going straight for breaking, but recent reports suggest that she first went to Vladivostok. She was last sighted at Vung Tao, Vietnam several years ago. IMO 5346502

REEF ESCAPE (built 1987 gross tonnage 1,815) was built by Carrington Slipways (yard number 182) at Newcastle, New South Wales, Australia as the LADY HAWKESBURY. She was renamed REEF ESCAPE in 1990 when purchased by Captain Cook Cruises. In 1997 she was registered under the Fijian flag as DRO KI CAKAU, but reverted to the name REEF ESCAPE in 2004. During Cyclone Mick in December 2009 she was deliberately beached on Naviti Island, with no loss of life, or injury to her passengers. The ship was refloated and towed to Suva, Fiji in January 2010, where she remains. She was sold to another Fiji owner but remains laid up. IMO 8512475

SPIRIT OF GLACIER BAY (built 1984 gross tonnage 1,471) was built in 1984 by Jeffboat Inc, at Jeffersonville, Indiana, USA as the NANTUCKET CLIPPER for Clipper Cruise Line. She was acquired in early 2006 by Cruise West and later renamed as the SPIRIT OF NANTUCKET. In 2008 she was renamed as the SPIRIT OF GLACIER BAY, and was one of the two ships laid up in 2009. Cruise West ceased trading in September 2010 and the ship remains laid up, but appears to be owned now by General Electric Capital Corporation. IMO 8883563

SUPPERCLUB CRUISE 02 (built 1962 gross tonnage 3,464) was built by Blohm & Voss (yard number 823) in Hamburg as the WAPPEN VON HAMBURG. She was renamed WAPPEN in 1964, ALTE LIEBE in 1966 and HELGOLAND in 1984. She became the Dutch-owned SUPPERCLUB CRUISE 02 in 2005 and had been laid up in Haifa for some time with a view to being converted into a polar expedition cruise ship for Amstelaviv Investments with the name POLAR GRACE. More recently she appears to have moved to Tuzla in Turkey. IMO 5386057

UNITED STATES (built 1952 gross tonnage 53,329), the fastest passenger liner ever built, has been languishing in various ports for more than 40 years, since she was withdrawn from service in 1969. She was built by the Newport News Shipbuilding and Drydock Company (yard number 488) in Newport News, Virginia, USA for the transatlantic service of United States Lines to partner the older and smaller AMERICA. She gained the Blue Riband for the fastest westbound and eastbound crossings of the North Atlantic in 1952 with an eastbound average speed of 35.53 knots, a speed not subsequently beaten by a conventional passenger ship. Withdrawn from transatlantic service in November 1969, she was laid up first in Newport News and later in Hampton Roads and then Norfolk. In June 1992 she was towed to Istanbul and in November 1993 moved to Sevastopol for the removal of asbestos. In May 1994 she returned to Istanbul (Tuzla) and in July 1996 was towed to Philadelphia. Norwegian Cruise Line acquired the UNITED STATES in April 2003, possibly in a spoiling move to prevent anyone else returning her to service in competition with NCL America. She remained laid up. In 2011 she was acquired from NCL for $3,000,000 by the SS United States Conservancy, who are currently evaluating options for the future of the ship. IMO 5373476

WANG FU (built 1961 gross tonnage 3,787) was built by Sudostroitelnyy Zavod im A Zhadov in Leningrad as the TADZIKISTAN, one of nine ships in the KIRGHIZISTAN class for Russia. She was sold in 1988, becoming the KISTAN, then the PORTO LEONE. She was renamed OLYMPIC FLAME in 1989 and passed to Chinese owners in 1992 when she became the CHANG SHENG. Further names under

United States at Philadelphia *(Rick Frendt)*

Yankee Clipper (Mark M Amielanczyk)

Chinese ownership were ALICE PRINCESS and SOUTHERN KINGDOM, both in 1993 before she was renamed WANG FU later that year. She was last reported laid up in China in 2005.

WILDERNESS EXPLORER (built 1969 gross tonnage c300) was built by Blount Marine Corporation, Warren, Rhode Island, USA as the WILDERNESS EXPLORER. She is recorded as being acquired by Glacier Bay Cruiseline in 2003. Glacier Bay Cruise Line failed in 2006 and the ship remains laid up. IMO 8978655

YANKEE CLIPPER (built 1927 gross tonnage 327) was built by the Krupp shipyard in Kiel, Germany as the armour plated private yacht CRESSIDA. Later she was renamed CRIMPER. She was later acquired by the Vanderbilts and renamed PIONEER. Windjammer Barefoot Cruises purchased the ship in 1965 and renamed her YANKEE CLIPPER I. She was renamed as the YANKEE CLIPPER in 1996. Windjammer filed for bankruptcy in 2008 and the ship is thought to be laid up. IMO 8845872

SECTION 6
Recent Departures

AMET MAJESTY (built 1975 gross tonnage 16,546) was built by Dubigeon-Normandie (yard number 143) at Nantes, France as the BORE STAR for Baltic ferry operator Bore Line of Finland, part of the Silja Line consortium, for service between Finland and Sweden. She later passed to consortium member EFFOA of Helsinki and was renamed SILJA STAR. She was refitted in Bremerhaven by Lloyd Werft in 1986 following her sale to Sealink (UK) Ltd, and became the cruise ferry ORIENT EXPRESS for service in the Mediterranean. Later that year she was chartered to Club Sea for Caribbean cruising as the CLUB SEA. She continued to operate as ORIENT EXPRESS on the termination of this charter for a further two years, also undertaking winter charters to Europe Cruise Line as the EUROSUN. In 1990 she reverted to the name ORIENT EXPRESS and cruised in the Mediterranean again. Later in the year she was registered under the ownership of Eurosun Ltd. In 1991 she passed to Sembawang Johnson Shipmanagement of Singapore for cruising from that port as the ORIENT SUN. She moved back to her original area and role in 1992, becoming the WASA QUEEN for Wasa Line's services between Sweden and Finland. She later passed back to Silja Line and continued to operate in the Baltic under the same name. In 2001 she was sold to Star Cruises, who operated her under the Cruise Ferries brand between Hong Kong and Xiamen in China. She subsequently operated day and overnight gambling cruises from Hong Kong. In 2009 she reverted to her original ferry role on charter to Ilion Lines for Adriatic service between Italy and Albania as the ARBERIA. In March 2011 she was acquired by Amet and converted into a combined training ship and cruise ship, entering service with a first cruise on 9 June 2011 as the AMET MAJESTY. She was largely unsuccessful and was sold to Indian shipbreakers at Alang, where breaking commenced on 25 May 2013. IMO 7360198

ARTSHIP (built 1940 gross tonnage 7,987) was built as the type C3P cargo and passenger liner DELORLEANS for Delta Line's New Orleans to Argentina service. Soon afterwards she was renamed as the USS CRESCENT CITY and put into service as a troop transport. She was laid up from 1948 to 1971, when she was refitted to become the California Maritime Academy's training ship GOLDEN BEAR. On her retirement in 1995 she was again laid up until 1999 when acquired by the Artship Foundation and renamed ARTSHIP with the aim of being converted into a floating cultural centre. She was laid up at Mare Island, California, until January 2012 when she was renamed PACIFIC STAR and towed to Esco Marine at Brownsville, Texas for breaking. IMO 8424666

ATLANTIC STAR (built 1984 gross tonnage 46,087) was ordered by Sitmar Line from Chantiers du Nord et de la Mediterranee (yard number 1436) at La Seyne, France as the FAIRSKY, as an alternative to converting the former Portuguese liner PRINCIPE PERFEITO into a luxury cruise ship. The FAIRSKY was the last major passenger vessel to be built with steam turbine machinery. Delivered in 1984, she was used on west coast USA cruises. Following the takeover by P&O in 1988 she was integrated into the Princess Cruises fleet and renamed SKY PRINCESS, although still under the ownership of P&O Lines. Ownership was transferred to Princess Cruises in 1994, and in 2000 the ship was transferred to P&O Cruises (Australia) and renamed PACIFIC SKY for cruising from Australia. In 2006 she was acquired by Pullmantur Cruises and repositioned to the Adriatic Sea for summer cruising under the new name, SKY WONDER. In June 2007 she was replaced on her Adriatic itineraries by the newly introduced ZENITH. She then moved to Barcelona to begin a series of one-week cruises, but by 2008 was back in the Eastern Mediterranean. She was withdrawn from service and laid up in December 2008, and it was widely thought that it was the end of her. However, in 2009, as the ATLANTIC STAR

Amet Majesty as ***Arberia*** in Bari *(William Mayes)*

Atlantic Star as ***Antic*** at Aliaga *(Jonathan Boonzaier)*

Club Harmony as ***Harmony Princess*** at Savona *(William Mayes)*

Coral in Barcelona *(William Mayes)*

Costa Allegra in Genoa *(William Mayes)*

Costa Concordia off Giglio *(Matthew Sudders)*

it was planned that she would become Pullmantur's first dedicated Portuguese cruise ship, based in Funchal and Lisbon. In the event the PACIFIC DREAM was used for the role, but the ATLANTIC STAR was called into service when the former ship broke down. She broke down too and remained laid up in Marseille, despite rumours of sale. In 2013 she was part-exchanged with STX St Nazaire when Royal Caribbean International placed the order for the third Oasis class ship. She was soon sold for scrap and was beached at Aliaga on 10 April 2013 under the name ANTIC. IMO 8024026

CHANG BENG (built 1978 gross tonnage ‡5926) was built in Shanghai. Continued existence in doubt. IMO 7741835

CHANG HE (built 1974 gross tonnage ‡5926) was built at the Hudong Shipyard in Shanghai. Continued existence in doubt. IMO 7741770

CHANG JIN (built 1974 gross tonnage ‡5926) is a product of the Hudong Shipyard in Shanghai. Continued existence in doubt. IMO 7741782

CHANG XIU (built 1974 gross tonnage ‡5926) was built in Shanghai by the Hudong Shipyard. Continued existence in doubt. IMO 7741823

CLUB HARMONY (built 1969 gross tonnage 25,558) was the first in a series of five container ships built by Wartsila (yard number 1169) at Turku, Finland for Johnson Line of Sweden; a sister to the ANNIE JOHNSON, she was named the AXEL JOHNSON. In 1985 she was sold to Lelakis-owned company Universal Glow Inc. and renamed the REGENT SUN. The plan to convert the ship for cruising was abandoned in 1986 and she was sold to Navyclup in Italy and renamed ITALIA. Two years later she was sold to Costa company Mediterranean Cruise Lines. A further two years elapsed before the new cruise ship emerged from the Mariotti shipyard at Genoa as the COSTA MARINA. She has subsequently operated in the Caribbean, Europe, Scandinavia and South America. From spring 2002 the COSTA MARINA became the first Carnival group ship to be dedicated to the growing German cruise market, offering cruises in the Mediterranean and Baltic Seas. Pioneering again, the COSTA MARINA became the first of the company's ships to be based in the Far East in 2006, returning to the Mediterranean Sea for the bulk of 2007, and where she remained until late 2010. In 2011 she operated in Northern Europe and the Mediterranean and was scheduled to move to Sharm el Sheik in March 2012, but was instead reported to have been sold to Korean company Polaris Shipping for whom she was renamed CLUB HARMONY, although she initially carried the name HARMONY PRINCESS. The venture was unsuccessful and the sale appears to have fallen through as the ship was again registered under Costa ownership. The ship was laid up but in September 2014 was sold for breaking at Alang. IMO 6910544

CORAL (built 1971 gross tonnage 14,194) was built by the Rotterdam Drydock Company (yard number 329) at Rotterdam in The Netherlands as the CUNARD ADVENTURER for Cunard Line's new venture into Caribbean cruising in purpose built ships. She was replaced by a larger ship and sold to Kloster's Norwegian Caribbean Cruise Line in 1977 when she was renamed SUNWARD II. In 1991 she was acquired by Epirotiki Lines and renamed TRITON for cruising in the Eastern Mediterranean. On the merger with Sun Cruises she became part of the new Royal Olympic fleet, but on the final demise of that business was sold at auction in April 2005 to Louis Cruise Lines. In May 2005 she was renamed CORAL. In 2011 she operated from Genoa and Marseilles, but did not operate at all in 2013. In November 2013 she was sold to Turkish breakers. IMO 7046936

COSTA ALLEGRA (built 1969 gross tonnage 28,597) was built by Wartsila (yard number 1170) at Turku in Finland as one of a class of five container ships for the Johnson Line of Sweden in 1969. As the ANNIE JOHNSON she served Johnson Line's North American service to Northern Europe until 1985, when she was sold to Peleus Marine Company of Cyprus (a company owned by Greek ship-owner Antonis Lelakis) who planned to convert her and two sisters into cruise-ships. She was renamed the REGENT MOON, but these plans eventually fell through, and in 1988 she was sold to the Swiss-based Mediterranean Shipping Company and renamed the ALEXANDRA. In 1990, following the successful conversion of the COSTA MARINA, Costa approached MSC and bought the ship, which was sent to the Mariotti shipyard in Genoa for conversion. In addition to the conversion the ship was lengthened by 13.5 metres and equipped with new engines, being re-delivered to Costa Crociere in September 1992 as the COSTA ALLEGRA. The COSTA ALLEGRA was chartered to a new Paquet Croisieres in the summer of 2010. In February 2012 she suffered an engine room fire while in the Indian Ocean and was eventually returned to Genoa, where she remained laid up until sold for scrap, arriving at Aliaga on 24 October 2012 under the name SANTA CRUISE. IMO 6916885

COSTA CONCORDIA (built 2006 gross tonnage 114,147) was ordered from Fincantieri in 2004, and was built in the Sestri yard (yard number 6122) at Genoa, Italy. She operated 7-night Western Mediterranean cruises from her homeport at Savona until the evening of 13 January 2012 when in an apparently mis-calculated sail past of the island of Giglio she hit rocks and subsequently partially sank with the loss of 32 lives. She was righted in September 2013, floated in June 2014 and eventually towed to Genoa for scrapping in July 2014 with the cost of the entire salvage operation estimated at €1 billion. IMO 9320544

DIPOLOG PRINCESS (built 1969 gross tonnage 3,787) was built by Onomichi Zosen KK (yard number 210) at Onomichi, Japan as the TOKYO MARU. She became the DON EUSEBIO in 1978 and passed to her current owner in 1989, when she was renamed DIPOLOG PRINCESS. She is used in the domestic trades around the Philippine Archipelago. The ship has a capacity for 1,261 passengers but the mix between berthed and deck is unknown. IMO 6924765

FORMOSA QUEEN (built 1970 gross tonnage 22,945) was built by Wartsila (yard number 392) at Helsinki, Finland as the SONG OF NORWAY for the new Royal Caribbean Cruise Line, one of an initial series of three revolutionary new ships. Two of the three ships, including the SONG OF NORWAY, were lengthened in 1978-1980. She was sold to Sun Cruises (Airtours) in 1997 and renamed as the SUNDREAM for cruises in the Mediterranean, the Caribbean and around the Atlantic Isles. Sun Cruises withdrew from cruising in 2004 and she was sold to Lance Shipping subsidiary, Tumaco Shipping, taking the new name DREAM PRINCESS. She was franchised to Caspi Cruises in April 2005 to undertake short cruises from Israel to Turkey, Greece and Cyprus. In early 2006 the ship was renamed DREAM. In November 2006 she was chartered by her owners to Gulf Dream Cruise to operate a cruise service between Karachi and Dubai. It is thought that only the first five-day voyage was completed before the venture collapsed. She ran for a while in 2007 for Israeli Caspi Cruises, but that came to an abrupt end with the ship almost sinking in the harbour at Rhodes following the failure of a ballast pump. She was acquired by the Danish Clipper Group and renamed CLIPPER PEARL. She was chartered to the Peaceboat Organisation from May to November 2008 and renamed CLIPPER PACIFIC, but her first circumnavigation was something of a disaster, as she was holed and had to put into New York, following which she was detained by the US Coastguard due to a number of safety issues. She eventually continued her voyage, but on arrival in Piraeus, still with mechanical problems, the passengers were loaded on to the hastily chartered MONA LISA to complete their journey. With the Peaceboat charter ended she was returned to Clipper Group and laid up in Istanbul, moving to Burgas, Bulgaria in April 2009. In early June she was renamed FESTIVAL, and following a major overhaul she returned to Caspi Cruises in July. The charter was ended early in September, and the ship was laid up again. For 2010 and 2011 she was chartered to Happy Cruises as the OCEAN PEARL for operation in the Western Mediterranean. Late in 2011 Happy Cruises filed for bankruptcy and the ship was laid up in Tilbury, England. She was later sold to Far East interests to operate as a cruise ship from Taiwan and China as the FORMOSA QUEEN, but it is not thought that she ever operated in this capacity. She was sold to Chinese breakers in late 2013, arriving at Jiangmen Yinhu Shipbreaking at Guangdong on 26 October. IMO 7005190

GEORG BUCHNER (built 1951 gross tonnage 11,060) was built by Cockerill (yard number 743) at Hoboken, Belgium as the CHARLESVILLE for Cie Maritime Belge for service from Antwerp to the Belgian Congo and Angola. She was the last ship in a series of five passenger/cargo liners, each with accommodation for around 200 first class passengers. In 1967 she was sold to the East German Merchant Marine for use as a cadet training ship and renamed GEORG BUCHNER, but by 1991 she had become a hotel ship in Rostock. After efforts to preserve her failed, she sank in the Baltic Sea while under tow to Polish breakers on 30 May 2013. She was named after Georg Buchner (1813-1837), the German author, playwright and academic. IMO 5068863

GEROI SEVASTOPOLYA (built 1965 gross tonnage 1,987) was built by Stocznia Szczecinska im A Warskiego (yard number B850/04) as the research vessel VASILIY GOLOVNIN, one of a series of eleven similar ships. She was renamed in 1991 as SVYATOY NIKOLAY and was probably converted for passenger use in 1999 when she was acquired by Sudostroyeniye and renamed GEROI SEVASTOPOLYA. She arrived at Aliaga for breaking on 17 October 2011. IMO 8929393

GOLDEN PRINCE (built 1973 gross tonnage 7,735) was built by KK Usuki Tekkosho (yard number 1165) at Saiki, Japan as the WAKASHIO MARU for local service in Japan. In 1979 she was renamed as the SUN FLOWER 7. She moved to Greek owners, Epirotiki, in 1991 as the APOLLON and was later converted for use as a day cruise ship. Minoan Lines acquired her in 1995, and renamed her PRINCE, later MINOAN PRINCE. She was sold to Golden Prince Cruises in 2002 and renamed GOLDEN PRINCE. She had been laid up for several years but eventually went for scrap, arriving at Aliaga on 14 April 2014. IMO 7323449

Formosa Queen as *Ocean Pearl* in Barcelona *(William Mayes)*

Golden Prince in Heraklion *(William Mayes)*

Island Adventure at Fort Lauderdale *(Rick Frendt)*

HAKON JARL (built 1952 gross tonnage 2,173) was built by Aalborg Vaerft (yard number 93) at Aalborg in Denmark as the Hurtigruten ship HAKON JARL. In 1983 she was briefly renamed HAKON GAMLE, but then reverted to her original name. She was renamed CHRISTIAN V in 1992, and DIAMOND PRINCESS in 1997, before reverting again to her original name in 2004. She operated as a restaurant ship in Oslo for some time, but in 1997 opened as the Diamond Princess Hotel in Antwerp. Eventually she closed and the authorities wanted the space so she was moved to another dock and may now have been broken up. IMO 5140300

ISLAND ADVENTURE (built 1976 gross tonnage 15,409) was built by Wartsila (yard number 1222) at Turku, Finland as the KAZAKHSTAN, the fourth in a series of five ships for the Black Sea Shipping Company of the Soviet Union. She was renamed UKRAINA in 1994 for BLASCO UK as her owners were then styled. In 1996 she became the ROYAL SEAS for Chastnaya Kompaniya Globus of Odessa and was chartered to Royal Seas Cruise Line of Florida. She reverted to the name UKRAINA in 1997 and was subsequently chartered to Sea Escape Cruises, taking the name ISLAND ADVENTURE. She was sold in 2008 following the bankruptcy of Sea Escape Cruises but does not subsequently appear to have traded. As ADVENTURE she arrived at Alang for breaking on 3 November 2011. IMO 7359486

LYUBOV ORLOVA (built 1976 gross tonnage 4,251) was built by Brodogradiliste Titovo (yard number 413) at Kraljevica in what was Yugoslavia for the Far Eastern Shipping Company of Vladivostok as one of a series of eight ships for various Soviet owners. She has been owned by Lyubov Orlova Shipping Company of Novorossiysk since 1996, but has been marketed as the ORLOVA by Quark Expeditions. She operated under charter to Cruise North Expeditions of Canada from the summer of 2007. In September 2010 the ship was arrested in St John's Newfoundland for non-payment of crew wages. In late 2012 the ship was sold for scrap and after two failed tows the ship was left drifting in the North Atlantic. She is believed to have sunk in late February 2013 about 700 miles off the coast of Ireland. Lyubov Orlova (1902-1975) was probably the most glamorous and popular actress of the Soviet cinema. IMO 7391434

MIRAGE 1 (built 1973 gross tonnage 14,264) was built by Dubigeon-Normandie (yard number 133) at Nantes, France as the BOLERO for Fred. Olsen Line, initially for service between Travemunde, Germany and Sodertalje, Sweden. In the event she was, instead, chartered to Prinz Linien for North Sea service. She soon travelled west for charters to Commodore Cruise Line in winter for Caribbean cruising, and Prince of Fundy Line in summer for the ferry service between Portland, Maine and Yarmouth, Nova Scotia. She moved back to Europe in 1976 and sailed between Bergen, Norway and Newcastle, England. From 1978 to 1981 she was on Stena Line's Gothenburg, Sweden to Kiel, Germany service as the SCANDINAVICA while that company was awaiting the very late delivery of some new ships. A planned charter to Brittany Ferries in 1981 didn't materialise, so the ship underwent a major refit to resume Olsen service. Her final days with the Norwegian company were spent on the Newcastle to Bergen service, which was sold, along with the BOLERO, to Norway's Color Line in 1991. She was renamed as the JUPITER and continued on the same route until 1994. After a short charter to Baltic Sea operator Viking Line, she moved to Central America for a service between Cristobal and Cartagena on charter to Promotora de Navigation as the CRUCERO EXPRESS. In 1997 she began operating from St Petersburg, Florida as the SEMINOLE EXPRESS. The following year she returned to Europe and after another refit became the MAGIC 1 of Magic Cruise Lines. She later served as a Haifa-based cruise ship before returning to the Caribbean to operate as the MIRAGE 1 for Ocean Club Cruises, a business that failed after only one season. ISRAMCO purchased the ship in March 2004. She had been reported as chartered to a subsidiary of Israeli travel company EGGED for summer 2005, and was operating under the marketing name of MAGIC 1. She later operated for Caspi Cruise Line, but was not thought to be in service when that company collapsed in September 2011. She arrived at Aliaga for breaking on 19 March 2012. IMO 7221433

NATIONAL GEOGRAPHIC POLARIS (built 1960 gross tonnage 2,138) was built by Solvesborgs Varv (yard number 55) at Solvesborg Sweden as the ORESUND, a passenger car ferry for service between Copenhagen, Denmark and Malmo, Sweden. In 1981 she was purchased by Salen Lines and chartered to Lindblad as the expedition ship LINDBLAD POLARIS. She was sold to ETICA in 1997 and renamed POLARIS, although still operated by Lindblad from time to time. Her name was lengthened in late 2007. She was broken up in Ecuador in 2010. IMO 5264704

OCEAN COUNTESS (built 1976 gross tonnage 16,795) started life as one of a pair of second-generation Caribbean cruise ships for Cunard Line. She was built by Burmeister & Wain (yard number 858) at Copenhagen, Denmark as the CUNARD COUNTESS, and served the company for twenty years before being sold for further service in the Far East as the AWANI DREAM 2. In 1998 she was acquired by Royal Olympic Cruises and renamed OLYMPIC COUNTESS for service mainly in the Mediterranean.

Lyubov Orlova at Tenerife *(Martin Grant)*

Mirage 1 in Limassol *(Rick Frendt)*

Ocean Countess at Cobh *(William Mayes)*

In 2002, under pressure from the International Olympic Committee, the company changed its name to Royal Olympia Cruises and the ship followed suit, becoming the OLYMPIA COUNTESS. Following the collapse of that company she passed to Majestic International Cruises in 2004, and was chartered to Globalia for the summer of 2005 as the OCEAN COUNTESS. She was then chartered to Holiday Kreuzfahrten as their second ship and renamed as the LILI MARLEEN. That company ran into financial difficulties and ceased trading in the summer of 2006. She was returned to her owners in late 2006 and took the name OCEAN COUNTESS for the second time. In 2007 she was chartered to Louis Cruise Lines, as the RUBY, as part of that company's replacement programme for the SEA DIAMOND. At the end of 2007 she took the name OCEAN COUNTESS again. For the summer of 2009 she was chartered to Quail Cruises of Spain and marketed as the NEW PACIFIC. In 2010 she started a two-year charter to Cruise and Maritime Voyages, it being the company's intention to run her year-round. In the event she was laid up for the winter of 2010/11 and reactivated in the spring of 2011 with a series of ex-UK cruises. The ship was returned to her owner in 2012 and did not operate during 2013. While being refitted for a charter, the ship caught fire on 30 November 2013 at Chalkis in Greece and was declared a total loss. IMO 7358561

OCEAN LIFE (built 1981 gross tonnage 12,709) was built by Stocznia Szczecinska (yard number B492/02) at Szczecin, Poland as the LEV TOLSTOY, the second in a series of six ships for the Black Sea Shipping Company of the USSR. In 1986 she underwent a major reconstruction at Lloydwerft, Bremerhaven, Germany. By 1991, with the break-up of the Soviet Union, she was flying the flag of Ukraine, and was chartered to Transocean Tours for a period of four years. She was subsequently laid up in Haifa, Israel, before being sold in 1998 to Columbus Leisure Cruises and renamed NATASHA. Later that year she was renamed PALMIRA and then undertook charters to two German travel companies. In 2001 she was sold to Zenith Cruises for operation by Mano cruises as THE JASMINE. In 2006 she passed to Arab Ship Management and was renamed FARAH for operation as a ferry in the Red Sea. In 2008 she was acquired by Easycruise and after refit entered service as the EASYCRUISE LIFE. In 2009 the company was sold to Greek Ferry operator Hellenic Seaways. The ship did not operate in 2010, but was chartered in September of that year to Indian company Blue Ocean Cruises, being renamed OCEAN LIFE. However on an early cruise, on 16 November 2010, she sustained a crack in her hull and was taken out of service for repairs. The ship re-entered service in the spring of 2011 but the resumption was short-lived and the ship was laid up in Piraeus. In 2014 the OCEAN LIFE was advertised by both the Odessa Shipping Company and Apex Tour of Turkey as starting a summer of Greek island cruises, but the start date came, and went and all reference to the ship was removed from both websites. Eventually the OCEAN LIFE left Piraeus under tow and arrived at Aliaga on 15 August 2014. IMO 7625809

OCEAN MIST (built 1956 gross tonnage 5,067) was built for the Italian liner and ferry operator Adriatica as the SAN GIORGIO by Cantieri Riuniti dell'Adriatico (yard number 1813) at Trieste, Italy and was used on Mediterranean Sea passenger/cargo services from Venice and Trieste to Istanbul, Izmir and Piraeus. Sometimes these voyages were extended to call at Alexandria and other Eastern Mediterranean ports. In 1976 this elegant little ship was sold to the Greek Kyriakis Group and converted for pure cruising in and around the Aegean Sea. She was rebuilt and renamed as the CITY OF ANDROS and operated under the Cycladic Cruises banner. In 1984 she passed to Ocean Cruise Lines, becoming the high-quality OCEAN ISLANDER. She then cruised in European waters in summer and in the Caribbean Sea in winter. Ocean Cruise Lines was sold to Paquet, the French cruise operator in 1990, but the OCEAN ISLANDER was sold to Star Line Cruises, renamed ROYAL STAR and put to work in the Indian Ocean under charter to African Safari Club. The ship's owners appear to have run into financial difficulty and the ship was laid up in Mombassa. In 2010 she was sold to Kenyan owners, PV Ocean Mist, and renamed OCEAN MIST. It is thought that she never re-entered service and was sold to Indian breakers at Alang, where breaking commenced on 9 March 2012. IMO 5309906

OLA ESMERELDA (built 1966 gross tonnage 11,209) was built for both dual purpose and dual ownership by Lubecker Flender-Werke (yard number 561) at Lubeck, Germany as the BLACK PRINCE. She initially served Fred. Olsen's services between Harwich and Kristiansand and Amsterdam and Kristiansand in summer and joined her sister, the BLACK WATCH, on the Canary Islands service in winter. She became jointly owned with the Bergen Line in 1970 and continued her dual role until the ending of the agreement in 1986. During this period she was named VENUS while on the North Sea services. Following her refit she was equipped with a retractable 'marina' that could be put out from the stern when at anchor for the provision of a number of sporting activities. Her refit had been designed to attract a younger and more active passenger. She was not very successful, and was withdrawn from cruise service. An attempt to employ her on a new ferry service between Copenhagen and Gothenburg, was spectacularly unsuccessful, primarily because her Philippine registry and

Ocean Life as *Easycruise Life* in Piraeus *(William Mayes)*

Ocean Mist as *Jason* in Piraeus *(Rick Frendt)*

Ola Esmerelda as *Black Prince* at Rothsay *(John Hendy)*

international crew had caused trouble with local trades unions. She was re-fitted again, but for a British market this time and became an enormous success, with a fiercely loyal following. Her sale to Servicios Acuaticos de Venezuela was confirmed in May 2009, but the ship continued to operate for Olsen until October of that year. On arrival in Venezuela the ship was prevented from operation on environmental grounds, thought to be wash damage to the islands through which she would sail, so she remained laid up for a while. The hurricane that wrought great destruction on the island of Haiti provided work for the ship as she was chartered to a UN relief agency as an accommodation ship for relief workers at Port au Prince. It is believed that the OLA ESMERELDA finally entered service on her intended itineraries early in 2011, but ceased operating in November 2012. She is thought to have been sold to breakers locally. IMO 6613328

OMEGA G (built 1965 gross tonnage 1,987) was built by Stocznia Szczecinska im A Warskiego (yard number B850/06) at Szczecin, Poland as the research ship FADDEY BELLINGSHAUSEN. She was one of the series of eleven ships of the NIKOLAY ZUBOV class. In 1996 she was renamed OMEGA, still under the Ukrainian flag, and in 2002 she became the OMEGA G. At some stage she was converted for passenger use. She was sold for breaking and arrived at Aliaga on 21 June 2012. IMO 8927735

PACIFIC (built 1971 gross tonnage 20,186) was built by Rheinstahl Nordseewerke (yard number 411) at Emden, Germany as the SEA VENTURE for Norwegian Cruiseships of Oslo. She was initially operated by Flagship Cruises between New York and Bermuda, but was soon sold to a joint venture between Oivind Lorentzen and Fearney & Eger. She was sold on to the Peninsular and Oriental Steam Navigation Company in 1975, becoming the PACIFIC PRINCESS for P&O subsidiary Princess Cruises. She was sold to Pullmantur in 2002 and renamed PACIFIC. The ship was operated in conjunction with CVC of Brazil on Brazilian coastal cruises until 2007. Summer cruises included the Fernando de Noronha Islands, while winter itineraries took in the River Amazon. From the summer of 2007 she returned to the Mediterranean Sea for a season based in Valencia, Spain. Subsequently the ship was sold to CVC, but chartered to Quail Cruises for the European summer. She is now owned by Quail Cruises and has operated for CVC during the northern winter as the NEW PACIFIC. It appears that she was in such poor condition on her return from Brazil in 2008 that she immediately went to Genoa for repairs. She remained there, under arrest and it is thought that she has been abandoned by her owner, Templeton International, a subsidiary of Quail Ship Management. After several abortive sales she finally arrived at Aliaga on 6 August 2013 under the name ACIF. IMO 7018563

PALM BEACH PRINCESS (built 1964 gross tonnage 6,659) was built by Wartsila (yard number 375) at Helsinki, Finland as the ILMATAR for Finska Angfartygs of Helsinki for its passenger and car ferry service from that city to Stockholm. From her earliest days, in addition to her ferry duties, she operated short cruises in the Baltic. In 1970, she appeared in Silja Line livery for the first time, although her owner had been trading as part of the Silja consortium for some years. For a change of route, and a greater emphasis on cruising, she was sent to Germany in 1973 for lengthening by about 20 metres, and for the installation of additional engines. She re-entered service, now trading between Helsinki and Travemunde as a three-screw vessel, and almost three knots faster than previously. Finska withdrew from the route in 1975 and the ILMATAR was used principally as a cruise ship. She was sold to Norwegian owners in 1980, but continued to offer a similar range of cruises encompassing the Baltic and Norway in summer and the Mediterranean and Atlantic Isles in winter. Her new owners were less than successful and she was laid up in 1982. Two years later she was sold to Grundstad Maritime Overseas to run gambling cruises from California, as the VIKING PRINCESS. She later moved to Florida where she continued to operate in a similar role as the PALM BEACH PRINCESS for the Palm Beach Casino Line. From 2008 she was owned by Mauro Sebben (Datasys International Corp). She completed her last cruise in February 2010 and was laid up at Palm Beach. She was to have been used as an accommodation ship in Haiti, but her creditors refused to allow the ship to sail. Eventually she left in April bound for Freeport, Bahamas. She was broken up by Blade Iron Group, Santo Domingo in 2014, having arrived in November 2012. IMO 6402937

PHILIPPINES (built 1952 gross tonnage 27,090) was built by Cantieri Riunite dell'Adriatico (yard number 1757) at Trieste in Italy as the AUGUSTUS for the Italian Line. She was the second major passenger ship to be delivered to the company as part of its post-war rebuilding programme and was immediately placed on the service to South America. Following the loss of the ANDREA DORIA, the AUGUSTUS was transferred to Italia's North Atlantic service in 1957. She returned to the South Atlantic in 1961 following the delivery of the new LEONARDO DA VINCI. She had a long career as a transatlantic liner until she was sold to Emilio Yap, owner of Philippine President Lines, in 1976. The ship then went into a semi-retirement at anchor in various Far Eastern ports. During this time she had frequent name changes including GREAT SEA, OCEAN KING, PRESIDENT, ASIAN PRINCESS and more

Pacific in Genoa *(William Mayes)*

Palm Beach Princess *(Rick Frendt)*

Princess Daphne in Istanbul *(William Mayes)*

recently, PHILIPPINES. Despite almost three decades of lay-up, the ship has always been well maintained and fully crewed. Her only voyages have been occasional private cruises for the Yap family and their friends, and trips to Subic Bay for dry-docking. In recent years the ship had been tied up at a pier next door to the Manila Hotel, where her public rooms were available for private parties. She was sold for scrap in September 2011 and was the last surviving former Italian passenger liner. Breaking commenced on 19 October 2011 at Alang. IMO 5030684

PRINCESS DAPHNE (built 1955 gross tonnage 15,833) was built by Swan, Hunter and Wigham Richardson (yard number 1827) at Wallsend on Tyne in England for Port Line as the passenger and cargo ship PORT SYDNEY. In 1972 she was sold to Greek owners for conversion to a passenger and car ferry, but although commenced, this conversion was never completed. While undergoing work she was renamed AKROTIRI EXPRESS. She was later rebuilt as a cruise ship, taking the name DAPHNE, and was operated unsuccessfully for a while and eventually chartered to Costa Line, along with her sister (the DANAE, similarly converted and now the PRINCESS DANAE). Costa later purchased the ships and in the late 1980's marketed them under the Prestige Cruises banner. In 1996 she was renamed SWITZERLAND after sale to Leisure Cruises, a Swiss based but Monaco controlled company. In 2000 she passed to Dreamline Cruises, a company under the same control, without a change of name. She was acquired by Majestic International Cruises of Greece in spring 2002 and briefly renamed OCEAN ODYSSEY before adopting the name OCEAN MONARCH. Hansa Kreuzfahrten chartered her in 2005, and in 2006 she ran for Golden Star Cruises in place of the arrested AEGEAN I. The OCEAN MONARCH was scheduled to operate for Monarch in 2007, but following the collapse of Holiday Kreuzfahrten and the unexpected availability of the OCEAN COUNTESS, she was dropped from the company's programme and was laid up. She was acquired by Classic International Cruises in 2008 and underwent a major refurbishment in Lisbon, from which she emerged as the PRINCESS DAPHNE. In the winter of 2010/11 she operated a series of cruises for Classic International in the Far East. She was in Northern Europe for much of the 2011 summer season on charter to Russia's Metropolis Tur. When Classic International Cruises filed for bankruptcy the ship was laid up in Crete. Subsequently, the ship was returned to the Potamianos family but finance was difficult to raise and the ship could not be refitted. She was later sold for scrap and sailed to Alang under the name DAPHNE. She arrived at Bharat Shipbreakers, Alang on 6 June 2014 and breaking commenced one week later. Daphne was the daughter of the River God Peneus. In Greek Mythology Daphne turns into a laurel tree to escape the unwelcome advances of Apollo. IMO 5282627

ROCHDALE ONE (built 1977 gross tonnage 7,662) was built by Dubigeon-Normandie (yard number 144) at Nantes, France as the AYVAZOVSKIY for the Soviet Danube Shipping Company of Ismail, for service in the Black Sea between Ismail, Yalta and Istanbul in connection with the Soviet owned Danube cruise vessels. She was christened by the wife of the then Soviet Ambassador to France. In 1992 her owners were re-styled as the Ukraina Danube Shipping Company. In 1996 she was renamed the KARINA for charter to the German tour operator Phoenix Reisen. She became the PRIMEXPRESS ISLAND; a Cyprus based casino ship in 2000 and was acquired by Kyprosun Marine Services of Limassol in January 2004 with intention of converting her into an accommodation ship. The work started in Greece, but could not be completed, so the ship sailed to Amsterdam, where the conversion was finished. She was renamed ROCHDALE ONE, after the housing association that operated her, for her service as an accommodation ship housing 200 students for the University of Amsterdam. The charter expired in 2009 and the ship remained laid up in Amsterdam. She was sold to Turkish breakers at Aliaga, where breaking commenced on 29 July 2013. IMO 7411959

RONG XIN (built 1978 gross tonnage ‡3857) was built by the Qiuxin Shipyard in Shanghai, China.This ship's continued existence is in doubt. IMO 8426573

RTS SINDBAD BITIC (built 1949 gross tonnage 637) was built by Trosvik Verksted (yard number 63) at Brevik, Norway as the coastal vessel SOROY. In 1966 she was renamed SKULE, in 1981 OSTFOLD and in 1991 GLOMMEN. She was acquired by Zambezi Shipping in 2004 and renamed as the RTS SINBAD in the following year. She passed to her current owner in 2007 for service as a training ship, carrying 30 cadets. She was renamed in 2008. After a short period of disuse she was sold for breaking and arrived at Gadani Beach on 4 February 2014. IMO 5334614

SAPPHIRE (built 1967 gross tonnage 12,263) had a long and interesting history. She was built by Cantieri Navale Felszegi (yard number 76) at Trieste, Italy as the ITALIA for Crociere d'Oltremare of Cagliari, Sicily. She was almost immediately chartered to the newly established Princess Cruises. She was marketed as PRINCESS ITALIA, but not renamed. In 1973 she was chartered to Costa Line for Caribbean cruising, and later that year Costa bought the ship. Seven years later she was sold to Ocean Cruise Lines and renamed OCEAN PRINCESS. In 1990 she was acquired by Croisieres Paquet for whom she operated until sold in 1993 to Ellis Marine of Greece, following a partial sinking after

Rochdale One in Amsterdam *(Rick Frendt)*

Sapphire *(Tony Davis)*

The Calypso at Santorini *(Rick Frendt)*

striking a wreck at the mouth of the Amazon, which rendered her a constructive total loss. She was refurbished in Piraeus and later renamed SEA PRINCE. Later she carried the name SEA PRINCE V, but reverted to SEA PRINCE before being sold to Louis Cruise Lines who renamed her PRINCESA OCEANICA. In 1996 she was chartered to UK tour operator Thomson Holidays for whom she was renamed SAPPHIRE. In 1999 France Croisieres chartered her and she subsequently operated on other charters and for Louis' own account. The SAPPHIRE did not operate during 2011 and was laid up in Eleusis Bay, Greece. She arrived at Alang for breaking under the name ASPIRE. Breaking commenced on 11 May 2012. IMO 6313994

SIRIUS (built 1967 gross tonnage 14,113), the third ship of the Texas Maritime Academy, was built by Swan, Hunter & Wigham Richardson (yard number 2016) at Wallsend on Tyne in the North East of England as the Royal Fleet Auxiliary's replenishment vessel LYNESS. She was acquired by the US Navy in 1980, but does not appear to have been renamed until 1997 when she was given the name SIRIUS. When decommissioned she was acquired by the Texas Maritime Academy in 2005, and refitted as a training ship. She was renamed as the TEXAS CLIPPER in 2007, and was laid up in 2009 at Beaumont, Texas under the name SIRIUS as part of the US Reserve Fleet. She arrived at Esco Marine, Brownsville, Texas for breaking on 30 May 2014. IMO 6706888

SOUNDS OF ORIENTS (built 1961 gross tonnage 5,230) built as the KHABAROVSK and last reported at Vladivostok more recently than the 1989 date that Lloyd Register suggests that she was broken up. After all this time, it is probably safe to assume that she has gone. IMO 5186196

THE CALYPSO (built 1967 gross tonnage 11,162) was built by Navalmeccanica (yard number 645) at Castellammare di Stabia, Italy as the car ferry CANGURO VERDE for Italian operator Traghetti Sardi. She sailed between Genoa and Sardinia in competition with Italian state owned operator, Tirrenia, and along with her sisters was eventually chartered to that company. In 1981 she was sold to a Saudi owner, renamed DURR and set to work as a pilgrim carrier. She was sold to Greek ferry operator Strintzis Lines in 1989, along with her sister, the YUM (previously CANGURO BRUNO) and was renamed as the IONIAN HARMONY. She spent two seasons on Adriatic Sea services before being sold again, this time to Danish Cruise Line. She was renamed SUN FIESTA for Caribbean cruising, but it is thought that she never actually entered service. In 1992 she was auctioned by the US Admiralty Marshall, acquired by the owner of Regency Cruise Line and towed to Greece. She was substantially rebuilt and emerged as the cruise ship REGENT JEWEL. She never actually entered service under that name and by the autumn of 1994 she was the CALYPSO, on charter to Germany's Transocean Tours. Her owners eventually collapsed and the National Bank of Greece seized the ship in 1999. Louis Cruise Lines purchased her in 2000, and she continued to operate short cruises in the Eastern Mediterranean. In April 2005 she was renamed as THE CALYPSO and in the following year, a season of cruising from Tilbury, England was severely curtailed following an engine room fire. From 2007 she was chartered to Thomson for part of the year for cruises in the Eastern Mediterranean and the Black Sea. Calypso was the daughter of Atlas, who in Homer's Odyssey entertained Odysseus for seven years. The Thomson charter finished in 2009 and THE CALYPSO was subsequently employed on short cruises from Piraeus and Cyprus. She was sold for breaking and arrived, under the name CALY, at Alang, where breaking commenced on 10 April 2013. IMO 6715372

THE EMERALD (built 1958 gross tonnage 26,428) was built as the SANTA ROSA by Newport News Shipbuilding and Dry Dock Company (yard number 521) at Newport News, USA for Grace Line of New York, and served the company's New York to Central America service for 13 years before being laid up at Hampton Roads. She remained there for 18 years until she was acquired by Coral Cruise Lines in 1989 and towed to Greece for rebuilding. She was renamed PACIFIC SUN, then DIAMOND ISLAND before finally coming back into service as the RAINBOW in 1992 for a Caribbean cruise programme. In 1993 she passed to Regency Cruises as the REGENT RAINBOW, but following the failure of that company she was laid up again. Louis Cruise Lines acquired her in 1996, renamed her THE EMERALD, and the following year began a long-term seasonal charter to Thomson Cruises. In the spring she usually operated for Louis Cruise Lines on short itineraries from Piraeus, but for Thomson's season she was based in Corfu for Aegean and Adriatic Sea itineraries. For the winter of 2007/2008 she was chartered to an Australian tour operator. Her 11-year seasonal charter to Thomson finished in 2008 and she returned to the Louis fleet, mainly operating from Cyprus. In 2011 she was not in service and remained laid up in Eleusis Bay, Greece. She was sold to breakers at Alang in 2012 and sailed on her delivery voyage as SS EMERALD. Breaking commenced on 1 August 2012. IMO 5312824

THE OCEANIC (built 1965 gross tonnage 38,772) was the first new ship to be built for Home Lines. She was constructed by Cantieri Riunite dell'Adriatico (yard number 1876) at Monfalcone, Italy as the OCEANIC for transatlantic service between New York and Italy. She later sailed between New York and

The Emerald in Venice *(Martin Grant)*

The Oceanic at Villefranche *(William Mayes)*

Venus at Aliaga *(Jonathan Boonzaier)*

Bermuda and was used extensively for cruising. She was sold to Premier Cruise Lines in 1985, when she became the ROYALE OCEANIC, but was renamed as the STARSHIP OCEANIC later that year. She reverted to her original name in 1998. In 2000 she was renamed BIG RED BOAT I, but reverted to her original name in December of that year, and two years later was sold to Pullmantur. She developed a loyal following on her weekly Western Mediterranean circuits from Barcelona. In 2009 she was to move to Valencia, from where she was to operate alternate 2- and 5-day itineraries. However, at short notice she was sold to Japan Grace for charter to the Peaceboat Organisation. She was renamed as THE OCEANIC in September 2009. She arrived in China for breaking on 17 June 2012. IMO 5260679

VAEANU (built 1967 gross tonnage 1,540) was built by J.J.Sietas (yard number 601) in Hamburg, Germany as the cargo vessel CADIZ. She was sold to Compagnie Polynesienne de Transport Maritime in 1980 and renamed ARANUI. She was converted to carry passengers in 1984. In 1991 she became the TUHAAPAE 3, and was acquired by her current owner and renamed VAEANU in 1993. She was scuttled on 15 February 2013. IMO 6726175

VENUS (built 1971 gross tonnage 16,710) was one of the first generation of purpose-built cruise ships, delivered by Cantieri Naval dell Tirreno e Riuniti (yard number 288) at Riva Trigoso in Italy as the SOUTHWARD for Kloster's Norwegian Caribbean Cruise Line. She served her owner well for almost 25 years before passing to UK tour operator Airtours, whose cruise operation later became Sun Cruises. In her new role she was renamed as the SEAWING. Ownership passed to the Louis group and she continued to operate for Airtours. When Airtours, by now renamed as My Travel, pulled out of cruising in 2004 she was earmarked for further use with Louis Cruise Lines, but was then switched to Louis Hellenic Cruises, as the PERLA. Following a charter to Golden Star Cruises in 2008 she was renamed THE AEGEAN PEARL, a name that she retained when she returned to Louis Cruises. THE AEGEAN PEARL then operated short cruises from Piraeus, but was sold in the Spring of 2010 to Eagles Shipholding SA, a Marshall Islands registered business, which appears to be connected in some way with Louis Cruises through subsidiary Core Marine Ltd. The ship was renamed RIO and chartered to Caspi Cruise Line. Caspi Cruise Line ceased trading in September 2011 and the ship was auctioned. In 2012 she came back into service for another Israeli company under the name VENUS, but was equally unsuccessful. She was sold for breaking and arrived at Aliaga on 28 March 2013. IMO 7111078

WINDWARD II (built 1964 gross tonnage 5,739) was built by Kaldnes Mekaniske Verksted (yard number 160) at Tonsberg, Norway as the VIKING II for Thoresen Car Ferries for service from Southampton. In 1977 she became Sealink's EARL WILLIAM and continued to operate on English Channel services. When sold in 1992 she was briefly renamed WILLIAM, but later that year became PEARL WILLIAM for Greek Owners. In 1996 she became the MER-JULIA and a year later was renamed CESME STERN. She took her current name in 2001 when acquired by Windward Lines of Barbados. For several years she served as the Ocean Pearl Hotel at Chaguaramas in Trinidad, but while under tow to the Dominican Republic in April 2011 she is believed to have sunk. IMO 641704

Other Changes since the previous edition

7107 Islands Cruise has not operated and is unlikely to do so.

Abercrombie & Kent no longer operate ships for their own account.

Adventure Cruise Lines is no longer operating.

Albatros Travel no longer operates its own ships.

Amet Cruises ceased trading in 2012.

Amstelaviv Investments did not start trading with POLAR GRACE.

Asia Cruises ceased operation.

Atlantic Shipping Corporation's ANTARCTIC DREAM is now operated by Turismo Nuevo Mondo.

Blue Ocean Cruises ceased trading in 2011.

Canodros and its ship were acquired by Silversea.

Caspi Cruise Line ceased trading in September 2011.

Caspian Cruise Line is thought never to have operated.

Classic International Cruises ceased trading.

Colombia Ecotourism no longer operates cruises.

Cruise North Expeditions seems to have been absorbed by Adventure Canada.

Cruise West ceased trading in 2010 and the fleet was later dispersed.

Diamond Princess Hotel closed.

Fantasea Adventure Cruises no longer operates any vessels that qualify for inclusion.

Golden Prince Cruises is no longer operating.

Granada Logistics sold the OMEGA G for scrap and no longer operates passenger ships.

Happy Cruises ceased trading in September 2011.

Harmony Yacht Club disposed of its ship.

Ihatai Nui Productions ceased trading and the ship was scuttled.

Inner Sea Discoveries has been re-branded as Un-Cruise Adventures.

Kristina Cruises ceased operating ocean cruises in December 2013.

Lord Nelson Seereisen did not recommence trading.

Manila Floating Hotel and Restaurant disposed of the PHILIPPINES in September 2011.

MS Georg Buchner was sold for scrap in 2013.

NDS Voyages is not operating its own programme.

Neptune Cruises appears to have ceased operating.

Ocean Pearl Hotel is no longer operating aboard the WINDWARD II.

Ola Cruises ceased trading in November 2012 and the OLA ESMERELDA was sold for breaking.

Oriental Dragon Cruises' ship is now operated by Metropolis Cruise.

Orion Expedition Cruises was acquired by Linblad Expeditions.

Paquet Croisieres no longer operates any ships.

Polar Star Expeditions filed for bankruptcy in 2011.

Phillipine Span Asia Carrier no longer operates any qualifying ships.

PV Ocean Mist is not thought to have operated.

RAK Training Ship Sinbad sold its ship for scrap.

S Continental is no longer operating the S C ATLANTIC.

Spirit of Adventure was absorbed into Saga Cruises in 2012.

Sudostroyeniye no longer operates pasenger ships.

Tropicana Cruises appears to have ceased trading.

Woningstichting Rochdale no longer operates the ROCHDALE ONE.

Bibliography

This edition has been updated using the following sources

Periodicals

Cruise and Ferry Info Shippax Information

Fairplay IHS-Fairplay

Lloyds List Informa Publishing

Marine News The World Ship Society

Sea Lines The Ocean Liner Society

Other sources

Company brochures and websites

Linerslist, a membership site on Yahoo Groups

www.maritimematters.com

www.simplonpc.co.uk

Sea Web – the on-line ships register from IHS-Fairplay

There are often discrepancies between sources of information and in these cases I have tried to select the most likely scenario. It is therefore possible that some errors have crept into this book. I would appreciate notification of any information that might be suspect, so that the next edition will be an even more accurate portrayal of the cruise ships of the world.

william.mayes@overviewpress.co.uk

Index of companies

Index of former names

CALEDONIAN STAR	NATIONAL GEOGRAPHIC ENDEAVOUR
CALYPSO	THE CALYPSO
CAMELIA	ECLIPSE
CAMPECHE SEAL	ATOLL EXPLORER
CANGURO CABO SAN JORGE	ORIENTAL PRINCESS
CANGURO VERDE	THE CALYPSO
CAP BON	KENNEDY
CAPE COD LIGHT	SEA DISCOVERER
CAPE HARRISON	CALEDONIA
CAPE MAY LIGHT	SEA VOYAGER
CAPTAIN OMAR	TURAMA
CARIBBEAN PRINCE	WILDERNESS ADVENTURER
CARIBE	AZORES
CARIBIC STAR	7107 ISLANDS CRUISE
CARL B DOWNS	ISABELA II
CARNIVAL DESTINY	CARNIVAL SUNSHINE
CARONIA	OASIA
CAROUSEL	OCEAN STAR PACIFIC
CELEBRATION	COSTA CELEBRATION
CELEBRITY GALAXY	MEIN SCHIFF 1
CELEBRITY MERCURY	MEIN SCHIFF 2
CENTURION	ARABELLA
CENTURY	CELEBRITY CENTURY
CESME STERN	WINDWARD II
CHANG LUI	ORIENTAL QUEEN
CHARLESVILLE	GEORG BUCHNER
CHRISTIAN IV	WIND PERFECTION
CHRISTIAN V	HAKON JARL
CHRISTINA	CHRISTINA O
CINDERELLA	VIKING CINDERELLA
CINDY BRILEY	ISABELA II
CITALIA	CAPRI
CITANIA	LA PINTA
CITY OF ANDROS	CAPRI
CITY OF ANDROS	OCEAN MIST
CIUDAD DE PALMA	ORIENTAL PRINCESS
CLELIA II	CORINTHIAN
CLIPPER ADVENTURER	SEA ADVENTURER
CLIPPER DISCOVERER	SEA DISCOVERER
CLIPPER ODYSSEY	SILVER DISCOVERER
CLIPPER PACIFIC	FORMOSA QUEEN
CLIPPER PEARL	FORMOSA QUEEN
CLIPPER VOYAGER	SEA VOYAGER
CLUB 1	SALAMIS FILOXENIA
CLUB CRUISE 1	SALAMIS FILOXENIA
CLUB MED 1	WIND SURF
CLUB SEA	AMET MAJESTY
COASTAL QUEEN 1	SEA VOYAGER
COASTAL QUEEN 2	SEA DISCOVERER
COLONIAL EXPLORER	SS LEGACY
COLUMBA	HEBRIDEAN PRINCESS
COLUMBIA	WILDERNESS EXPLORER
COLUMBUS 2	INSIGNIA
COLUMBUS CARAVELLE	TURAMA
COMMODORE	WIND SOLUTION
CONSTELLATION	CELEBRITY CONSTELLATION
CONSTELLATION	LAUREN L
CONTESSA	ALASKAN DREAM
CONTINENTAL WORLD	LEISURE WORLD
COOK HMAS	MARIA KOSMAS
CORAL CAT	CORAL PRINCESS II
CORINTHIAN	LAUREN L
CORINTHIAN II	SEA EXPLORER
COSTA EUROPA	THOMSON DREAM
COSTA MARINA	CLUB HARMONY
COSTA OLYMPIA	NORWEGIAN SKY
COSTA ROMANTICA	COSTA NEOROMANTICA
COSTA TROPICALE	OCEAN DREAM
COSTA VOYAGER	ZHONG HUA TAI SHAN
CRAIGAVON	CARIB VACATIONER
CRESCENT CITY USS	ARTSHIP
CRESSIDA	YANKEE CLIPPER
CRIMPER	YANKEE CLIPPER
CRISTAL	LOUIS CRISTAL
CROWN	ALBATROS
CROWN DYNASTY	BRAEMAR
CROWN JEWEL	GEMINI
CROWN MAJESTY	BRAEMAR
CROWN MONARCH	VOYAGER
CROWN ODYSSEY	BALMORAL
CROWN PRINCESS	PACIFIC JEWEL
CROWN PRINCESS VICTORIA	AMUSEMENT WORLD
CRUCERO EXPRESS	MIRAGE 1
CRUISE MUHIBAH	AMBASSADOR II
CRUISE ONE	AEGEAN PARADISE
CRYSTAL HARMONY	ASUKA II
CT NEPTUNE	STARRY METROPOLIS
CUNARD ADVENTURER	CORAL
CUNARD CONQUEST	GOLDEN IRIS
CUNARD COUNTESS	OCEAN COUNTESS
CUNARD PRINCESS	GOLDEN IRIS
DALMATINO	ORIENTAL PRINCESS
DANA GLORIA	ISLAND BREEZE
DANA GLORIA	JUPITER
DANAE	LISBOA
DAPHNE	PRINCESS DAPHNE
DARLI	DICLE
DAUNTLESS USS	SS DELPHINE
DELFIN CARAVELLE	TURAMA
DELFIN STAR	SILVER EXPLORER
DELORLEANS	ARTSHIP
DELOS	AURORA
DELPHIN RENAISSANCE	AZAMARA QUEST
DELPHIN VOYAGER	AEGEAN PARADISE
DIAMOND ISLAND	THE EMERALD
DIAMOND PRINCESS	HAKON JARL
DIOGENIS V	HARMONY V
DISKO	POLARIS
DISKO II	QUEST
DMITRIY SHOSTAKOVICH	NEW IMPERIAL STAR
DOLMAR	PICTON CASTLE
DOLPHIN	AEGEAN ODYSSEY
DOMINO EFFECT	VICTORY CHIMES
DON EUSEBIO	DIPOLOG PRINCESS
DOUBLE FORCE	PEGASUS
DOULOS	DOULOS PHOS
DREAM	FORMOSA QUEEN
DREAM 21	SILVER EXPLORER
DREAM PRINCESS	FORMOSA QUEEN
DREAMWARD	SUPERSTAR GEMINI
DRO KI CAKAU	REEF ESCAPE
DRONNING INGRID	AFRICA MERCY
DUNBOYNE	A F CHAPMAN
DURR	THE CALYPSO
EAGLE	ROYAL IRIS
EARL WILLIAM	WINDWARD II

EASYCRUISE LIFE	OCEAN LIFE
EASYCRUISEONE	CRUISEONE
ECSTASY	CARNIVAL ECSTACY
EDWIN & MAUDE	VICTORY CHIMES
ELATION	CARNIVAL ELATION
ELBE 2	ATLANTIS
ELOISE	ROYAL IRIS
EMERALD SEA	KRONPRINSESSE MARTHA
EMPIRE FORTH	VITYAZ
EMPRESS OF THE NORTH	AMERICAN EMPRESS
EMPRESS OF THE SEAS	EMPRESS
ENDEAVOUR	NATIONAL GEOGRAPHIC ENDEAVOUR
ENTERPRISE	KENNEDY
EQUATOR	VITYAZ
EUROPA	SAGA SAPPHIRE
EUROPEAN STARS	MSC SINFONIA
EUROPEAN VISION	MSC ARMONIA
EXECUTIVE EXPLORER	ALASKAN DREAM
EXPLORER II	MINERVA
EXPLORER STARSHIP	OCEAN DIAMOND
FADDEY BELLINGSHAUSEN	OMEGA G
FAIRSKY	ATLANTIC STAR
FAITHFUL	AURORA
FANTASEA AMMARI	AMMARI
FANTASY	CARNIVAL FANTASY
FANTASY WORLD	LEISURE WORLD
FASCINATION	CARNIVAL FASCINATION
FASECO NO 3	TRINITY BAY
FEDOR DOSTOEVSKIY	ASTOR
FERNHILL	OCEAN DIAMOND
FERRY LAVENDER	OCEAN ROSE
FESTIVAL	FORMOSA QUEEN
FLAMENCO	OCEAN DREAM
FLAMENCO I	OCEAN DREAM
FORCE TIDE	BERAKAH
FRANCA C	DOULOS PHOS
FRANCESCA	OCEAN ENDEAVOUR
FRANKFURT	ALEXANDER
FRIDTJOF NANSEN	AZORES
FRONTIER SPIRIT	BREMEN
FUJI MARU	MIRA 1
FUTURE SEAS	EMPRESS
G D KENNEDY	A F CHAPMAN
GALAPAGOS EXPLORER	SILVER GALAPAGOS
GALAXY	MEIN SCHIFF 1
GANN	SJOKURS
GANN	SANDNES
GLACIER BAY EXPLORER	PACIFIC MONARCH
GLOBETROT PRINCESS	JIA RI
GLOMMEN	RTS SINBAD BITIC
GOLDEN BEAR	ARTSHIP
GOLDEN ODYSSEY	REX FORTUNE
GOLDEN PRINCESS	BOUDICCA
GOPLO	SIGNORA DEL VENTO
GRAND CELEBRATION	COSTA CELEBRATION
GRAND LATINO	BOUDICCA
GRAND MAGIC	DUBAI MAGIC
GRAND MISTRAL	COSTA NEORIVIERA
GRAND VOYAGER	ZHONG HUA TAI SHAN
GREAT RIVERS EXPLORER	NATIONAL GEOGRAPHIC SEA LION
GREAT SEA	PHILIPPINES
GROSSHERZOG FRIEDRICH AUGUST	STATSRAAD LEHMKUHL
GRUZIA	SALAMIS FILOXENIA
GUNES DIL	SAVARONA
GUSTAV VASA	LOGOS HOPE
GWAREK	ROYAL CLIPPER
HAINAN EMPRESS	AEGEAN PARADISE
HAKON GAMLE	HAKON JARL
HAMMONIA	SAGA PEARL II
HANS CHRISTIAN ANDERSON	DISCOVERY PALAWAN
HAPPY DOLPHIN	AEGEAN PARADISE
HARALD JARD	SERENISSIMA
HARDANGERFJORD	DICLE
HARLEKIN	BLUE DAWN
HARMONY A	VARIETY VOYAGER
HARMONY PRINCESS	CLUB HARMONY
HEBRIDEAN SPIRIT	CALEDONIAN SKY
HELGOLAND	GALAPAGOS LEGEND
HELGOLAND	SUPPERCLUB CRUISE 02
HOLIDAY	GRAND HOLIDAY
HOLIDAY DREAM	SAGA SAPPHIRE
HOMERIC	OCEAN MAJESTY
HOMERIC	THOMSON DREAM
HOTU MATUA	ANTARCTIC DREAM
HUMBER GUARDIAN	TROPIC SUN
HUSSAR	MANDALAY
HUSSAR	SEA CLOUD
HYUNDAI KUMGANG	BOUDICCA
HYUNDAI PONGNAE	ORIENTAL DRAGON
HYUNDAI PUNGAK	DISCOVERY
ILLYRIA II	CALLISTO
ILMATAR	PALM BEACH PRINCESS
IMAGINATION	CARNIVAL IMAGINATION
INFINITY	CELEBRITY INFINITY
INGRID	AFRICA MERCY
INSPIRATION	CARNIVAL INSPIRATION
IONIAN HARMONY	THE CALYPSO
IONIAN KING	OCEAN ROSE
ISLAND HOLIDAY	ENCHANTED CAPRI
ISLAND PRINCESS	DISCOVERY
ISLAND SUN	SEA EXPLORER
ISLAND VENTURE	DISCOVERY
ISLANDER	NATIONAL GEOGRAPHIC ISLANDER
ISTRA	PORTO
ITALIA	CLUB HARMONY
ITALIA	SAPPHIRE
ITALIA I	AZORES
ITALIA PRIMA	AZORES
JALINA	JI MEI
JAUN MARCH	OCEAN MAJESTY
JIN JIANG	JI MEI
JUBILEE	HENNA
JULES VERNE	VOYAGER
JULIA	WIND PERFECTION
JUNIATA	MILWAUKEE CLIPPER
JUPITER	MIRAGE 1
KALYPSO	STAR PISCES
KAMBUNA	KRI TANJUNG NUSANIVE
KANMIN MARU	PUTERI MAHSURI
KARELIYA	STARRY METROPOLIS
KARINA	ROCHDALE ONE
KATTEGAT	EXPEDITION

KAZAKHSTAN	ISLAND ADVENTURE	MELODY	QING
KAZAKHSTAN II	DELPHIN	MELTEMI II	HARMONY II
KHABAROVSK	SOUNDS OF ORIENT	MER-JULIA	WINDWARD II
KIELER FORDE	CARIB VACATIONER	MERCATOR ONE	ALEXANDER
KILCHERNAN HMS	BRAHE	MERCURY	MEIN SCHIFF 2
KIMA	O'MEGA	METANGULA	PRINCESSA ELENA
KIMBERLEY EXPLORER	HAUMANA	MIDNATSOL	NATIONAL GEOGRAPHIC
KING OF SCANDINAVIA	WIND AMBITION		EXPLORER
KING OF SCANDINAVIA	JUPITER	MIDNATSOL II	NATIONAL GEOGRAPHIC
KONSTANTIN CHERNENKO	OCEAN ATLANTIC		EXPLORER
KONSTANTIN SIMONOV	OCEAN ENDEAVOUR	MIKHAIL SUSLOV	OCEAN JEWEL OF ST
KOSTER	KRONPRINSESSE		PETERSBURG
	MARTHA	MILLENNIUM	CELEBRITY MILLENNIUM
KRISTINA BRAHE	BRAHE	MINERVA II	ADONIA
KRISTINA KATARINA	OCEAN ENDEAVOUR	MING FAI PRINCESS	METROPOLIS
KRISTINA REGINA	BORE	MINISEA	BIRGER JARL
KUNGSHOLM	VERONICA	MINOAN PRINCE	GOLDEN PRINCE
KYPROS STAR	OCEAN MAJESTY	MISTRAL	COSTA NEORIVIERA
LA FAYETTE	WIND SURF	MONA LISA	VERONICA
LADY DI	MEGASTAR TAURUS	MONACO	ISLAND BREEZE
LADY DIANA	MEGASTAR TAURUS	MONARCH OF THE SEAS	MONARCH
LADY HAWKBURY	REEF ESCAPE	MOONTA	LYDIA
LADY SARAH	THE TAIPAN	MORMACTIDE	EMPIRE STATE
LARVIKSPILEN	GALAPAGOS LEGEND	MOSTAR	HARMONY II
LE DIAMANT	OCEAN DIAMOND	MOTIVE EXPLORER	HAUMANA
LE LEVANT	TERE MOANA	MTS DISCOVERER	OCEAN QUEST II
LEEWARD	LOUIS CRISTAL	MUNSTER	AMBASSADOR II
LEISURE WORLD I	DUBAWI	MURRAY EXPLORER	CAPTAIN COOK'S
LEONID BREZHNEV	STARRY METROPOLIS		EXPLORER
LEV TOLSTOY	OCEAN LIFE	MUSSON	SEVASTOPOL-I
LILI MARLEEN	OCEAN COUNTESS	N F TIGER	EXPEDITION
LINDBLAD POLARIS	NATIONAL	N KAZANTZAKIS	METROPOLIS
	GEOGRAPHIC POLARIS	NANTUCKET CLIPPER	SPIRIT OF GLACIER BAY
LINDMAR	NATIONAL GEOGRAPHIC	NANUYA PRINCESS	DISCOVERY ADVENTURE
	ENDEAVOUR	NARCIS	AEGEAN ODYSSEY
LION PRINCE	WIND SOLUTION	NARVIK	GANN
LION QUEEN	AMUSEMENT WORLD	NASSAU	CARIB VACATIONER
LISTER	ARTEMIS	NATASHA	OCEAN LIFE
LONG JIE	ORIENTAL DRAGON	NAUTICAN	VOYAGER
LORD OF THE HIGHLANDS	NATIONAL	NEDERLAND	ROAD TO MANDALAY
	GEOGRAPHIC ISLANDER	NEPTUNE	STARRY METROPOLIS
LOUIS MAJESTY	THOMSON MAJESTY	NEVA	IGOR FARKHUTDINOV
LU XING JIA	ORIENTAL QUEEN	NEW SHOREHAM I	PACIFIC MONARCH
LUISELLA	ESMERELDA	NEW SHOREHAM II	ADMIRALTY DREAM
LYNGEN	NATIONAL GEOGRAPHIC	NEW YORK FORTUNE 1	ISLAND BREEZE
	EXPLORER	NEWPORT CLIPPER	SAFARI ENDEAVOUR
MACAU SUCCESS	REX FORTUNE	NIEUW AMSTERDAM	THOMSON SPIRIT
MAGIC 1	MIRAGE 1	NINIKORIA	POLYNESIAN PRINCESS
MAHROUSSA	EL HORRIYA	NJORD	POLAR STAR
MAJESTIC EXPLORER	NATIONAL	NOORDAM	THOMSON CELEBRATION
	GEOGRAPHIC SEA BIRD	NORDIC EMPRESS	EMPRESS
MALCOLM BALDRIGE	USHUAIA	NORDIC PRINCE	OCEAN STAR PACIFIC
MARBURG	NATIONAL GEOGRAPHIC	NORDIC SUN	AMBASSADOR II
	ENDEAVOUR	NORPAC II	BERAKAH
MARIA ALEKSANDRA	ESMERELDA	NORRONA	LOGOS HOPE
MARINA	CALLISTO	NORTH STAR	NATIONAL GEOGRAPHIC
MARINA TSVETAYEVA	ORTELIUS		ENDEAVOUR
MAURY USNS	GOLDEN BEAR	NORTHWEST EXPLORER	BARANOF DREAM
MAVI MARMARA	GAZI M	NORWEGIAN CROWN	BALMORAL
MAYAN PRINCE	WILDERNESS DISCOVERER	NORWEGIAN DREAM	SUPERSTAR GEMINI
MAZOWIA	ANKARA	NORWEGIAN DYNASTY	BRAEMAR
MEDINA	DOULOS PHOS	NORWEGIAN MAJESTY	THOMSON MAJESTY
MEGASTAR CAPRICORN	CALEDONIAN SKY	NORWEGIAN SEA	SUPERSTAR LIBRA
MEGASTAR SAGITTARIUS	SEA SPIRIT	NORWEGIAN STAR	ALBATROS
MEIN SCHIFF	MEIN SCHIFF 1	NORWEGIAN STAR I	ALBATROS

NORWEGIAN WIND	SUPERSTAR AQUARIUS	PANDAW	PAUKAN 1947
OCEAN EMPRESS	OCEAN JEWEL OF ST	PARADISE	CARNIVAL PARADISE
	PETERSBURG	PATRIA	SEA CLOUD
OCEAN ISLANDER	OCEAN MIST	PATRICIA	AMUSEMENT WORLD
OCEAN KING	PHILIPPINES	PATRIOT	THOMSON SPIRIT
OCEAN MONARCH	PRINCESS DAPHNE	PCE 830	BRAHE
OCEAN ODYSSEY	PRINCESS DAPHNE	PEACE	SIGNORA DEL VENTO
OCEAN PEARL	FORMOSA QUEEN	PEARL OF SEYCHELLES	FIJI PRINCESS
OCEAN PRINCESS	ORIENTAL PRINCESS	PEARL WILLIAM	WINDWARD II
OCEAN PRINCESS	OCEANA	PENTHEON	PAN ORAMA II
OCEAN PRINCESS	SAPPHIRE	PERLA	VENUS
OCEAN VILLAGE	PACIFIC PEARL	PETR PERVVY	OCEAN JEWEL OF ST
OCEAN VILLAGE TWO	PACIFIC JEWEL		PETERSBURG
OCEANIC	THE OCEANIC	PETREL	CALEDONIA
OCEANIC GRACE	SILVER DISCOVERER	PETREL V	CALEDONIA
OCEANIC II	VERONICA	PETRONELLA	MARE FRISIUM
OCEANIC ODYSSEY	SILVER DISCOVERER	PILGRIM BELLE	SS LEGACY
OCEANIC PRINCESS	OCEANIC	PILOTO PARDO	ANTARCTIC DREAM
	DISCOVERER	PINTA 1	LA PINTA
ODESSA SKY	SALAMIS FILOXENIA	PIONEER	YANKEE CLIPPER
OISEAU DE POLYNESIA	ARGUS	PLATINUM	DISCOVERY
OKEAN	MINERVA	POLAR STAR	AURORA
OLAU BRITANNIA	WIND PERFECTION	POLII	ARTEMIS
OLVIA	STARRY METROPOLIS	POLYNESIA	ARGUS
OLYMPIA COUNTESS	OCEAN COUNTESS	PONGNAE	ORIENTAL DRAGON
OLYMPIA EXPLORER	EXPLORER	PORT MELBOURNE	LISBOA
OLYMPIA VOYAGER	ZHONG HUA TAI SHAN	PORT SYDNEY	PRINCESS DAPHNE
OLYMPIC	OCEAN MAJESTY	PRESIDENT	PHILIPPINES
OLYMPIC COUNTESS	OCEAN COUNTESS	PRIDE OF ALOHA	NORWEGIAN SKY
OLYMPIC EXPLORER	EXPLORER	PRIMEXPRESS ISLAND	ROCHDALE ONE
OLYMPIC VOYAGER	ZHONG HUA TAI SHAN	PRINCE	GOLDEN PRINCE
OMAR II	REX FORTUNE	PRINCE ALBERT	HARMONY II
OMAR III	ORIENTAL DRAGON	PRINCE ALBERT II	SILVER EXPLORER
OMAR STAR	CHINA STAR	PRINCESA OCEANICA	SAPPHIRE
OMEGA	OMEGA G	PRINCESS DANAE	LISBOA
OPATIJA	POLYNESIAN PRINCESS	PRINCESS MAHSURI	BERLIN
OPERA	LOUIS CRISTAL	PRINCESSE RAGNHILD	JI MEI
ORANGE MELODY	BERLIN	PRINSESSAN BIRGITA	WIND AMBITION
ORANGE MOON	BLUE DAWN	PRINSESSAN CHRISTINA	WIND SOLUTION
OREGON	EMPIRE STATE	PRINSESSE RAGNHILD	BAHAMAS
ORESUND	NATIONAL GEOGRAPHIC		CELEBRATION
	POLARIS	PRINZ OBERON	AMBASSADOR II
ORIENT EXPRESS	AMET MAJESTY	PROFESSOR KHROMOV	SPIRIT OF ENDERBY
ORIENT QUEEN	LOUIS AURA	PUTRI BINTANG	AMUSEMENT WORLD
ORIENT SUN	AMET MAJESTY	PYOTR PERVVY	OCEAN JEWEL OF ST
ORIENT VENUS	AEGEAN PARADISE		PETERSBURG
ORION	NATIONAL GEOGRAPHIC	QUEEN ODYSSEY	SEABOURN LEGEND
	ORION	R EIGHT	ADONIA
ORION II	CORINTHIAN	R FIVE	NAUTICA
OSIJEK	HARMONY II	R FOUR	OCEAN PRINCESS
OSTFOLD	RTS SINBAD BITIC	R ONE	INSIGNIA
PACIFIC EXPLORER	BERAKAH	R SEVEN	AZAMARA QUEST
PACIFIC PRINCESS	PACIFIC	R SIX	AZAMARA JOURNEY
PACIFIC SKY	ATLANTIC STAR	R THREE	PACIFIC PRINCESS
PACIFIC STAR	AMUSEMENT WORLD	R TWO	REGATTA
PACIFIC STAR	OCEAN DREAM	RADISSON DIAMOND	CHINA STAR
PACIFIC STAR	AURORA	RAGNVALD JARL	SJOKURS
PACIFIC STAR	ISLAND BREEZE	RAINBOW	THE EMERALD
PACIFIC SUN	HENNA	RAPTURE	SAFARI EXPLORER
PACIFIC SUN	THE EMERALD	REEF TREK	HAUMANA
PACIFIC WARRIOR	BERAKAH	REGAL PRINCESS	PACIFIC DAWN
PALAU	WIND SOLUTION	REGENT JEWEL	THE CALYPSO
PALMIRA	OCEAN LIFE	REGENT MOON	COSTA ALLEGRA
PALOMA	NEW IMPERIAL STAR	REGENT RAINBOW	THE EMERALD
PALOMA I	NEW IMPERIAL STAR	REGENT SUN	CLUB HARMONY

REGINA MARIS	ALEXANDER	SEA PRINCESS	VERONICA
REGINA RENAISSANCE	SEA EXPLORER	SEA TRAVELLER II	LA PINTA
REMBRANDT	ROTTERDAM	SEA VENTURE	PACIFIC
RENAI I	SEA EXPLORER	SEABOURN GODDESS I	SEADREAM I
RENAI II	ISLAND SKY	SEABOURN GODDESS II	SEADREAM II
RENAISSANCE	DUBAWI	SEABOURN LEGEND	STAR LEGEND
RENAISSANCE EIGHT	ISLAND SKY	SEABOURN PRIDE	STAR PRIDE
RENAISSANCE FIVE	SEA SPIRIT	SEABOURN SPIRIT	STAR BREEZE
RENAISSANCE FOUR	CORINTHIAN	SEABOURN SUN	PRINSENDAM
RENAISSANCE SEVEN	SEA EXPLORER	SEALORD	BLUE DAWN
RENAISSANCE SIX	CALEDONIAN SKY	SEASPIRIT	SAFARI ENDEAVOUR
RENAISSANCE THREE	SILVER GALAPAGOS	SEAWARD	SUPERSTAR LIBRA
RENAISSANCE TWO	CRUISEONE	SEAWING	VENUS
RESEARCHER	USHUAIA	SEMINOLE EXPRESS	MIRAGE 1
RHAPSODY	GOLDEN IRIS	SENSATION	CARNIVAL SENSATION
RINJANI	KRI TANJUNG FATAGAR	SHANGRI-LA WORLD	LEISURE WORLD
RIO	VENUS	SHEARWATER	POLARIS
RIVAGE MARTINIQUE	FIJI PRINCESS	SHIRETOKO MARU	METROPOLIS
RIVAGE ST MARTIN	AMMARI	SIKKER HAVN	SAKARYA
RIVAGES GUADELOUPE	NATIONAL	SILJA OPERA	LOUIS CRISTAL
	GEOGRAPHIC ISLANDER	SILJA STAR	AMET MAJESTY
RIVERSIDE AMMARI	AMMARI	SITIA	ISLAND BREEZE
ROMA	DOULOS PHOS	SITMAR FAIRMAJESTY	PACIFIC PEARL
ROYAL MAJESTY	THOMSON MAJESTY	SJOKURS	GAMLE SALTEN
ROYAL ODYSSEY	ALBATROS	SJOKURS	SANDNES
ROYAL PRINCESS	ADONIA	SKULE	RTS SINBAD BITIC
ROYAL PRINCESS	ARTANIA	SKY PRINCESS	ATLANTIC STAR
ROYAL SEAS	ISLAND ADVENTURE	SKY WONDER	ATLANTIC STAR
ROYAL STAR	OCEAN MIST	SKYWARD	LEISURE WORLD
ROYAL VIKING QUEEN	SEABOURN	SOCIETY ADVENTURER	HANSEATIC
	LEGEND	SOL CHRISTIANA	OCEAN MAJESTY
ROYAL VIKING SEA	ALBATROS	SONG OF AMERICA	LOUIS OLYMPIA
ROYAL VIKING SKY	BOUDICCA	SONG OF FLOWER	OCEAN DIAMOND
ROYAL VIKING STAR	BLACK WATCH	SONG OF NORWAY	FORMOSA QUEEN
ROYAL VIKING SUN	PRINSENDAM	SOROY	RTS SINBAD BITIC
ROYALE OCEANIC	THE OCEANIC	SOUTHERN CROSS	OCEAN DREAM
ROYALE STAR	NEW IMPERIAL STAR	SOUTHWARD	VENUS
RTS SINBAD	RTS SINBAD BITIC	SOVEREIGN OF THE SEAS	SOVEREIGN
RUBY	OCEAN COUNTESS	SPICE ISLANDER	CORAL PRINCESS II
RUSS	OCEAN ATLANTIC	SPIRIT OF 98	SS LEGACY
RYFYLKE	KRONPRINSESSE MARTHA	SPIRIT OF ADVERTURE	BERLIN
S C ATLANTIC	OCEAN ATLANTIC	SPIRIT OF ALASKA	BARANOF DREAM
SAFARI LEGACY	SS LEGACY	SPIRIT OF COLUMBIA	ADMIRALTY DREAM
SAFE CHRISTINA	WIND SOLUTION	SPIRIT OF DISCOVERY	WILDERNESS
SAGA PEARL	MINERVA		EXPLORER
SAGA RUBY	OASIA	SPIRIT OF ENDEAVOUR	SAFARI ENDEAVOUR
SALLY ALBATROSS	LOUIS CRISTAL	SPIRIT OF GLACIER BAY	PACIFIC MONARCH
SALLY CARAVELLE	TURAMA	SPIRIT OF LONDON	OCEAN DREAM
SALLY CLIPPER	SILVER EXPLORER	SPIRIT OF NANTUCKET	SPIRIT OF
SALTEN	GAMLE SALTEN		GLACIER BAY
SAN GIORGIO	OCEAN MIST	SPIRIT OF OCEANUS	SEA SPIRIT
SANTA ROSA	THE EMERALD	SPIRIT OF YORKTOWN	YORKTOWN
SAQQIT ITTUK	QUEST	SPORT ROVER	KRONPRINSESSE
SARPIK ITTUK	OCEAN NOVA		MARTHA
SCANDINAVIA	ISLAND ESCAPE	SS CLIPPER	MILWAUKEE CLIPPER
SCANDINAVICA	WIND AMBITION	STAFFORD	ISLAND BREEZE
SCANDINAVICA	MIRAGE 1	STAR ODYSSEY	BLACK WATCH
SEA BIRD	NATIONAL GEOGRAPHIC	STAR PRINCESS	PACIFIC PEARL
	SEA BIRD	STARDANCER	ISLAND ESCAPE
SEA GODDESS I	SEADREAM I	STARSHIP ATLANTIC	QING
SEA GODDESS II	SEADREAM II	STARSHIP MAJESTIC	OCEAN DREAM
SEA LINER	LA PINTA	STARSHIP OCEANIC	THE OCEANIC
SEA LION	NATIONAL GEOGRAPHIC	STARWARD	LOUIS AURA
	SEA LION	STEINFOREST	PICTON CASTLE
SEA PRINCE	SAPPHIRE	STELLA DALMATIAE	MONET

STENA FINLANDICA	GALAPAGOS LEGEND	TOSHIMA	O'MEGA
STENA NORDICA	WIND SOLUTION	TRILLINGEN	SAKARYA
STENA OCEANICA	AMUSEMENT WORLD	TRITON	CORAL
STENA SAGA	AMUSEMENT WORLD	TROPIC BIRD	CORAL I
STENA SCANDINAVICA	WIND AMBITION	TROPIC STAR	ISLAND BREEZE
STOCKHOLM	AZORES	TROPICALE	OCEAN DREAM
STORMONT HMCS	CHRISTINA O	TUHAAPAE 3	VAEANU
SUMDREAM	FORMOSA QUEEN	TURA	HARMONY V
SUMMIT	CELEBRITY SUMMIT	TURNSTEIN	PICTON CASTLE
SUN	SEA EXPLORER	TURQUAZ	HARMONY V
SUN BAY	XPEDITION	TYDEMAN	PLANCIUS
SUN BAY II	LAUREN L	UKRAINIA	ISLAND ADVENTURE
SUN FIESTA	AMUSEMENT WORLD	UTSTRAUM	PICTON CASTLE
SUN FIESTA	THE CALYPSO	VACATIONER	CARIB VACATIONER
SUN FLOWER 7	GOLDEN PRINCE	VAN GOGH	SALAMIS FILOXENIA
SUN JO 1	LA PINTA	VASILIY GOLOVNIN	GEROI SEVASTOPOLYA
SUN PRINCESS	OCEAN DREAM	VELMA	MANDALAY
SUN VIKING	ORIENTAL DRAGON	VELMA LYKES	KENNEDY
SUN VIVA	SEA SPIRIT	VENUS	WIND AMBITION
SUN VIVA II	CALEDONIAN SKY	VENUS	OLA ESMERELDA
SUNBIRD	LOUIS OLYMPIA	VICTORIA	LORD OF THE GLENS
SUNBORN	THE YACHT HOTEL	VICTORIA	VERONICA
SUNFLOWER	AL SAID	VICTORIA II	LORD OF THE GLENS
SUNNHORDLAND	BRAHE	VICTORIAN EMPRESS	SS LEGACY
SUNSHINE FUJI	MABUHAY SUNSHINE	VIKING II	WINDWARD II
SUNWARD	BOUDICCA	VIKING POLARIS	POLARIS
SUNWARD II	CORAL	VIKING PRINCESS	PALM BEACH PRINCESS
SUPERSTAR ARIES	SAGA SAPPHIRE	VIKING SAGA	LOUIS CRISTAL
SUPERSTAR CAPRICORN	BOUDICCA	VIKING SERENADE	ISLAND ESCAPE
SUPERSTAR EUROPE	SAGA SAPPHIRE	VIKINGFJORD	SANDNES
SUPERSTAR GEMINI	GEMINI	VINCENTE PUCHOL	7107 ISLANDS CRUISE
SUPERSTAR LEO	NORWEGIAN SPIRIT	VISTAFJORD	OASIA
SUPERSTAR LIBRA	NORWEGIAN STAR	VISTAMAR	ORIENT QUEEN II
SUPERSTAR SAGITTARIUS	ORIENTAL DRAGON	VLADIMIR CHIVILIKHIN	KAY
SUPERSTAR SCORPIO	NORWEGIAN DAWN	VOLKERFREUNDSCHAFT	AZORES
SUPERSTAR TAURUS	LOUIS CRISTAL	VOYAGER	ZHONG HUA TAI SHAN
SVEA CORONA	JUPITER	VOYAGER	ISLAND BREEZE
SVEA JARL	PRINCE	WAKACHIBA MARU	EVOLUTION
SVYATOY NIKOLAY	GEROI SEVASTOPOLYA	WAKASHIO MARU	PACIFIC LINK
SWITZERLAND	PRINCESS DAPHNE	WAKASHIO MARU	GOLDEN PRINCE
TADZIKISTAN	WANG FU	WALRUS	VOYAGER
TAHITIAN PRINCESS	OCEAN PRINCESS	WAPPEN	SUPPERCLUB CRUISE 02
TANNER USNS	STATE OF MAINE	WAPPEN VON HAMBURG	AURORA
TAVERNER	PACIFIC AURORA	WAPPEN VON	
TDI KARADENIZ	DREAM	HAMBURG	SUPPERCLUB CRUISE 02
TEMPTRESS EXPLORER	BERAKAH	WASA QUEEN	AMET MAJESTY
TEMPTRESS VOYAGER	SAFARI VOYAGER	WATERWITCH HMS	HALAS 71
TERAAKA	POLYNESIAN PRINCESS	WELLAMO	JUPITER
TETYS	PICTON CASTLE	WESTERDAM	THOMSON DREAM
THE AEGEAN PEARL	VENUS	WESTWARD	BLACK WATCH
THE AZUR	ROYAL IRIS	WILLIAM	WINDWARD II
THE EXPLORER	ATOLL EXPLORER	WINDWARD	SUPERSTAR AQUARIUS
THE IRIS	OCEAN ENDEAVOUR	WORLD DISCOVERER	SILVER EXPLORER
THE JASMINE	OCEAN LIFE	XANADU	AURORA
THE MERCURU	DUBAWI	YAO HUA	ORIENT PRINCESS
THE NEPTUNE	CRUISEONE	YASAWA LEGEND	DISCOVERY ADVENTURE
THE SCHOLAR SHIP	VERONICA	YORKTOWN CLIPPER	YORKTOWN
THERIOT OFFSHORE IV	NORDIK EXPRESS	YUSHAR	MONET
THERISOS EXPRESS	LISBOA	YUWA MARU	EVOLUTION
THOMSON DESTINY	LOUIS OLYMPIA	ZI DING XIANG	ARAFURA LILY
TI'A MOANA	SALUZI		
TIGER	EXPEDITION		
TOKYO MARU	DIPOLOG PRINCESS		
TOM KYLE	BLUE DAWN		

Index